Hume and
the Problem of Causation

Hume and
the Problem of Causation

TOM L. BEAUCHAMP
ALEXANDER ROSENBERG

New York Oxford
OXFORD UNIVERSITY PRESS
1981

Copyright © 1981 by Oxford University Press, Inc.

Library of Congress Cataloging in Publication Data

Beauchamp, Tom L
Hume and the problem of causation.

Includes index.
1. Hume, David, 1711–1776.   2. Causation.
I.   Rosenberg, Alexander, 1946–   joint author.
II.   Title.
B1499.C38B4   122   80-20259
ISBN 0-19-520236-8

Printed in the United States of America

For
Stephen F. Barker

Preface

This work is an exposition and defense of David Hume's theory of causation. Hume's treatment of this problem proved to be the single most distinctive and influential achievement in a career of celebrated philosophical accomplishments. Virtually all parties to current disputes about causation consider Hume's account a live option, but the conclusions we reach in this volume are far more supportive. Indeed they vindicate Hume. We argue that Hume's account constitutes the most adequate general theory of causation yet to appear in the literature on the subject.

Our early chapters are largely interpretative and exegetical. We attempt to expound Hume's actual views about causation, cautiously extending his theory to questions about causation that he never explicitly faced, but which test the adequacy of his theory. This interpretative and expository undertaking in itself constitutes a sustained argument on behalf of Hume's theory of causation, for it enables us to undercut objections to the theory that rest on misunderstandings of its details and objectives. Our aims are not exclusively exegetical, however, and throughout we undertake to defend Hume's account of causation against substantive philosophical objections. While many of these objections were not explicitly anticipated by Hume himself, the viability of the Humean theory depends on its ability to counter all compelling alternative accounts. No adequate defense of a philosopher's general view can rest on retreat to a dignified silence in the face of pressing issues merely because those issues were not directly addressed in the philosopher's writings.

The interpretative and the philosophical elements of this work are a unified whole, so that any attempt to identify these discrete elements by chapter contents would at best be artificial. Nevertheless, the structure of our presentation reveals a transition from matters almost wholly textual to issues that involve successively larger interpretative extensions and applications of Hume's original doctrine. Thus, the first chapter attempts to settle a longstanding controversy about Hume's two definitions of "cause," and the second challenges an equally longstanding orthodoxy about his views on induction. Chapter 3 is devoted to an exposition and defense of the regularity theory of causal connectedness, and Chapter 4 treats Hume's account of the causal laws underlying these connections. In these chapters our objectives bring us face to face with powerful contemporary arguments against Hume's views, arguments that turn on the alleged primacy of singular causal sequences, the prospects of causal indeterminism, and the nature of nomological necessity. In Chapters 5 and 6 Hume's discussion of spatiotemporal relations among causes and effects is reconstructed and defended, and attacks on his appeal to temporal priority as the ground of causal directionality are examined.

By this stage in our treatment expositional matters have receded, and most of the discussion involves issues of contemporary concern. Hume's insights are extended to new areas as much in the spirit of the text as in its letter. Thus, for instance, at the end of Chapter 6 we consider whether Hume need have been committed to the asymmetry or directionality of causation. The seventh chapter is almost entirely free of exegetical matters, addressing questions about logical form and ontology that have only assumed their present form in the last few decades. Finally, in Chapter 8 we apply Hume's theory to questions about causal judgment and explanation, assessing the adequacy of his treatment of causation by its implications for ordinary causal judgments and for explanation in the natural and social sciences. A brief synopsis of the arguments in each of these chapters is found in the Analytical Table of Contents.

Our book, then, is both a treatise on Hume's theory of causation and a Humean theory of causation. Overall it represents a radical departure from the traditional interpretation of Hume's views, and some may think that we have defended the Humean theory only by indelicate reconstruction. If our exegetical claims are correct, however, this accusation cannot be sustained. Post-

Humean philosophy seems to us to have framed a picture of Hume's position that he would only have recognized as a caricature. If our exposition is at least as plausible as those traditionally offered, philosophers interested in assessing Hume's contributions should be led to a closer examination of his arguments and their interconnections.

Mendocino, California   T.L.B.
Syracuse, New York   A.R.
March 1980

Acknowledgments

The history of this book stretches over a decade, and the intellectual debts we have incurred during that period are extensive. Our interest in causation and in the work of Hume was initially encouraged in the late 1960s by Stephen Barker and Max Deutscher. At the same time Harry Silverstein's tenacious arguments helped improve our ideas. Although it has been more than a decade since we last had the advantage of criticism and advice from these three friends, virtually every chapter has been shaped by their formative influence.

In the years that followed, our interests took somewhat different courses. One of us specialized in the intricacies of Hume's text and the philosophical controversies generated by its commentators; the other critically investigated contemporary alternatives to Hume's analysis of causation. Despite this divergence of interest, we both came increasingly to hold the conviction that when properly interpreted Hume's analysis can withstand the arguments of his many critics. We tested this hypothesis in a series of papers, some written separately, some together, and some with other philosophers. A few of these papers have legacies in parts of the present work and are acknowledged below.

The program of work which led to this book was first outlined at a conference on the philosophy of causation sponsored by Canada Council and Dalhousie University, held over several weeks in the summer of 1973. We owe thanks both to the supporting agencies and to the participants for the opportunity and the stimulation provided during these weeks of discussion. Particularly valuable in the formulation of our views at this conference were conversations with David Braybrooke, Donald

Davidson, Jaegwon Kim, Robert Martin, Alex Michalos, David Sanford, and Fred Wilson—all of whom have continued to offer valuable suggestions in the years after this conference.

Among those whose critical comments helped improve our papers or arguments over the years, we must also name and thank Monroe Beardsley, Jonathan Bennett, Martin Bunzl, Richmond Campbell, Nicholas Capaldi, Arnold Davidson, John Earman, Ernest LePore, Larry Lombard, J. L. Mackie, Thomas Mappes, Joseph Margolis, Thomas McKay, Graham Nerlich, Nicholas Rescher, Daniel N. Robinson, Donald Seldin, Terry Tomkow, Stephen Toulmin, Peter van Inwagen, and Jane Zembaty. (Davidson effectively served as a silent partner on parts of the concluding section of Chapter 7.)

Finally, we must thank many persons for their comments on portions of the manuscript as it neared completion. Their generosity in criticizing our views—which they often strongly opposed—helped us improve exposition and assessment of views in their own domain of expertise. Their efforts saved us from a large number of infelicities and errors. Any remaining errors persist in spite of the best effort of these philosophers to convince us otherwise. We hope our stubbornness will not be taken for ingratitude. These correspondents and colleagues include Jerrold Aronson, Wayne Davis, Herbert Feigl, Antony Flew, Steven Kuhn, James Lesher, David Lewis, J. L. Mackie, David Sanford, and David Stove. Although no footnotes in Chapter 2 reflect the fact, we were influenced in revising this chapter by an advance copy of David Fate Norton's forthcoming volume *David Hume: Common Sense Moralist; Sceptical Metaphysician* (Princeton University Press, 1982).

Our depth of indebtedness to John Mackie deserves special notice. Several years ago, in a review of his *The Cement of the Universe* (Clarendon Press, 1974), we wrote that "No member of the current philosophical generation has produced a body of work on the concept of causality more impressive and more influential than J. L. Mackie's contributions on the subject." The reader will find this claim confirmed by the frequency with which we are compelled, in the pages ahead, to confront his views about causation. Despite our frequent disagreements, we owe as much to him for our understanding of issues in the philosophy of causation as to any other contemporary philosopher. We also thank him and his publisher for permission to use, on page 127 of this book, diagram vi from page 218 of *The Cement of the Universe*.

We wish also to thank the editors and publishers of several journals for permission to use material that originally appeared in articles they published. While material from these articles has been thoroughly revised before inclusion in this volume, the original sources are as follows: "Causation and Recipes: The Mixture as Before?" *Philosophical Studies* 24 (1973), pp. 378–85; "Hume's Two Theories of Causation," *Archiv für Geschichte der Philosophie* 55 (1973), pp. 281–300; "Mill and Some Contemporary Critics on 'Cause,'" *The Personalist* 54 (1973), pp. 123–39; "On Causal Irregularity: A Reply to Dretske and Snyder," *Philosophy of Science* 40 (1973), pp. 285–87; "Hume on Causal Contiguity and Causal Succession," *Dialogue* 13 (1974), pp. 271–82; "On Kim's Account of Events and Event-Identity," *Journal of Philosophy* 71 (June 13, 1974), pp. 327–37; six "Introductions" in *Philosophical Problems of Causation* (Encino, Calif.: Dickenson Publishing Co., 1974); "Vincula Revindicata" in *Philosophical Problems of Causation* (Encino, Calif.: Dickenson Publishing Co., 1974), pp. 217–22; "Is Hume Really a Sceptic about Induction?" *American Philosophical Quarterly* 12 (1975), pp. 119–29; "Propter Hoc, Ergo Post Hoc," *American Philosophical Quarterly* 12 (1975), pp. 245–54; "Singular Causal Statements: A Reconsideration," *Philosophical Forum* 5 (1975), pp. 611–18; "Concrete Occurrences vs. Explanatory Facts," *Philosophical Studies* 31 (1977), pp. 133–40; "Critical Notice of *The Cement of the Universe*," *Canadian Journal of Philosophy* 7 (1977), pp. 371–404; "Causation and Counterfactuals: Lewis' View Reconsidered," *Dialogue* 18 (1978), pp. 209–19; "The Extensionality of Causal Contexts," *Midwest Studies in Philosophy* 4 (1979), pp. 401–8. In the case of three of the above articles, coauthors must be acknowledged for allowing us to use material that in its original form they have as much right to call their own as do we. These coauthors are David Braybrooke, Thomas Mappes, and Robert M. Martin.

Finally, for many stylistic and philosophical improvements we are indebted to R. Jay Wallace, Jr., who read and criticized every section of the manuscript. Several students also contributed to the development of this book in a seminar on the manuscript. These students were Rolland Pack, Emilie Fox, and Linda Rambler. Mr. William Pitt made the very substantial contribution of compiling the index. Similarly, we must thank Cynthia Anderson, Mary Baker, Emilie Dolge, Mary Ellen Timbol, and Carole Wenthen who assisted with the preparation and correction of the manuscript. Apart from their scrupulous efforts, successive versions of our work might not have been intelligible to the two of us, let alone to its ultimate readers.

Contents

Analytical Table
of Contents

6 The Nature of Causal Directionality 201

The causal relation is universally agreed to be asymmetrical, but there has been no agreement on the nature of causal asymmetry. Hume seems to have attributed the direction of causation to the temporal priority of causes, but several alternatives have recently been advanced.

7   Events, Facts, and the Extensionality
of Causal Contexts   247

Hume does not treat the problem of causal relata, but his theory may
be placed in the context of recent theories of the ontology of causation.

8   Causal Judgment and Causal Explanation   283

Causation and explanation present substantially different problems.
Nonetheless, there are important connections between them, and it
has been widely held that Hume's theory of causation is inadequate
for the analysis of causal judgment and causal explanation.

Abbreviations

The abbreviations used in this volume and the editions they represent are as follows:

A   *An Abstract of a Treatise of Human Nature,* ed. J. M. Keynes and P. Sraffa (Cambridge: Cambridge University Press, 1938).

D   *Dialogues Concerning Natural Religion,* ed. Norman Kemp Smith (Edinburgh: Thomas Nelson and Sons, Ltd., 1947; as reprinted by Bobbs-Merrill).

EHU   *An Enquiry Concerning Human Understanding,* ed. L. A. Selby-Bigge (Oxford: Clarendon Press, 1894; Second Edition 1902), Third Edition as revised by P. H. Nidditch, 1975.

EPM   *An Enquiry Concerning the Principles of Morals,* ed. L. A. Selby-Bigge (Oxford: Clarendon Press, 1894; Second Edition 1902), Third Edition as revised by P. H. Nidditch, 1975.

T   *A Treatise of Human Nature,* ed. L. A. Selby-Bigge (Oxford: Clarendon Press, 1888), Second Edition as revised by P. H. Nidditch, 1978.

Hume and
the Problem of Causation

I

Hume's Two Theories of Causation

DAVID HUME'S theory of causation is an analysis of the causal relation; it is not an analysis of the logical subtleties of the ordinary employment of the word "cause." Many writers on causation have taken him to provide such an analysis, but we shall argue that this understanding is a fundamental misconception. Hume certainly does examine the circumstances under which ordinary speakers *believe* their causal claims to be true, but his real interest is the actual circumstances under which they *are* true. Hume is never primarily interested in the analysis of ordinary linguistic meanings,[1] and his metaphysical views are heavily influenced by epistemological considerations concerning the empirical meanings of important philosophical concepts. This is as true of his analysis of causation as it is of his other metaphysical theories.

Notoriously, Hume holds that the real meaning of a term is the idea to which it refers. To each idea there corresponds one or more impressions, of which the ideas are copies. In his examination of causation, Hume's procedure is to identify those sensory impressions that compose the complex idea of causation.

1. Hume repeatedly rejects as inadequate the ordinary meanings of important philosophical terms. The following is an example: "These words ["force," "power," "energy"], as commonly used, have very loose meanings annexed to them; and their ideas are very uncertain and confused" (EHU, Sec. 6on). The many passages in Hume's writings to this effect are thoughtfully analyzed by James Noxon, *Hume's Philosophical Development* (Oxford: Clarendon Press, 1973), pp. 134f.

Armed with this doctrine about meaning, Hume eventually isolates three empirical relations—*contiguity, succession,* and *constant conjunction*—and proclaims them the essential elements of the idea of causation. Additionally, and somewhat surprisingly, he cites an apparently nonempirical element as essential to causation: *necessary connection.* Hume's theory of causation largely consists of a close analysis of these four relations, where special attention is given to constant conjunction and necessary connection, the latter of which Hume believes to be subjective in origin, but which he nonetheless believes of "much greater importance" than either contiguity or succession (T, 77). There is no better summary of his basic doctrine than that which he provides in *An Abstract of a Treatise of Human Nature* (A, 11f, 22f):

Here is a billiard-ball lying on the table, and another ball moving towards it with rapidity. They strike; and the ball, which was formerly at rest, now acquires a motion. . . . There was no interval betwixt the shock and the motion. *Contiguity* in time and place is therefore a requisite circumstance to the operation of all causes. 'Tis evident likewise, that the motion, which was the cause, is prior to the motion, which was the effect. *Priority* in time, is therefore another requisite circumstance in every cause. But this is not all. Let us try any other balls of the same kind in a like situation, and we shall always find, that the impulse of the one produces motion in the other. Here, therefore is a *third* circumstance, viz. that of a *constant conjunction* betwixt the cause and effect. Every object like the cause, produces always some object like the effect. Beyond these three circumstances of contiguity, priority, and constant conjunction, I can discover nothing in this cause. . . .

In the considering of motion communicated from one ball to another, we could find nothing but contiguity, priority in the cause, and constant conjunction. But, besides these circumstances, 'tis commonly suppos'd, that there is a necessary connexion betwixt the cause and effect, and that the cause possesses something, which we call a *power,* or *force,* or *energy.* The question is, what idea is annex'd to these terms? If all our ideas or thoughts be derived from our impressions, this power must either discover itself to our senses, or to our internal feeling. But so little does any *power* discover itself to the senses in the operation of matter . . . [and] our own minds afford us no more notion of energy than matter does. . . . Upon the whole, then, either we have no idea at all of force and energy, and these words are altogether insignificant, or they can mean nothing but that determination of the thought, acquir'd by habit, to pass from the cause to its usual effect.[2]

At the end of his analysis, Hume provides two definitions of "cause," one of which emphasizes constancy of conjunction and the other of which emphasizes necessary connection in the form of a "determination of thought":

(Df_1) We may define a CAUSE to be "an object precedent and contiguous to another, and where all the objects resembling the former are plac'd in like relations of precedency and contiguity to those objects, that resemble the latter."

(Df_2) [We may define a CAUSE to be] "an object precedent and contiguous to another, and so united with it, that the idea of the one determines the mind to form the idea of the other, and the impression of the one to form a more lively idea of the other." (T, 170)

A multitude of connected problems are submerged in this account of causation.[3] The primary problem is that of determining which of these two apparently different definitions expresses Hume's theory of causation. Some of Hume's expositors maintain that he holds a regularity theory of causation, while others maintain that he holds a modified necessity theory. Still others, appealing to apparent incompatibilities between these two views, conclude that Hume holds no consistent theory of causation whatever, and even that such a theory was not among his objectives. We contend, against all these interpretations, that Hume maintains neither of these two theories explicitly, but that implicitly he is committed to both—a tension in his work unresolvable by textual analysis alone. However, we think this tension can be resolved by nontextual considerations, and we shall eventually defend *both* of Hume's theories in the form of a single unified theory.

The problems discussed in this chapter have escaped the notice of many of Hume's expositors because they have failed to

2. Reprinted by permission of Cambridge University Press from the 1938 edition, edited by J. M. Keynes and P. Sraffa.

3. We take Hume at his word when he claims to offer *definitions* of "cause." Wade Robison has argued, however, that Hume's "precise definition of cause and effect" (T, 169) is not an attempt at a definition or analysis of *causation*, but rather is a definition of causal judgment. See his "Hume's Causal Scepticism," in *David Hume: Bicentenary Papers* (Edinburgh: Edinburgh University Press, 1977), esp. p. 157.

grasp both the diversity of aims embedded in Hume's analysis and the limitations placed by certain of his epistemological principles on analysis of causation. In order to support this claim, a brief interpretation of Hume's aims will first be presented. His commentators' mistakes will then be considered. Finally, the alleged incompatibilities between his theories will be explored, and it will be explained why his philosophical principles lead to two definitions and to two theories of causation.

I

In the *Treatise* Hume seems to regard necessary connection as the most essential element in the idea of causation because it provides the foundation for inference from cause to effect or from effect to cause; that is, it underlies our claim that whenever the cause is present the effect *must* follow (T, 73–77, 89, 165). But since he also maintains that no quality of necessity in objects is empirically observable, Hume is faced with the task of giving an empiricist explanation of the derivation of this idea from experience. He must track down the primal impression. Ultimately, of course, he finds that the idea of necessary connection is directly derived from an internal impression and indirectly derived from a constant conjunction of objects.

If one reads Hume as a sceptic about causation, it is tempting to suppose that he actually denies that causes are necessarily connected with their effects, or perhaps even that causes exist. Richard Taylor, for example, contends that Hume can easily be interpreted as eliminating entirely the idea of necessity from the idea of causation, while A. H. Basson takes Hume to be attempting to explain how people are mistaken in supposing that causation involves necessary connection in addition to uniform sequence.[4] Hume certainly wishes to deny that there is any necessary connectedness between objects themselves. But does he wish to deny that a genuine *cause* is in any sense necessarily connected with its effect? It is more difficult to understand Hume

---

4. A. H. Basson, *David Hume* (Baltimore: Penguin Books, 1958), pp. 73–76. Richard Taylor, "Causation," *The Encyclopedia of Philosophy*, Vol. 2, p. 58, and "Causation," *The Monist* (1963), p. 291.

on this point than is generally recognized. On the one hand, he normally maintains that the idea of necessary connection is central to the notion of causation. On the other hand, his definitions of "cause" do not specifically mention the idea of necessary connection. Furthermore, he frequently intimates that the idea of necessary connection, together with its near synonyms and cognates, is the product of a universal propensity unnoticed even by philosophers to graft mind-dependent relations onto nature.

This matter may be clarified by introducing the distinction between philosophy as description and philosophy as revision. Is Hume attempting to describe the idea of causation by listing its essential features, or is he attempting to revise it after pointing to unwarrantable suppositions submerged in the common idea? The latter would be a reconstructive analysis which cared little for what some users of the language have in mind and still less about an analysis of the ordinary meaning. It is perhaps a subtle conflict between these two tasks of describing and revising common ideas that leads to perplexity on the question whether causes are, in his analysis, necessarily connected with effects.

One can easily be led to misapprehend Hume's actual goals by overemphasizing his repeated assertion that the main thrust of his investigation is to explain what it means to say that there are necessary connections. His aim is twofold: (1) to describe the common concepts "cause" and "causal necessity" and (2) to explain what "necessary connection" *means* by tracing it to the impression which is its source. These are different tasks, yet both are conceptual investigations. The first isolates the essential elements in the ordinary idea of cause, analyzes each one, and shows the idea of necessary connection to be a central element. But the second and not the first task is Hume's primary interest, for it alone provides the revision of the ordinary meaning that reflects Hume's discoveries of the truth conditions for causal statements. The second is an investigation into those basic experiences from which the common idea is derived; the "more precise meaning"—the revisionary meaning—is sought (EHU, Sec. 49). When captured, it may provide a solid basis for revising the ordinary concept in addition to overcoming its obscurity. The first task is a commitment to describe in what sense the idea of necessary connection is essential to the ordinary idea. The second task presupposes the first but carries no similar commitment. Revising the meaning is, for Hume, revising both the ordinary concept of causation and incorrect philosophical concepts; but this revision entails neither revision of the way in which the term "cause" is ordinarily used for purposes of inference nor revision of the ways in which causes are identified. Rather, a revision of what Hume calls the "inveterate prejudices of mankind" is demanded (T, 166). It is not the ordinary use of the term, but rather the common conception or belief about causes that needs revision; and Hume is equally concerned to refute the philosophical account of causation given by rationalists, as we shall later see.

Hume's task of describing how the idea of necessary connection is essential to the idea of causation is carried out by showing that the latter idea would be disastrously diminished were the former removed and that there would then be no basis for causal inference (EHU, Sec. 22). Hume's descriptive work, like his quest for an impression of connection, is indirect; he studies necessary connection largely through the inferences based upon it (T, 88). An example will make this clearer. Suppose a person A were simply to mention or itemize the empirical features of contiguity, succession, and constant conjunction to his colleague B. It is quite possible that B would not understand at all that a statement asserting a causal relation was being uttered. If A were to say that a train's rumble every morning at 7:00 slightly precedes and is contiguous with poor lighting in his bathroom, B would not know whether the statement is a causal one, a statement of coincidence, or merely a report. Obviously something is missing; in Hume's view it is the element of necessary connection or power (T, 88, 155). If A says the rumble *causes* the poor lighting, B understands him to mean that, given the rumble (presuming normal conditions prevail), the poor quality of the light *must* occur.

Hume here points out that the term "necessity" is used to express belief that, given a cause, only one outcome can be expected in the circumstances. If two or more mutually exclusive outcomes were in prospect, we would say any particular outcome is merely possible or probable. Saying that X and Y are *necessarily* connected is our way of proclaiming the "impossibility," given nature's uniformity, of any *x* being succeeded by a non-*y* (cf. EHU, Sec. 47). By regarding nature in this way, we are certainly not presupposing the rationalist view that causes entail effects. Only philosophers would even speculate on the parallel. Rather, belief in necessary connectedness is belief in the order and regularity of a universe where like effects follow like causes just as regularly as conclusions follow from appropriate premises (EHU, Sec. 59). The term "necessity" is used to express this belief.

As Hume fully realizes, his description of the ordinary use of the term fails to answer the important philosophical question —no doubt recondite to the common user—wherein the necessity lies. However, his revisionary work leads to a definite stance on such issues. His strategy, at least in the section of the *Enquiry* (VII) devoted to necessary connection, is first to determine how essential that idea is to causation, then to trace the idea to an impression source, and finally to assert the paradox that the idea *seems* meaningless:

> One event follows another; but we never can observe any tie between them. . . . The necessary conclusion *seems* to be that we have no idea of connexion or power at all, and that these words are absolutely without any meaning. (EHU, Sec. 58)

But immediately after propounding the paradox, Hume begins to dispel this overly sceptical view by a "method" showing that "when we say . . . that one object is connected with another, we mean only that they have acquired a connexion in our thought" (EHU, Sec. 59). He of course traces the idea and the connection to an impression of *reflection*. This is the more precise meaning promised at the beginning of Section VII (Sec. 49).

Hume intends to say not that ordinary statements about necessary connections between objects are meaningless and consequently to be eliminated, but rather that, philosophically speaking, the idea is more obscure than usually supposed and sometimes carries the false supposition that necessary connections exist in or between the objects themselves. There simply are no experiences to justify the latter claim. There is, however, an experience of associating objects (the "new impression") that justifies the way we ordinarily use terms to make causal inferences. That *usage* is not mistaken, and the terms so employed are not meaningless. A mistake occurs only when there is psychological projection of compulsion from the internal to the external and when causal terms are improperly used to refer to the external region. In his revisionary work Hume fulfills his initial promise to deliver a precise meaning of "necessary connection." But in his descriptive work he seems to grant that the way causal terms are commonly employed is meaningless only to the extent that an internal impression is taken to be an impression of sensation (cf. T, 168).

The task of revising causal notions begins to supplant the task of description with the development of the negative thesis that *there are no* necessary connections in objects independent of experience, a claim Hume refers to as the most "violent" of "all the paradoxes" in the *Treatise* (T, 165–67). ("Paradox" here seems to mean a thesis contrary to common belief and so entailing certain revisionary conclusions.)

In studying precisely how Hume's search for the original impression of necessity leads to conclusions that revise or reconstruct the common concept of causation, it is crucial to keep the following question in mind. After Hume has introduced the notion of constant conjunction, does he mean to revise the common concept by dropping the idea of necessity-in-objects as essential and substituting necessity-in-mind, or by dropping the idea of necessity altogther and substituting constant conjunction? Is he maintaining that causal relatedness consists essentially in: (1) a *necessary connection* between constantly conjoined objects *made by the mind,* a modified necessity theory that would merely revise certain common ideas about the nature of connectedness, or (2) a *constant conjunction* between disconnected successive objects, a pure regularity theory that would radically revise the common idea, or (3) both 1 and 2?

The textual evidence for Hume's revisionist position is characteristically difficult to untangle, yet it acquires a certain clarity when approached from two different, but compatible, perspectives:

(1) as a *genetic account* of the acquisition of causal beliefs;
(2) as a *reductionist account* of the idea of causation.

As a genetic account, Hume's argument may be divided into the following theses: the mind notices several similar pairs of objects that are constantly conjoined; this discovery leads to a new internal impression of which the ideas of necessary connection and power are copies; this internal impression is gradually attributed to external objects, leading us to believe mistakenly that necessary connections and powers exist between objects themselves and to make that belief an essential factor in our idea of causation. The correction of this mistake is the first project in Hume's task of revision. His conclusion at this stage includes a denial of the common belief in natural necessities independent of experience but does not include a denial of the common belief that necessity is essential to causation.

As a reductionist account, Hume's analysis attempts to show that the idea of causation is chiefly based on and is virtually reducible to the idea of necessary connection, which is then shown to be based on and to be reducible to connection in thought (customary imaginative transition). The connection in thought, in turn, is shown to be based on ("arises from," in Hume's language) the experience of constantly conjoined similar objects. So far as the relation apart from experience is concerned, the "connection" is entirely reducible to similar sets of separate objects repeatedly conjoined. At this stage necessity seems to be eliminated entirely as a criterion of causation, and Hume's theory appears to advance beyond the mere correction of a mistaken belief about causal connection to a positive reconstruction of the nature of causation that is quite different from ordinary ideas.

This distinction between Hume's reductionist and his genetic aims, we may tentatively hypothesize, accounts for the differences noted above in Hume's two definitions of cause.

II

But significant textual problems arise at this point. As Antony Flew points out, Hume curiously eliminates all mention of necessary connection in his definitions of "cause." After devoting a whole section to tracing the original of the idea, and finding it, we expect his definitions to reflect the "something more" than mere constant conjunction. Instead, says Flew, "he writes rather as if he had shown: not that talk of necessity does after all have some sense here, and what sense it has; but that really it has little or none, and arises from a misconception—

the projection of a mental association out on to a physical conjunction."[5] Flew's argument could be strengthened by mention of another puzzling fact. Hume says, both before and after the passages in the *Enquiry* and the *Treatise* where the definitions are formulated, that no adequate definition of cause can possibly be given "without comprehending, as a part of the definition, a *necessary connection* with its effect" (T, 77ff, 407; EHU, Sec. 74).

However, Flew's objection can be met. While it is true that neither the term "necessary connection" nor the *idea* (or copy) is mentioned in Hume's definitions, the impression (or original) is not entirely omitted. Hume's second definition in the *Enquiry* is "an object followed by another, and whose appearance always *conveys the thought* to that other" (EHU, Sec. 60, italics added). He mentions, in introducing the definition, that we have experience of this "customary transition." Flew seems to confuse the absence of the term with the absence of the term's meaning. The comparable definition in the *Treatise* similarly mentions mental *determination*. Hume appears in both cases to be defining causation in terms of the relevant empirical features of objects and a feature of mind. It is true that the first definition omits explicit reference to the crucial impression, but it should be noticed how Hume introduces that definition in the *Enquiry* (Sec. 60, italics added):

> Similar objects are always conjoined with similar. Of this we have experience. *Suitably to this experience,* therefore, we may define a cause to be an object, followed by another, and where all the objects similar to the first are followed by objects similar to the second.

The italicized prefatory remark qualifies the definition and perhaps further removes the force of objections such as Flew's. It must be admitted, however, that it is not entirely clear how this introduction should be construed. It may indicate that an object can be a cause only if suitably experienced, or it may merely mean that through experience we know there to be instances of similar objects constantly conjoined.

5. Antony Flew, *Hume's Philosophy of Belief* (London: Routledge & Kegan Paul, 1961), p. 123.

III

In any case, the problem raised by Flew is merely an introductory one that foreshadows a more disturbing interpretative question. J. A. Robinson has argued in detail the thesis that Hume's two definitions are neither intensionally nor extensionally equivalent, that only the first definition really defines the causal relation, and that the first alone is a philosophical analysis while the second is a statement of an empirical psychological theory mistakenly described by Hume as a definition. Robinson argues, specifically against Norman Kemp Smith, that Hume's theory of causation is intended to be a pure regularity theory that does not rest on a psychological theory of association. Kemp Smith's contention is that

> Hume is no supporter of what is usually meant by the "uniformity" view of causation. As he is careful to insist, causation is more than sequence, and more also than invariable sequence. We distinguish between mere sequence and causal sequence; and what differentiates the two is that the idea of necessitation (determination or agency) enters into the latter as a quite essential element.[6]

Robinson believes this interpretation confuses philosophical analysis of the concept of causation with psychological explanation of belief in necessary connection. Against all such interpretations, Robinson thinks Hume holds a pure regularity theory:

> [Df$_1$] is Hume's *definition* of the cause-effect relation, embodying his analysis of it as nothing more than an instance of a general uniformity of concomitance between two classes of particular occurrences, and as quite independent of any associations of ideas which may or may not exist in human minds.[7]

6. Norman Kemp Smith, *The Philosophy of David Hume* (London: Macmillan, 1941), pp. 91–92 (and quoted in Robinson, p. 41, fn. 7 below). Cf. also the statements by Kemp Smith on pp. 369 and 401. For a similar view, cf. R. W. Church, *Hume's Theory of the Understanding* (London: Allen and Unwin, 1968), pp. 81–84, and D. G. C. MacNabb, *David Hume* (Oxford: Basil Blackwell, 1966), 2nd ed., p. 106. A quite different view that accepts Kemp Smith's basic line of interpretation is offered in Barry Stroud, *Hume* (London: Routledge & Kegan Paul, 1977), pp. 88–92.
7. J. A. Robinson, "Hume's Two Definitions of 'Cause,'" *The Philosophical Quarterly* 12 (1962); reprinted in V. C. Chappell, ed., *Hume* (Garden City, N.Y.: Doubleday and Co., 1966: reissued by University of Notre Dame Press), pp. 129–47, with a "Reconsideration," pp. 162–68. Above quotation: pp. 138f.

Robinson buttresses this claim with two textual citations. First, he relies heavily on a passage notoriously exploited to exhibit Hume's belief that certain relations among external objects are mind-independent (T, 167–69). Secondly, Robinson correctly points out that, using the terminology of the *Treatise*, the second definition treats causation as a *natural* relation, while the first treats it as a *philosophical* relation. A philosophical relation involves only a comparison between two ideas, whereas an association between them is made in a natural relation (T, 170). Robinson compares this section of the *Treatise* with an earlier portion (10–15) where Hume explains the natural-philosophical distinction. Hume there enumerates seven genera of philosophical relations, which include the three natural relations of resemblance, cause-effect, and contiguity. Robinson takes Hume to mean that *all* relations are by definition philosophical, while the three natural ones happen also, in Hume's words, to "produce an association among ideas" (11). According to Robinson, Hume's explanation in the later sections, where causation is defined, turns attention from the ideas associated to the objects themselves and asks whether there is some property of the relation between these objects that accounts for the produced association between the ideas. In other words, is there something in the relation that explains the *"setting up* or *inducing* in the subject's mind of dispositions to pass" from one idea to another?[8] This question leads to Robinson's most distinctive interpretation of Hume's notion of natural relation:

> *Naturalness* is then simply the property of any relation R between a thing or event A and a thing or event B (*not* between the *idea* of A and the *idea* of B) whereby the observation of A and B standing to each other in the relation R is enough to induce an association between the idea of A and the idea of B. . . .
> Hume's notion of naturalness is *dispositional* in character: A's relation to B is *natural* if observation of A and B standing to each other in the relation in question would produce an association between the idea of A and the idea of B. This allows A and B to be naturally related without ever having been observed.[9]

Robinson claims that the existence of these natural relations is a contingent matter of fact discovered by psychology. By con-

---

8. *Ibid.*, p. 136.
9. *Ibid.*, pp. 136f, 164.

trast, relations discovered by philosophy would exist even in the absence of any natural ones:

> To say that a relation R is "philosophical" is to make a factually empty statement; all relations are philosophical. . . . It must not be thought that here we have a classification of all relations into two kinds, philosophical on the one hand and natural on the other. Thus the cause-effect relation, being a relation, is ipso facto a philosophical relation, and therefore to define it "as" a philosophical relation is, simply, to define it.[10]

Predictably, Robinson further contends that Hume wanted to show by his first definition that it is a "philosophical error" to include necessary connection in the analysis of the causal relation and that he only sought to explain, in terms of natural relations, why the error was committed by (pseudo-) definition Df_2.[11]

Robinson's interpretation is certainly inviting. It is well grounded in some regions of the Treatise, neatly holds together Hume's psychology and philosophy, and has other advantages as well. Similar analyses have subsequently been offered by Nicholas Capaldi and Terence Penelhum.[12] Unfortunately, the textual evidence against this interpretation is equally strong. This apparently paradoxical situation is to be explained, we shall argue, by the dual presence in Hume's system of: (1) the conjunction of his analysis of the common concept of causation and his genetic account and (2) his revision of the concept as prescribed by his reductionistic account. Hume's prevalent habit of both advancing and restraining his reductionism is the source of the problem.

But before passing to these deeper issues, several reasons for questioning Robinson's interpretation should be noted. First, as previously mentioned, Hume insists both before and after giving the definitions that "necessity makes an essential part of causation" (T, 407). He does not say an essential part merely of the idea, as consistency would require were Robinson's inter-

---

10. Ibid., p. 138.
11. Ibid., p. 140; cf. Basson, op. cit., pp. 73f.
12. Nicholas Capaldi, David Hume: The Newtonian Philosopher (Boston: Twayne Publishers, 1975), esp. pp. 120–23. Terence Penelhum, Hume (New York: St. Martin's Press, 1975), esp. pp. 46f, 53–57.

pretation correct. Similarly in the *Enquiry,* Hume defiantly challenges anyone to "define a cause without comprehending *as a part of the definition,* a necessary connection with its effect" (Sec. 74, our italics). These statements cannot be interpreted as isolated and casually expressed fragments, since in both books Hume follows them with the claim that removal of necessity removes causation.

Second, Hume's discussions of necessary connection seem dedicated to the discovery of an original impression that would *justify* use of the term "necessity." It would appear that Hume rightly should speak of something more than constant conjunction in his definitions. Perhaps, then, Robinson's thesis could be reversed—the second definition being the only true definition and the first mistakenly so regarded. The passages mentioned in the previous paragraph support this suggestion, as might the qualifying clauses already cited in regard to Flew, since they arguably tend to incorporate the impression of mental expectation into every definition in the *Enquiry.*

Third, Robinson's claim that for Hume causal relations among external objects are mind-independent may be regarded with suspicion, since there is no statement in the *Treatise* that explicitly affirms the existence of causal relatedness independent of experience. In the only place where Hume forthrightly says "Thought may well depend on causes for its operation, but not causes on thought" (T, 167), he uses the statement, and some similarly explicit ones, as an argument an *adversary* might adduce against the paradoxical character of his own theory. Hume's imaginary opponent is also represented as saying:

What! the efficacy of causes lie in the determination of the mind! As if causes did not operate entirely independent of the mind, and wou'd not continue their operation, even tho' there was no mind existent to contemplate them, or reason concerning them. (T, 167)

Hume does not explicitly maintain the directly opposite thesis —that causes do *not* operate independently of the mind—but he does introduce his imaginary adversary's objection as a notion contrary to his own sentiments. At any rate, it seems curious that the sole statement unquestionably supporting Robinson's claim is expressly introduced as the reactionary outburst of an opponent. Hume does say, on the very next page, that "As to what may be said, that the operations of nature are independent of our thought and reasoning, I allow it" (168); but he does not here say that *causal* relations are independent of thought, despite an acknowledgment that contiguity and succession exist independently. Also, it must be remembered that later in the *Treatise* Hume provides a psychological theory to explain why we suppose there to be an external universe. Hume's "admission" in the passage just cited (168) may only be his acknowledgment of what we must psychologically believe.

There is a still more important problem with Robinson's mind-independent argument. The passages he cites from Hume are actually *irrelevant* to Robinson's major thesis. If causation consists purely in constant conjunction, then it is unimportant, for purposes of *defining* causation (in Robinson's sense of definition), whether or not these constant conjunctions exist independently of experience. Whether the objects are constantly conjoined in experience or are so conjoined external to experience, they are all alike causally related. That they might be associated by an experiencing mind is, as Robinson puts it, a contingent psychological matter, not a definitional consideration.

Fourth, if one looks for even implicit support of Robinson's larger thesis in the *Treatise,* one is unlikely to find more than suggestive but distressingly ambiguous statements. The bulk of Book I, relevant to causation, is devoted to theories of mental activity, especially to the nature of necessary connection, causal inference, and belief. Having surveyed these subjects, Hume inserts the following rather puzzling remark immediately prior to the formal framing of his definitions:

'Tis now time to collect all the different parts of this reasoning, and by joining them together form an exact definition of the relation of cause and effect, which makes the subject of the present enquiry. This order wou'd not have been excusable, of first examining our inference from the [causal] relation before we had explain'd the relation itself, had it been possible to proceed in a different method. But as the nature of the relation depends so much on that of the inference, we have been oblig'd to advance in this seemingly preposterous manner. . . . (T, 169)

Numerous passages such as this one leave it unclear both whether causal relatedness depends at least in part on connection in thought and whether Hume is confusing his genetic inquiry with his reductionist purposes.

And, fifth, should the *Treatise* be set aside in favor of the briefer but author-touted *Enquiry,* not the slightest corroboration for Robinson's interpretation can be found. Hume neither introduces nor relies upon the philosophical relation-natural relation distinction; he simply enumerates three "principles of connection" in the opening sections (EHU, Sec. 19). Yet, as Robinson admits, the definitions themselves remain substantially the same.

IV

In spite of these preliminary objections to Robinson's pure regularity *interpretation,* we are prepared to go some way toward accepting his *conclusions.* The main barrier to accepting Robinson's arguments is the oversimplified way in which he sweeps aside countervailing passages, for Hume's several enterprises are never successfully drawn together in the neatly consistent package Robinson presents.[13] To obtain a clearer picture of what seems an inadvertent ambivalence in Hume's reflections on causation, his overall enterprise (as depicted above, in Section I) and its direction must first briefly be recalled.

After identifying the essential "idea of necessary connection," Hume directs his efforts toward discovering its original impression. The entire investigation is so far genetically directed. This context of inquiry does not itself dictate a revisionary or paradoxical theory of causation, for he might have followed certain predecessors in the nonparadoxical thesis that we have impressions (of sensation) of power, force, energy, etc. and that it is from these impressions that the idea of necessary connection is derived. Finding this thesis untenable, Hume turns instead to the category of impressions of reflection. The genetic quest for an original impression thus seems complete. But Hume feels impelled to explain further *why* the internal impression arises; he does so by citing experienced constant conjunctions.

13. Robinson does find some confusion in Hume's failure to distinguish "empirical psychology" from "philosophical analysis" and says this failure misleads readers. But Robinson also thinks, mistakenly, that the misleading feature can be corrected and Hume rendered consistent by *textual* analysis. We argue in later chapters that only a reconstruction of Hume's arguments can eliminate the tensions between his various enterprises.

The latter explanation is introduced as an extension of the genetic investigation. It locates the nonmental or purely sensory source of the idea being traced. But Hume's citations of constant conjunction often seem to play a second role over and above their function in the genetic account. Hume has a tendency (especially in the *Treatise*) to ignore momentarily the context of investigation and to speak as though causation could be reduced entirely to repetition of sequence; i.e., he is sometimes inclined to say that causes are *nothing but* similar objects constantly conjoined with their associates. This tendency appears only infrequently. Apart from the first definition, the following are the passages most clearly exemplifying the reductionistic strain in his writings:

Relation of cause and effect is a seventh philosophical relation, as well as a natural one. (T, 15)

We have no other notion of cause and effect, but that of certain objects, which have been *always conjoin'd* together, and which in all past instances have been found inseparable. We cannot penetrate into the reason of the conjunction. (T, 93)

Where objects are not contrary, nothing hinders them from having that constant conjunction, on which the relation of cause and effect totally depends. (T, 173)

Had it been said, that a cause is *that* after which *any thing constantly exists*; we should have understood the terms. For this is, indeed, all we know of the matter. (EHU, Sec. 74n)

Since these reductionistic sentiments carry Hume away from his immediate investigation, he never develops them and is always faithful in returning to the topic at hand. Moreover, his reductionist-seeming statements are all so unguarded that they veil rather than clarify his intentions; and they only appear exclusively reductionistic when isolated from their contexts. As previously mentioned, some statement of necessary connectedness in the mind always accompanies statements of the sort quoted above.

If one turns from the *Treatise* to the *Enquiry*, one finds striking passages to illustrate these problems. Consider the following quotations from the section on "Liberty and Necessity" (EHU, Secs. 75, 74n; cf. T, 399f):

Necessity may be defined two ways, conformably to the two definitions of *cause*, of which it makes an essential part. It consists either
in the constant conjunction of like objects, or in the inference of the
understanding from one object to another. Now necessity, in both
these senses, (which, indeed, are at the bottom the same). . . .
Constancy forms the very essence of necessity, nor have we any
other idea of it.

These passages seem entirely incompatible with many of Hume's
statements on the nature of causal necessity. He almost always
insists that necessity is "nothing but an internal impression of
the mind" (T, 165) and cannot consist in the relation of constant
conjunction. Perhaps, in asserting this equivalence, he *means*
to say what he says in a parallel portion of the *Treatise*: " 'Tis
the constant conjunction of objects, along with the determination of the mind, which constitutes a physical necessity" (T,
171). But the former passage, as it stands, is not consistent with
the latter.[14]

Such confusing passages seem the product of Hume's conviction, presented while *describing* the idea of causation and re-
inforced by his genetic investigation, that necessary connection
is an absolutely essential ingredient of the common idea. Whenever he discusses causes, even following the presentation of his
revisionary and genetic theses, he seems implicitly to presuppose
a thesis of the order of "necessary connectedness is a logically
necessary condition of causal relatedness." His reductionist
tendencies come to the foreground only to the extent that he
uncritically relaxes or suppresses this thesis, as his revisionary
efforts tend naturally to allow.

To put the point briefly, perhaps oversimply, Hume's text
harbors two incompatible lines of thought:

(1) Similar objects constantly conjoined with others, considered
apart from experience, are not causes; they are properly
causes only if necessarily connected.

---

14. This incompatibility charge is challenged in Robert McRae, "Hume on
Meaning," *Dialogue* 8 (1970), esp. pp. 488–91. McRae claims that while there
are two impression-sources of the idea of necessity (constant conjunction and
mental determination), there is only one *idea*. There are then two different
definitions of the same object. We cannot agree with his proposals, because
we cannot see that Hume's argument requires or even implies that there is
only one idea of necessity.

(2) Similar objects constantly conjoined with others, considered
apart from experience, are causes; the mind imposes a necessary connection when it discovers this relation.

Unfortunately, Hume never explicitly argues for or against (2),
a pure regularity theory, or (1), a modified necessity theory, in
a way that would indicate his true doctrine.
The real depth of Hume's hesitation between (1) and (2) can
only be appreciated when it is realized that he is actually committed to both accounts by certain of his key philosophical principles—a conclusion for which we shall argue in the next two
sections.

V

Let us now consider exclusively Hume's tendency toward a
pure regularity theory. In addition to the philosophical relations-
natural relations distinction, which Robinson rightly regards as
evidence for a pure regularity interpretation, Hume seems committed to this theory by the circularity of his definitions, by his
comments on "unknown causes," by his criticisms of causal
beliefs, and by his Rules. These four aspects of his work deserve
individual assessment as pillars for the pure regularity hypothesis.
  First, as several interpreters have observed, the second definition is circular and parasitic upon the first.[15] In both the
Treatise and the *Enquiry*, Df_2 is explicated in terms of constantly
conjoined objects plus their effect on the observer (T, 165).
"Determination of the mind" and "conveyance of thought" are
the effect words employed. The mind acquires this habit by
observation of constantly conjoined objects, which elsewhere are
said to "influence" it and to "produce" an association among
ideas (T, 155, 163, 172). X is the cause of Y partly because their
regular conjunction *causes* another event Z (a feeling). Since
the only way to understand such causal language is through
Df_1, Hume must mean that the habit of mental expectation
regularly follows and is temporally contiguous with certain ob-

---

15. Cf. C. J. Ducasse, "Critique of Hume's Conception of Causality," *Journal
of Philosophy* 63 (1966), p. 142, and reprinted in Tom L. Beauchamp, ed.,
Philosophical Problems of Causation (Encino, Calif.: Dickenson Publishing
Co., 1974). Cf. also Penelhum, *op. cit.*, p. 55.

servations of the first among constantly conjoined objects. His second "definition," on this reading, is not a definition at all, but an application or instance of the first definition.[16]

Second, as Robinson notices, Hume frequently indicates that on those occasions when the cause of some event is "secret," "unobserved," or "unknown," the event nonetheless *has a cause,* or at least we presuppose that it has a cause. Despite his insistence on restricting the use of induction, Hume praises those philosophers who adopt this "maxim" of uniformity rather than submit to the vulgar notion that there is fortuitous "irregularity in nature" (EHU, Secs. 47, 67f; T, 132). In this context "cause" seems to mean "pure regularity," because application of the uniformity maxim to concealed events presupposes causes where there are no observers to have feelings of determination.

Third, suppose momentarily that Hume actually does hold a modified necessity theory based on his genetic account. This theory would amount to nothing more than an explanation of the way in which causal beliefs are formed; it could not be construed in any sense as a framework for *justifying and criticizing* causal beliefs. Yet numerous passages clearly indicate that Hume regards himself both as a critic of causal beliefs and as a codifier of procedures for the justification of causal beliefs. When he criticizes theology, the evidence of the senses, education, dogmatism in all forms, belief in immortality, miracles, etc., he is clearly doing more than merely explaining how such beliefs are formed. He speaks of correcting factual beliefs about causal reasoning, so as to render the evidence of sensory experience "proper *criteria* of truth and falsehood" (EHU, Sec. 117), and his short section on "Rules by which to judge of causes and effects" (T, I.iii.15) is primarily intended to provide procedures for justifying causal beliefs.

Fourth, it appears that the feeling of expectation required by

16. Flew (*op. cit.,* pp. 122f) argues that the circularity charge is unfounded. He thinks "determination" and "conveys" are technical terms "for the alleged impression of habitual association" and are not *causal* terms. Of course, "determination" and its synonyms do refer to the impression, but Flew fails to see that they are also effect words for Hume, since the observation of *x* is regularly followed by the feeling *z*. (In private correspondence Professor Flew writes that "I have never been happy with either what I published or what I wrote and rejected in earlier drafts. And I am uneasy now." Correspondence of August 24, 1979.)

a necessity interpretation need play no role in verifying the existence of causal relations. This can be seen by considering the Rules section of the *Treatise*. Hume's intention in that section is to "fix some general rules, by which we may know when [causes and effects] really are so" (T, 173). The task is to specify the conditions that warrant causal statements. One needs rules if one is to determine the objective validity of such statements; Hume provides eight, the first four of which will suffice for present purposes. They form a set of individually necessary and jointly sufficient specifications of the truth of causal assertions:

(1) The cause and effect must be contiguous in space and time.

(2) The cause must be prior to the effect.

(3) There must be a constant union betwixt the cause and effect. . . .

(4) The same cause always produces the same effect, and the same effect never arises but from the same cause. (T, 173)

Hume treats rules (1) and (2) as stating the conditions of *conjunction* of cause and effect. They may be combined into one rule:

(1a) The cause and effect must be conjoined.

(3) and (4) also may be combined, as follows:

(2a) All objects of Type C are conjoined with objects of Type E; all objects of Type E are conjoined with objects of Type C.

According to (2a), causal relations are expressible in the form of universal generalizations (general laws). The "always" in Hume's formulation has tenseless reference to the complete set of particular sequences constituting instances of the laws; "all" performs this function in (2a). Singular causal statements, if questioned, could be supported by evidence corroborating the generalization relevantly satisfying (2a). If one knew that both of these specifications were fully satisfied in the case of particular objects x and y, he would know that "x causes y" is a true statement and that the inference from its antecedent to its consequent is warranted.

Hume's Rules seem to recognize that the validity of causal inferences does not depend on whether observers, when placed in the relevant circumstances, acquire the feeling of determination. Any observer who knew (*per impossibile*) that the above specifications were satisfied could make valid inferences without the occurrence of any internal impression of determination. Thus, no necessary connection, in Hume's psychological sense, need be involved in the causal relation, even if the idea of necessary connection is essential to the ordinary idea of the relation. Since satisfaction of the warrant-generating specifications provides all the evidence needed for the verification of causal statements, feelings of expectation add nothing essential and might even be misleading or mistaken (cf. Rule 6, p. 174).

According to this general analysis, Hume is committed to the position that any singular causal statement "x causes y" implies, indirectly perhaps, two conditions satisfying the above specifications:

(1a') x is conjoined with y.
(2a') All objects relevantly resembling x similarly are conjoined with objects relevantly resembling y.

This analysis perfectly conforms to definition Df_1—cause considered as a philosophical relation. Of course in ordinary causal statements, where an association is made between two objects, the asserter might know that (1a') obtains, but could only presuppose and not know the truth of (2a'). This person's presupposition would be manifested in a determination of the mind to pass automatically or "naturally" to y when x is present. This second analysis conforms closely to definition Df_2—cause considered as a natural relation.

Our analysis of Hume's commitments in his discussion of Rules thus generally accords with the *conclusions* reached in Robinson's analysis of the definitions, though our separate means to those conclusions differ markedly. Hume is committed, according to our pure regularity interpretation, to the claim that the actual warranting conditions of general causal statements ("X always produces Y") are different from the incomplete, inductively derived, warranting conditions ordinarily used ("X in all observed cases is known to have produced Y"). Both singular and general statements of the form "X causes Y" are true only when (1a') and (2a') are true, even though "x causes y" is ordinarily taken to be true whenever (1a') is true and (2a') is presupposed true in such a way that X is invariably associated with Y.

VI   C. 1

The four arguments discussed in Section V favor a pure regularity theory, according to which Hume's second definition reduces to the first. By emphasizing others of Hume's principles it is possible to reverse these conclusions. It can be argued that the first definition reduces to the second and that a modified necessity theory is textually plausible. Especially important in this regard are Hume's theories of meaning, relations, and inductive generalization.

Consider first Hume's theory of meaning, while keeping in mind Robinson's claim that Hume's two definitions are neither intensionally nor extensionally equivalent. According to Hume's theory, the meaning of a word is the idea for which it stands, and all meaningful ideas are traceable to parent impressions. In the case of "causation," what is meant is the set of impressions to which the idea of causal relatedness is traceable. This set seems to involve essentially and irreducibly the feeling of expectation to which the idea of necessary connection is traceable. Nothing either more or less metaphysical can be meant, since the limits of what can be meant are set by experience, and there exists no other impression source. Accordingly, "x causes y" seems to *mean* "X's are constantly conjoined with Y's and normal observers feel x necessitating y."

In pursuit of this suggestion, a distinction must be introduced between observed constancy of sequence and unobserved constancy of sequence. By Hume's own admission, observed constancy of sequence provides an insufficient basis for calling a sequence "causal" unless a feeling of determination accompanies it:

I . . . enlarge my view to comprehend several instances; where I find like objects always existing in like relations of contiguity and succession. At first sight this seems to serve but little to my purpose. The reflection on several instances only repeats the same object; and therefore can never give rise to a new idea. But upon farther inquiry I find, that the repetition is not in every particular the same, but produces a new impression. . . . (T, 155)

Within the context of Hume's empiricism the project of revising an idea that has such good experiential roots, by reducing it to the idea of something fundamentally different (loose, separate constancy of conjunction), seems doomed from the start. No impression can be identified that would show either that the idea under investigation *means* constancy or that it could (psychologically) be made to mean constancy. Yet the pure regularity intepretation takes us directly down this trail.

Moreover, it cannot plausibly be argued that Robinson's strategy of deemphasizing the notion of observed constancy, which seems to require a natural relation in order to be "considered" causal, while concentrating on unobserved constancy (i.e., constancy itself) as a philosophical relation, will improve the situation. Unobserved things are, of course, unexperienced; yet the notion of unobserved cases of *causation* can only be *understood* by means of immediately experienced impressions. The reductionistic analysis of causation is parasitic in meaning, then, on the genetic revisionary analysis, which gives the all-important experiential basis of causation. Accordingly, even if Robinson is correct in maintaining that the two definitions are neither intensionally nor extensionally equivalent, Hume's own theory of meaning or definition leads to the conclusions that the *second* is a primary definition and that Robinson's distinction between the first as a philosophical analysis and the second as an empirical psychological theory is tenuous at best.

This line of argument may be used to weaken the pillars supporting the pure regularity interpretation. First, the claim that correct inferences *could* be made without feelings of mental determination can be challenged. This is a logical "could"; correct inference without such feelings is logically possible. But Hume's theory of inductive inference runs against this logical grain. He indicates that no observer could, psychologically, make valid inferences without feeling determination. The contradictory of this contingent statement of psychological fact is, of course, logically possible; but Hume seems clearly to believe that ,if the relevant conditions were satisfied, any normal observer would experience an impression of determination and that independently of this feeling, no observer would be *motivated* to arrive at causal conclusions. Accordingly, the evidence needed to verify causal claims, as required by Hume's specifications, could not be recognized as evidence independently of feelings of expectation.

Second, Robinson assumes that for Hume philosophical relations are independent of mental processes. Hume has remarkably little to say about this matter, but his few comments on relations between objects (as distinct from "relations of ideas") indicate that philosophical as well as natural relations are the products of the mind's comparison of objects (T, 13f, 170). Philosophical relations obtain, on this interpretation, only if there exists an observer who does the comparing, for there is nothing in the ideas themselves on which the relation depends and to which it can be reduced. If this account of Hume's theory of relations is correct, it has important consequences for Robinson's interpretation. As Donald Gotterbarn has pointed out,[17] Df_1 describes constant conjunction in terms of resembling objects. Since resemblance is a philosophical relation, a mental comparison seems required even by Df_1. More importantly, if mental acts are required for causal relations, then the two definitions may be extensionally (though not intensionally) equivalent after all. It is not likely that Hume would admit resembling conjunctions actually recognized as constant conjunctions to be extensionally distinct from those conjunctions accompanied by feelings of mental determination. Unfortunately, Hume's passages on relations are sufficiently opaque that they make it difficult to interpret his other theories in their light. Nonetheless, the mind-dependence interpretation has at least as plausible a textual basis as the mind-independence interpretation.

Third, Rule (2a), which is crucial for the pure regularity interpretation, requires that causal relations entail the existence of unrestricted universal generalizations. But Hume here confronts the problem encountered by logical positivists who held a strict verifiability theory of meaning. Since meaning is dependent upon verification by an impression or set of impressions, any meaningful statement entails and is entailed by a set of impression statements. Unfortunately, this demand cannot be met in the case of unrestricted universal generalizations, since they are

17. Donald Gotterbarn, "Hume's Two Lights on Cause," *The Philosophical Quarterly* 21 (April, 1971), pp. 168–71; "Hume's Definitions of Cause: Skepticism with regard to Lesher's Two Senses," *Journal of the History of Philosophy* 14 (January, 1976), pp. 99f; and "How Can Hume Know Philosophical Relations?" *The Journal of Critical Analysis* 4 (1973), pp. 133–41, esp. 135f, 139. Many problems in the interpretation of Hume on these matters are explored in Alan Hausman, "Hume's Theory of Relations," *Nous* 1 (1967), pp. 255–82.

not logically reducible to a finite set of impression statements. The problem is exacerbated in Hume's case by his scruples concerning laws of nature. He argues that we cannot *in principle* confirm those unobserved cases of causal relatedness required by Rule (2a). The evidence for such cases reduces completely to actually observed cases. But no universal generalization satisfying (2a) is fully confirmable by this evidential base, because there is no guarantee that the future will be "conformable to the past" (EHU, Secs. 30–32). To reduce causal statements to statements of uniformity of sequence independent of experience, then, is to reduce them to statements (causal laws) that are meaningless on Hume's account.

This modified necessity interpretation of Hume might be thought to carry a hidden benefit for anyone seeking to render Hume more consistent. Even though the second definition (Df$_2$) is, according to this second interpretation, Hume's true definition, the tension between the two definitions could be eased somewhat by regarding the first as a mere forerunner of the second. The second, then, would be considered Hume's only *complete* definition. Robinson's charge that the two definitions are mutually exclusive could be blunted in this way by a proponent of the necessity interpretation. In any case, by arguing for both interpretations we have tried to show thus far that Hume is committed, by different principles, to *both* definitions as true and primary. In reaching this conclusion we do not deny, of course, that there may be important relations between the two definitions.

VII

Our contention that there are two theories of causation and two resultant definitions of "cause" in Hume's text can be supported and extended as a defense of Hume by further considering his account of meaning.

We have seen that Hume says, "Necessity may be defined two ways conformably to the two definitions of *cause*" (EHU, Sec. 75), and that these two definitions of necessity state the word's two "senses." Hume's treatments of "necessity" and "cause" are but two examples of his standard approach to problems of meaning and definition. He has a general theory of definition, and he employs it for the analysis of all terms: words obtain meaning through their customary association with ideas (T, 20–22), and all ideas derive from impressions. Determining the meaning of obscure terms is a matter of discovering the original impressions of which the ideas they name are copies. To define or give the meaning of a word, then, is to state what may be called its impression-source. That Hume finds two different impression-sources for the idea of necessity is understandable. His reductionistic account describes only the external impression-sources (impressions of sensation), as in Df_1; while the genetic account describes both the external and the internal (reflective) impression-sources, as in Df_2.

If this interpretation is correct, it follows that Hume's analysis *requires* that there be two definitions, two meanings, and two senses of "cause," just as Hume always says when he turns his attention explicitly to the number of definitions and meanings. And this is equally true of both "cause" and "necessity," as James Lesher has perspicaciously pointed out:

> In the discussion of "necessity," Hume recognizes two *senses* (EHU, p. 97) of the term because there are two separate conditions which give rise to the idea, and since he is quite aware that neither constant conjunction nor mental determination is what is ordinarily meant by the term, he says that "as long as the meaning is understood, I hope the word can do no harm" (EHU, p. 97). . . . Since there are distinct experiences, there are distinct impressions, and hence distinct ideas of cause, or like "necessity," distinct senses of "cause."[18]

Lesher's interpretation is correct in all essentials, but needs modest clarification. Lesher might be taken to mean that distinct (and not merely distinguishable) *experiences* of constant conjunction and of mental determination eventuate in distinct impressions and ideas of causation. That view is of course incorrect. The idea of causation does not derive immediately from the experience of constant conjunction. For Hume there cannot (psychologically) be an experience of constantly conjoined causal

18. James H. Lesher, "Hume's Analysis of 'Cause' and the 'Two-Definitions' Dispute," *Journal of the History of Philosophy* 11 (July, 1973), pp. 387-92, esp. 391. Through correspondence with Lesher we have been significantly aided in structuring the clarification that follows this quotation (Correspondence of September 21, 1979).

items without an attendant mental determination, but philosophical analysis can distinguish the two different sets of
impression-sources. To track down a word's meaning is for
Hume not merely to trace an idea or a term to an impression-
source, but also to reduce complex impression-sources to their
simplest ingredients. Because he holds that the relationship between words and ideas is purely conventional, two quite different
kinds of things may be called "causes," if we so choose to make
the designation. The word can have two perfectly good senses
even if a cause in one sense is always accompanied by a cause
in the other sense. "Necessity," according to this analysis, means
both (1) constant conjunction, which can be analyzed into a
repetition of resembling impressions contiguously and successively related,[19] and (2) the impression of mental determination
produced by the constant conjunction. The two definitions of
"cause" are shown to be extensionally nonequivalent by *analysis
into* these two different impression-sources, which are coextensive in the *experience* of cause and effect.

This interpretation makes it possible to explain why there is
both an intensional and an extensional nonequivalence. Lesher's
argument leads correctly to the conclusion that there are two
distinct senses of "cause" and hence an intensional nonequivalence. The two are extensionally nonequivalent, however, only
if the elements of their different extensions can be distinguished
by reductive analysis of the complex idea of cause. The extension of cause in sense Df_2 can on this interpretation be seen to
have the additional ingredient of mental determination. This
appears also to be the grain of truth in Robinson's otherwise
incorrect claim that Hume's first definition is a philosophical
analysis and the second merely a psychological theory.

This interpretation of Hume's account of definition has still
other implications for theories such as Kemp Smith's and Robinson's, each of whom accepts the view that the two definitions

19. There are confusing aspects to this claim, since there is no impression
of the conjunction of similar objects, as several philosophers have pointed
out. Cf., e.g., Church, *op. cit.*, p. 85, and Jaegwon Kim, "Causation, Nomic
Subsumption, and the Concept of Event," *The Journal of Philosophy* 70
(1973), pp. 217f. Kim points out that constant conjunction is a relation of
types of events and "makes no clear or nontrivial sense when directly applied to spatiotemporally bounded individual events."

are neither extensionally nor intensionally equivalent and that Hume has only one correct or primary definition. If we are correct, their respective claims that one definition is primary are unacceptable, precisely because there are two correct and primary meanings. Accordingly, it is not an unresolvable paradox, as Robinson seems to think, that *the* causal relation is definable in two extensionally nonequivalent ways.

On the other hand, we do not wish to claim too much for this interpretation as an account of Hume's text. In explicating the Modified Necessity Theory in the previous section we attributed only *one* of the two definitions to Hume. We did so in order to emphasize those Humean principles that tend to support the Modified Necessity interpretation. Our present conclusions in this section show, of course, that this single-definition emphasis need not be made in interpreting Hume. Our general conclusion is that the two theories of causation deeply embedded in Hume's text determine the two different definitions. The text does not allow us to decide, however, which of the two theories is the deeper or more important.

VIII

In this chapter it has been argued that Hume's text contains two distinct theories of causation and two distinct definitions of "cause." However, it has only been argued that Hume is implicitly committed by his philosophical principles to both theories. It has not been argued that Hume intended to advance two different theories, or even that he explicitly maintains either theory. Indeed quite the opposite seems likely: Hume wanted a unified theory of causation and intended to provide one. In subsequent chapters we shall argue that Hume's writings on causation can rationally be reconstructed so that a unified theory emerges that is faithful to his intentions. As a conclusion to this chapter, these arguments may be anticipated by sketching an entirely different perspective from which the two theories and the two definitions may be viewed.

Robinson and most all recent writers on causation believe that Hume holds a pure regularity theory of causation. For instance, J. L. Mackie, who allies himself with Robinson, has dubbed this theory "heroic Humeanism," interpreting it to mean that statements of causal connection are nothing but statements of *de facto* constant conjunction.[20] This "Humean" theory has been subjected to intense scrutiny in contemporary philosophy. It has been found deficient because it is unable to distinguish causal laws from statements of *de facto* regularity. No doubt an unguarded statement of heroic Humeanism is philosophically objectionable. But is heroic Humeanism Hume's position? After all, there is the second definition of "cause," which escapes serious notice in the Robinson-Mackie interpretation despite Hume's repeated assertion that, "According to my definitions, necessity makes an essential part of causation" (T, 407). We have seen that Hume even boldly challenges other philosophers to provide a definition of "cause" without "comprehending, as a part of the definition, a *necessary connexion*" (EHU, Sec. 74). If these passages are taken seriously, and not explained away in terms of Hume's reductionistic tendencies and the single sense of "necessity" accompanying them, then he can only be interpreted as thinking that heroic Humeanism is false. And if his second definition of "cause" is read simply as his insistence that necessity in a second sense must play a role in any correct theory of causation, then we think it is possible to construct a unified and defensible Humean theory of causation. This is the view we shall defend as the account most faithful to the spirit of Hume's intentions.[21]

20. J. L. Mackie, *The Cement of the Universe: A Study of Causation* (Oxford: Clarendon Press, 1974), pp. 198f.
21. See below pp. 139ff, esp. pp. 140 and 156f.

2

Causal and Inductive
Scepticism

IN THIS CHAPTER we turn to the interpretation of Hume's philosophy as a sceptical account of causation and of induction (causal inference). The first section links our treatment of Hume's two definitions in the previous chapter with the question of whether Hume is a sceptic about causation and inductive reasoning. We there argue that Hume is not a sceptic about the causal relation; and, in the remainder of the chapter, we show that he is not a sceptic concerning inductive inference and the claims of reason generally.

These arguments should lend considerable weight to the claims of Chapter 1. The attribution to Hume of what Mackie calls "heroic Humeanism" appears plausible largely because Hume's account of causation is generally considered an indivisible part of a general sceptical program. For example, Mackie and others say that Hume is a sceptic both about induction and about the inclusion of any sense of "necessity" in his definitions of "cause"—and that he is a sceptic about both for the same reasons. We argue that this interpretation cannot be substantiated and that Hume's only major complaint about induction and causal necessity is that rationalists have misunderstood the nature of causation and inductive inference.

I

There are a number of possible ways to formulate the notion that Hume is a sceptic about causation. One way is to derive some type of scepticism from one or both of the definitions of "cause" examined in Chapter 1. Such a tactic has been perspicuously outlined by Wade Robison:

> One tradition opts for D_1 and treats Hume as a proponent of the Uniformity Thesis. . . . On this view the focus of Hume's scepticism is the problem of induction: if we cannot distinguish causal from casual regularities, how can we justify inferring unobserved events from observed ones?
>
> The other tradition opts for D_2 and commits Hume to a subjectivist thesis. . . . On this view Hume's scepticism centres not on how we can determine when we have got an objective causal relation, but on how we can even say that there could be one.[1]

That Hume is not a sceptic in the first sense is demonstrated in later sections of this chapter, where it is argued that he makes a general distinction between experientially or inductively well-grounded beliefs and purely artificial or associational ones (cf. esp. Sec. IV, point 4). That he is not a sceptic in the second or "subjectivist" sense can be seen by a brief recapitulation of the argument in the first chapter. It was there argued that Hume is sceptical about both the common man's and the rationalists' beliefs in the objective existence of necessary connections in nature. In this regard Hume is sceptical about certain views that posit the existence of necessary connections among objects. This scepticism focuses only on the *nonmental* existence of necessary connectedness. In other respects Hume is neither sceptical nor even revisionary in the account of causation he develops.

On the other hand, given the argument of Chapter 1, the following interpretation *is* a correct attribution to Hume of "sceptical" views: on neither of Hume's theories of causation is the existence of an objectively necessary connection between objects a logically necessary condition of their being related as cause

1. Wade L. Robison, "Hume's Causal Scepticism," in *David Hume: Bicentenary Papers*, ed. G. P. Morice (Austin: University of Texas Press, 1977), pp. 156–57. A variant of the second type of scepticism is mentioned and rejected by Barry Stroud, *Hume* (London: Routledge & Kegan Paul, 1977), p. 92. Robison's broader program for interpreting Hume as an inductive sceptic is found in two other articles: "David Hume: Naturalist and Metasceptic," in D. W. Livingston and J. T. King, eds., *Hume: A Re-Evaluation* (New York: Fordham University Press, 1976), pp. 23–49; and "Hume's Scepticism," *Dialogue* 12 (1973), pp. 87–99.

and effect; yet, by his own admission, the idea of an objectively necessary connection is an essential part of causal relatedness in the ordinary sense of "cause." Since Hume's arguments delete this condition, he has significantly altered the meaning of the term "cause." But what follows from this "sceptical" view? One possible conclusion is that Hume meant to embrace something approximating Russell's declaration that the notion of causation as ordinarily understood is a "relic of a bygone age" that therefore deserves "complete extrusion from the philosophical vocabulary."[2] If this position is Hume's, as Ducasse claims,[3] then clearly he is a sceptic about causation in a significant sense.

It is one thing to say that Hume is sceptical concerning the commitments of the *common concept* of cause, or the *rationalists' use* of cause, and quite another to suggest that he seeks to expunge the notion altogether. The argument sketched in the previous paragraph shows at most that Hume is a sceptic about certain features of the ordinary and rationalistic conceptions of cause, which features he rejects; the argument does not show that he is sceptical about the existence of the causal relation. A similar assessment holds if his "scepticism" is formulated in more general ways, such as those D. C. Stove and Terence Penelhum have proposed. They hold that Humean scepticism is the position that "no proposition which is not itself observed to be true is rendered more likely to be true by the citation of evidence from experience."[4] Whether Hume is a sceptic about *causation* in this sense depends on how the "proposition" about causation is formulated. If the proposition is "There are causal relations in the ordinary sense or in the rationalistic sense of objectively necessary connections," then Hume does reveal a sceptical attitude about such relations. But if the proposition is "There are true causal statements," then we have seen that Hume is nonsceptical, for there are causes in his philosophy. Even though this proposition is "not itself observed to be true," it is rendered more likely by the evidence of constant conjunctions.

2. Bertrand Russell, "On the Notion of Cause," *Mysticism and Logic* (Garden City, N. Y.: Doubleday, 1917), p. 174.
3. C. J. Ducasse, *Causation and the Types of Necessity* (Seattle: University of Washington Press, 1924; New York: Dover Publications, 1969), p. 50.
4. This formulation is from Terence Penelhum, *Hume* (New York: St. Martin's Press, 1975), p. 50. Stove's views are treated in detail in Section V below.

All things considered, it seems both less confusing and more accurate to say that Hume provides a revisionary rather than a sceptical analysis of causation. His revisionary analysis, after all, is not merely a linguistic proposal concerning proper use of the word "cause." He attempts to discover the true nature of the causal relation. His conclusion cannot fairly be described as a sceptical one if he is thus understood as providing truth conditions for causal statements. In contrast to the interpretations of Robison, Penelhum, and Stove, a more reasonable approach was suggested by Thomas Reid, perhaps Hume's severest antisceptical critic.[5] Whereas Reid saw Hume as endorsing an "absolutely sceptical" system of philosophy, he thought Hume simply had a different *notion* of causation than did other philosophers. Reid thus did not take Hume to be sceptical about the *existence* of causal relations. As Reid recognized, Hume's scepticism extends to the definitions of cause that both ordinary language and philosophical tradition had handed down.[6] But Hume was not sceptical about the existence of causal relations, as *he* defined them. Doubts to the contrary rest largely on the belief that Hume is a sceptic about induction, a topic to which we now turn.

II

Irrespective of whether Hume is sceptical about causal connection, is he sceptical about causal or inductive reasoning? The answer to this question, we shall argue, is essentially the same as the one just provided about causation: Hume is sceptical about *rationalist claims* concerning the power and scope of

5. Thomas Reid, *Philosophical Works,* Hamilton edition, with an Introduction by Harry Bracken (Edinburgh 1895 printing, Georg Olms Verlagsbuchhandlung, 1967), pp. 83 (Letters to Gregory), 456f (*Intellectual Powers*), 604, 627 (*Active Powers*).
6. Even more charitable interpretations of Hume than Reid's do exist. For example, Harry Silverstein has suggested to us that insofar as the ordinary use of "cause" allows that necessity may be internal, Hume's attempt to make the meaning more precise may be regarded as a clarification and/or explanation, and not necessarily as revisionary. Also, a balanced and useful interpretation of Hume's general scepticism is found in James Noxon, *Hume's Philosophical Development: A Study of his Methods* (Oxford: Clarendon Press, 1973), pp. 8–16.

causal reasoning, but not sceptical about causal reasoning itself. We proceed now to a series of arguments in defense of the following interpretation: Hume may in many respects be a sceptic, but he is not a sceptic about induction. In those passages commonly said to exhibit scepticism about induction, Hume's intentions have been misinterpreted. He is concerned to show that inductive reasoning can provide neither self-evident certainty nor the logical necessity that uniquely characterizes demonstrative reasoning (*a priori* reasoning), and also that demonstrative reasoning cannot prove matters of fact by its own resources alone. Thus, the problem of induction, as that problem is conceived today, is simply not to be found in Hume's philosophy. (Following modern usage, we use the expressions "inductive reasoning" and "inductive inference," rather than "causal reasoning" or "causal inference.")

Most of Hume's final views on causal inference are presented in Sections IV–V.i of the first *Enquiry*. His earlier views are sprinkled throughout the *Treatise* and then collated in a remarkably succinct summary in the *Abstract*. These passages are the source of his fame as the discoverer of the modern problem of induction. But on our reading of Hume, his expositors and critics have unwittingly collaborated to present a confused and mistaken picture of his views both on the problem of induction and on the related problem of providing rational support for inductively derived conclusions. In general, these expositors claim that Hume is a complete sceptic about induction. Specifically, they contend: (1) that he thinks no inductive procedures provide rational justifications, (2) that he thinks there are no rational justifications of inductive procedures, (3) that he does not distinguish between rational and irrational belief, (4) that he advances an epistemology which implies that our factual "knowledge" is reducible to an irrational faith, and (5) that his critique of induction undermines his own empirical method. These claims are made by philosophers as diverse as Will, Kneale, Popper, Stove, Penelhum, and Bennett. We shall refer to their interpretations, as revealed in the following passages, as "the received view" of Hume's positions on inductive justifications and on the rationality of inductive procedures:

The standard argument for complete inductive scepticism, for the belief that inductive procedures have no rational and no empirical justification whatever, is the one stated in a small variety of ways in the writings of Hume. . . . We have, accordingly, no reason for believing any of these inferences; they are all a matter of . . . "animal faith."[7]

F. L. Will

Hume was unable or unwilling to make any distinction between rational and irrational belief, and so for him there could be no hope of an escape from irrational confidence to something better. . . . What shocks us is Hume's assertion that induction can be no more than the association of ideas without rational justification.[8]   *William Kneale*

[Hume was] a believer in an irrationalist epistemology. . . . Our "knowledge" is unmasked as being not only of the nature of belief, but of rationally indefensible belief—of *an irrational faith.*[9]   *Karl Popper*

[Hume held that] "All predictive-inductive inferences are unreasonable." This captures the nonpsychological, the evaluative, and the unfavourable meaning of Hume's conclusion [that] even *after* we have had experience of the appropriate constant conjunction, it is not reason (but custom, etc.) which determines us to infer the idea (e.g of heat) from the impression (e.g. of flame).[10]   *D. C. Stove*

Hume certainly holds that because inductive inference is formally invalid, it lacks rational justification. This conclusion, however, divides into at least three contentions: (1) that inductive conclusions are incurably vulnerable (inductive fallibilism); (2) that there is real possibility that the course of nature may change in the future from what it has been in the past; (3) that no evidence, however great in quantity, can contribute any likelihood to the conclusion of any inductive inference (inductive scepticism). Each is thought by him to be established by the formal invalidity of induction. Clearly (2) is more radical than (1). . . . Clearly (3) is more radical than (2). . . . Their combination is a total scepticism about induction.[11]   *Terence Penelhum*

In considering any belief's intellectual standing, all Hume will do is demand its birth-certificate. . . . Hume's over-insistence on our in-

7. F. L. Will, "Will the Future Be Like the Past?" *Mind* 56 (1947); reprinted in *Logic and Language*, Second Series, ed. by A. Flew (Garden City, N.Y.: Doubleday, 1965), pp. 249f, 253.

8. William Kneale, *Probability and Induction* (Oxford: Clarendon Press, 1949), p. 55.

9. Karl Popper, *Objective Knowledge* (Oxford: Oxford University Press, 1972), pp. 4f.

10. D. C. Stove, *Probability and Hume's Inductive Scepticism* (Oxford: Clarendon Press, 1973), pp. 34, 31.

11. Penelhum, *op. cit.*, p. 52.

tellectual passivity also ignores the causal judgments which look interrogatively rather than confidently towards the future. . . . His theory does not cover non-credulous, tentative, interrogative predictions. He clearly thinks that beliefs are the whole story.[12]   *Jonathan Bennett*

Various reasons in support of such interpretations are cited by these authors, but generally their accounts rest on one, or both, of the following reconstructions of Hume's arguments:

Argument I
   (1) All factual beliefs are based solely on instinct and not on justifying reasons.
   (2) If all factual beliefs are based solely on instinct and not on justifying reasons, then all factual beliefs are irrational.
∴ (C_1) All factual beliefs are irrational.
   (3) All inductively derived beliefs form a subset of the set of factual beliefs.
   (4) If all factual beliefs are irrational and all inductively derived beliefs form a subset of the set of factual beliefs, then no inductive conclusion can be rationally justified.
∴ (C_2) No inductive conclusion can be rationally justified.

Argument II
   (1) The entire institution of inductive reasoning cannot be rationally justified.
   (2) If the entire institution of inductive reasoning cannot be rationally justified, then no inductive conclusion can be rationally justified.
∴ (C) No inductive conclusion can be rationally justified.

These arguments, which reach the same conclusion, are certainly valid, but are they Hume's? We contend that both premise (1) of Argument I and premise (1) of Argument II are incorrect depictions of Hume's views and that both lead to a final conclusion that is an equally incorrect depiction of Hume's views.

In order to show the mistaken character of these two reconstructions of Hume's arguments, it is necessary to introduce a preliminary distinction between *external* and *internal* justifications. The received view holds that Hume's "critique" of induc-

12. Jonathan Bennett, *Locke, Berkeley, Hume* (Oxford: Oxford University Press, 1971), pp. 300-2.

tion is radical in that it demands a justification of inductive reasoning in general—the whole institution of inductive procedures and standards. This radical demand for an external justification of inductive reasoning must be distinguished from a demand for internal justification of particular inductive conclusions, as evaluated within the institution of inductive reasoning. We shall refer to problems of internal justification as *internal problems.* They are answerable only in reference to established standards of inductive evidence. We shall refer to the problem of external justification as the *external problem.* It involves a radical challenge to all internal standards of inductive reasoning, and it demands a noncircular justification, one that does not rely on inductive reasoning. This problem will be understood as the request for a noncircular demonstration of the rational justifiability of the entire institution of inductive reasoning. Any internal problem assumes the legitimacy of some inductive policies and only questions the rational justifiability of a particular inductive conclusion.

However one construes Hume's stance on the external problem, it would be precipitous to label his philosophy as a whole— or even his epistemology—irrationalist. One major reason for this conclusion is that Hume expressly advocates standards for the resolution of *internal* problems. He quite clearly believes some inductive conclusions rational and others irrational, as assessed by a set of appropriate inductive standards that even such critics as Ducasse acknowledge him to have pioneered.[13] (We document Hume's commitment to inductive standards and his entitlement to this commitment in Section IV.) Nonetheless, the received view of Hume's position on the *external* problem leads to the suspicion that a crucial inconsistency haunts his philosophy: his celebrated "critique" of induction seems to undercut the inductive methodology he both employs and defends. It must be conceded that if Hume does in fact hold either premise (1) of Argument I or premise (1) of Argument II, he is mired in inconsistency. But, as we shall now argue, he holds neither premise, and so is not guilty of such inconsistency. We begin our argument to this conclusion by demonstrating the

13. C. J. Ducasse, "Critique of Hume's Conception of Causality," *The Journal of Philosophy* 63 (1966), pp. 145f.

implausibility of Argument II as an interpretation of Hume's views.

III

An examination of Argument II must answer two closely related questions: (A) Does Hume explicitly raise the external problem— i.e., does he demand a rational justification of the entire institution of inductive procedures? (B) Does he advance a sceptical answer to the external problem, and thereby undermine the internal use of the very inductive standards he otherwise supports? The received view answers affirmatively to (A), and it is thereby disposed, we suggest, to answer (B) in the affirmative as well.

But an affirmative answer to either (A) or (B) depends on a misinterpretation. It was never Hume's intent to question the entire institution of inductive procedures and standards. His argument is a frontal attack on rationalist assumptions that at least some inductive arguments are demonstrative; it is not a demand for a wholesale justification of induction and a fortiori not a sceptical assault on induction. It is an argument that rejects rational intuition or understanding, while proceeding from premises about imagination, custom, and perception. Moreover, if considered as an attack on reason, Hume's critique is directed specifically against the rationalistic conception of reason. It is not an unrestricted scepticism concerning what today we often call "reason" and "rational justification." Hume sometimes uses the word "reason" and its analogs in a narrower way than is common today, and he often substitutes terms such as "experience" and "custom" where we would likely use "reason." Perhaps because of such tendencies, commentators have transformed his claim that no inductive inference can be supported and hence justified rationally, in the narrow a priori sense, into the far different claim that no inductive inference can be justified rationally, in the broader contemporary sense of "rationality." This interpretation transplants an alien equivocation into Hume's philosophy. His scepticism concerns only rationalistic uses of "reason," not the sagacious use of what he calls "reasoning from matters of fact." Thus, in his discussions of inductive inference (EHU, Secs. 20–38; cf. T, 77–93), his arguments are intended to show that pure reason cannot demonstratively prove matters of fact and that induction cannot provide demonstratively certain knowledge. The case for this reading of Hume may be supported in two ways: (1) by a consideration of Hume's anti-rationalist concerns, as informed by the longstanding rationalist-empiricist clash; (2) by a close textual analysis of Hume's arguments concerning induction.

1. Hume's Anti-Rationalism

In Hume's era pure reason was often considered capable of deriving sweeping factual conclusions. Norman Kemp Smith has incisively described (and documented) this use of "reason" by rationalist philosophers:

> One consequence, inevitably resulting from the mathematical method, is the identification of . . . causation with explanation. If all things follow from their grounds in the same way that the different properties of a triangle follow from its definition, the one possible form of connection between real existences must be that of logical dependence. And that all-important consequence (implied though not openly recognised in Descartes' system) Spinoza states in the most explicit manner. Like Leibniz, he takes the principle of causality as being a necessary truth of reason, and as identical with the principle of ground and consequent. The effect is that which can be deduced with logical necessity from the notion of the cause. When no such necessary conceptual relation exists between phenomena, they cannot be causally related.[14]

Because such views were then flourishing, a broad use of the term "reason" was anathema to eighteenth-century empiricists, and Hume was understandably hesitant about employing the term in any way that might have rationalistic associations (cf. EHU, Sec. 36n; T, 64, 639). The single most important rationalistic view under scrutiny in his work is the Cartesian (and even

---

14. Norman Kemp Smith, "The Cartesian Principles in Spinoza and Leibniz," in his *Studies in the Cartesian Philosophy* (New York: Macmillan, 1902), pp. 143f. Several other influential philosophers and scientists of the time who shared these views are canvassed in Donald W. Livingston, "Hume on Ultimate Causation," *American Philosophical Quarterly* 8 (1971), esp. pp. 63ff; Julius Weinberg, *Ockham, Descartes, and Hume* (Madison: University of Wisconsin Press, 1977), pp. 94, 115ff; Barbara Winters, "Hume on Reason," *Hume Studies* 5 (1979), pp. 26ff; and Eric Steinberg, "Introduction" to Hume's *An Enquiry Concerning Human Understanding* (Indianapolis: Hackett Publishing Co., 1977), p. xiii.

Lockean) belief that there can be synthetic *a priori* knowledge about the world derived from self-evident first principles. Hume repeatedly argues that induction is nondemonstrative; his model of a demonstrative argument is one that proceeds from self-evident *a priori* premises to a conclusion certified by deductive logic. Just as one of Newton's ambitions was to eliminate this procedure in the natural sciences (and Hume's science in the *Treatise* is notoriously Newtonian), so the larger purpose of Hume's treatment of induction is to attack this rationalistic conception of reason. Hume shows first that demonstrative reasoning does not yield factual results and, second, that induction is not marked by the logical necessity attending demonstrative reasoning. This two-part demonstration concludes Hume's argument against rationalism, and his argument against rationalism is the whole point of his "critique" of induction. Far from being a sceptical challenge to induction, then, Hume's "critique" is little more than a prolonged argument for the general position that Newton's inductive method must replace the rationalistic model of science.[15]

It is thus easy to see why Hume restricts "reason" to *a priori* reason in those contexts where he directly discusses the nature of induction (and also why he incorporates restrictions to disallow synthetic *a priori* reasoning). Apart from these special contexts, he refers to inductive inference as "a true species of reasoning" (T, 97n) and uses the term "reason" in a looser sense approximating our ordinary usage in these contexts today. Hume stipulatively confines the scope of reason to the discernment of ideas and their relations (i.e., to deductive reasoning and intuitive derivation of nonsynthetic *a priori* propositions), but he does so only where there is a danger of misuse. Stipulation can be commendable when one has a good reason for it, and Hume has several good reasons. As a consequence he is committed to speaking as though there are no justifications for empirical claims. This commitment, however, concerns merely a terminological point, and it reflects a clarity rather than a confusion in his intentions.

An appreciation of these anti-rationalist intentions is essential

---

15. An attractive explanation of the Newtonian influence on Hume is found in Nicholas Capaldi, *David Hume* (Boston: Twayne, 1975), pp. 39–42 and 49ff.

for a proper understanding of Hume's statements about reason. The following excerpt contains Hume's typical "sceptical" arguments pertaining both to induction and to the limits of human reason (EHU, IV.2; cf. T, 91–93):

Even after we have experience of the operations of cause and effect, our conclusions from that experience are *not* founded on reasoning, or any process of the understanding . . . it seems evident that, if this conclusion [that similar causes produce similar effects] were formed by reason, it would be as perfect at first, and upon one instance, as after ever so long a course of experience. But the case is far otherwise. . . . [An inductive] inference is not intuitive; neither is it demonstrative. Of what nature is it, then? To say it is experimental, is begging the question.

Hume here uses "reason" in his stipulatively restricted sense. He is not attacking what *elsewhere* he calls "experimental reasoning." Moreover, Hume never reaches harsher conclusions about the poverty of reason. While he occasionally does inject similarly condemnatory language, one generally finds it only in the early and self-confessedly brash work of the *Treatise*. Here are his least guarded statements:

. . . *even after the observation of the frequent or constant conjunction of objects, we have no reason to draw an inference concerning any object beyond those of which we have had experience.* (T, 139)

When I give the preference to one set of arguments above another, I do nothing but decide from my feeling concerning the superiority of their influence. (T, 103)

[It is not] by any process of reasoning [that one] is engaged to draw this [inductive] inference . . . understanding has no part in the operation. (EHU, Sec. 35)

Never are Hume's indictments of reason sterner. Usually he is reserved, cautious, and totally disinclined to speak about irrationalism, or even about unreliability. As he repeatedly emphasizes, his intention is only to show that "there can be no *demonstrative* arguments to prove, *that those instances, of which we have had no experience, resemble those, of which we have had experience*" (T, 89; all italics his).

Apparently Hume's interpreters and critics have found it all too tempting to seize on passages such as the above and declare them exhibitions of a philosophy of irrationalism. This interpretation entirely misses his point.[16] His theses are *anti-rationalist*, never *irrationalist*, and he usually surrounds even his apparently most extravagant comments with a softer protective belt. For example, Hume says at one point that the inventions of inductive reasoning "must be entirely arbitrary" (EHU, Sec. 25). In context his point is simply that if, as rationalists claim, we conjectured entirely *a priori* about the effect an object or event would cause, then causal reasoning would be entirely arbitrary. This proposition is not only quite understandable; it is true.

2. *Hume's Arguments concerning Induction*

Hume entitles his most extensive and concentrated discussions of induction—both located in the *Enquiry* (IV–V)—"Sceptical Doubts concerning the Operations of the Understanding" and "Sceptical Solution of these Doubts."[17] In these sections the received view has always interpreted Hume as proclaiming his scepticism concerning the external problem. This interpretation is perfectly represented by the following quotation from Wesley Salmon:

It is well known that Hume's answer to this problem was essentially skeptical. . . . Hume's position can be summarized succinctly: We cannot justify any kind of ampliative inference. If it could be justified deductively it would not be ampliative. It cannot be justified nondemonstratively because that would be viciously circular. It seems, then, that there is no way in which we can extend our knowledge to

16. See a reply to our earlier published arguments by Adi Parush, "Is Hume a Sceptic about Induction?" *Hume Studies* 3 (1977), esp. pp. 4–5. We believe that Parush misses the point as fully as his predecessors.

17. An important linguistic point about eighteenth-century usage of "scepticism" has been made by Mary Shaw Kuypers, in *Studies in the Eighteenth Century Background of Hume's Empiricism* (New York: Russell and Russell, 1966), Pt. II, iv, esp. pp. 85f. She offers evidence that there is "a curious identification of scientific method with scepticism" as early as Locke and that "Hume subscribed to it." She also *suggests* that Hume's full acceptance of empiricism and rejection of rationalism is closely tied to the usage of "scepticism" in his philosophy. Obviously the traditional reading of Hume would have been quite different had he entitled his section on induction "Scientific Doubts concerning the Operations of the Understanding." But it would have been a more apt title.

the unobserved. We have, to be sure, many beliefs about the unobserved, and in some of them we place great confidence. Nevertheless, they are without rational justification of any kind![18]

We consider this interpretation entirely implausible. Neither of Hume's discussions in the first *Enquiry* either raises the external problem or argues for a sceptical answer to it. Each section is divided into two parts (IV.1, IV.2, V.1, V.2), the first three of these four subsections constituting the core of his "critique" of induction. Their structure and major contentions may be outlined as follows:

(IV.1) *Demonstrative reasoning (a priori reasoning), which is purely a product of the understanding, cannot from its own resources alone prove matters of fact.*

(IV.2) *Inductive reasoning (factual reasoning) is not a product of the understanding and cannot provide the logical necessity that uniquely characterizes demonstrative reasoning.*

(V.1) *Inductive reasoning is not a product of the understanding (the source or "principle" of a priori reasoning) but rather is a product of custom (the source or "principle" of factual reasoning).*

It is important to note that this reconstruction locates the unity of Hume's subsections in his arguments concerning the scope and limits of the faculty of understanding. Our interpretation thus accords well with his section title, "Sceptical Doubts concerning the Operations of *the Understanding*." But now we must demonstrate that these reconstructions are accurate. Since our interpretation of IV.2 will undoubtedly prove the most controversial, we shall first treat the less troublesome subsections, beginning with V.1.

The following excerpts from Subsection V.1. capture Hume's usual arguments for a "sceptical solution" of his earlier "doubts":

[34] . . . in all reasonings from experience, there is a step taken by the mind which is not supported by any argument or process of the understanding. . . .

[36] The conclusions which [Reason] draws from considering one

18. Wesley Salmon, *The Foundations of Scientific Inference* (Pittsburgh: University of Pittsburgh Press, 1966), pp. 7, 11.

circle are the same which it would form upon surveying all the circles in the universe. But no man, having seen only one body move after being impelled by another, could infer that every other body will move after a like impulse. All inferences from experience, therefore, are effects of custom, not of reasoning. . . .

[38] What, then, is the conclusion of the whole matter? A simple one; though, it must be confessed, pretty remote from the common theories of philosophy. All belief of matter of fact or real existence is derived merely from some object, present to the memory or senses, and a customary conjunction between that and some other object.

That inductive reasoning is based on custom rather than on the understanding is clearly the point of these largely psychological contentions. Nowhere does Hume raise the external problem, and the "sceptical solution" of his earlier doubts cannot be construed as a sceptical solution of the external problem (cf. also T, I. iv. 1), for it is merely "scepticism concerning the operations of the understanding."

The external problem is also absent from Subsection IV.1, which constitutes the first part of Hume's "sceptical doubts" concerning the understanding. Here are his most typical contentions in this subsection:

[21] *That the sun will not rise to-morrow* is no less intelligible a proposition, and implies no more contradiction, than the affirmation, *that it will rise.* We should in vain, therefore, attempt to demonstrate its falsehood. Were it demonstratively false, it would imply a contradiction. . . .

[23] . . . knowledge of [a causal] relation is not, in any instance, attained by reasonings *a priori*; but arises entirely from experience, . . . nor can our reason, unassisted by experience, ever draw any inference concerning real existence and matter of fact. . . .

[25] . . . every effect is a distinct event from its cause. It could not, therefore, be discovered in the cause, and the first invention or conception of it, *a priori,* must be entirely arbitrary.

Hume's thought in this subsection moves to the conclusion that demonstrative reasoning, which is purely a product of the understanding, cannot be employed to prove matters of fact, since factual knowledge arises "entirely from experience" and never *a priori.* Again, nowhere is the external problem raised and nowhere is there exhibited any scepticism concerning the foundations of factual reasoning in general. Rather, the foundations are located in custom and imagination. Hume's "sceptical doubts" center solely on the scope and powers of the understanding (the faculty of *a priori* reasoning), not on the justifiability of inductive reasoning.

We must now consider the passages in Subsection IV.2, where Hume has always been thought to raise most directly the external problem and also to manifest his sceptical leanings. Against the received view, we shall argue that the following reconstruction of this subsection both includes Hume's major lines of argument and excludes no major point of his concern: *Neither demonstrative nor inductive reasoning can be employed successfully to provide a proof of the supposition that the future will be conformable to the past. Since this supposition cannot be proved, it cannot legitimately serve as an intermediary that certifies the* understanding *to arrive at inductive inferences characterized by logical necessity. There also seems to be no other logical connecting medium that so certifies the understanding. Accordingly, inductive reasoning is not a product of the understanding and cannot provide the logical necessity that uniquely characterizes demonstrative reasoning.* We contend that the following set of passages is sufficient, without introducing either textual distortion or rearrangement of order, to confirm this reconstruction.

The Problem Outlined:

[28] I shall content myself, in this section, with an easy task, and shall pretend only to give a negative answer to the question here proposed. I say then, that, even after we have experience of the operations of cause and effect, our conclusions from that experience are *not* founded on reasoning, or any process of the understanding.

[29] [Why past] experience should be extended to future times . . . is the main question on which I would insist. The bread, which I formerly eat, nourished me; . . . but does it follow, that other bread must also nourish me at another time . . . ? The consequence seems nowise necessary. . . . [There is] an inference, which wants to be explained. . . . There is required a medium, which may enable the mind to draw such an inference, if indeed it be drawn by reasoning and argument. What that medium is, I must confess, passes my comprehension. . . .

[30] [The demand is for a] connecting proposition or intermediate step, which supports the understanding in this conclusion.

Connecting Proposition Not Provable Demonstratively:

[30] That there are no demonstrative arguments in the case seems evident; since it implies no contradiction that the course of nature may change. . . .

Connecting Proposition Not Provable Inductively:

[30] All our experimental conclusions proceed upon the supposition that the future will be conformable to the past. To endeavor, therefore, the proof of this last supposition by probable arguments, or arguments regarding existence, must be evidently going in a circle, and taking that for granted, which is the very point in question.

No Other Logical Connecting Medium Apparent:

[31] [If any causal or inductive] conclusion were formed by reason, it would be as perfect at first, and upon one instance, as after ever so long a course of experience. But the case is far otherwise.

[32] The question still recurs, on what process of argument this *inference* is founded? Where is the medium? . . . the inference is not intuitive, neither is it demonstrative. . . . To say it is experimental, is begging the question . . . no enquiry has yet been able to remove my difficulty. . . .

Conclusion:

[33] . . . it is not reasoning which engages us to suppose the past resembling the future, and to expect similar effects from causes which are, to appearance, similar. This is the proposition which I intended to enforce in the present section.

It must not be thought that this interpretation applies only to the first *Enquiry*. In the *Treatise* (Book I, Part III, Sec. vi) there corresponds a virtually identical argument. On the critical pages (86–92) Hume argues that it is not the understanding that allows us to infer from the cause to the effect, and thus that causal inference is not an *a priori* movement of reason (pursuant to experience of causes and effects): "If reason determined us, it wou'd proceed upon that principle, *that instances, of which we have had no experience, must resemble those of which we have had experience, and that the course of nature continues always uniformly the same*" (T, 89). Because this premise cannot be proved demonstratively or causally without circularity, reason cannot ground or discover the premise, and so the understanding cannot act on it. Only the imagination can.

The question may be raised whether our reconstruction does

justice to certain celebrated passages that the received view associates with the external problem, especially those passages where Hume speaks of the circular, question-begging character of induction if used to justify itself—e.g., the above excerpts from Sections 30 and 32 (cf. also T, 89). Adherents of the received view focus on these passages because they believe that Hume's treatment of the "supposition" that the future will resemble the past manifests a sceptical concern with the external problem. They rightly point out that Hume concludes that neither demonstrative nor factual argument can substantiate this supposition. Nonetheless, it must not be thought that Hume is requesting a rational justification of the entire institution of inductive reasoning. Rather, he is simply requesting a justification of the supposition that the future will conform to the past. He issues this request not in order to question the institution of induction, even though the institution can, of course, plausibly be construed as resting on such a principle of uniformity. Rather, he issues the request in order to question the rationalistic assumption that factual reasoning is characterized, at least in some cases, by logical necessity. And this request expresses the substance of his sceptical doubts concerning the understanding. More precisely, Hume requests, with sceptical intent, *only* a justification of the assumption that the future will be conformable to the past. He does so because rationalistically inclined thinkers must assume this or some similar principle, as a "medium," in order to ground their view that causal inferences can be drawn with the force of logical necessity. Hume is merely arguing that this assumption is unwarranted, not that the institution of induction is unwarranted. Nor is he attacking other uses of the principle as a medium. When the principle is assumed in the ordinary course of inductive reasoning—as Hume's own methodology in the *Treatise* requires—he does not challenge the principle. Of course, he *might* have challenged the principle in this context, in which case he would have broached the external problem. He then would have had to provide some general justification; but this, we have argued, is not his concern.

Our overall conclusion may still be resisted. Some will claim that our interpretation is too paradoxical; it seems to do violence to the robustness and the incisiveness of Hume's "critique" of induction. We would counter by turning such an objection upon its own adherents: contrary arguments advanced by the received view are appreciably more paradoxical and less compatible with Hume's major philosophical objectives. Hume is the most influential and consistent figure in modern empiricism, and his *Treatise* extols the empirical method from its Introduction to its Appendices. It would be a truly extraordinary oversight were he to bind himself to a procedure whose conclusions cannot be given "rational justification of any kind" (Salmon) and to proclaim sceptically that it has "no rational and no empirical justification whatever" (Will).[19]

Kneale and Popper even argue that Hume—who wrote specifically to overcome the errors and methodological confusions in previous philosophy—thought that no philosopher, himself included, was able to overcome irrationalism. Popper and Will, in addition, suggest that Hume considered his own philosophy to have attained a level of conceptual rigor no higher than that of animal faith—a stunning conclusion about the author of the *Dialogues* and the *Natural History of Religion*, two books where "reasoning" by animal faith is repeatedly reprimanded. And surely the accounts by Bennett and Kneale will seem odd to anyone familiar with Hume's discussion of superior degrees of inductive evidence in the *Enquiry* and of proper inductive analogy in the *Dialogues*—both of which conclude with the observation that "a wise man proportions his belief to the [inductive] evidence" (EHU, Sec. 87; cf. D, II). It would seem to us, then, that the greater onus of proof is on these interpretations. Each denies what Hume is most concerned to affirm: the inductive method as used in science is the sole method for placing philosophy on the road to well-grounded truth. We hasten to add that our view is not, as one critic has suggested,[20] that these Hume scholars are themselves inconsistent in the very way they have taken *Hume* to be inconsistent. Our view is simply that they mistakenly attribute inconsistency to Hume.

19. The claim that Hume tried to erect his science on a sceptical foundation that could not bear the weight is found in J. A. Passmore, *Hume's Intentions* (Cambridge: Cambridge University Press, 1952), p. 151. Noxon has argued, correctly in our view, that this attack would be correct if Hume held such views, but he does not. Noxon, *op. cit.*, p. 14.

20. See Parush, *op. cit.*, p. 9. For a reaction to these traditional interpretations as incredulous as our own, see Julius Weinberg, *op. cit.*, pp. 95, 100, 102.

We conclude that the reconstruction of Hume's views presented in Argument II is incorrect, for it is based on the mistaken notion that Hume raises the external problem and argues for a sceptical answer to it.

IV

We can now turn to an investigation of Argument I, where Hume's commitment to standards for the resolution of *internal problems* of justification assumes prominence. If the initial premise of this argument is taken as a correct depiction of Hume's views, it would be difficult not to attribute to Hume the conclusion of Argument I: No inductive conclusion can be justified rationally. But the first premise seriously misconstrues Hume's position. The premise may be divided into two distinct claims: (A) All factual beliefs are based solely on instinct; (B) No factual beliefs are based on justifying reasons. Adherents of the received view generally attribute (B) to Hume because they hold that he argues for (A). But never does Hume argue that factual beliefs are based *solely* on instinct. He does indeed maintain that all factual beliefs are based on instinct, but he also regards some factual beliefs as additionally based on what are today commonly called "justifying reasons."

We suggested in Section II and shall now argue (against the received view) that Hume expressly commits himself, without inconsistency, to what we would today call "rational inductive procedures." Our argument consists in showing: (1) that there are at least five prominent features of his philosophy that appeal directly to a distinction between mere factual belief and justified factual belief and that provide criteria for distinguishing the two; (2) that Hume's commitment to these criteria is perfectly compatible with his psychological thesis that all factual beliefs are based on instinct.

1. *Hume's Criteria of Justified Belief*

First—as we argued in Chapter 1—Hume's section "Rules by which to judge of causes and effects" (T, I.iii.15) is expressly designed to provide inductive methods for justifying or eliminating causal beliefs. His intention is to "fix some general rules by which we may know when [causes and effects] really are so" (T, 173). These Rules indicate that the correctness of causal inference is a matter of objective support and does not depend on custom or animal faith or observers who acquire feelings of determination. When judgment conflicts with errant imagination, says Hume, we must observe "some general rules, by which we *ought* to regulate our judgment concerning causes and effects" (T, 149; our italics). Since satisfaction of the warranting conditions provides all the evidence needed to verify causal statements, "instinctual" feelings of expectation add nothing essential and might even be misleading or mistaken (cf. Rule 6, 174 and also 149).

Second, Hume's account "Of the probability of chances" (T, I.iii.11) inquires whether inductive arguments attain different degrees of evidence, some being superior to others. He begins by suggesting that we

distinguish *human reason* into three kinds, viz, *that from knowledge, from proofs, and from probabilities.* By knowledge, I mean the assurance arising from the [*a priori*] comparison of ideas. By proofs, those arguments, which are deriv'd from the relation of cause and effect, and which are entirely free from doubt and uncertainty. By probability, that evidence, which is still attended with uncertainty. (T, 124, first italics ours; cf. EHU, VI, fn. 1)

He goes on to argue that there exists a "gradation from probabilities to proofs" which is in "many cases insensible" (i.e., undetectable) even though it is easy to see the "difference betwixt kinds of evidence" when widely varying experiences and types of generalization are compared (T, 131; cf. EHU, Sec. 87). These distinctions, coupled with the section on Rules, provide Hume's basic criteria for the resolution of internal problems of justification. Note also that in the above passage Hume ventures a belief that there are two kinds of certainty—knowledge derived from the understanding through deductive reasoning and empirical proofs derived from the inductive inferences of the imagination. From Hume's perspective, rationalists deny imagination its significant role in knowledge (cf. Descartes and Spinoza, e.g.). They wrongly insist that there is only one kind of certainty, and so mistakenly evaluate induction by standards appropriate only to deduction.

Third, in the important section "Of the probability of causes" (T, I.iii.12), Hume indicates that whenever the source of some event is secret, unobserved, or unknown, we should proceed on the hypothesis that the event fits a pattern of causal uniformity, even if we are disposed to believe otherwise (T, 132f; EHU, Secs. 47, 67f). "Deliberation" is said properly to displace "habitual determinations":

[In deliberation] we commonly take knowingly into consideration the contrariety of past events; we compare the different sides of the contrariety, and carefully weigh the experiments, which we have on each side: Whence we may conclude, that our reasonings of this kind arise not *directly* from the habit, but in an *oblique* manner. (T, 133)

Hume recommends the application of his Rules in such circumstances and, contrary to Bennett's interpretation, explicitly develops an account of hypotheses and "non-credulous, tentative, interrogative predictions":

The circumstance, on which the effect depends, is frequently involved in other circumstances, which are foreign and extrinsic. The separation of it often requires great attention, accuracy, and subtilty. (EHU, Sec. 84n)

Fourth, Hume distinguishes between experientially or inductively well-grounded beliefs and those that are purely artificial or associational. Inference-drawing, he says, is often "rash" and unjustified by deeper experience (T, 113). He accounts for this phenomenon by attributing it to the difference between wide, varied acquaintance and limited acquaintance. The reflective life of wide experience enables one to *test* customs and displace them with more adequately grounded beliefs (T, 113, 133). Hume expresses this point by saying that mere belief produced by the unsupplemented workings of the imagination is capricious and must be assisted by the application of general rules of judgment (T, 149). Kemp Smith has nicely captured Hume's meaning:

Hume's real position is not that custom (or habit) as such is king: it has no manner of right to lay claim to any such dignity. It is experience—and custom only in so far as it conforms to and is the outcome of experience—which is, and ought to be, the ultimate court of appeal.[21]

21. Norman Kemp Smith, *The Philosophy of David Hume* (London: Macmillan, 1941), p. 382.

It must not be thought that Hume's normative views in regard to the justification and correction of belief come only as late as the Rules section of the *Treatise* or in the superficial form of an *ad hoc* appendix. Such standards prevail throughout his philosophy. The *Treatise* is subtitled *An Attempt To Introduce the Experimental Method of Reasoning into Moral Subjects* and is intended as a whole to be an inductive science of human nature. The *Enquiry* mirrors the *Treatise* in this regard and applies inductive standards in sections that take up new subjects—most notably in the discussion of miracles. And the *Dialogues* appeal to such standards throughout.

Fifth, Hume has an often overlooked but nonetheless instructive theory of education. He generally uses the word "education" in so negative a way that it not only carries a force of disapproval but comes virtually to mean "indoctrination." In the *Treatise* Hume says that the teaching of other people often "commands our assent beyond what experience will justify" (113) and then comments that

. . . education is an artificial and not a natural cause, and as its maxims are frequently *contrary to reason* [factual reason], and even to themselves in different times and places, it is never upon that account recogniz'd by philosophers; tho' in reality it be built almost on the same foundation of custom and repetition as our reasonings from causes and effects. (T, 117; our italics)

By "recogniz'd" Hume means "assented to"; acceptance of the maxims of education is nothing less than acquiescence to uncritical assumptions. In his *Natural History of Religion* the fancies and customs of primitive belief are called the "prejudices of education" and are opposed to what we would today ordinarily call, and what Hume himself refers to as, *rational inquiry*.[22] As we might expect, Hume opposes experience to education and extols experience as the corrective of the dangers of education.

2. The Compatibility of Psychological Explanation and Rational Justification

On the basis of the above considerations, both the crucial first premise and the conclusion of Argument I seem plainly to be

22. From *Hume on Religion*, ed. by Richard Wollheim (New York: Meridian Books of the World Publishing Co., 1964), pp. 31, 96.

misrepresentations. Why, then, would anyone maintain that Argument I accurately reconstructs an argument in Hume's philosophy? The justification offered by adherents of the received view generally takes the following form: since for Hume all factual beliefs are based *solely* on instinct, and thus not on rational faculties, he has systematically excluded all possibility that such beliefs could be based on justifying reasons. This interpretation was eloquently and unflatteringly expressed by Kant. Kant's assessment and that of the twentieth-century philosophers quoted in this chapter lead to the conclusion that despite any endorsement Hume may give to inductive standards, he is not *entitled* to adopt them. In short, Hume's psychology commits him to premise (1) of Argument I, and this, in turn, commits him to the conclusion of Argument I.

This reconstruction might be acceptable if premise (1) were an accurate depiction of Hume's views. But it is not. Hume never argues that all factual beliefs are based *solely* on instinct. To his way of thinking, it is in no way inconsistent that a given factual belief may be based at once on both instinct and justifying reasons. *All* factual beliefs are based on instinct; *some* factual beliefs additionally satisfy criteria that render them justified. The former thesis is psychological, the latter epistemological. According to Hume's psychology all operations of human imagination are instinctual. Some conclusions reached by imagination (but not all) additionally satisfy inductive criteria derived from extensive observation and experience (T, 108, 149, 225). Hume clearly believes that satisfaction of these additional specifications is a necessary condition of any justified factual belief (cf. T, 84, 89, 173ff; EHU, Secs. 36n, 84n). As previously established, the imagination must often be supplemented or corrected by general rules employed by the faculty of judgment (T, 147–49). This fact prompts Hume to proclaim that one can reason either "justly and naturally" or only "naturally" (T, 225f).

Finally, it should be noticed that we are not arguing that Hume abandons his account of causal and psychological determinism, whereby experience is sovereign. As might be expected of one who holds a compatibilist account of freedom and determinism, Hume finds causal explanations *compatible with and not destructive of* what we now commonly call "rational justifications." It is precisely this point that the received view neglects, yet without understanding it one really cannot begin to understand Hume's larger philosophical enterprise, including his treatment of induction. Nor will it suffice to argue, as Bruce Aune does, that Hume does have standards of rationality that allow him to judge failures to use induction as irrational, but that these standards themselves are "merely matters of custom."[23] Here we must be careful in our use of the term "custom." If the standards were merely customary, without reference to the logical criteria used to criticize customary formations of belief, Hume could not hold the position we have sketched throughout this section. Hume does of course have a naturalistic psychological theory of the mind that explains the operation of the rules, and to develop such a psychological theory while expounding a logical theory may seem peculiar to modern philosophers. On the other hand, both Arthur Pap and Frank Ramsey seem to take precisely this approach in their work, including acceptance of Hume's theory of habit.[24]

We conclude that the reconstruction of Hume's views presented in Argument I is incorrect, for it relies on the mistaken notion that Hume considers all factual beliefs to be based solely on instinct and not on justifying reasons.

V

An approach to Hume's scepticism that may seem similar to ours is the celebrated naturalistic interpretation of Norman Kemp Smith, to whose authority we appealed only a few pages back.[25] Kemp Smith's views have recently been buttressed in an imaginative book by Barry Stroud. The hallmarks of their naturalistic

23. Bruce Aune, *Rationalism, Empiricism, and Pragmatism* (New York: Random House, 1970), p. 59.
24. Frank Ramsey, *The Foundations of Mathematics,* ed. R. B. Braithwaite (London: Kegan Paul; New York: Harper, 1931), pp. 196f; Arthur Pap, "Disposition Concepts and Extensional Logic," in *Minnesota Studies in the Philosophy of Science,* ed. H. Feigl, *et al.* (Minneapolis: University of Minnesota Press, 1958), p. 220; and also Arthur W. Burks, *Chance, Cause, Reason* (Chicago: University of Chicago Press, 1977), pp. 616–18.
25. Kemp Smith, *The Philosophy of David Hume* and "The Naturalism of Hume," *Mind* n.s. 54 (1905), pp. 149–73, 335–47.

interpretation are the acceptance, but minimization, of Hume's scepticism, conjoined with a conception of his larger enterprise as that of providing scientific causal explanations of mental and moral phenomena, a science that Hume used to challenge rationalistic metaphysics. They attempt to rebut the overly sceptical interpretations of Thomas Reid, Thomas Hill Green, and others.[26] Stroud claims to have produced "a more systematic and more consistent naturalistic interpretation" than Kemp Smith's, but nonetheless acknowledges his deep indebtedness to that commentator. They find common ground in the view that Hume's thought has its roots in the scientific work of Newton and the philosophical work of Francis Hutcheson.[27] As their conclusions are superficially in agreement with our own and are important in their own right, their arguments must now be considered.

Stroud and Kemp Smith regard Hume's philosophy as "a systematic generalization of Francis Hutcheson's views on aesthetics and morals."[28] In Hutcheson's system of philosophy, moral and aesthetic judgments are based on our natural capacity to feel certain sentiments, quite independently of reasoning and reflection. Consistently invoking this background, Kemp Smith argues that "Hume's philosophy is not fundamentally sceptical; it is positive and naturalistic, and . . . humanistic in tendency."[29] Yet he also sees Hume as defending the epistemological view that "Reason is and ought to be subordinate to our natural beliefs," where belief is understood as a passion, feeling, or sentiment.[30] These beliefs are not acts of knowledge or reflective insights; rather they are subrational passions fixed by the constitution of our nature. Indeed, Kemp Smith argues that through Hutcheson, Hume came to the view that judgments of knowledge themselves rest on feeling, and not on the insights either of *reason* or of empirical *evidence*.[31] Because reason is thus to serve strictly "in the service of feeling and

26. Kemp Smith, "Naturalism," pp. 150ff; *The Philosophy of David Hume*, pp. 79f.
27. Kemp Smith sees these two influences as occasionally coming into conflict. *The Philosophy of David Hume*, pp. 73ff.
28. Barry Stroud, *Hume* (London: Routledge & Kegan Paul, 1977), p. 10.
29. Kemp Smith, *The Philosophy of David Hume*, p. 155.
30. *Ibid.*, pp. 11f, 44.
31. *Ibid.*, pp. 13, 44, 86f.

instinct," Kemp Smith regards Humean causal inference as merely "so-called causal inference"; it turns out "not to be inference at all." It is causally conditioned in belief, "not logically or evidentially conditioned."[32]

There is, [Hume] argues, no such thing as causal *inference*. When the mind passes from an idea or impression of one object to that of another, it is the imagination which is operating, not the understanding. It is custom and not reason, habit and not evidence, which is at work.[33]

Inevitably, says Kemp Smith, Hume is led to a "moderate scepticism" as the necessary supplement to his naturalistic teaching.[34]

Stroud has brought this general interpretation still closer to the concerns of our volume:

In Hume's hands the denigration of the role of reason and the corresponding elevation of feeling and sentiment is generalized into a total theory of man. Even in the apparently most intellectual or cognitive spheres of human life, even in our empirical judgments about the world and in the process of pure ratiocination itself, feeling is shown to be the dominant force. . . .

Hume usually looks first for the "foundation in reason" of the beliefs and attitudes he examines, and only after demonstrating that they have none does he then proceed to his positive causal explanation of their origin. . . . [Yet] virtually nowhere does he argue that a particular belief or attitude is unjustifiable, unreasonable, or without rational foundation *because* it is simply caused in such-and-such a way by discoverable features of our minds and the world.[35]

Naturally we find the concluding sentences in this quotation congenial. Stroud admirably appreciates the fact that Hume's sustained attack on reason is *largely* an attempt to discredit his-

32. Kemp Smith, "Naturalism," pp. 151f (cf. 164 and 166), 372.
33. Kemp Smith, *The Philosophy of David Hume*, pp. 375, cf. 350. Contrast the strange interpretation in "Naturalism," pp. 171, 173.
34. Kemp Smith, *The Philosophy of David Hume*, pp. 130–32, 378. In "Naturalism" Kemp Smith seems to argue the still more nontraditional view that because certain factual beliefs are natural they are "thus removed beyond the reach of sceptical doubts" (p. 152) and that "Hume is thus no sceptic as to the powers of reason, but quite positive that its sole function is practical" (p. 155). Yet, as he states Hume's position, it is one sceptical of induction (p. 162), and more sceptical than necessary (p. 168).
35. Stroud, *op. cit.*, pp. 10f, 15.

torically influential views about human nature and rationality
from Aristotle to the Continental Rationalists. He sees the
substance of this challenge as Hume's "revolutionary" view. But
the first few lines of Stroud's statement repeat the errors of
the received interpretation. Moreover, he goes on to argue that
Hume rejects reason entirely as the source of inductive inferences, thus leading to his "most famous sceptical result." "And,"
says Stroud, "there is no doubt that it was meant to be sceptical."[36] Nonetheless, he argues, Hume does not stop with scepticism, for he integrates his theory of imagination into his experimental, naturalistic study of human nature, so as to show that
induction is based on the imagination. On these grounds Stroud
erects a broad naturalistic interpretation that sees Hume's negative purpose as a sceptical argument "directed against the claims
of a certain traditional conception of reason or rationality" and
his positive argument as consisting in the larger Newtonian
purpose of the *Treatise*.[37]

There are several flaws in the interpretation offered by Kemp
Smith and Stroud. We shall here concentrate on Kemp Smith's
statement, because it is the bolder and more extensive of the
two. Our general line of argument, however, applies as well
to Stroud as to Kemp Smith.

Consider Kemp Smith's general interpretation of Hume's account of causal inference:

Hume's teaching [is] that judgments of causal connexion express
not insight but *only* belief, resting *not* on the apprehension of any
relation (other than mere sequence), *but on a feeling or sentiment* in
the mind.[38]

The italicized words echo the mistakes of the received view; and,
though it harbors the critical issue, the parenthetical qualification is brushed aside throughout Kemp Smith's work. Our
claim is that a proper interpretation of Hume's views on the
relation of sequence or constant conjunction, together with an
understanding of the section on rules in the *Treatise*, provides
sufficient grounds for concluding that Hume did not consider

36. *Ibid.*, p. 52.
37. *Ibid.*, p. 60. Cf. 9–15, 53, 68.
38. Kemp Smith, *The Philosophy of David Hume*, p. 44 (italics added). Cf.
Stroud's somewhat more cautious statements, *op. cit.*, pp. 69, 76f, 92.

causal inference to be based *merely* on custom and belief. This interpretation may be seen as a consistent development of Kemp Smith's useful distinction between custom and experience. Had Kemp Smith pursued the notion of experience further, he might have come to terms with Hume's view of the rational assessment of evidence. But it is precisely here that Kemp Smith's interpretation founders, for like others who regard Hume as a sceptic about induction, Kemp Smith claims that Hume lacks a theory of *evidence*. And this, we have argued, he most certainly does not lack. Kemp Smith is also led by his interpretation to the mistaken view that there is no factual *knowledge* for Hume, since it is "properly speaking" mere opinion.[39] Kemp Smith seizes upon the classic passages for the sceptical interpretation of Hume—such as the passage in the *Abstract* that proclaims " 'Tis not, therefore, reason which is the judge of life, but custom" (A, 16)—and concludes that factual belief is a matter of "brute necessity for which there is no evidence whatever except its own psychological compulsiveness; and that, of course, is not *evidence* at all."[40] Our disagreement could scarcely be more complete.

When Kemp Smith confronts the issue that, he agrees with us, is "the critical point in Hume's argument"—viz. how truly causal sequences are to be distinguished from apparently causal sequences—he again turns to Hutcheson for a clue to Hume's solution. (Stroud denies that Hume makes this distinction at all[41] —a problem we treat in Chapter 4.) Hume argues the Hutchesonian line, according to Kemp Smith, that one must look in the observer for the answer. There one finds the impression of necessity, and it is this impression that turns the merely uniform into the causal.[42] Kemp Smith here repeats the mistake we identified in Chapter 1 regarding his views about Hume's two definitions. Furthermore, his interpretation is at odds with the Humean texts discussed in the previous sections of this chapter. He fails to explain the presence of the section on rules—which Stroud also repeatedly ignores—and neglects Hume's discussions

---

39. Kemp Smith, *The Philosophy of David Hume*, p. 46. Contrast "Naturalism," p. 165.
40. Kemp Smith, *The Philosophy of David Hume*, p. 46 (italics in original).
41. Stroud, *op. cit.*, pp. 66, 93-95.
42. Kemp Smith, *The Philosophy of David Hume*, p. 48.

of how custom and imagination are to be corrected when causality is attributed to uniform sequences through a mistaken
belief accompanied by a feeling of necessity. Again, it appears
as though Kemp Smith correctly grasps the distinction between
custom and broad experience, but does not link experience to
factual reasoning in the way Hume does. Stroud appends the
observation that, for Hume, "the repeated observation of similar
phenomena precludes our thinking of them as occurring together
merely coincidentally."[43] This strained interpretation is without
the slenderest foundation in Hume's text. On the contrary, Hume
exhibits a keen sensitivity to the importance of inductive re-
straint and the application of rules in the face of custom and
accidental conjunction. This much even Kemp Smith seems to
have appreciated. (We return to a fuller treatment of this issue in
Chapter 4.)

The shortcomings of the Kemp Smith interpretation are
further reflected in his account of "experience in the normative
sense" in Hume's philosophy. He acknowledges that Hume often
wishes to correct custom in order to identify habits and beliefs
that are reliable and beneficial. Hume, he says, even "concedes
that not all regularities are reliable, that not all customs are
good customs," and so calls upon "reflective powers" of causal
inference to distinguish truly causal from accidental uniformities.[44] Kemp Smith recognizes that this tendency in Hume's text
is at odds with his own interpretation, but this variance he
attributes to Hume's "excessive emphasis upon custom" in the
early sections of the *Treatise*.[45] He offers the extraordinary interpretation that in those early sections Hume thinks "beliefs
are neither true nor false, because they simply occur or do not
occur." Later in the text, he proposes, experience becomes both
reflective and normative of what we ought to believe.[46]

Following our interpretation of the text, by contrast, there

43. Stroud, *op. cit.*, p. 93. Stroud's interpretation was anticipated and rejected by Julius Weinberg, *op. cit.*, pp. 99f. An equally unfortunate predecessor of Stroud's interpretation is H. A. Prichard's alleged paraphrase of
Hume: "There is no such thing as believing something for a bad reason."
Knowledge and Perception (Oxford: Oxford University Press, 1950), p. 184.
44. Kemp Smith, *The Philosophy of David Hume*, pp. 382–88.
45. *Ibid.*, p. 387.
46. *Ibid.*, p. 388.

is no significant difference between the early and later parts of the *Treatise*. The problem lies not with Hume; it lies with Kemp Smith. He fails to understand that only the rationalistic sense of reason is under attack and that custom must be corrected by reflection and scientific inquiry in Hume's constructive work throughout the first book. Kemp Smith and Stroud rightly interpret Hume in light of his Newtonian and naturalistic goals, but they do not see that the way Hume understands these very goals—as entailing careful inductive practices—undermines their interpretation of his text. To maintain that for Hume, causal inference is "not logically or evidentially conditioned," is to disregard both the general conclusions of his philosophy and the methodology employed in arriving at those conclusions. Most especially Kemp Smith misunderstands how Hume uses "reason" when he is not attacking the notion in its rationalistic sense. This contention deserves further analysis.

Hume repeatedly appeals to the need for what he calls "accurate and just *reasoning*" (EHU, Sec. 7) in metaphysics, in order to distinguish science from popular superstition. He laments that "eloquence" rather than "reason" has won the prize in past debates in philosophy (T, xviii). The goal of deliberate factual reasoning is the one he sets for himself in the first *Enquiry*, just as a Newtonian investigation of human nature is the proclaimed goal of the *Treatise*. He links reason directly to the "experience and observation," involving "careful and exact experiments," that constitute the method of inquiry in the *Treatise* (xviii–xxiii). Reason is the faculty that permits inference from the observed to the unobserved (T, 155). His use of the terms "reason" and "reasoning" in these contexts goes unmentioned by Kemp Smith and Stroud, and indeed it has largely been ignored by generations of Hume scholars. Yet Hume praises this inductive sense of "reasoning," apparently never supposing that his standard sense of the term could be confused with the rationalistic sense so constantly under attack.

Throughout his work Hume attributes a sweeping and constructive role to inductive reason: "We infer a cause immediately from its effect; and this inference is not only a true species of reasoning, but the strongest of all others" (T, 96n). Reason is said to be the faculty whereby we may correct inaccuracies in sensory experiences, in beliefs, and in the passions (T, 413f, 416,

583; EHU, Sec. 117; EPM, Secs. 137, 143, 185, 234f). As Páll Árdal has painstakingly shown in his work on Hume's theory of reason and the passions, reason (understood within Humean naturalism) would in our modern vernacular properly be interpreted as the virtue of being reasonable—a view ultimately tied to Hume's ideal observer account of morality, according to which moral agents must assume a universal and objective point of view.[47] Moreover, Hume's rules of inductive inference are said to constitute "the LOGIC I think proper to employ in any reasoning" (T, 175). Although instinct, feeling, and belief lead to unreliable expectations, these can be rendered more accurate by causal reasoning (T, 73, 89f). In the section "Of the reason of animals," Hume argues that beasts, like men, are capable of using their "reasoning faculties" for ends that exhibit "extraordinary instances of sagacity," which in turn can be understood by reference to breadth of observation and experience at making causal inferences (T, 176–8). When he later returns to this subject in the first *Enquiry*, where "reasoning" concerning causes and effects is under consideration, he ponders the criteria that distinguish a genius from a brute, since "men so much surpass animals in reasoning." He argues that this distinction arises because humans formulate rules of induction, broaden experiences by the use of language, carefully distinguish causes from mere conditions, and reflectively generalize through experimental reasoning (EHU, Sec. 84n; cf. T, 131).

The position Hume everywhere advocates is that our ideas and beliefs are the products of our natural constitution. The position he nowhere takes (at least consistently or in detail) is Kemp Smith's interpretation that reason is simply an instinctual faculty. True, Hume is led by his goal of naturalistic explanation to say that reason is the slave of the passions (T, 415) and an "instinct in our soul" (T, 179)—passages seized upon by Stroud and Kemp Smith.[48] But in these same pages he says, e.g., that "reason is nothing but the discovery of" causal connection (T, 414). When he discusses the corrective function of causal reasoning, as

47. Páll S. Árdal, "Some Implications of the Virtue of Reasonableness in Hume's *Treatise*," in Livingston and King, eds., *op. cit.*, pp. 91–108.

48. See Stroud, *op. cit.*, pp. 11, 77; Kemp Smith, "Naturalism," pp. 157, 335, 346; and also J. L. Mackie, *Hume's Moral Theory* (London: Routledge & Kegan Paul, 1980), pp. 52f, 60.

contrasted with a psychological explanation of its basis, he sharply distinguishes reason from passions and instinct, which reason both corrects and guides. Causal reasoning and probable reasoning are explicitly cited for this role (T, 73, 103, 459).

Hume certainly holds that we have natural tendencies to factual beliefs, but he does not say that any belief is true *because* we are caused to embrace it by our passions or feelings. To be sure, Hume continues to be interpreted, along Kemp Smith's line, as concluding that "true belief is just belief in which the feeling of conviction occurs appropriately." But, as even this commentator—W. H. Walsh—admits, "Hume never does this explicitly."[49] Again following Kemp Smith, Walsh maintains that the "Hutchesonian account of moral and aesthetic judgments" applied to Hume's matter of fact reasoning leads naturally to this conclusion. But Hume's theories of both truth and certainty are not based on or exhausted by this psychological theory of belief, and are therefore not reducible to subjectivism in the way Walsh suggests.

In this regard Hume is to be distinguished from his own contemporary critics, such as Thomas Reid, who is often taken as a leading defender of reason against Humean scepticism. Reid and his commonsense contemporaries held that what must unavoidably be believed must be true (and in some cases must be true with certainty). Reid held as well that we are entitled to accept without proof certain foundations of knowledge that are necessary to our constitution.[50] Reid supports his conclusions with an account of our natural constitution; there is no appeal to reason. Hume did not accept such views about truth and knowledge, and his experience-based account is neither sceptical nor naturalistic in the ways so typical of his Scottish contemporaries. For both Hume and Reid, of course, any judgments reached through principles of human nature are believed because constitutive features of our nature compel belief. But for Hume beliefs unavoidably generated by the constitution of our nature are not thereby certain or true. Truth is independent of human thought,

49. W. H. Walsh, "Hume's Concept of Truth," in *Reason and Reality,* Royal Institute of Philosophy Lectures, Vol. 5 (London, 1972), p. 112.
50. See Reid's *Essays on the Intellectual Powers of Man,* ed. Baruch Brody (Cambridge, Mass.: M.I.T. Press, 1969), esp. Essay VI, Chapters IV and VI, pp. 596, 654–55.

and it is the business of reason to search after it. In Hume's philosophy the scope of reason encompasses "the inferring of matter of fact" (T, 463, and linked to probable reasoning at 413). His general position on *truth* is consistent with this account of *reason*, for he maintains that truth is an agreement "either to the *real* relations of ideas, or to *real* existence and matter of fact" (T, 458; also EHU, Secs. 30, 132; EPM, Sec. 237). "Truth is of two kinds, consisting either in the discovery of the proportions of ideas, consider'd as such, or in the conformity of our ideas of objects to their real existence" (T, 448). The normative rules for judging causes and effects are our tools for discovering real existence, and thus are the means for replacing belief with knowledge (T, 173).

Hume uses a confusing variety of terms to describe this function of "reason." "Inference" and "understanding" are among the more frequent substitutes. Whatever the word selected, the function referred to remains constant in Hume's philosophy: reason (or inference or understanding) is the faculty that judges of truth; the constitution of our nature may determine our beliefs, but truth is not determined thereby, and beliefs may always be rationally corrected; our beliefs are true if and only if they correspond to the way the world is; no belief is true because we believe it. *That* alone is the Humean philosophy of belief and truth. It is consistent with naturalism and determinism, but it is a correspondence theory not exhausted by them.

Kemp Smith, then, rightly emphasizes the normative role of causal reasoning for Hume; he simply fails to see its critical place in the very foundations of Hume's enterprise. As Barbara Winters has recently argued, any univocal reading of "reason" and "reasoning" in Hume's work will fail to account for major sections of his work and will distort his overall philosophical enterprise. Yet a nonunivocal view is perfectly compatible with a radical interpretation of his naturalism.[51] Our nonunivocal in-

51. Barbara Winters, "Hume on Reason," *Hume Studies* 5 (1979), pp. 20–35. Winters's view suffers, however, from acceptance of the Stroud-Kemp Smith thesis that in reasoning we never have good or justified reasons for our beliefs (cf. pp. 30, 32). It may be that there are at least three senses of "reason" in Hume, but it is impossible to understand the rules section and other parts of Hume's work apart from what Kemp Smith rightly calls the normative sense.

terpretation has the virtue of rendering consistent what would otherwise be literally thousands of textual inconsistencies, ones which must otherwise be attributed to Hume's sloppiness and ambivalence. At the same time, our interpretation makes sense of both Hume's critical and his constructive tasks.

VI

In the preceding sections we have attempted to controvert the received view of Hume's treatment of induction, as typified in the writings of Will, Kneale, Popper, Penelhum, and Bennett, and as modified by Kemp Smith and Stroud. In recent years perhaps the most sustained interpretation of Hume's "inductive scepticism" has been that advanced in D. C. Stove's lucid book, *Probability and Hume's Inductive Scepticism*.[52] This more extended interpretation of Hume is directly opposed to ours, and we must now see what lies at the bottom of our disagreement.

In general, Stove takes Hume's view to be that inductive arguments do not even render their conclusions probable, for evidence gained from experience never increases the likelihood that empirical arguments are true. His instrument for analyzing Hume's "sceptical" argument is a version of the theory of logical probability. Stove construes "Hume's inductive scepticism" as resting on the following philosophical claim (34, 35):

(1) All predictive-inductive inferences are unreasonable.

He then expresses this statement's purport in the following formal terms (64, 61):

(1′) For all e and h such that the argument for e to h is inductive, $P(h,e{\cdot}t) = P(h,t)$.

Here the form $P(A,B)$ is translatable as "the logical probability of A, given B" and is to be understood above as "the degree of conclusiveness of the argument from e to h" [e stands for statements of evidence and h for hypothesis, following Carnap (8f); and the propositional variable t takes only tautological values (15)]. This construal (1′) is a position of absolute probabilistic

---

52. Stove, *op. cit.* In this section all references placed in parentheses are to this book.

irrelevance, since it effectively asserts that, for the class of all statements satisfying this form, the probability of *e* in no way affects the (prior) probability of *h* (where neither *h* nor –*h* is entailed by *e*).[53]

Stove argues that this inductive scepticism follows from two other positions he believes Hume held (106), one explicitly and one implicitly in the form of a suppressed premise. First, Stove thinks Hume explicitly embraced "inductive fallibilism." Stove formulates this notion as follows [where "valid" strictly means "its premiss logically implies its conclusion," as in deductive logic, and where "to judge it invalid is to affirm that $P(A,B) < 1$" (13)]:

(2) All predictive-inductive inferences are invalid.

Claim (2) is then translated into the following notation (64):

(2′) For all e_1, e_2, and *h* such that the argument from e_1 to *h* is inductive and e_2 is observational, $P(h,e_1 \cdot t) < 1$ and $P(h,e_1 \cdot e_2 \cdot t) < 1$.

This formulation effectively says that in the case of predictive-inductive inferences, the addition of observational evidence e_2 cannot create a probability of 1, and hence such inferences are always invalid.[54] That is, inductive reasoning, no matter how well supported, must remain deductively invalid, as there is a permanent possibility of falsity. Stove thinks Hume relied not only upon this claim, but also on a suppressed premise, which Stove dubs "deductivism":

(3) All invalid arguments are unreasonable.

Deductivism is thus the view that no argument rationally certifies a conclusion unless the inference to its conclusion is deductively valid. This claim is also given a formal statement (64):

(3′) For all *e* and *h*, such that the argument from *e* to *h* is invalid, $P(h,e \cdot t) = P(h,t)$.

53. Stove recognizes the probabilistic irrelevance. Cf. his "Hume, the Causal Principle, and Kemp Smith," *Hume Studies* 1 (1975), pp. 6–8.
54. Some useful expansions in this account of inductive fallibilism are found in Stove's "Why Should Probability Be the Guide of Life?" in Livingston and King, eds., *op. cit.*, pp. 50–68, especially Section II. Some rather different glosses are found in Penelhum, *op. cit.*, pp. 51ff.

Stove argues that each of these three statments is logically inde-pendent, but that the first follows *validly* from the second and the third. He then goes on to produce a "valid" argument (68f) to show that the third is false, and hence that "Hume's inductive scepticism" (1) is false, even though inductive fallibilism (2) is true and significant.

There are at least two ways to show that Stove's contentions are mistaken. The first is to attack his translations of 1–3 to 1'–3' as incorrectly comprehending the English language meaning of 1–3 (independent of Hume's meaning). Stove has his own no-tion of probability, and it is controversial whether he succeeds in demonstrating the adequacy of his translations. This strategy, however, should be taken up by those interested primarily in the theory of logical probability, and it is therefore beyond the scope of our present discussion. The second way to attack Stove is to challenge the adequacy of 1–3 as interpretations of Hume's text or to attack 1'–3' as inadequate translations of *Hume's* meaning if he held 1–3. We will not bother to consider 1'–3' here—though we are highly doubtful that Stove's translations into the notation of logical probability are adequate in any of the three cases. Instead, we will show that Stove's argument is short-circuited at a much earlier and more fundamental point, viz., his claim that Hume held 1 and 3. By controverting this claim, we shall also undercut J. L. Mackie's critique of Hume's account of causal inference, as it appears in the first chapter of *The Cement of the Universe,* for that critique—like Penelhum's —is erected almost entirely on the foundations of Stove's argu-ment.

If the analysis of the first four sections of this chapter is correct, it is clear that Hume does not hold 3 (deductivism), or any-thing remotely like it; but if he does not hold 3, then Stove's "valid" deduction of 1 from 2 and 3 is forestalled. We have also given independent reasons for thinking that Hume does not hold 1 (inductive scepticism). The interesting question is: On what textual evidence do Stove and Mackie rely in order to as-sert that Hume does hold 3 (deductivism) and 1 (inductive scepticism)? Surprisingly, they advance very little in the way of textual evidence, despite their abundant textual citations in other contexts (cf. 5, 34–37, e.g.). We say surprisingly because Stove in particular explicitly asserts that analysis of the text itself is the sole basis for deciding between his and other interpretations (15).

So far as we are able to reconstruct Stove's rationale for attributing 1 and 3 to Hume, it is the following: He says that "Hume only ever gave one argument." He then proceeds to diagram this single argument, relying heavily on an interpretation of the many passages in Hume that resemble the (previously cited) one from the *Enquiry:* "nor is it by any process of reasoning, [that we are] engaged to draw this [inductive] inference" (EHU, Sec. 35). Stove takes these passages to be a close paraphrase of the *Treatise* (T, 139): "Even *after* we have had experience of the appropriate constant conjunction, it is not reason (but custom, etc.) which determines us to infer the idea (e.g. of heat) from the impression (e.g. of flame)" (31). In his book, Stove translates this statement to mean "All predictive-inductive inferences are unreasonable" ("Hume's inductive scepticism," or 1 above), and in his later Hume Bicentennial Address[55] he says it also means "that we cannot learn *even from* experience."

Though Stove makes not a single reference to Hume's text in order to justify this translation, he does give the following argument for it: Hume's statements about "reason" may *appear* to be psychological claims concerning a mental faculty. But they do not so *function* in his text, for his interest is logical and evaluative, not psychological:

[Hume] asserts logico-philosophical theses in the guise of remarks about the constitution of the human mind. . . . [They are] evaluative, in some sense, of a certain class of inferences (viz. predictive-inductive ones). Not just any evaluation would do, of course. For there can be no doubt that Hume intends by [his inductive scepticism] an extremely unfavourable evaluation of the inferences which are its subject. (33)[56]

No further textual citations are marshalled to support this interpretation. If it be asked why Stove so strongly believes "that Hume intends . . . an extremely unfavourable evaluation of [inductive] inferences," the following is the only explanation to be found:

55. D. C. Stove, "The Nature of Hume's Scepticism," *McGill Hume Studies* (San Diego: Austin Hill Press, 1979), p. 220.
56. Cf. also Stove, "Hume, the Causal Principle, and Kemp Smith," pp. 7, 21.

Hume certainly thought of himself as having advanced, about inductive inferences, some proposition of a sceptical kind; of a kind, that is, which is shocking to common beliefs, and unfavourable to men's pretensions to knowledge. Nearly all of Hume's readers must also have thought that he did so. I shall therefore take this point as granted. (27; cf. 38)

On the basis of this and similar passages, it appears that Stove merely *assumes* that Hume is a sceptic, and uses the theory of logical probability to *explain* in what his scepticism consists.[57] But if the argument in earlier sections of the present chapter is correct, then Stove's entire enterprise, as an account of Hume, is beside the point. It evades begging the question only by asking the entirely different question, "Is probabilistic inductive scepticism (a view not held by Hume) a sustainable philosophical position?"

More importantly, it is possible to locate precisely where Stove goes wrong. His fatal assumption is that for Hume "reason" governs the process of induction in a way that forces Hume to conclusions 1 and 3 above. That is, Stove thinks that Hume's use of "reason" is such that he holds *both* deductivism and, derivatively, inductive scepticism. This assumption permits Stove to claim that inductive scepticism (1) follows from deductivism (3) and inductive fallibilism (2). We have previously shown, however, that Hume does not intend "reason," in these contexts, to denote factual reasoning at all, but rather to apply only to demonstrative reasoning. The implications for Stove's argument are the following. On one construal of deductivism, Hume *is* a deductivist. He does believe that "all invalid arguments are unreasonable," which for him strictly means that such arguments are the products of the faculty of the imagination, not of reason, and hence are nondemonstrative. It follows validly from *this* understanding of deductivism and from inductive fallibilism that "All predictive-inductive inferences are unreasonable" in the sense of not being the products of demonstrative rationality. But, *pace* Stove's account of Hume's use of "reason," Hume's arguments are not in general evaluative; they are evaluative only

57. Stove describes his method in precisely these terms in his "The Nature of Hume's Scepticism." In this paper (pp. 213ff) he also cites other Hume passages in support of his interpretation. However, these citations are mere page references, not interpretations of the text.

of the rationalistic use of "reason." So while Hume does hold all the premises attributed to him by Stove, nothing follows in regard to his being an inductive sceptic, for the simple reason that *he is not discussing or critically evaluating inductive reason.*[58]

One striking feature of Stove's interpretation is that it is not supported by the very text Stove says is the "version" of Hume's analysis "to which my account of the argument corresponds most closely" (30), viz. the *Abstract* account:

> It is not any thing that *reason* sees in the cause, which makes us *infer* the effect. Such an inference, were it possible, would amount to a *demonstration,* as being founded merely on the comparison of ideas. But no inference from cause to effect amounts to a demonstration. Of which there is this evident proof. The mind can always *conceive* any effect to follow from any cause, and indeed any event to follow upon another: whatever we *conceive* is possible, at least in a metaphysical sense: but wherever a demonstration takes place, the contrary is impossible and implies a contradiction. There is no demonstration, therefore, for any conjunction of cause and effect. (A, 13f, some italics added)

"Reason" is used here, even more explicitly than elsewhere in Hume's work, in a fashion confined to *demonstrative* inference. Stove correctly explains Hume's use of the word "demon-

---

58. Even if our interpretation of Hume's use of "reason" is incorrect, Stove's interpretation would not thereby be rendered more plausible. One of Stove's more perceptive reviewers, Donald Livingston, apparently holds a different interpretation of Hume from ours, yet sees the same problems with Stove's interpretation:

> [It may be that as a matter of historical scholarship Hume uses] "rationality" in some sense completely unlike that of "degree of conclusiveness." Stove considers but rejects this objection on the ground that "so far almost nothing has been said to make the concept of rationality determinate; we do not yet know what properties we are to credit this magnitude with" (p. 70). This may be, but it will not do as an interpretation of Hume. The Hume scholar's task is diligently and empathetically to seek out the various senses of rationality in Hume's writings that might have a bearing on his conception of inductive scepticism. Stove's interpretation is, unhappily, not the result of such work.

Review, *Journal of the History of Philosophy* 13 (July, 1975), pp. 413f. For further useful commentary on Hume's senses of "reason" and "reasonableness," see Winters, *op. cit.,* and Wade Robison, "Hume's Scepticism," *Dialogue* 12 (1973), p. 99, note 16. Robison's support for the position Livingston and we are proposing is especially intriguing because of Robison's own interpretation of Hume as a sceptic. Robison also makes reference to support in both Kemp Smith and Árdal.

strative" (35),[59] but strangely fails to link it to "reason" in the way Hume does. It also deserves note that the *Abstract* resists Stove's interpretation in other interesting passages. For example, Hume prides himself on his analysis of "probabilities, and those measures of evidence on which life and action intirely depend" —measures, he observes, neglected in the "common systems of logic" (A, 7–8). Stove's translation, then, distorts Hume's meaning, and it is in doing so that his mistakes arise. If this assessment is correct, it should, on Stove's own admission, decide the issue against him. For he says that if Hume does not hold the *one* statement of inductive scepticism that he attributes to Hume, then "there is no inductive scepticism in Hume" (34).

The same conclusions may be reached in regard to J. L. Mackie's interpretation, which is a slightly mitigated version of Stove's:

Hume's premiss that "reason" would have to rely on the principle of uniformity holds only if it is assumed that reason's performances must all be deductively valid. . . . Reasonable but probabilistic inferences, then, have not been excluded by Hume's argument, for the simple reason that Hume did not consider this possibility.[60]

So far Mackie's account is modestly preferable to Stove's, for Mackie correctly notices that Hume does not even consider using "reason" in a probabilistic or inductive sense. But Mackie goes on to say that Hume embraces "the more sweeping conclusions" that causal inferences "are not even reasonable or probable, that they are to be ascribed to imagination, custom, and habit rather than to reason, that it is out of the question to try to justify them on any ground except that they are natural, instinctive, and unavoidable."[61] At this point, Mackie agrees with Stove on the following two conclusions: (1) Hume believes causal inferences are based solely on unavoidable natural instinct and therefore are not reasonable; (2) Hume thinks it is out of the question to justify causal inferences except on grounds of unavoidable natural instinct.

59. Cf. also Stove's perspicacious formulation in his "The Nature of Hume's Scepticism," p. 211. Stove first analyzed Hume's meaning in "Hume, Probability, and Induction," pp. 196ff (see note 64 below).
60. J. L. Mackie, *The Cement of the Universe* (Oxford: Clarendon Press, 1974), p. 15.
61. *Ibid.*, p. 18.

Consider (2) first. We have argued that Hume does not assert that natural instinct or any other factor justifies causal inferences in general. The question never arises. Hume does, of course, ask whether *a priori* causal inferences, which are purely a product of the understanding, can be justified. When he appeals to custom and instinct, he is providing an explanation, not a justification. It is therefore odd that Mackie should complain that Hume "never really justified, but only explained" causal inference. Hume only sought to explain how causal inferences are made, not to justify or to criticize the institution of induction. It follows that Hume does not hold "Hume's inductive scepticism"; and if we are correct that his sceptical doubts center only on the understanding as rationalistically conceived, then he does not hold "deductivism" either. Moreover, if as we claim, he distinguishes between inductively well-grounded beliefs and purely associational beliefs, then he is opposed to the forms of scepticism and deductivism imputed to him by Mackie's conclusion (1).[62]

Despite our critical estimate of the Stove-Mackie interpretation, we may end this section on a more conciliatory note. The third of the propositions Stove attributes to Hume is "inductive fallibilism," and we would agree with Stove both that Hume held this position and that it is not, as some have alleged, trivial. Indeed Stove's claim conforms to our thesis that Hume's "scepticism concerning rationalism" is a measured and proper antidote to the excesses of that philosophical view. In effect, what Stove refers to as "inductive fallibilism" alone describes the "sceptical" position we attribute to Hume. Furthermore, in the end, the position we have defended is compatible with a larger purpose of Stove's book. By attacking Hume, Stove hopes to show that philosophers who cite Hume as the forerunner of

---

62. Stove does say that "I do not suggest that Hume, even in his philosophical works, is an inductive sceptic consistently. That is obviously not so." ("Hume, the Causal Principle, and Kemp Smith," pp. 8f; cf. 11f, 17f.) This admisssion is minor, since it is effectively an assertion of inconsistency. Our problem is that we cannot locate inductive scepticism in Stove's sense anywhere in Hume, whereas Stove's position is that Hume's inconsistencies result from his acceptance of radical scepticism, on the one hand, and his attempt "to evade a charge of 'scepticism' against his writing on the other hand." This evasiveness, Stove charges, leads Hume to be "insincere" in his statements of his own views! (*Ibid.*, p. 18.)

their own "inductive scepticism" have appealed to an unsound source, and have been led astray as a result. In this connection Stove has Karl Popper most prominently in mind. Our view, of course, is that Popper is simply a misled exegete of Hume.[63] So we may conclude by inviting Stove to join us in rejecting Popperian excesses, and we offer him another reason for doing so, viz. that Popper misreads Hume. If our view of Hume's treatment of induction is correct, then Stove can adopt it, and still pursue his program of showing that inductive scepticism is an untenable position. Stove is concerned to argue that Hume's "refutation of I. P. [inductive probabilism] is an entirely imaginary episode in the history of philosophy."[64] Our agreement with this claim could not be more complete, even if our reasons for holding it could scarcely be more diverse.

VII

An interesting philosophical question might yet be raised. Though Hume does not concern himself with what we have called the external problem, one might still wonder whether an empiricist philosophy such as his could, without inconsistency, muster the resources to resolve the problem. For this reason it might not be frivolous to show that Hume's philosophy is capable of resolving the external problem and hence that Hume *could* on empiricist grounds construct a suitable philosophical foundation for his well-developed views on inductive standards and internal problems of justification. Such a resolution of the external problem would provide a general framework for the logical rules Hume uses as criteria to distinguish between reasoning merely "naturally" and reasoning "justly and naturally."

We have maintained that Hume does not argue for a sceptical

63. Stove also agrees that Popper and others are misled exegetes. See his *Probability and Hume's Inductive Scepticism*, pp. 125–32. A remarkably stern rebuke is found in "Why Should Probability Be the Guide of Life?" p. 56, note 8. See also "The Nature of Hume's Scepticism," pp. 211f. The compatibility of our views with Stove's, against both Popper and Carnap, becomes especially apparent on pp. 214f, 219f of the latter paper, and in Stove's book, Chapters 7–8.
64. Stove, "Hume, Probability, and Induction," as reprinted from *The Philosophical Review* 74 (1965), in V. C. Chappell, ed., *Hume* (Garden City, N. Y.: Doubleday, 1966), pp. 189, 195, 208f, 211.

approach to the external problem. It is not difficult to show, in addition, that his empiricism is capable of directly confronting this problem and, with complete consistency, of taking any one of several plausible paths toward its resolution. We shall proceed in this demonstration by considering two recently influential treatments of the traditional problem of induction: (1) Dissolution Arguments and (2) Pragmatic Justification Arguments. It is significant that most of the philosophers we cite below as advocates of these approaches comfortably label themselves empiricists, and even as Humeans.

(1) Dissolution or pseudo-problem arguments are in no respect incompatible with Hume's philosophy. Proponents of this approach maintain that one cannot coherently ask whether inductive procedures are rational; they conclude that the traditional problem is one whose resolution comes only through dissolution. Both Antony Flew and A. J. Ayer have taken this position, and both correctly see the compatibility of their approach with the broader perspective of Hume's empiricism. They are mistaken only in thinking that Hume is a sceptic whose scepticism needs correction. Flew, for example, erroneously interprets Hume to be raising the traditional problem of induction and objects that "this is tantamount to enquiring what reason there is for insisting that our expectations should be shaped by experience. This insistence just is rational. There can be no sense in asking for any further or more ultimate reason why."[65] Flew rightly believes his own dissolution perfectly compatible with Hume's empiricism. He wrongly thinks this answer would save Hume from scepticism, for on our view Hume needs no such salvation. But had he been concerned with the external problem, he might well have taken the course recommended by Flew.[66] Much the same can be said concerning A. J. Ayer, who similarly believes that he need not sacrifice empiricist principles in order to take the dissolution approach. In *The Problem of Knowledge* he

65. Antony Flew, *Hume's Philosophy of Belief* (London: Routledge & Kegan Paul, 1961), p. 89.
66. According to Barry Stroud's interpretation of Strawson and the dissolution approach (*op. cit.*, pp. 64–66), Hume could not have found their views congenial. Stroud would be right if his understanding of Strawson's theory were correct, but we find it so distant from Strawson as to be scarcely more than a caricature (esp. p. 65).

quickly dismisses what he takes to be Hume's problem of induction and remarks, while speaking of the inductive sceptic in general, that

his demand for justification is such that it is necessarily true that it cannot be met. But here again it is a bloodless victory. When it is understood that there logically could be no court of superior jurisdiction, it hardly seems troubling that inductive reasoning should be left, as it were, to act as judge in its own cause.[67]

There has been an unfortunate tendency among many adherents of the dissolution approach to flail away at Hume on the pretense that he has generated a pseudo-problem by severely restricting the term "reason" and then asking whether the institution of inductive reasoning is reasonable. We have seen that Hume does indeed restrict the term "reason" but that he never proceeds to call the entire institution of inductive reasoning into question. Once Hume's commitments are thus understood, we can see that Hume might himself argue the line taken, for example, by P. F. Strawson (who is often thought to be arguing against Hume):

What reason have we to place reliance on inductive procedures? . . . It is our habit to form expectations in this way; but can the habit be rationally justified? . . . The doubt has its source in a confusion. . . . The demand is that induction should be shown to be a rational process; and this turns out to be the demand that one kind of reasoning should be shown to be another and different kind.[68]

Hume, who was principally concerned to discriminate between inductive and demonstrative reasoning, would easily have felt at home with the last sentence of this argument. What could be more absurd, from Hume's anti-rationalistic perspective, than the demand that "one form of reasoning should be shown to be another and different kind"? Strawson himself has noted the compatibility of his views with those of Hume, and is among the few to observe the consistency of Hume's rules section with

67. A. J. Ayer, *The Problem of Knowledge* (Baltimore: Penguin Books, 1956), p. 75. Ayer's careful statement of what he takes to be Hume's sceptical position is found in *Probability and Evidence* (New York: Columbia University Press, 1972), Chapter 1, esp. pp. 4f.
68. P. F. Strawson, *Introduction to Logical Theory* (London: Methuen and Co., 1952), pp. 249f.

his naturalistic account of inference. For Hume, he cogently argues, "it is a requirement of Reason that our beliefs should form a coherent system. Committed by nature to the 'basic canons' of induction, we are led by Reason to elaborate our procedures and policies on this basis. Reason is and ought to be, the slave of the passions."[69]

(2) Other contemporary neo-Humeans such as Reichenbach, Feigl, and Salmon insist on solutions rather than dissolutions and offer a pragmatic justification, or vindication, of induction (while admitting that any validation of the method of induction is impossible). They attempt to show that, presuming a desire to make correct predictions, one ought to adopt the rule of induction. It is rational to adopt this rule, they maintain, because it is uniquely suited as a means to attain correct predictions, and so is preferable to all known forms of inference, or is at least as good as any alternative.

Again, this approach is entirely compatible with Hume's philosophy. Although its proponents also share the misconception that Hume held a sceptical position in regard to the external problem, they clearly see that Hume's empiricism need not be sacrificed in order to escape scepticism. Feigl, speaking of his own pragmatic justification of induction, remarks that "the conclusion reached may seem only infinitesimally removed from Hume's scepticism" and that "it is the final point which a consistent empiricist must add to his outlook." Although Hume is not a sceptic in the way Feigl implies, he might nonetheless have wanted, as a consistent empiricist, to add this final point to his outlook.[70]

---

69. P. F. Strawson, "On Justifying Induction," *Philosophical Studies* 9 (1958), pp. 20f. Strawson's views are favorably compared to Hume's text in Farhang Zabeeh, "Hume's Problem of Induction," in Livingston and King, eds., *op. cit.*, esp. pp. 84–87.

70. Herbert Feigl, "De Principiis Non Disputandum . . . ?" in *Philosophical Analysis*, ed. Max Black (Ithaca, N. Y.: Cornell, 1950), p. 131. Wesley Salmon's ingenious essay, "An Encounter with David Hume," is apparently intended to show that Hume raised penetrating and correct questions about induction which find their best solution in those "pragmatic justifications" that derive from Reichenbach. The essay is found in Joel Feinberg, ed., *Reason and Responsibility*, 4th ed. (Belmont, California: Wadsworth Publishing Company, 1979).

VIII

The conclusions we have reached in this chapter concerning Hume's views on induction bear directly on his theory of causation in a way that deserves reemphasis. These conclusions make it clear why Hume takes up the nature of inductive inference at the points in his work where he discusses the place of necessity in causal relatedness. An examination of the former is clearly a part of his exposition of the latter. He must attack the idea that objectively necessary connection provides the medium for inference that is required by rationalism. Additionally, our conclusions undercut the suggestion that Hume's larger philosophical enterprise in analyzing causation and inductive reasoning is purely critical and sceptical. We have not shown, of course, that Hume is not sceptical in others of his teachings; and we have certainly not shown that leading interpretations of Hume's writings as sceptical—such as Richard Popkin's seminal work[71]—are without merit. But these interpretations fail to capture either the letter or the spirit of his philosophy of causation. We are confident that it can be shown that these interpretations are misguided by citing the texts and using the approach instanced in this chapter.[72] That undertaking, however, is a major one far afield from the philosophy of causation.

Having reached the conclusion in our first two chapters that Hume's aim is fully as constructive as it is critical, we turn in the next chapter to a closer examination of his constructive enterprise.

---

71. Richard H. Popkin, *The High Road to Pyrrhonism* (San Diego: Austin Hill Press, 1980). Included in this collection of papers is Popkin's classic article "David Hume: His Pyrrhonism and His Critique of Pyrrhonism," *The Philosophical Quarterly* 1 (1951). Robison's work cited in footnote 1 above deserves the same careful study.

72. This nonsceptical interpretation has already been argued for in three papers by Fred Wilson: "Is Hume Really a Sceptic with Regard to Reason?," unpublished; "What Pyrrho Taught and Hume Renewed," unpublished; and "Hume's Theory of Mental Activity," *McGill Hume Studies, op. cit.,* pp. 101–20.

3
Causal Laws
and Causal Instances

HUME'S AIMS, strategies, and conclusions were examined in the first two chapters. In this chapter we turn to an exposition, analysis, and defense of major implications of his views. In particular we consider the relation between singular statements about particular causal relations and universal statements about general causal relations.

Hume's theory represents a profound and in some ways permanent shift in the history of philosophy, in which causal laws replaced causal instances as the real locus of controversy about the causal relation. Hume's predecessors had supposed that the causal relation was to be analyzed in terms of a particular item's inherent power, efficacy, or agency—or perhaps in the transmission of some quantity like energy, which an inherent power made possible. They also believed that causal laws are derived and established through the repeated experience of particular sequences of phenomena independently recognized as causal in character. We have already seen that Hume's own brand of Copernican revolution reverses this picture: individual cases of causation are to be analyzed in terms of constant conjunctions, while the powers we accord to them are assimilated to the terms of a mental association.

Hume's Copernican shift obliges him to provide first an account of the nature of these laws, second a justification for the claim that the truth of singular causal statements depends on the truth of law statements (instead of the reverse), and third an explanation of why we sometimes correctly make singular causal claims without knowing the allegedly relevant laws and sometimes in the absence of previous acquaintance with the items of the sort causally related. We intend to discharge these and others of Hume's obligations in our analysis of his treatment of the relation of law and instance.

I

Hume's denial of the primacy of individual causal sequences in understanding causal relations is not so much a consequence of his regularity theory as its starting point. His denial that we can learn what causation consists in by attending to particular sequences hinges on the claim that nothing is observable in these cases to distinguish them from accidental sequences. That is, we experience no quality or relation common and peculiar to individual sequences deemed causal, and we therefore cannot determine what causes and effects there might or must be by the minutest inspection of a particular event, state, or condition (T, 75). Specifically, the power, efficacy, or agency other philosophers accord to causes to explain the occurrence of their effects, is something we are incapable of detecting. As Hume puts it, "there is nothing in any object, considered in itself, which can afford us a reason for drawing a conclusion beyond it" (T, 139).

The empiricist strictures of Hume's ideas and impressions doctrine nudges him from this purely negative claim to his positive regularity theory of causality. It is sometimes contended that Hume's march can be stopped well short of his regularity account if only we refuse to grant his negative, empiricist claim that causality cannot be detected in the individual case. Gertrude Anscombe so argues:

[A]s to the statement that we can never observe causality in the individual case. Someone who says this is just not going to count anything as "observation of causality." This often happens in philosophy; it is argued that "all we find" is such-and-such, and it turns out the arguer has excluded from his idea of "finding" the sort of thing he says we don't "find." And when we consider what we are allowed to say we do "find," we have the right to turn the tables on Hume, and say that neither do we perceive bodies, such as billiard balls, approaching one another. When we "consider the matter with the utmost attention" we find only an impression of travel made by successive positions of a round white patch in our visual fields . . . etc.[1]

Anscombe's aim is to argue for the primacy of individual causal sequences. Her strategy is to attack Hume's epistemology, hoping that its inadequacies will cast a pall over his theory of causation. Anscombe is quite wrong to suggest, however, that from the fact that we do perceive physical objects, *pace* Hume's theory of perception, the conclusion can be reached that we also perceive "a lot of causality." Quite apart from interpretative issues regarding whether Hume doubts that we perceive physical objects, it is clear that Hume does not deny that we observe cases of causal sequence and identify them on the basis of current and past observation. There is of course also a sense in which causality is not observable, and Anscombe herself admits that in this sense Hume was correct, though she does so in terms calculated to show Hume mistaken. Hume's standard challenge to his opponents was, "produce some instance, wherein the efficacy is plainly discoverable to the mind, and its operations obvious to our consciousness or sensation" (T, 157–58). Anscombe accepts the challenge:

Nothing is easier: is cutting, is drinking, is purring not "efficacy"? But it is true that the apparent perception of such things may be only apparent: we may be deceived by false appearances. Hume presumably wants us to "produce an instance" in which *efficacy* is related to sensation as *red* is. It is true that we can't do that; it is not *so* related to sensation. He is also helped, in making his argument that we don't perceive "efficacy," by his curious belief that "efficacy" means much the same thing as "necessary connection"![2]

For the purposes of Hume's argument that particular causal sequences cannot directly and immediately be recognized, all that is required is the admission that "efficacy," or power or agency, or productive force, or any of the cognates of causation, is not related to sensation in the way "red" is, whatever way that may be. That these former terms are not so related to sensation is indeed a consequence of Hume's epistemology and

1. Gertrude Anscombe, "Causality and Determination," as reprinted in Ernest Sosa, ed. *Causation and Conditionals* (Oxford: Oxford University Press, 1975), pp. 68–69.
2. *Ibid.*, p. 69.

theory of perception. It is, however, also a consequence of a large number of other such theories, including some specifically mentioned and rejected by Hume himself. In any event, so far as Hume's "curious belief" is concerned, the notion that efficacy provides the necessary connection Hume's opponents hoped to find is a tentative *concession* Hume makes to his opponents in order to increase the plausibility of their argument; it is not a gratuitous assumption he himself embraces.

The passage quoted above is found in that section of the *Treatise* in which Hume examines all possible senses of necessary connection, and all possible attributions to causal sequences that might perform the functions accorded to necessary connection. Anscombe's attack represents a common mistake among Hume's critics, who suppose that defects in one of his theories must vitiate the central and distinctive features of other parts of his philosophy. It may be true that Hume's epistemological views and his theory of meaning first led him to a regularity account of causation, but the latter account may be assessed independently of his theories of knowledge and language. Indeed, his own arguments may consistently be expounded outside those contexts. (Moreover, any alternative to Hume's regularity approach ideally should explain why there is no directly or indirectly detectable property common and peculiar to causal sequences. Anscombe's view does not count as such an alternative, because her view is that the notion of causation is altogether unanalyzable. Her view can only be refuted by producing a successful and complete alternative analysis.)

Because Hume thinks no third thing is ever to be observed besides the two conjoined events called cause and effect, he is led to the view that there is a connection of meaning between the truth of a singular causal statement and the truth of one or more statements reflecting the regularity observed. A semantical entailment between singular causal statements and lawlike statements is required by both of Hume's two definitions. These two definitions reflect Hume's commitment to the primacy of laws over individual cases in the analysis of causation, for to regard an individual sequence as causal is *ipso facto* to regard it as an instance of a general law; to confirm that a sequence is causal is tantamount to confirming that a general statement is a law. The universality Hume thus finds within the particularity of individual causal sequences replaces the necessity conceived earlier in the history of philosophy as that which is most central to the concept of cause. But what exactly is the relationship between the singular statement and the law whose truth is a semantically necessary condition for the singular statement's truth? This putative relation must be squared with the evident fact that all —Humeans included—are willing to offer singular causal statements as true without knowing the laws that are allegedly their necessary conditions.

II

We must first discuss the Humean notion of a causal law. Unfortunately, Hume never explicitly states the conditions a statement must meet to qualify as a causal law; moreover, he leaves even darker what kind of entity qualifies as a causal instance. In this section we reconstruct Hume's tacit commitments on both scores. First, however, we discuss the meanings of the indefinite label "law of nature," which Hume uses only rarely and then without careful attention to its meaning.

In scientific discourse "law of nature" covers less territory than in common discourse, for in the latter it may be applied to causal uniformities only crudely formulated and understood. Science, of course, recognizes some noncausal laws, but when words such as "law" and "lawlike generalization" or "nomological generalization" (to distinguish laws from other universal statements) are used in this chapter, they should be understood as including only the class of *causal* laws and generalizations. This class we take to have extensive membership and not to be coincident with the class of *scientific* laws. Any universal causal generalization qualifies if it is true and either is inferred from its instances or is deducible from another generalization or is derived analogically from other laws (cf. EHU, Sec. 26). Statements such as "Open flames cause dry newspaper to burn" are law statements in our stipulative, restricted sense of the term. (Cf. Hume's use of the terms "law" and "general fact"; EHU, Secs. 90, 132, 47.) Causal laws in this sense need not contain the verb "cause" or its cognates. The laws could be stated, for example, in the language of contiguity and succession or expressed in verbs and other parts of speech that reflect causal connections. Thus "Open flames burn dry newspapers" is as much a causal law as the previous expression employing the word "cause." But, however formulated, every expression of a causal law is governed by a set of definitive specifications, a set we shall now examine in detail. To a large extent these specifications constitute the stock in trade of contemporary discussions of causal law. Nevertheless, it will be useful to collect them all here, and to find their warrant in the Humean corpus.

In the first place, Hume's emphasis on *constant* conjunction makes it patent that an irregularity of conjunction among particular sequences is impossible. Accordingly, a first specification for any causal law, *c*, is the *Uniformity Specification:*

(1) *c* states a uniform relation of contiguity and succession between relevantly similar pairs of particular entities (x_1, y_1), $(x_2, y_2) \ldots (x_n, y_n)$.

This specification is obviously insufficient, since Hume demands that *all* genuine instances of the type X be so related to an instance of type Y. Whenever and wherever a genuine antecedent condition X appears, a consequent condition Y follows (though *y*'s may conceivably occur without *x*'s). A second specification, then, is the *Universality Specification:*

(2) *c* is universally quantified and has the form of a universal conditional.

According to Hume's first definition of causation (Df$_1$), after which these first two specifications are patterned, it is a conceptual truth that causal laws are exceptionless. Statements describing regularities that "generally" or "frequently" hold do not qualify as laws. Nomological generalizations always have the general form "X is succeeded without fail by Y." But this formula is still too simple. Hume is committed to the formula "Same cause *x*, same effect *y*" *provided that* the causally relevant conditions surrounding *x* and *y* are also the same. A fuller analysis of this theory of causal laws, then, would read as follows: "Whenever an instance of *x* and causal conditions *o* coexist, an instance of *y* follows contiguously." Hume would undoubtedly insist that any full formulation of a causal law would include the complete set of jointly sufficient conditions, and many criticisms of Hume seem plausible only because they miss this important point.

Causal laws must also take the form of universal *conditionals*. Laws are often thought to be appropriately expressed, at least to a first approximation, in the universal conditional form "All A's are B's," where "A" and "B" are schematic letters for descriptive predicates. Construed as $(x)(A_x \supset B_x)$ this form may seem satisfactory. There are, however, several reasons why a Humean might object to it, unless further specifications are mentioned. First, causal laws express a strong universal relation of succession that is masked by the atemporal and purely material conditional "All A's *are* B's." Second, accidental regularities share an identical logical form. Third, the descriptive terms themselves might involve dispositional concepts or causal relations that simply shift the analysis to a different level. Accordingly, it is better to begin with the looser form "Whenever condition A obtains, then condition B obtains," where it is understood that causal predicates cannot be substituted for "A" and "B," and that these descriptive predicates are logically independent. Even though modern logic recognizes no difference between "all" and "whenever," the latter more closely reflects Hume's specifications. Moreover, since Hume regards cause and effect as perfectly distinct and separable events, symbolization of causal generalizations might well recognize this logical difference by means of two quantifiers. The following is therefore an initially attractive rendering of *c*:

$$(x) [Ax \supset (\exists y) (By \cdot Syx)]$$

This formula expresses the structure of a statement to the effect that whenever there exists an instance of A, it is succeeded by an instance of B. The variable "*x*" ranges over causes described by predicate "A," and the variable "*y*" ranges over effects described by predicate "B." ("S" symbolizes the relation of contiguous succession. "A"—which here includes both X and O as distinguished above—and "B" are usually highly complex predicates.) This first-order symbolization for *c* still reflects a presumption that the causal force of a law is at least in part expressible by means of a truth-functional conditional such as material implication; yet it is now generally conceded that the material conditional is not an appropriate logical connective to express causal sufficiency.[3]

Temporarily laying aside problems of logical form, our analy-

3. See, e.g., Davidson's work cited in footnote 11 below.

sis of laws as universal conditionals is still incomplete, for such statements could describe accidental conjunctions (sharing the same logical form), and they could be false. The problem of accidental sequence is not dispelled by the Universality and Uniformity Specifications—a major problem confronted throughout Chapter 4. False statements must, of course, be excluded; and since the Universality Specification covers all cases, there must at no time be a falsifying instance. A third specification, then, is

(3) c is omnitemporally true.

This condition requires elaboration. The omnitemporality qualification is redundant: all nonindexical expressions that have truth-value have it omnitemporally, and causal laws cannot satisfy the universality and uniformity conditions if ineliminably indexical terms figure in their expression. The qualification is included here to emphasize the requirement that laws be totally exceptionless. It must also be borne in mind that (3) is not an epistemic requirement. (3) does not require c be known to be true, or even that it be believed true. Indeed, (3) does not describe *any* conditions for the acceptance of c as lawlike. (These epistemic issues will be treated in Chapter 4.)

Finally, a universal causal conditional describes a constant conjunction of instances that fulfill, as a matter of contingent fact, the succession expressed by the statement. *De facto* universality is integral to Hume's attack on rationalism and provides a fourth specification:

(4) c is contingent.[4]

This specification requires that statements of causal connection not be logically necessary. Although the nature of causal laws is such that, by definition, they are exceptionless, any particular causal generalization can be denied without self-contradiction. As shown in the previous chapter, it is a fundamental point in

---

4. In accordance with this specification, the truth-functional formulas mentioned under specification number 2 would have to be amended to show that a cause and an effect are not members of the same class. This is not to deny that there are analytically true general causal statements such as "Fatal illnesses cause death" or perhaps "Vacuum bottles cause liquids to remain warm." Whether these statements are nomological generalizations and related questions are discussed in later chapters.

Hume's philosophy that causal connections cannot be discovered by "reasonings *a priori*," since knowledge of such relations "arises entirely from experience" of constant conjunctions, or comes analogically or by education. Causal generalizations, then, are contingent in the sense that their truth or falsity depends on (is contingent on) empirical truth conditions (EHU, Secs. 21–23).

Although Hume never broaches the subject, his use of terms such as "always" and "constantly" strongly suggests that he would agree with those modern philosophers who insist that law statements in the present tense are statements of *unrestricted universality*.[5] This additional specification is essential for two related reasons. First, causal laws are not mere substitutes for lists of proper names. They state that there has never been, is not, and never will be an exception to the regularities they express. This is true even if the classes mentioned in the law no longer have members—e.g., "All mastodons are tooth-bearing." Accordingly, all laws are formulable in the present tense and refer to open or infinite classes of instances rather than to closed or finite classes. (Laws that refer exclusively to past instances describe classes believed to be contingently closed to further augmentation.) Second, in asserting a law statement, we seem at least implicitly to be saying either that no finite number of observed instances composes the exhaustive class of the law's instances or that it cannot be known that an enumerated set is exhaustive. Laws stated in the present tense, then, are contingent, unrestricted universal statements of uniform succession believed to be true on the basis of some observed instances.

III

Two problems confronting the above specifications deserve immediate attention: the problem of plural causes and the problem of ultimate causes.

Plural Causes. There may be a looseness in the Uniformity Specification due to Hume's neglect of the problem of a plurality of causes. He holds that "the same effect never arises but from

5. Cf. K. Popper, "A Note on Natural Laws and So-called Contrary-to-Fact Conditionals," *Mind* (January, 1949). Reprinted in *Philosophical Problems of Causation*, ed. T. Beauchamp (Encino, Calif.: Dickenson Publishing Co., 1974).

the same cause" (T, 173). This declaration, forming part of Hume's Fourth Rule "by which to judge of causes," is never given argued support. He does not carefully consider whether some difficulty may be generated by holding the counterclaim that there can be two causal generalizations, "Whenever X, then Y" and "Whenever Z, then Y," where X and Z are both logically separate and individually sufficient conditions of Y, and where Y is fully described in each case. He merely suggests, in his Fifth Rule, that "where several different objects produce the same effect, it must be by means of some quality, which we discover to be common amongst them" (T, 174). This claim that in certain cases there are not (or, more difficult still for Hume, could not be) a plurality of causes has struck some philosophers, both friendly and antagonistic, as implausible.[6] C. J. Ducasse's reaction is typical:

"Where several different objects produce the same effect," what immediately and obviously does follow is that *as a bare matter of experience nature is then not uniform.* . . . [What does not follow is] that these different objects have some common quality, as Hume asserts.[7]

Hume's Single Agreement criterion may be poorly formulated, but Ducasse and others have missed his point. The point is that to assume the general principle "same cause, same effect," is to assume that there is a "common quality" among "plural causes" (T, 173). Whether it is appropriate to make this assumption is a matter for experimentation to decide, not theory. An example of an unresolved problem may help illustrate our meaning. Suppose three different drugs produce apparently identical types of hallucination, and it is not known why. Despite our condition of partial ignorance, we are inclined to say that the effect in each instance is the same. This case is not significantly different from a situation in which apparently identical states of drunkenness are produced by mescal, brandy, and vodka. While mescal is distilled from the juice of the American aloe, brandy from the grape, and vodka chiefly from rye, we know that there is a

6. Cf. J. L. Mackie, "Causes and Conditions," *American Philosophical Quarterly* 2 (October, 1965), pp. 245–64, and A. Pap, *An Introduction to the Philosophy of Science* (New York: Free Press, 1962), pp. 255–58.
7. C. J. Ducasse, *Causation and the Types of Necessity* (Seattle: University of Washington Press, 1924; New York: Dover, 1969), p. 15.

distillate "common quality," relevant to all three causes, that produces the single effect. Hume is arguing the simple, and we think correct, point that our past successes in isolating such *common* qualities among apparently different causal sources leads us to predict that we can be similarly successful in handling such new plurality cases as those involving drugs.

Hume is here thinking of inductive reasoning by analogy. Much the same account is still widely prevalent in ongoing work in inductive logic and the theory of lawlikeness. Far from making the substantive point (which would be synthetic *a priori*) that there *cannot* be cases of plural causes, Hume is making the common sense methodological point that experience teaches us to look for common qualities and not to rest content with such a simple view of experience as that advanced by Ducasse. At best, Ducasse's argument leads to a stalemate, and at worst it makes him appear to be an opponent of inductive reasoning, which in fact he is not. As Juhani Pietarinen has perceptively pointed out,

Inference by analogy is closely connected with the problem of lawlikeness. A prerequisite for a growth of the degree of belief in a generalization is that certain (usually a great number of) properties are believed to a large extent to be irrelevant. But the analogical reasoning is not all that counts. The degree of learning depends essentially on certain assumptions about the "regularity" of the phenomena which the generalizations are concerned with.[8]

Since Hume's regularity theory of causation is neither crucially impaired by removal of his Fourth Rule nor significantly enhanced by its retention, there is no need to assess its shortcomings in detail. It should not be overlooked, however, that Hume intends his "Rules by which to judge of causes and effects" more as guiding principles to the discovery and verification of causal relations and claims than as firm theoretical principles that are either true or false. Their own warrant is inductive— the successes of their past employment. Hume would probably not contest the view that most of these rules, if in any sense true, are contingently and not analytically so (though at least some are conceptual truths, if his definitions of "cause" are presupposed). But he *would* challenge a defender of the plurality thesis to produce an example that is more than speculative. Short

8. Juhani Pietarinen, *Lawlikeness, Analogy, and Inductive Logic* (Amsterdam: North Holland Publishing Co., 1972), pp. 10–11.

of such an example, his Rules seem at least to be trustworthy; and it deserves notice that those who use the objection from causal pluralism provide no alternative explanation to account for the alleged fact of pluralism.

Ultimate Causes. Hume's discussions of ultimate causes also present a problem. He argues that one of reason's chief functions is to grasp "general causes" which explain "many particular effects." He pursues his point with the following argument:

As to the causes of these general causes, we should in vain attempt their discovery; nor shall we ever be able to satisfy ourselves, by any particular explication of them. These ultimate springs and principles are totally shut up from human curiosity and enquiry. Elasticity, gravity, cohesion of parts, communication of motion by impulse; these are probably the ultimate causes and principles which we shall ever discover in nature; and we may esteem ourselves sufficiently happy, if, by accurate enquiry and reasoning, we can trace up the particular phenomena to, or near to, these general principles. The most perfect philosophy of the natural kind only staves off our ignorance a little longer. (EHU, Sec. 26)

If this passage is interpreted in accordance with Hume's own theory of causation, a search for causes of general causes would indeed be "in vain." One might search for underlying and general regularities, which explain a wide variety of phenomena; but it would be a category mistake to seek the causes of general causes. Hume has been accused of committing this mistake by John Passmore:

Take the case where A *always* goes with B. How, on this definition of "cause" [Df₁], can Hume intelligibly speak of such universal contiguities as having a cause? Just because the contiguity of A and B is universal, there is nothing prior to it. . . . It is meaningless to talk, as Hume does, of "the *cause* of attraction" (T, 13). In his sense of the word "caused," it is unintelligible to speak of attraction as "caused"; it could have a cause only if at one time bodies did not attract one another—in which case the laws of attraction would no longer be universal.[9]

9. J. A. Passmore, *Hume's Intentions* (Cambridge, England: Cambridge University Press, 1952), p. 30. Passmore is referring to *mental* attraction between ideas. (In addition to T, 13, cf. T, 92f, 169, 179, and EHU, Secs. 9, 26, 36.) For a much more favorable interpretation than Passmore's, see Donald Livingston, "Hume on Ultimate Causation," *American Philosophical Quarterly* 8 (1971), esp. pp. 66f.

This criticism betrays a misunderstanding of Hume's argument and its aim. Just prior to the above quotation from the *Enquiry*, Hume speaks of ultimate causes as powers and attacks the Lockean position that if the ultimate atomic constituents of things were exposed, their operations could *fully* be understood (by some rationalist standard of intelligibility). Hume contends that even following discoveries of the most general regularities, such as Newton's Law of Universal Gravitation or his own "universal laws of cohesion among ideas," we still find ourselves unable fully to understand phenomena that are subsumable under those laws or to "penetrate into the reason of the conjunction" (T, 12f, 169; EHU, Sec. 26). Such discoveries fail to explain what causes one event to succeed another, in Locke's sense of cause. Only succession is observed, never what makes the succession happen. In place of the false hope extended by Locke, Hume is offering his readers no more than a nonparadoxical, deductive-nomological account of explanation—viz., that deductive explanations, in those cases where the explanandum consists in a general law, subsume the explanandum under other laws of *wider* scope. This is what Hume means when he says "we must endeavour to render all our principles as universal as possible, by tracing up our experiments to the utmost, and explaining all effects from the simplest and fewest causes . . ." (T, xvii).

Hume's point is that repeatedly subsuming natural phenomena under causal laws of broader scope provides no comprehension of *Lockean* ultimate causes, for even the most basic laws only "stave off our ignorance" until discovery of their "general causes," i.e., general regularities from which they are deducible. The small thread of truth in Passmore's criticism is that Hume uses the term "general cause" sloppily, perhaps because he has Locke in mind. To render his language consistent Hume should say "general law" instead of "general cause." However, he does not fall into the deeper confusion Passmore attributes to him. He never commits himself to the view that general causes have prior and contiguous causes; he holds only that any general regularity expressed by a nomological generalization may itself be grounded in other, "more ultimate" regularities. The problem of ultimate causes thus turns out to be identical to the problem of fundamental laws.

IV

Bearing in mind the four specifications of general laws developed in Section II, we shall now consider the relation between laws that meet these specifications and singular causal statements. The obvious problem is that the causal generalizations that follow directly from reflection on common singular causal statements cannot always meet the requirements of Hume's theory. For example, the singular causal statement "the shelving of a copy of Hegel's *Phenomenology* caused the bookshelf to break" does not entail a general law to the effect that bookshelves break whenever copies of Hegel's *Phenomenology* are placed on them. The former statement might be true in virtue of the presence of a copy of that great classic being contingently necessary for the breaking, while the latter lawlike statement is not true. A predicate such as "shelving copies of Hegel's *Phenomenology*" might be among the antecedents of some lawful conditional, but it does not describe any part of the antecedent of the law that subsumes the particular causal sequence here described. After all, any other book or object of equal or greater weight would have been sufficient on the occasion for the breakage, though none would have been necessary. The causally relevant factor for purposes of generalization is weight, yet it goes unmentioned in the true singular statement. In what way, then, could the singular statement in question entail a law that involves considerations unmentioned in the singular statement? How could irrelevant predicates be employed to pick out correctly the causal sequences the singular statement reports? And in what sense are such singular statements "implicitly general"?

Donald Davidson has offered an appealing answer to these questions.[10] He distinguishes between stronger and weaker versions of the thesis that singular causal statements are implicitly general. On the strong version, a singular causal statement, employing predicates "X" and "Y" to describe its relata (the par-

10. Donald Davidson, "Causal Relations," *Journal of Philosophy* 64 (1967), pp. 691f, 697, 701f. Cf. also his "Actions, Reasons, and Causes," *Journal of Philosophy* 60 (1963), pp. 685–700, as reprinted in B. Berofsky, ed., *Free-Will and Determinism* (New York: Harper & Row, 1966), pp. 236f. Some features of Davidson's analysis were anticipated by Hume's Scottish successor, Thomas Brown (1778–1820). See his *Inquiry into the Relation of Cause and Effect* (London, 3rd ed., 1818).

ticular cause, x, and its effect, y), entails a general statement of conditional form, whose antecedent and consequent predicates consist in, or at least include "X" and "Y." On a weak interpretation of the condition of implicit generality, the truth of the singular statement entails that there are some true descriptions of x and y, the cause and effect, and that there is some general law employing the predicates that figure in these descriptions, from which the singular statement in question follows, on appropriate substitution of co-referential descriptions. This interpretation is weaker than the former because no particular law employing predicates "X" and "Y" is directly entailed by ordinary statements that employ these predicates, and the truth of such a statement can be defended without having to defend any particular law.

Davidson's suggestions focus attention on the crucial, but easily overlooked, point that a distinction must firmly be drawn between causes (those events, states, or conditions that actually bring about an effect and that would be mentioned in one or more true causal laws) and those features of causal occasions generally cited in our *descriptions* of a cause and its effect. Following Davidson's lead, it is useful for us to distinguish further between the laws actually entailed by true singular causal statements and the general statements our descriptions of those causal occasions would entail if the singular statements were generalized. In Hume's formula "all the *objects similar to x* are followed contiguously by *objects similar to y*," common sense will lead one to focus attention on objects similar to x (under a certain description). Even ordinary causal generalizations reflect this fact (e.g., "life preservers—or aluminum boats, or buoys, or logs—cause persons to float"). But any universally true causal law will focus attention not on the objects but on the relevant similarities x possesses in common with other objects (e.g., its shape, density of material, etc.). In short, the Uniformity and Universality Specifications must be tightened to assert that a condition of causal laws is formulation *purely* in terms of universally connected features. Accordingly, the terms ordinarily used to describe causally connected objects may differ radically from the descriptive predicates that appear in those causal laws governing the cited sequences. In most cases, only precisely formulated laws that refer to specific but quite general features will not violate the Uniformity and Universality Specifications.

The relation of Hume's two specifications to singular causal statements may now be clarified further. The Uniformity Specification governs instances as follows: the antecedent condition terms in a constant conjunction statement of law c may be employed to describe correctly one or more features of each instance of c's antecedent, and the consequent condition terms in c correctly describe one or more features of each instance of c's consequent. The Universality Specification relates to instances as follows: if s is a singular causal statement of the form "x caused y," then s may entail no particular law but it does entail that there exists a universally quantified conditional statement, containing among its antecedents a predicate x instantiates and as its consequent a predicate y instantiates.

Although it is not clear whether Davidson explicitly attributes either the strong or the weak version of the claim of implicit generality to Hume's writings, it is plausible to attribute the more acceptable of these two accounts to Hume. Two passages in particular support this contention. First, in the section on Rules, Hume offers two principles, which, he says, "hang upon" what we have called uniformity-universality requirements:

(5) Where several different objects produce the same effect, it must be by means of some quality, which we discover to be common amongst them. . . .

(6) The difference in the effects of two resembling objects must proceed from that particular, in which they differ. . . . When in any instance we find our expectation to be disappointed, we must conclude that this irregularity proceeds from some difference in the causes. (T, 174)

In some late sections of the first *Enquiry,* Hume augments these familiar inductive principles with a warning against carelessly attributing irrelevant conditions to causes:

When we infer any particular cause from an effect, we must proportion the one to the other, and can never be allowed to ascribe to the cause any qualities, but what are exactly sufficient to produce the effect. . . . If the cause, assigned for any effect, be not sufficient to produce it, we must either reject that cause, or *add to it such qualities as will give it a just proportion to the effect.* (EHU, Sec. 105, emphasis added)

Hume misleads us somewhat by saying we ascribe causation "wherein we discover the resemblance." Davidson correctly maintains that we may discover a shared quality of causal instances, yet not have hit upon true causal features. Still, Hume's broad formulation produces no major problem. Perhaps he means "discoverable common quality" (as at EHU, Sec. 68, for instance), not "discovered common quality." He commonly assumes a distinction between causal ascriptions and correct causal ascriptions, as the passage from the *Enquiry* suggests. At any rate, it seems obvious that Hume would not quarrel with Davidson's constructive claims (cf. T, 139, 175).

Moreover, Hume appears to anticipate Davidson's views in his discussions of unknown and hidden causes. Hume often admits that there may be qualities that account for causal relatedness other than the "superficial qualities" we commonly cite (EHU, Secs. 29, 31). Sometimes it appears that Hume is not serious and might be parodying Locke in his comments on hidden causes. But at other points, he is clearly pressing a thesis. He argues, for example, that while we often attribute causal agency to objects that only "irregularly and uncertainly" produce a particular effect (opium irregularly causes sleep), *philosophers* do not presume that such objects, as experienced, are causes. Rather, they suppose that there are "some secret causes in the structure of the parts" that are either operative or prevent the operation (EHU, Secs. 47, 67; T, 132). The causal laws of which such cases are instances he also proclaims secret, i.e., undiscovered. In such cases as "pestilence, earthquakes, and prodigies," says Hume, we believe there is a causal relation, yet we are "at a loss to assign a proper cause" (EHU, Sec. 54). He explains this loss as follows: "The circumstance, on which the effect depends, is frequently involved in other circumstances, which are foreign and extrinsic. The separation of it often requires great attention, accuracy, and subtilty" (EHU, Sec. 84n). Hume is again arguing that one may be aware of particular causal sequences without being aware either of exact causal factors or of the causal laws governing the sequences observed.

Hume's conclusion seems to be the one Davidson argues for: while singular causal statements do not entail any particular law, they do entail that there is a law. Perhaps the first clause in this conclusion should be elaborated in the following way: one may know that particular causal sequences occur without knowing the precise causal laws that govern them; and, furthermore, the *meaning* of singular causal reports of such sequences does not include the citation of a particular law. Hume's insistence that there is no well-founded attribution of causal relatedness to individual sequences without the support of past experience, analogical reasoning from such experience, or belief acquired through education, is thus clearly compatible with Davidson's approach to implicit generality. While Davidson's argument centers on the meaning of causal statements and Hume's on a claim about the epistemic basis of such statements, they are perfectly complementary.

Moreover, Davidson's clarification of the relations between causal laws and causal instances and our extension of it serve to undercut two important objections that have been lodged against Hume's regularity theory. The first may be called the Irregular Cause Problem, and the second the Singular Cause Problem. We consider them in turn in the next two sections.

V

The Irregular Cause Problem. It has repeatedly been claimed by philosophers that some true causal citations do not conform to the requirement of regular succession. One particularly interesting example of this objection has been advanced by Fred Dretske and Aaron Snyder. They provide alleged counterexamples to Hume's view, which they in turn use to support a theory of causal irregularity. The chief counterexample involves a randomizing device R that proceeds, upon activation, to one of its one hundred different terminal states (each equiprobable). Attached to R is a revolver that fires when and only when the terminal state is number 17. If we place this device next to a cat, point the revolver at the cat, activate R, and the cat is killed, then according to ordinary causal thinking we have killed the cat, even though the improbable has occurred. The distinctive Snyder-Dretske thesis emerges from this example:

Though we designate our actions as the cause, and the cat's death as the result, there is no regular or uniform connection between actions of *the first sort* and results of the latter sort. If we should perform in the same way under *identical circumstances,* more often than not (roughly 99% of the time) the cat would survive. . . . [Here] in identical circumstances something of type C will not even generally be followed by something of type E.[11]

In one important sense the described circumstances do provide an example of causal irregularity. But the authors fail to answer the pertinent and most difficult questions forced by the Hume-Davidson analysis. Consider again Hume's discussions of unknown and hidden causes. As we saw, he contends that while we often attribute causal efficacy to objects that only "irregularly and uncertainly" produce a particular effect, philosophers suppose there to be "some secret causes, in the structure of parts," that are either operative or preventive. Because the causal laws are also undiscovered, we should distinguish, in cases such as the Snyder-Dretske example, between the regularities entailed by true singular causal statements and the general statements our descriptions of those causal occasions would entail if the known singular relation were generalized. No proponent of the Regularity Theory would unguardedly admit that the antecedent conditions Dretske and Snyder describe as type C events are relevantly similar to the conditions that actually cause the death of the cat. Regularity theorists would insist that until the description of type C events is divided into types $C_1, C_2, \ldots,$ C_{100}, one has merely described some obviously causal occasion without identifying the exact cause.

The peculiarities of a randomizing device fail to diminish the force of this argument. An advocate of the regularity theory would not concede that the criteria for a proper nomological description of events of type C are satisfied by a description such as "activating a randomizing device." This event is *part* of the cause—indeed it is a contingently necessary condition—but adequate and precise descriptions of type C events would include both the sufficient and the necessary conditions for type E events. In the case of a randomizing device the conditions would have to be those sufficient both for landing in state number 17 and for killing the cat. Here several laws might be involved.

Holding to their objection from causal irregularity, Dretske and Snyder have responded to one possible line of criticism as follows:

11. F. I. Dretske and A. Snyder, "Causal Irregularity," *Philosophy of Science* 39 (1972), p. 70 (emphasis added).

. . . it is unclear how we could redescribe our action so as to include conditions "sufficient both for landing in state number 17 and for the killing of the cat"—since, so far as is known, there are no conditions which are sufficient (in the sense of "subsumable under causal laws") for the electron's landing in state number 17. . . . [If the suggestion is] that we can redescribe *what we did* as "putting the electron in state number 17" and, under this description, have something that is part of some causally sufficient condition for the cat's death, [this] is certainly right. But [it] implicitly concede[s] the very point for which we were arguing. For if we can be said to have put the electron in state number 17, despite the acknowledged lack of any causal regularity, then we can also be said to have killed the cat. The conclusion remains that either we can do things that bear no causal connection to our immediate actions, or else causal connections do not require regularity.[12]

This conclusion is fallaciously drawn, even though Dretske and Snyder do correctly see the line of argument a defender of the regularity theory must take. Suppose one can, as they suggest, redescribe the agent's action as "putting the electron in state number 17." We know, based on what they say, that the following causal generalization is true:

Whenever the electron is put in state number 17, then (given the stipulated circumstances) the cat dies.

We also know that a generalization based on any other activating action (e.g, putting the electron in state number 16) is false. These formulations demonstrate that when we are sufficiently precise in our descriptions of events and reach a true causal generalization, we have located the cause, and when we are sufficiently imprecise we say something that is either false or misleading. They also reveal the irrelevance of injecting, as Dretske and Snyder do, the reminder that there is an "acknowledged lack of any causal regularity." At the appropriate link in the chain from activation of R to the cat's death there is no lack of causal regularity at all, for the generalization cited above is universal, uniform, and true. There is, of course, a *noncausal* irregularity in their example between activating the machine and its landing in state number 17, since (as they hy-

12. F. I. Dretske and A. Snyder, "Causality and Sufficiency: Reply to Beauchamp," *Philosophy of Science* 40 (1973), p. 289.

pothesize) there was an "event which was perfectly random and had no cause."[13] But this noncausal occurrence is irrelevant (as they correctly see) to whether the activator caused the cat's death (he did); nor does it figure in any way in the proper causal law. In short, the randomizing device example is irrelevant and is shown to be irrelevant, as was originally suggested, by a correct redescription of the human action as one of placing the electron in state number 17 (where, of course, there is a perfect causal regularity with the death of the cat). Because of this regularity we recognize that the action is the cause of the cat's death; if there were no such regularity, then either the actor did not cause the death or else the death resulted from some other action (describable using the appropriate terms).

Dretske and Snyder may have still another rejoinder, one which they seem to anticipate. They argue that if one focuses on the effect "landing in state number 17," and asks for its cause, it appears that the activation of the machine caused the effect of landing in state number 17, even though these two events are irregularly connected. And this is indeed a somewhat more interesting example than the cat's death, because there is without question an irregular relation between activating R, and the device's landing in state 17. Dretske and Snyder argue that there is a causal relation here, too, because "there are no conditions other than C [the activating act] which are necessary for E [landing in 17] *for which C is not already sufficient.*"[14] Hence, C is causally sufficient for E.

But this claim too is mistaken. It may be admitted that the act of activating R at least partially *explains* why R landed in state 17, once we understand both how randomizing devices operate and that the probability of landing in 17 was 0.01. But we would not say that the activating act *caused* R to land in state 17. The action in question, activating R, may be described as the event that caused the electron to land in one of the one hundred terminals, but not to land in 17 in particular.

This perhaps unappealing claim does not simply beg the question by insisting on a regularity account while invoking Davidson's theory of redescription. It follows from what Dretske and

---

13. Dretske and Snyder, "Causal Irregularity," p. 70.
14. Dretske and Snyder, "Causality and Sufficiency," p. 291.

Snyder themselves say. They say that settling in state number 17 was a "random event" that was "not causally determined." Yet, they say, it was not an uncaused event: "our activating the device was causally sufficient for its settling in state number 17, and consequently for the cat's death, in the sense that nothing further was necessary, in that particular case, for either of those results." But something else was necessary in that particular case, viz., a random occurrence. According to their own account of causation, after which the previous quotation is patterned, "in calling a condition S sufficient for E, we mean that there are no conditions other than C which are necessary for E *for which C is not already sufficient.*"[15] The question, then, is whether C was "already sufficient" for the random occurrence that led to E. The answer seems obviously to be that it was not causally sufficient, no matter what account of sufficiency one employs. For nothing could, on their own definition, be *causally* sufficient for the *purely random* occurrence. It is a random, accidental occurrence; hence, the act of activating the device does not *cause* the landing in 17. At most it causes R to land in some terminal or other. And this is good regularity doctrine, whether Hume's or Davidson's. [Note also that the Dretske-Snyder analysis of causal sufficiency comes precariously close to begging the question by repeating "sufficiency" in the analysans.]

Dretske and Snyder have perhaps confused causal irregularity with causal accidentality. If, during an air raid, bombs are dropped that cause the unanticipated deaths of children in regions remote from the target, the deaths will be described as an accident (in part because their probability is low) but not as a case of causal irregularity. It may be that the case of killing the cat is similarly improbable, but not irregular. The air raid example again illustrates the importance of a proper description of the actions involved. None would deny that bombing under the fully described conditions always results in the death of distant children. Similarly we should not deny that activating a randomizing device under the appropriate description (say, Dretske's and Snyder's "putting the electron in state number 17") will always result in the death of appropriately distant cats.

15. *Ibid.*

The real problem of randomness is at once more and less serious than proponents of causal irregularity recognize. Where there is genuine randomness, there is no causation at all, as Dretske and Snyder seem to recognize: an "event which [is] perfectly random . . . [has] no cause."[16] It is therefore no counterexample to the regularity thesis that causation consists in regularities that are not just nonrandom, but strictly universal. But suppose, as the current orthodoxy in the interpretation of quantum mechanics suggests, that the fundamental laws of nature are not strictly universal, but are irreducibly statistical. What will the upshot be for the Humean? Here the problems of causal irregularity become more serious than philosophers such as Dretske and Snyder have imagined. Suppose it turns out that all events are related to one another in the irreducibly stochastic way that a quantum mechanical randomizing device's states are alleged to be related. If the fundamental laws of physics are statistical in character, then the apparently deterministic phenomena at the macroscopic level will correctly be described by statements, deducible from the statistical quantum laws, that are themselves only deterministic in the unattainable limit, as Planck's constant approaches zero by comparison to values of macroscopically measured values.

This possibility, not envisioned by Hume, must have serious repercussions for his theory of causation, because it appears to deny the existence of the constant conjunctions in which causation consists. Thus, given an event of either macro- or microphysical character, the most fundamental law of working will not restrict its successor to one and only one kind, but will at best specify a class of different kinds of successors with varying degrees of probability. Because at the level of macroscopic events the probability distribution is so heavily skewed that the probability of one particular successor approaches 1.00, we mistake the sequence for a deterministic one when in fact it is essentially statistical. But if there are no true universal and uniform laws, there is no Humean causation, anywhere. If in the light of this conditional we nevertheless embrace the truth of at least one singular statement of causal relatedness between two particular events, we are *ipso facto* committed to rejecting Hume's account of causation as false.

16. *Ibid.*

How can the Humean reply to this argument? The safest reply is that the philosophy of physics is currently in an unsettled state, and problems surrounding the interpretation of quantum mechanics remain insufficiently resolved to enable one particular view of this theory to refute a theory of causation that has so much to recommend it. For it is by no means agreed that quantum mechanics is most plausibly construed as irreducibly statistical or indeterministic. Numerous exponents of hidden variable theories claim that underlying deterministic mechanisms may eventually be found to which quantum phenomena are reducible. Others, following Ernest Nagel,[17] argue that in all important respects quantum mechanics is a deterministic theory after all. Nagel points out that the Schrödinger wave equation expressing the fundamental regularity of the theory is not a probability formula, but a differential equation of the same form (providing single-valued time dependent solutions) as the equations expressing deterministic Newtonian mechanics. The difference between Newtonian and quantum mechanics, in Nagel's view, rests on differences between the state-descriptions that the two theories both deterministically relate. The fundamental states of objects in Newtonian mechanics are given by their values of momentum and position; the parallel states for quantum mechanical objects are given by the so-called Ψ-function. The appearance of irreducible probability is generated for quantum mechanics by the fact that the only plausible interpretation available for the Ψ-function involves treating the square of its absolute value as a measure of the probability that an object will have the classical state-variable properties at a given time. The Humean may take over this argument and claim that if the states accorded to objects by quantum mechanics can satisfy the requirements of spatiotemporal contiguity and succession, then the deterministic character of the fundamental equation of quantum mechanics assures that these objects will engage in causal relations of the sort Hume envisaged.

The trouble with this line of counterargument, aside from the fact that it rests on an interpretation of quantum mechanics at least as controversial as the one attributed to anti-Humeans,

17. Ernest Nagel, *The Structure of Science* (New York: Harcourt, Brace & World, 1961), Chapter 10.

is that it is uncertain whether objects can satisfy the requirements of contiguity and succession. That is, these requirements were initially established in the light of Newtonian assumptions that the fundamental states of objects are their exact position and momentum. The deterministic interpretation of quantum mechanics obliges us to surrender this assumption, and to replace it with the supposition that objects are fundamentally characterized by their Ψ-functions. But at present the Ψ-function is either uninterpreted or interpreted in terms of irreducible objects having only probable position and momentum. In the former case, we cannot tell whether objects satisfy the requirements of spatiotemporal location that position and momentum provide, while the latter alternative obviously renders quantum mechanics incompatible with the Humean account of deterministic causality. This dilemma for the Humean illustrates why it is perhaps best simply to say that arguments from quantum mechanics involve premises that are too controversial to settle any matters in the present connection.

Other Humean responses to the absence of strictly universal and uniform laws also deserve consideration. One strong rejoinder is to admit that without such laws there is no causality whatever, and that the concept of cause will then have no correct application to any actual sequence. Of course the Humean will only agree to this admission if his opponents accept the challenge of showing, in the absence of universal and uniform laws, what difference there is between the causal sequences they seek to retain and accidental sequences. If Humean arguments to show our inability to distinguish causal sequences from accidental ones without appeal to regularities are sound, opponents will be unable to substantiate their claim that causality obtains in an indeterministic world, because they will be unable to distinguish causal and accidental sequences.

It will not do to argue in reply that causation obtains in any sequence reflecting a probabilistic regularity at some particular level above chance. There will be no detectable difference between accidental sequences that reflect the particular level of probability in question and the most fundamental (and therefore unexplainable) statistical regularity of quantum mechanics associating kinds of events at exactly the same level of probability. We cannot ground causation on irreducible statistical laws, quantum mechanical or otherwise, for the fundamental status of these laws excludes their nomological explanation as surely as the accidental status of a nonnomological statistical regularity excludes its wholly nomological explanation. Under these circumstances causal and accidental sequences will be indistinguishable. The following conclusion is the one we have suggested the Humean should support: if the fundamental "laws" of nature turn out to be statistical and not uniform and universal, there is no causation, and the concept has no correct applicability.

It is worth emphasizing again that Hume's is not an inquiry into the meaning of the expression "cause" as it figures in ordinary language. Appeals as to what we should say in ordinary or extraordinary contexts have little weight for Hume. He is concerned not with what we *believe* is true when a singular causal statement is true, but with what *is* invariably true when such a statement is true. If it turns out that on the only tenable account of the matter, given the facts of an ineliminable indeterminism, all singular causal statements are false, the analysis Hume offers will in no way be vitiated. His philosophical views do not entail the existential claim that there are true singular causal statements. To announce that there are paradigm cases of true singular causal statements is no part of an analysis of the notion of cause, unless the announcement is accompanied by an account of the differences between sequences that make the paradigm cases true and sequences that are noncausal. The latter endeavor transcends appeal to intuitions about particular cases.

VI

The Singular Cause Problem. It has been argued that since Hume restricts inquiry into causation to the search for laws, his work makes no contribution to the analysis of singular causal statements as such or to inquiry concerning the character of the events, states, and conditions among which the causal relation obtains. This misconception of Hume's theory is due to an emphasis on causal laws out of proportion to their actual place in Hume's writings. C. J. Ducasse is representative:

If the engine of my car stops, and I ask *"Why?"*, I am not asking for a statement of invariable succession or of a law, even though one may, conceivably, be inferable. . . . What I want to know is . . . the single *difference* between the circumstances of the engine at the moment when it was running, and at the moment when it was not. . . . Constant conjunctions . . . would follow as a matter of course, if the cause and the conditions were repeated. But constant conjunction is then *a possible corollary, not the definition,* of causation. *To have mistaken it for the latter was Hume's epoch-making blunder.* . . . [Hume and Mill believe] inquiry into causation *is* inquiry into laws. The truth is on the contrary that it is directly and primarily an inquiry concerning *single, individual events.*[18]

This interpretation is not entirely groundless, but it obscures important subtleties in Hume's analysis. In Ducasse's interpretation Hume thinks causal inquiry is directly concerned with constant conjunctions and is not concerned, or is only indirectly concerned, with single cases. This emphasis is Ducasse's primary misconception.

Ducasse fails to see that on Hume's view even if a singular statement about an instance entails that a law exists, it is no less a singular statement about the instance. Saying "This hole in the radiator caused the car to break down" is on Hume's analysis neither equivalent to a law statement nor the result of an inquiry into a law, though the truth of the statement does entail that there is a universal law, known or unknown, subsuming the sequence described. Hume simply holds that whereas some relations are inherently relations between individuals regardless of the class to which they belong (spatial relations, e.g.), the causal relation holds between *individuals as instances* of specifiable classes. This analysis involves more than a mere verbal quibble with Ducasse. Hume grants that in any particular case what we "want to *know*," as Ducasse puts it, is the single difference between one set of circumstances and another. Indeed, one of Hume's previously cited passages could be mistaken for a quotation from Ducasse: "the circumstance, on which the effect depends, is frequently involved in other circumstances, which are foreign and extrinsic. The separation of it often requires great attention, accuracy, and subtilty" (EHU, Sec. 84n; cf. T, 148, 175). Hume affirms through his rules of induction the importance of inquiry into single differences and would agree that, as a matter of practical need, we are commonly interested in

---

18. C. J. Ducasse, *Causation and the Types of Necessity,* pp. 19, 21; also cf. p. 10. (Passages slightly rearranged, and some italics added.)

single differences and in single cases. He denies only that single differences can be *known* from absolutely singular cases.

This last observation points to a second difference between Hume and Ducasse, one regarding the conditions of causal knowledge. Hume's "epoch-making" epistemological twist is his claim that there is no identification, detection, or recognition of a causal relation without an appropriate background of experience. Ducasse disagrees. He thinks both that a sequence occurring only once can be causal and also that a particular sequence can be *known* through observation to be causal, even though it is unique, and therefore independent of any regularity or analogy to another regularity. Ducasse maintains that the individual causal sequence is primary and the general regularity secondary in the order of knowledge, and consequently in the analysis we may offer of the meaning of the concept. In this respect he is in agreement with Anscombe. Unlike Anscombe, however, Ducasse substantiates this commitment with an argument for the perceivability of causation. He claims that a set of changes C, composed of changes $c_1, c_2, \ldots c_n$, is the cause of an event E, in circumstances S (composed of C, E, and the set of irrelevant causal conditions I), if and only if C and E are the *only* two changes in S, and C can be distinguished from elements in I *by perception* in singular cases: "In any such concrete case observed, the causation which occurred was *not inferred* but was as literally *perceived* as were the concrete events it connected." Ducasse admits that perceptual mistakes are sometimes made about causation, but he attributes them to the fact that we have not succeeded in isolating the *only* change in circumstances:

It is difficult to make sure that no other occurred; but it is likewise difficult to make sure by observation that there is at a given time no mosquito in a given room, or no flea on a given dog. . . . Thus, theoretically, all that observation can yield is probability. . . . In many cases it is difficult or impossible to attain certainty that what we observe really conforms to the definition of the [causal] relation.

Ducasse has, in effect, described Mill's Method of Difference, which he takes to be a description or definition of the causal relation itself, not just a method for discovery or proof.[19]

19. *Ibid.*, pp. 147ff, and C. J. Ducasse, *Nature, Mind, and Death* (LaSalle, Ill.: Open Court, 1951), pp. 95, 105–7, 118–21. The two quotations are, respectively, from the former, p. 151, and from the latter, p. 119.

Ducasse is well aware of criticisms that it is difficult to ascertain the true cause by perceptual observation. He argues that if any doubt as to the conformity between observation and the definition of causation arises, then "additional observation can often dispose of the doubt and thus increase the probability."[20] This argument defends Ducasse's claims only by weakening them to the degree that Hume rests unrefuted. Hume never denies that hypotheses about proper causes can be framed on the basis of single occasions; and he notoriously agrees that experience in the form of "additional observations" increases the probability of accuracy. Hume merely denies that the relation itself is ever directly perceived or that we know by single perception which changes are the causal ones. It is the second of these claims that Ducasse must refute, and yet he fails to do so. Even certain of Ducasse's proponents have apparently recognized this defect. Among them, Edward Madden and James Humber write:

In perceiving the complex change, . . . did we directly observe the causal relation? Ducasse answers "yes" because we experienced what was in fact sufficient to E, even though what we experienced was more than sufficient. It seems to us, however, that the correct answer is "no" because there is a difference between experiencing the cause of E and experiencing something as the cause of E. Ducasse confuses the two notions. He is right in saying that one has perceived what is the cause of E but wrong in thinking that one thereby has perceived x as the cause of E. Given any complex change, one cannot claim to have experienced the whole of it or any part of it as the cause of E because what the cause of E is can be known in such cases only inferentially.[21]

In order to show both that causation is perceivable in particular sequences and that it is not an unanalyzable notion, Ducasse would have to show precisely which features of *perceptual* experience distinguish causes from noncauses. It would not suffice to show which features merely distinguish causes from irrelevant conditions or from changes that are accidental concomitants. Otherwise the initial question of how we are to distinguish causal and noncausal changes in a non-Humean way

20. Ducasse, *Nature, Mind, and Death*, pp. 113–25. Quotation p. 119.
21. Edward Madden and James Humber, "Nonlogical Necessity and C. J. Ducasse," *Ratio* 13 (1971); and reprinted in Beauchamp, ed., *Philosophical Problems of Causation, op. cit.,* p. 170.

is begged. Ducasse never provides such differentia' as features of immediate perceptual experience alone, and his explanations invariably make tacit appeal to influential knowledge from other cases. In the end his account seems indistinguishable from Hume's.

In order to test Ducasse's views against Hume's, imagine a quite ordinary case of "perceiving" causation. Suppose an apprentice painter adds a blue substance to a can of white paint and stirs. He notices that the paint gradually thickens after these two initial changes. The blue substance, he thinks (or should we say perceives?), is not only coloring the can's contents but is also thickening them. He repeats the experiment with the same result. But now he wants a can of white paint, so he stirs the original paint without adding any of the blue substance. To his surprise it thickens in the same way, and just as rapidly. The stirring, not the added ingredient, has caused the thickening. Hume's Rules (Mill's Methods) tell the apprentice how to obtain this result ("with probability"), but how is he to know it on Ducasse's account? Following the latter, he would know by perception that the thickening is caused by the blue agent *or* the agent together with the stirring, since these are the only changes introduced; but he would not know that the stirring alone is the cause.

The fact that we thus relinquish our initial causal beliefs based on perception if similar instances prove us wrong simply reflects Hume's analysis and its commitments to generality in causal knowledge. The fact that one genuine counterinstance proves us wrong in such cases tends to show that we implicitly think regularities are involved. Our powers of perception in singular cases are sufficient, then, to inform us which changes are causes. Matters only become more difficult as the changes in circumstances S are multiplied, for an increasing number of tests will be needed to discriminate causally relevant changes from irrelevant ones.[22] But if this is what Ducasse means in the passage above about "additional observation," then his account and Hume's still remain indistinguishable.

This example is not one unfairly foisted on Ducasse, for his own examples encounter the same problem:

22. In Hume, cf. EHU, Secs. 105, 84n; T, 173–75.

The other day, the dash lamp of the automobile I was in failed to light on my turning the switch. But when I fumbled at random in the mess of wires under the dash, the light flickered on. *Postulating* then that neither the barking of the dogs on the other side of town, nor any of the other changes which I did not observe taking place *were causally relevant* to the light's flickering on, I at once *concluded* that "what I had done" was the cause of it. Having thus identified the cause perceptually. . . .[23]

In this example the mentioned extraneous feature is obviously irrelevant, but if other changes had simultaneously obtained inside the car, could the "cause" have been so readily ascertained? Moreover, as Hume noticed, the "perception" of causation commonly requires sorting relevant and irrelevant features through analogy from previous experience of constant conjunctions. Ducasse may be revising the meaning of "perception" to include processes of reasoning, such as the elimination of alternative hypotheses, but then his theory clearly caves into Hume's. However, this interpretation of "perception" is not plausible as a rendering of Ducasse's meaning, for he often argues that knowledge of constant conjunctions and causal generalizations has nothing to do with the perception of causation. Indeed, Hume's "epoch-making blunder" allegedly lies in his failure to distinguish the two.

In addition to these problems concerning perception, it is doubtful that an analysis in terms of individual changes in preceding circumstances captures what is ordinarily meant by "cause," despite Ducasse's claim to have done so. In the first place, cause is not commonly distinguished from conditions in the way he suggests. The immediate single difference is not causally sufficient, by his own admission; and in many contexts it is not generally thought to be the cause at all. Suppose a roll of thunder is followed by the bursting of a dam—a structure, it is discovered, which was inadequately designed and built below specifications. Both the actions of the designer and contractor and the standing bulk of water are causal conditions capable of being isolated as the cause. There is a temporal gap between the former causal occasion and the cited effect, while the water and the construction materials are standing conditions in the set of

23. Ducasse, *Causation and the Types of Necessity*, p. 78. (Italics added.)

irrelevant conditions I just before the occurrence of the effect, not changes in C. Furthermore, the roll of thunder may or may not be causally relevant. Suppose a long-term erosion of concrete is actually the precipitating factor. Are we to say that only the last slight chink of erosion is causally sufficient? Even if we knew that this latter change alone had occurred in the circumstances, would it be the cause? We argue in Chapter 5 that Hume has a convincing answer to these questions, based on his account of contiguity and succession—a thesis on which he and Ducasse may in the end agree. That point, however, is presently irrelevant. We wish only to observe that Ducasse's analysis fails to capture the ordinary meaning of "cause," despite his oft-repeated claim to have done so and thereby to have bested Hume.

In at least one further respect Ducasse's view is indisputably at variance with Hume's. Ducasse insists that the cause of an engine's stopping is the single difference between "the circumstances of the engine at the moment when it was running, and at the moment when it was not." If this change is the sole instance of its type, and constituted the sole change in the circumstances, then it is the cause regardless of whether the sequence would or would not occur in exactly similar circumstances. Up to a point the regularity theorist agrees that qualitatively unique and unrepeated sequences may be causal. Regularity accounts say only that apart from analogical reasoning we cannot *know* that such sequences are causal, even though they may be unique instances of regularities. The Humean, then, will disagree specifically with Ducasse's claim that "the observing of . . . recurrence is theoretically *unnecessary* to the *identification* of cases of causation." If there can be no analogical comprehension whatever under "any known species," as Hume puts it, then there can be no "conjecture or inference at all" (EHU, Sec. 115). Humeans need not disagree that recurrence is theoretically unnecessary to the sequence's *being* a causal instance. The metaphysical issue for Hume is not the contingent matter of whether the type of sequence in question is in fact repeated, but whether the type of sequence instanced is invariable and unconditional regardless of *de facto* repetition.

This disagreement hinges on Ducasse's modal claim that an unrepeated sequence would be causal even were it not to recur at other times and places *where the same circumstances obtain.*

This view entails the dubious claim that causal statements fail to support counterfactual conditional statements. The disagreement thus depends on the character of modal and counterfactual claims and their bearing on singular factual ones. This matter will be taken up in the next chapter. It may now be observed, however, that the present dispute is not limited to a disagreement between Humeans and anti-Humeans similar to Ducasse. The dispute is between Ducasse and all others interested in analyzing causation, including many of Hume's most formidable opponents. It is now everywhere acknowledged that causal claims have counterfactual force. The issues that currently separate philosophers concern the explanation of this force. Perhaps these philosophers are mistaken on this fundamental matter, but we find no argument in Ducasse or elsewhere to support such a view.

VII

One passage in the *Treatise* seems inconsistent with Hume's teaching that more than one experience is required for knowledge of causal relatedness. This passage may seem to sustain Ducasse's view of the matter:

'Tis certain, that not only in philosophy, but even in common life, we may attain the knowledge of a particular cause merely by one experiment, provided it be made with judgment, and after a careful removal of all foreign and superfluous circumstances. (T, 104; cf. EHU, Sec. 84n)

Hume recognizes that if causation consists in *de facto* constancy, and if causal inference requires customary expectation acquired by repetition of sequence, then multiple instances would be essential and causal knowledge would therefore seem inexplicable in cases of singular causation. He responds to this objection with the argument that

tho' we are here suppos'd to have had only one experiment of a particular effect, yet we have many millions to convince us of this principle; *that like objects, plac'd in like circumstances, will always produce like effects;* and as this principle has establish'd itself by a sufficient custom, it bestows an evidence and firmness on any opinion, to which it can be apply'd. (T, 105)

Employing an argument independent of those previously considered, Ducasse vigorously attacks this line of reasoning. He argues that this passage presupposes his own common sense singularism and constitutes an inconsistency in Hume's regularity theory. He alleges inconsistency because the principle to which Hume appeals would allow the generalizing of any observed singular sequence whatsoever—causal or accidental. Hume's stipulation about careful removal of superfluous circumstances fails to resolve the problem, Ducasse argues, for how could the superfluous conditions be identified on the basis of a single experiment? Such a procedure would have to involve the separation of relevant causal conditions from irrelevant ones, as occurs according to Ducasse's own theory. Yet the principle of same cause, same effect cannot itself provide this singular knowledge. From these premises Ducasse reaches two conclusions: (1) Hume's principle has "valid applicability" not for the discovery of causal sequences but only for their generalization after they have been discovered; (2) If causal relations can be discovered by single experiences, then causal relatedness may entail, but does not consist in, constancy of sequence.[24]

If Ducasse's interpretation of Hume were correct, his critical conclusions could not be gainsaid. But Hume has again been misinterpreted. He never allows that causal relations are discovered or even suspected in the case of objects with which an observer is entirely unfamiliar. Indeed, he steadfastly adheres to a principle which, he says, "admits of no exception": "Let an object be presented to a man of ever so strong natural reason and abilities; if that object be entirely new to him, he will not be able, by the most accurate examination of its sensible qualities, to discover any of its causes or effects; . . . nor can our reason, unassisted by experience, ever draw any inference" (EHU, Sec. 23). Ducasse apparently interprets Hume to have maintained that an observer need only be mentally equipped with the principle "like causes, like effects" and need not have previous knowledge of the object itself or of the circumstances in which it is found in order to infer causal relations. But Hume is not

24. Ducasse, *Nature, Mind, and Death*, pp. 96f; *Causation and the Types of Necessity*, pp. 10–13; and "Critique of Hume's Conception of Causality," *The Journal of Philosophy* 63 (1966), pp. 144f, as reprinted in *Philosophical Problems of Causation, op. cit.*, pp. 8f.

tempted by this view; he consistently argues that all reasoning concerning matters of fact is based on the relation of cause and effect *and analogy therefrom*. We interpret Hume to mean that knowledge of three distinct sorts is required for causal inference in single cases. Such inferences can occur only if the observer is acquainted with the causal irrelevance of certain background conditions, the observer is capable of some identifying "judgments" about the object prior to the actual experiment, and the observer is capable of reasoning analogically, within this epistemic framework, from the principle "like causes, like effects."[25]

An example will illustrate these three epistemic elements. Suppose Karl, who has only a common knowledge of fruits, is handed a young persimmon by his friend Ludwig, who requests that he taste it and give his reaction. Since Karl has just subjected his mouth to an astringent mouthwash, he waits until this "foreign circumstance" is no longer capable of spoiling the experiment. Meanwhile, he checks for bruises that would distort the natural taste. And since he is aware that the juice of some fruits tastes rather different from the fruit itself, he carefully slices a sector and only then deposits it in his mouth. He immediately experiences the tart bitterness and puckering sensation produced by persimmons. He thinks every bite of a persimmon will produce the same result. Why? Roughly, we maintain, for the reasons Hume gives. Karl does not think he is being deceived by the experiment because he was meticulously cautious in probing and eliminating foreign circumstances. He expects the same result to follow in a similar experiment because he has found this principle to obtain so regularly in the past. Of course he does not yet know all the relevant variables that could contribute to his knowledge of the fruit's qualities. He is not aware, for example, that the persimmon must not be softened by frost since after softening it turns sweet and delicious. This knowledge can be obtained only through further experimentation.

A similar single-experiment pattern is employed in applied sciences. All known variables are kept perfectly constant prior

25. On the importance of analogy in general for Hume, see James Noxon, *Hume's Philosophical Development: A Study of His Methods* (Oxford: Clarendon Press, 1973), Part III, Sec. 4.

to the introduction of some new factor. A scientist working on the effects of a chemical substance, for example, may go to elaborate lengths before the experiment to determine the health status of his rats, the nutritional value of their food, the purity of their genetic strain, the uniformity of their cages, the regularity of their handling, etc. If the rats immediately die, and it is known that needle injections themselves cause no harm, the scientist will be confident that his chemical substance and no other factor is the cause. If instead of death he merely observes a chromosome breakage several days after the injection, he may be less confident of a causal relation. But in either case he would probably be willing, if requested, to hypothesize certain undetected conditions which might have been present and which, if discovered, would refute the causal claim, even though he has at present no reason to suspect that such undetected conditions actually obtain.

On Hume's argument causal inference through analogical reasoning beyond immediate experimental contexts is not precluded, and may be useful in the formulation of testable hypotheses. His larger point seems to be that it is possible to reason by elimination of alternative hypotheses until the sole relevant causal factor is reached, provided that (1) the context is relatively simple (cf. EHU, Sec. 84n), (2) some features of the objects involved are known, and (3) belief in the principle that like causes produce like effects is present. This appeal to elimination is to be expected from a defender of the regularity theory.[26]

VIII

One potential problem in this defense of Hume lies in the insufficiently analyzed phrase "relevant respects"—or essential rather than accidental circumstances, in Hume's language. Richard Taylor has argued that regularity theorists fail on at least two counts in their use of this notion. On the one hand, Taylor argues, the notion is otiose as an analysis of the causal relation, for to analyze causation in terms of causally relevant respects

---

26. In addition to our arguments, J. L. Mackie correctly points out that causal generalizations provide vital evidence of the *irrelevance* of various changes in the spatiotemporal vicinity of the causal relation. *The Cement of the Universe* (Oxford: Clarendon Press, 1974), p. 122.

simply begs the question. Furthermore, according to Taylor, the constant conjunction theory cannot satisfactorily explain how irrelevant conditions are to be distinguished from relevant ones, for some irrelevant conditions present in accidental (noncausal) constant conjunctions would have to be declared causally relevant by defenders of a pure regularity theory. A diverse set of true general statements about constantly conjoined features with plural instances could thus be constructed that we would know to be noncausal, but that the regularity doctrine would nevertheless identify as causal. For example, says Taylor, suppose a carload of matches has some unique combination of marks that distinguishes the matches (omnitemporally) from all other matches: "we could then rub each in a certain way and, if all of them in fact ignited, it would then be *true* that *any* match that has those properties ignites when rubbed in that fashion." Taylor concludes from this argument that the upholders of the constant conjunction tradition cannot legitimately account for the crucial distinction between relevant and irrelevant features, even though they have repeatedly resorted to its use.[27] This objection to Hume is at least as old as Thomas Reid's but is no more convincing for its updated terminology. Hume's Rules are attempts to specify experimental procedures in accordance with which it can be determined whether some set of features of objects is *always* conjoined with another set. Using these Rules, an assumption of invariability (i.e., a causal relevance hypothesis) can be made prior to actual *belief* in causal relatedness and can subsequently be tested experimentally (T, 149, 173). Hume admits that this inductive procedure may be tedious, complex, and sometimes unsuccessful (EHU, Sec. 84n; T, 148f), but the most one can ask is that good evidence be presented for causal claims. Hume's Rules are his attempt to specify a procedure for the discovery of such evidence. The methods of eliminative induction, which he somewhat too economically expounds, stand in need of considerable improvement;[28] but there

---

27. Richard Taylor, "Causation," *Monist* 47 (1963), pp. 287–313, esp. pp. 293–96. Quotation p. 295.
28. The Methods of Eliminative Induction, as applied to causation within the framework of a regularity theory, have been developed by J. R. Lucas, "Causation," in *Analytical Philosophy*, 1st Series, ed. R. J. Butler (Oxford: Basil Blackwell, 1962), and by J. L. Mackie, "Causes and Conditions," *op. cit.*, Section V, and *The Cement of the Universe*, Appendix.

is no philosophical problem with his basic suggestion that good eliminative procedures do succeed in eliminating irrelevant factors and suffice quite adequately as practical criteria of causal relevance. No question is begged. On the contrary, the constancy feature of the constant conjunction theory is taken seriously and given additional content, viz., that the genius of causal inquiry consists in discounting differences while recognizing similarities.

Undoubtedly critics of Hume such as Taylor would deny such a rebuttal. Methods of elimination, they would say, are used precisely to find causal laws that specify what would and would not happen under certain conditions. The notion of counterfactual sequence thus underlies Taylor's arguments from accidental relations, and it seems to him clearly incompatible with Hume's emphasis on *de facto* conjunction:

> Sometimes difficulties of the kind suggested have been countered by introducing the idea of a *law* into the description of causal connections. . . . [Causes] must, according to this suggestion, be exactly similar in certain respects only, and can be as dissimilar as one pleases in other respects. But here we shall find that, by introducing the idea of a law, we have tacitly re-introduced the idea of a necessary connection between cause and effect—precisely the thing we were trying to avoid. A general statement counts as a *law* only if we can use it to infer, not only what does happen, but what would happen if something else were to happen, and this we can never do from a statement that is merely a true general statement.[29]

What Taylor here claims can never be accomplished using a constant conjunction theory is precisely what Hume, or his modern followers at least, must and can do with consistency. The next chapter as a whole is an argument to defend this claim.

In this chapter we have marshaled arguments, building on those of the first two chapters, to expound Hume's doctrine of the implicit generality of singular causal instances. We first offered a Humean account of the laws that make for this implicit generality. Then we turned to counterexamples and counterarguments that suggest the primacy of causal instances over causal laws. We have been pulled progressively away from conceptual issues concerning the nature of laws and their relation to causal sequences, and have been drawn progressively closer

29. Taylor, "Causation," pp. 294–95.

to the epistemic conditions underlying our causal beliefs. This direction of argument should not be surprising. Attacks on Hume's conception of the implicit generality of causal sequences have rarely been based on a rejection of the truth conditions Hume poses for singular causal statements and laws. Rather, his opponents have appealed to certain basic beliefs about causal sequences and causal laws, on the assumption that some of these beliefs are both true and incompatible with the Humean theory of causation. The beliefs in question are, most prominently, the counterfactual ones to which Taylor appeals in the passage above. In accounting for these beliefs, a Humean too must shift the focus; from the truth conditions of causal claims attention must be directed to the *evidence* we marshal on behalf of these claims.

In the next chapter we turn to the question of whether the regularity theory can explain the counterfactual force of causal statements. Our intent is to supplement the answers offered in this chapter. In later chapters we shall add a Humean theory of the *relata* of singular causal sequences, as well as further arguments against the objections to Hume canvassed so far. These inquiries bulk large as answers to the questions posed in this chapter. In this respect our defense of the Humean theory about the relation between causal laws and causal instances will not be complete until the final chapter.

4

Law, Accident, Necessity, and Counterfactuals

WE HAVE SEEN how Hume substitutes implicit generality for the necessary connection alleged by his predecessors to obtain between the objects of causation. Accidentally conjoined events, by contrast, instantiate no law, and it is in their failure to do so that their accidentalness consists. If there are true contingent statements that are universal in form and that describe a uniform relation of *accidental* conjunction, then it may seem that Hume's specifications on the laws distinguishing causal from accidental sequences are inadequate, and thus that his theory of causation is seriously deficient. If in addition laws governing causal connections could be shown to reflect a nonpsychological necessity—some sort of necessity in the objects of causation—then Hume's entire program would be undermined.

The attempt to find a non-Humean necessity either in general laws or in the causal sequences that instantiate them has recently focused on the relation between singular causal statements, laws, and counterfactual statements about the objects mentioned in the singular statements. The relevance of singular counterfactual statements to singular indicative causal statements hinges on the virtually universal conviction that a singular sequence of particular events, c and e, is a causal sequence only if there is some sense in which, if c had not occurred, e also would not have occurred. The sequence c,e is merely accidental, if, in this same sense, had c not occurred, e nevertheless might have. The relevance of singular counterfactual statements to laws rests

119

on a somewhat less widespread conviction that a true universal general statement of the form "Whenever some object *x* has property F, then *x* or some other object *y* has property G" is a universal of law *only if* it is the case that some object *a*, which does not have property F, were to have F, then there would be at least one object (*a* itself or some other object *b*) that would have property G. A universal statement is not a universal of law, but merely a report of an accidental or coincidental uniformity of greater or lesser *de facto* generality, if the counterfactual conditional just cited is false of objects that do not manifest property F.

The conviction that both singular causal statements and general laws bear these relations to counterfactuals, while reports of accidental sequences and accidental generalizations do not, must either be explained by a theory of causation, or explained away by such a theory. Hardly anyone thinks these convictions can simply be explained away as unwarranted superstition or unintelligible speculation. Yet explanations of them that accord universals of law a modal force beyond anything that uniformity and universality permit, and which attribute a necessary connection to those singular sequences that support their associated counterfactuals, seem to be utterly at variance with Hume's account of causation. This problem has been widely touted as unresolvable on Humean grounds. In this chapter we examine the most influential explanations of the alleged counterfactual content of laws and singular statements, and show that to the extent that they are incompatible with Hume's treatment of causation and causal necessity they are unacceptable; and to the extent that they do provide explanations of these convictions, the explanations were embraced by Hume in a way compatible with the regularity theory he defends.

I

The contemporary *locus classicus* of the new necessitarian attack on the regularity theory is the work of William Kneale,[1] al-

---

1. William Kneale makes special reference to Hume, as an object of attack, in *Probability and Induction* (Oxford: Clarendon Press, 1949), pp. 7f, 78, and in his "Universality and Necessity," *The British Journal for the Philosophy of Science* 12 (1961), pp. 89f, 97f.

though, as we shall see, his work has affinities to historically significant theories offered by Descartes, Locke, and Kant.

Kneale argues that nomological generalizations are properly expressed as modal statements while *de facto* universals are properly expressed as categorical statements. He holds that the common empiricist distinction between unrestricted and restricted universals of fact insufficiently distinguishes laws from non-laws. He agrees with defenders of the regularity theory that laws are not established *a priori* and are not experientially certain.[2] But he also contends that one of the essential functions of laws is to describe boundaries on empirical possibility: If "All X's are followed by Y's" is a genuine nomological statement, then anyone who asserts the law thereby rules out a situation where an X is not followed by a Y.[3] Thus Kneale concludes that generalizations of law express the factually necessary relation, "Whenever X, Y *must* ensue."

It is widely supposed that Kneale regards laws as "logical necessities somehow embodied in the structure of things."[4] Kneale's view seems to be, however, that nomological necessity is *sui generis*, and not to be confused with logical necessity.[5] He does say that the notion of necessity used in both logic and natural science is identical in one respect—viz. they alike express "the notion of a situation without alternatives"[6]—but causal laws are not otherwise comparable to logical necessities. Laws assert connections that are weaker than logically necessary connections, Kneale seems to say, but stronger than mere contingent conjunctions. Kneale does not challenge Hume's view that universal statements are either logically necessary or logically contingent. But he does contend that a distinction is to be

---

2. Kneale, "Universality and Necessity," p. 99.

3. Kneale, *Probability and Induction*, pp. 78ff.

4. The interpretation is Antony Flew's, in *Hume's Philosophy of Belief* (London: Routledge & Kegan Paul, 1961), p. 135. Other philosophers who similarly misinterpret Kneale include J. Bennett, "Some Aspects of Probability and Induction," *The British Journal for the Philosophy of Science* 7 (1956–57), pp. 320f, and K. Popper, *The Logic of Scientific Discovery* (London: Hutchinson & Co., 1959), p. 430. Kneale's terse manner of stating his views leaves room for this confusion.

5. Cf. Kneale, *Probability and Induction*, p. 92, and "A Reply to Mr. Bennett," *The British Journal for the Philosophy of Science* 8 (1957–58), pp. 61f.

6. Kneale, "A Reply to Mr. Bennett," p. 62.

drawn between two types of logically contingent universal statements, namely (1) factual statements that merely express accidental, invariable conjunctions and (2) nomological generalizations that express empirically necessary connections.[7] Kneale regards the modal component as irreducible and not further explicable, and he conceives it as the type of necessary connection Hume attempted to discredit, and hence as an embarrassment to regularity analyses of causation.[8]

Kneale's central anti-Humean argument relies on the notion of counterfactual conditional statements. The concept of a law, he alleges, is incompletely captured by reduction to universal statements of antecedent-consequent form, because this analysis fails to explain why laws sustain counterfactuals. According to Kneale, Hume's analysis allows one to translate the unrestricted universal statement "All X's are followed by Y's" as "There is not an *x* which is not followed by a *y*." This latter statement is exhaustively analyzable into a conjunction of three temporally distinct statements:

(1) All past X's were followed by Y's.
(2) All present X's are followed by Y's.
(3) All future X's will be followed by Y's.

Kneale insists that this set of statements will not support the counterfactual "If an X were to occur, it would be followed by a Y"; yet the counterfactual is precisely the sort of statement laws must support. Kneale concludes that status as a law is not entirely dependent upon the truth of categorical statements of fact and that the question whether true universal generalizations are nomological is independent of the question whether they categorically assert facts. A modal terminology is needed to express the strength of the connection in laws that is lacking in statements of mere factual concomitance. Kneale thus holds that en-

---

7. Kneale, "Universality and Necessity," pp. 102, 89–91, and *The Development of Logic* (Oxford: Oxford University Press, 1962), pp. 648f.
8. Kneale, "Universality and Necessity," pp. 90f, 101f. Roderick Chisholm earlier made a similar suggestion, but his statement of it was rather hesitant and he never endorsed natural necessity *conclusions*. Cf. his "The Contrary-to-Fact Conditional," as reprinted in H. Feigl and W. Sellars, eds., *Readings in Philosophical Analysis* (New York: Appleton-Century-Crofts, Inc., 1949), esp. pp. 496 and 486. (The original source is cited in footnote 51 below.)

tailment of counterfactuals is a logically necessary condition of lawlikeness and that Hume's analysis is deficient because it fails to satisfy this condition.[9] (This argument may not be entirely original to Kneale. Its roots are also found in seminal articles on counterfactuals by Roderick Chisholm and Nelson Goodman mentioned later in this chapter. It is Kneale, however, who most thoroughly and imaginatively turns the analysis in the direction of Hume and causation.)

Although Kneale's theory may seem intuitively satisfactory, his explanation of the difference between laws and accidental generalizations in terms of an irreducible nonlogical, natural necessity remains obscure. As R. B. Braithwaite points out, such an ultimate ontological category is comparable to Locke's depiction of substance as "something I know not what."[10] In those few places where Kneale attempts to explicate the notion of "natural necessity" he uses synonymous modal expressions of equal obscurity, such as "must occur"; and when he characterizes natural necessity as the relation holding between entities connected by law, he in effect underlines the problem without resolving it. Similarly, when the subjunctive conditional is *defined* in terms of an irreducible connection between the logically distinct properties of natural entities, the nature of the connection itself is not further illuminated, whether it be referred to as "real," "ontological," or "natural."

Kant was among the first to complain that Hume's empiricism failed to account for nomological generalizations taking the modal form "If X, then Y *must* follow." Laws with this modal force seemed to Kant presupposed by Newtonian science, and Kneale's problem with empiricism is substantially the same as Kant's. But, unlike both Hume and Kant, Kneale does not locate the necessity attributed to these laws in the mind. Rather, as he explicitly notes, his philosophy represents a return to Locke.[11] Locke held the quasi-rationalistic view that although

9. Kneale, "Universality and Necessity," pp. 89f, 97ff. *Probability and Induction,* pp. 55, 71–78, 89. Especially clear is his earliest treatment in "Natural Laws and Contrary-to-Fact Conditionals," *Analysis* 10 (1950), pp. 121–25 *passim.*

10. R. B. Braithwaite, *Scientific Explanation* (New York: Harper Torchbook, 1953), p. 294. Cf. Hume, EHU, Sec. 60.

11. Kneale, *Probability and Induction,* p. 71.

finite creatures reason inductively and accordingly cannot acquire certain knowledge of laws, a nonfinite being acquainted with the "real essences" of things could see the connection between cause and effect to be as necessary as that between logically inseparable entities. Contemporary philosophers of a rationalistic persuasion have similarly argued that there is a "linkage between the characters a and b" in a necessary causal relation (A causes B), because the *nature* of A's is such that they have inherent causal properties that an a could not lack and still be an a.[12] Although Kneale eschews this robust rationalism, his view reflects a kindred metaphysical doctrine. His claim that natural necessity is both irreducible and distinct from logical necessity commits him to a plainly antiempiricist position.

Kneale sometimes uses the phrase "principles of necessity" to explain his views, and his few remarks on the nature of these principles suggest a Cartesian theory of laws and possible worlds. Descartes conceived of natural laws as divinely supported rules of cosmic order governing all natural changes. They are so basic that "even if God had created more worlds, there could have been none in which these laws were not observed."[13] For Descartes's laws apply in all worlds because God so made the universe, not because the universe limits God's activity. But, setting aside Descartes's theological convictions, his universe is governed by a system of structural principles with which empirical entities in all possible worlds must accord. Kneale's view is similar, as is revealed in his treatment of theories propounded by Tarski and Popper.[14] Tarski holds the following view of logical necessity: a statement is logically necessary if and only if it is deducible from a statement function satisfied by every model or interpretation of the function. Such universally valid statement functions are true in all logically possible worlds. Popper explicates the notion of *natural* necessity in a parallel

12. Brand Blanshard, *Reason and Analysis* (La Salle, Ill.: Open Court, 1962), p. 469. Cf. A. C. Ewing, "Causality and Induction," in his *Non-Linguistic Philosophy* (London: George Allen & Unwin, 1968).

13. René Descartes, *Discourse on Method*, Part V, trans. John Veitch, in *The Rationalists* (Garden City: Doubleday Dolphin, 1960), p. 71. Cf. also Descartes's "The World; or Essay on Light," Chapter VII.

14. Kneale, "Universality and Necessity," esp. p. 99, and *The Development of Logic*, p. 643.

fashion: a statement is *naturally* necessary if and only if it is deducible from a statement function satisfied by the class of worlds differing from ours only by having different initial conditions. Such "universally valid" statements are true in all worlds that are members of this limited class.[15]

The possible worlds formula is a device used to exclude accidental universals. These universals are not necessary, because they are false in at least one such possible world. The truth of a genuine *law* does not vary with changes in initial conditions, but the truth of an accidental generalization does. Kneale finds Popper's interpretation of natural necessity "acceptable," because "it connects the notion of natural law with that of validity for states of affairs other than the actual; . . . what holds for all possible worlds is obviously necessary."[16] This modernized form of Cartesianism eliminates reference to God and pares down the class of "possible worlds." If we are right in placing Kneale in the Lockean and Cartesian traditions, it is not surprising that he finds Hume a natural antagonist, for these necessitarians first excited Hume to his sceptical challenges. Subsequent to the publication of Kneale's and Popper's views, much has been made in the literature on causation about possible worlds in the analysis of counterfactuals and causation. Later in this chapter we take up these themes and assess their consequences for Hume's theory. But we must first pursue Kneale's notion of natural necessity and its influence on contemporary philosophy, for a tenable version of his claim would be devastating to a Humean analysis, and many have believed that his views are more cogent than Hume's.

II

At least one philosopher has found merit in Kneale's notion that universal statements are laws only if they reflect a natural necessity in the objects of causation: J. L. Mackie. But Mackie has

---

15. Popper, *op. cit.*, pp. 432f. This formula is deficient in ways that need not concern us here. Cf. G. Nerlich and W. A. Suchting, "Popper on Law and Natural Necessity," *The British Journal for the Philosophy of Science* 18 (1967), pp. 233–35, and Popper's reply, "A Revised Definition of Natural Necessity," in the same volume (1968), pp. 316–21.
16. Kneale, "Universality and Necessity," p. 99.

found no more acceptable than we the obscurity of the notion of natural necessity as Kneale advances it. He therefore attempts to reconstruct Kneale's argument with a view to revealing the sort of necessity in the objects of causation that Hume failed to notice. He expects thereby to distinguish laws from true but accidental universals. Mackie begins his reconstruction by admitting the force of Humean complaints against the sort of necessities in nature advocated by Kneale. Mackie then attempts to propound an empirical counterpart to such rationalistic natural necessities, an account that yet describes the causal necessitation Hume claimed could not be provided. Mackie's argument, initially cast in opposition to Kneale, begins as follows:

[Kneale explains] natural laws . . . by their association with *transcendent hypotheses,* such as wave or particle theories in physics. These hypotheses introduce new terminology, they are "concerned with things which are not observable even in principle," and they concern only "structures" which can be expressed in the language of mathematics. . . .

The suggestion, then, is that we advance beyond a view of causation as mere regular succession when we conjecture that there really is some causal mechanism underlying the succession and explaining it. But must this be a matter of conjecture, of *transcendent* hypotheses? Would it not be even better actually to uncover and observe the mechanism? And yet, if we did so, would not Hume's criticisms again have force: what, in the operation of a mechanism, however delicate and ingenious, could we see except the succession of phases. . . . The question must still be answered: what *is* there in it except the succession of phases? . . .

I find that Kneale's transcendent hypotheses [need] . . . an empirical counterpart of the rationalists' necessity.[17]

Mackie's willingness to advance the discussion by putting it on an empirical basis and providing further arguments certainly seems an improvement over the obscure status of natural necessity in Kneale's writings. But is the "empirical counterpart" he substitutes acceptable?

Mackie proposes that natural necessity consists in the qualitative or structural continuity or persistence exhibited by processes that obey basic "laws of working," such as Newton's laws: "We

17. J. L. Mackie, *The Cement of the Universe* (Oxford: Clarendon Press, 1974), pp. 216–17, 223.

may speculate, then, that what could count as necessity or intelligibility here is some *form of persistence,*" and "if our specu-
lations are correct, a singular causal sequence instantiates some
pure law of working which is itself a form of partial persistence;
the individual sequence therefore is, perhaps unobviously, identical with some process that has some qualitative or structural continuity."[18]

In defense of these claims, Mackie invites us to consider the
simplest of all causal sequences, a single particle free from inter-
ference and moving in a straight line in accordance with Newton's first law.

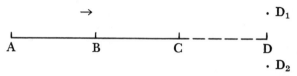

Of this case Mackie writes, "if the particle moves continuously
from A to B, from B to C, and from C to D, these being all equal
distances, in equal times, it is in a very obvious sense keeping on
doing the same thing. It is not of course logically or mathe-
matically necessary. . . . But it may well seem expectable that
it should go on doing as nearly as possible the same thing . . .
if nothing intervenes to make it do anything else."[19]

Furthermore,

if after going from A to B and from B to C the particle had then gone
not to D but, say, to D_1, this would have been prima facie surprising:
since D_1 is placed asymmetrically with respect to the line ABC, we
might say that if it were to go to D_1 it might as well go rather to D_2,
similarly placed on the other side of the line; since it cannot go to
both, it ought not to go to either, but should confine itself to the con-
tinuation of its straight path through D.[20]

These facts, Mackie suggests,

cast some doubt on Hume's claim that "If we reason *a priori,* anything
may appear able to produce anything"; or even that "Any thing may
produce any thing." Perhaps it *may;* but at least in some cases some
outcomes are less intrinsically surprising than others; and yet this is

18. *Ibid.,* pp. 218, 229.
19. *Ibid.,* p. 218.
20. *Ibid.,* p. 220.

a matter of *a priori* considerations, it does not depend on any appeal, either open or covert, to our actual experience of or familiarity with processes of the kind in question. . . . We may suggest, then, that basic laws of working are, in part, forms of persistence. . . . This sort of causing plays a larger part, underlying processes that at the perceptual level are cases of unrelieved change, of a cause being followed by an utterly different effect. A match is struck . . . and a flame appears: on the face of it this effect has nothing in common with its cause. But if we were to replace the macroscopic picture with a detailed description of the molecular and atomic movements with which the perceived processes are identified by an adequate physico-chemical theory, we should find far more continuity and persistence. And this is part of the point of micro-reduction, of the transcendent hypotheses of which Kneale speaks. . . . What is called a causal mechanism is a process which underlies a regular sequence and each phase in which exhibits qualitative as well as spatio-temporal continuity.[21]

The conclusion is that the absence of "qualitative" persistence— the "tie" between causes and effects—underlies the difference between merely accidental, noncausal sequences (even when universal in their instantiation) and nomological regularities or causal sequences.

To assess these claims, let us return to Mackie's original example. It is, he says, more intelligible or expectable that the particle, having moved from A to B and B to C, should continue to do the same thing, should go to D, rather than go somewhere else. But what does "expectable" mean here, and what constitutes "doing the same thing"? As Hume asks, how can we have expectations about the matter except in the light of previous experience? If our previous experience in the matter is exhausted by our single sequential experience(s) of the motion of the particle from A to B and B to C, then the inference that it will go to D is simply an inductive one—weak, but nevertheless stronger than any other inference. This expectation is plainly not *a priori*.

Do we have any expectations about the motion of the particle between C and D, or between A and B for that matter, before we have observed its motion at all (or been given theoretical reasons supported by experience)? That we do not becomes clear, if we consider what constitutes "doing the same thing." All we know about the particle's path is its course between A and C. This being the case, of course Mackie is correct: we would be surprised to see the particle move to D_1. However, if the particle's path before reaching A does not describe a straight line, but involves slight deflections at upward intervals of the length of A–C, then "doing the same thing" in such a case requires that the particle move towards D_1, instead of D. But we would still be surprised to see the particle move to D_1. In general, whether we say something is "doing the same thing" or not is relative to a period of observation, and so our expectations in the matter are inductive and not *a priori*.

Mackie argues that "a body's moving uniformly in a circular orbit is not *in itself* intelligible in the same way as rectilinear motion is."[22] Why? No doubt because Newtonian mechanics equates rectilinear motion with rest, and requires the presence of forces to produce circular motion—in contrast to Aristotelian conceptions of celestial motion, which accord circular motion as much intelligibility as rectilinear motion. We could, however, just as well work out a scheme in which circular motion requires no continuous presence of forces while rectilinear motion does. Thus, the "intelligibility" of rectilinear motion depends on the particular contingent theory we embrace to account for our experience. Consider again Mackie's claim that if the particle had gone to D_1, "this would have been prima facie surprising: since D_1 is placed asymmetrically with respect to the line ABC. . . ." It would have been perfectly intelligible for the body to have gone towards D_1, if its path previous to ABC involved similar deflections; that is, it need not have been surprising with respect to other lines of motion. (Suppose, e.g., that one is observing a small section of motion along a regular polygon.) To deny this is tantamount to assigning persistence solely on the basis of "where we came into the sequence," so to speak.

Persistences are inferred from experience, and in particular from experiences of regularities. We suggest that isolating patterns of persistence actually presupposes prior causal determinations, and therefore can hardly serve as a basis on which to distinguish them from noncausal sequences. (Consider the history of mechanics from Aristotle to Newton, where causal sequences

22. *Ibid.*, pp. 219–20.

such as those occurring on a billiard table were distinguished before such underlying structural persistences as conservation of momentum were isolated: everyone knew that pushing a pendulum bob caused it to swing, though before Galileo they knew nothing about the structural persistences that actually underlie this phenomenon.) Hume seems to us correct when he says that "if we reason *a priori,* anything may appear able to produce anything." The persistence involved in or underlying causal sequences is not a matter either of *a priori* expectedness or intelligibility. Whether the detection of persistences contributes to our understanding of causal sequences is another matter, but one that is irrelevant to whether it is a necessary feature of causation "in the objects." What is it, we may ask, that distinguishes persistences from noncausal sequences? Hume's challenge is still unanswered. If persistences are not *a priori* intelligible or expectable, then there is no noninductive reason to suppose that we can find a "mark" of causality in them that is not present in universal but merely accidental regularities.

Our conclusion seems substantiated by Mackie's own rationale for rejecting Kneale's arguments. His fundamental complaint about Kneale is that the latter's analysis leaves too wide an opening for a decisive Humean counterattack:

But must [Kneale's] causal mechanism be a matter of conjecture, of *transcendent* hypotheses? Would it not be even better actually to uncover and observe the mechanism? And yet, if we did so, would not Hume's criticisms again have force: what, in the operation of a mechanism, however delicate and ingenious, could we see except the succession of phases? It may be to avoid this reply that Kneale stresses the transcendent character of the hypotheses; but whether the mechanism is observable or not, the question must still be answered: what *is* there in it except the succession of phases?[23]

This same question can now be put to Mackie's analysis: Is there anything in persistence that constitutes what Mackie describes as "the long-searched-for link between individual cause and effect which a pure regularity theory fails, or refuses, to find"? If we are correct that persistences are experientially derived from constant conjunctions, the answer is "no." And since Mackie has rightly rejected Kneale's transcendent hypothesizing in favor of empirical laws of working, his interpretation of

23. *Ibid.,* p. 217.

Kneale provides no transcendent grounds for objecting to Hume. Interpreted as a refutation of Hume, Mackie's nonrationalist reconstruction of Kneale's theory is thus rendered implausible by arguments that Mackie himself advances.

We conclude that the notion of natural necessity is as elusive in the hands of Kneale, even as refurbished by Mackie, as Hume proclaimed it to be in the hands of his contemporaries and predecessors. But is this defense of Hume adequate? After all, Kneale introduced the notion of natural necessity in order to explain counterfactual claims. The differences between those counterfactual claims we believe and assent to, and those we do not, is based on our belief that causal and accidental sequences are distinct. As Mackie correctly says, "the major issue" is whether the regularity theory can explain this data, and thereby draw a binding distinction.[24] For Mackie, the Humean must ultimately maintain either that he can make the distinction purely on regularity grounds or that "it was only an unwarranted prejudice that there should be any such distinction . . . between regularities . . . which could be called accidental, and those which would be counted as causal laws or laws of nature."[25] Mackie is right in considering these two alternatives exhaustive of the possibilities open to the Humean, and he is correct in suggesting that, save for certain "heroic Humeans," most of Hume's defenders would prefer to make the distinction compatible with their system of ideas.

We shall begin to explore this issue by arguing that the challenges offered by Kneale and Mackie are not successful, partially because of a failure on their part to appreciate the power of the explanation Hume himself offers of the law-accident distinction. We shall describe views about this distinction that can directly be attributed to Hume, and then we shall defend his account against the theories of Kneale and Mackie.

III

As we read Hume, he defends the view that there are two necessary and sufficient conditions of *lawlikeness:* (1) the Condition of Inductive Support and (2) the Condition of Predictive Confidence. "Lawlike" generalizations, if true, describe a genuine

24. *Ibid.,* p. 105.
25. *Ibid.,* pp. 198–99.

law, where the notion of law is understood in terms of the conditions of a law of nature discussed in Chapter 3 (Sec. 2). Lawlike generalizations, then, are formulations intended to express genuine laws, though they may fail in this attempt. Laws are also to be distinguished from the regularities they describe. Lawlike generalizations are epistemically well-grounded *attempts* to formulate universals of law correctly, and are thus more than poorly grounded general hypotheses. In turn, universals of law are general propositions that *in fact* satisfy the four conditions delineated in Chapter 3. These propositions describe regularities among events in nature, events and regularities that are, of course, nonpropositional. Thus, there are three distinct classes of law-connected items under discussion, each of which corresponds to a class of accident-connected items:

An Epistemological Distinction:
    Lawlike Generalizations — Accidental Generalizations

A Metaphysical Distinction (A Distinction among Propositions):
    Universals of Law   — Universals of Accident

An Ontological Distinction (A Distinction "among the Objects"):
    Causal Regularities   — Accidental Regularities

There has been considerable confusion in the literature on causation regarding these different categories. The expression "causal law," for example, has been confusingly used to refer to all three law-connected categories. Except when quoting and discussing the theories of other philosophers, we shall hereafter employ the above terminology exclusively. Hume himself addresses the law-accident distinction through a consideration of lawlike and accidental generalizations, rather than through a consideration of laws, as we shall now see.

    The Condition of Inductive Support. Philosophers sympathetic to Hume have commonly countered necessitarian interpretations of the law-accident distinction by an appeal to the different kinds of evidence supporting unrestricted generalizations.[26]

---

26. Braithwaite, *op. cit.,* Chapter 9, and A. Pap, *An Introduction to the Philosophy of Science* (Glencoe, Ill.: Free Press, 1962), pp. 301ff. A pragmatic account of laws and causal necessity is found in Brian Skyrms, *Causal Necessity* (New Haven: Yale University Press, 1980).

The nature of this support, however, is not uniformly described. Several philosophers refer to direct instantial evidence, indirect confirmability (indirect deducibility from laws of broader scope), and nonfalsified hypotheses. But the dominant contention is that acceptance of unrestricted universal statements as lawlike—as nomological generalizations—is dependent on their place within a body of scientific theory, where they are embedded in a system of mutually reinforcing principles that are not independently derived. The generic distinction between universals of law and universals of accident, as urged by Kneale, is judged inappropriate by these philosophers, because they believe the pertinent and epistemically warranted distinction is one between poorly supported generalizations and well-supported, universal statements. Those philosophers who subscribe to this approach have generally dismissed Hume's psychologically rooted theory of necessity as an expendable eccentricity.[27] Yet, if one sets aside his psychological account of mental determination, Hume can be seen to be arguing the line taken by these philosophers. It would be a mistake to regard the later accounts as somehow generically different from Hume's own explication of the law-accident distinction, or even as advances on it, although a few sophisticated maneuvers have since been developed.

What now is Hume's account of the distinction between lawlike and accidental generalizations? Let us begin by looking again at the section of the *Treatise* on "Rules by which to judge of causes and effects." Besides listing general rules and procedures by which "we learn to distinguish the accidental circumstances from the efficacious causes" (T, 148–49), Hume adds that testing a number of instances under a variety of circumstances produces "degrees of evidence" and instills further confidence that generalizations "really are" lawlike (T, xxiii, 149, 153, 173f). Hume thus tends to think of induction to lawlike generalizations exclusively in terms of direct experience. But lawlike generalizations may additionally be the deductive consequences of other well-confirmed generalizations, and Hume considers such indirect confirmation satisfactory, so long as the

---

27. Cf. Ernest Nagel, *The Structure of Science* (New York: Harcourt, Brace & World, 1961), p. 56, and Karl Popper, *Conjectures and Refutations* (New York: Harper Torchbooks, 1968), pp. 42–46.

fundamental generalizations are themselves experientially confirmed (cf. T, 141f, 154, 173f).[28]

Hume's arguments also touch on the problem of support for counterfactual conditionals. "All hypothetical arguments," he says, are "reasonings upon a supposition" (T, 83); sufficient experience through repeated encounters naturally disposes us to regard lawlike generalizations as supporting inferences "beyond the actual," including indicative predictions and counterfactual assertions (cf. T, 134f; EHU, Secs. 25, 59). Once one has become convinced that "Every X is succeeded by Y," one does not hesitate to endorse an imaginative prediction that "If so-and-so were an X, it would be succeeded by a Y."[29] Such "foreseeing of consequences," Hume maintains, is often an operation of custom performed without conscious reflection (T, 103f, 133; EHU, Sec. 33). But when reflection on consequences is involved, Hume points out, we mark the law-accident distinction by expressing ourselves in modal terminology:

Perfect habit . . . makes us conclude in general, that instances, of which we have no experience, must *necessarily* resemble those of which we have. (T, 135; second italics added; cf. 104)

As the first imagination or invention of a particular effect . . . is arbitrary, where we consult not experience; so must we also esteem the *supposed* tie or connection between the cause and effect, which binds them together, and renders it *impossible* that any other effect could result from the operation of that cause. (EHU, Sec. 25; italics added)

Hume also insists that we suppose like causes to be connected with like effects even when the inference from one object to another involves an extension to objects that "lie *beyond the reach of our discovery*" (T, 91f, italics added). It is of course fundamental to his empiricist epistemology that law-governed counterfactuals neither augment our knowledge nor state neces-

28. Cf. Braithwaite's Humean way of arguing this point, *op. cit.*, Chapter 9. There are problems in attributing this view to Hume without qualification, since hypotheses that transcend immediate empirical verification might be used to deduce laws, and these hypotheses would on some interpretations of Hume be ruled out by his empiricism.

29. Although Hume does not specifically consider subjunctive conditional expressions, it would be unreasonable to think they are excluded from the inferential uses which he clearly regarded nomological generalizations as serving (EHU, Secs. 25, 38, 59–61; T, 133–35, 170).

sary factual connectedness, for counterfactual assertions must depend on and derive content from what is already known or believed—even though they do more than simply describe that existing data (cf. T, 103f, 139).[30]

Some examples should illuminate this account of Hume's distinction between causal (lawlike) and noncausal (accidental) generalizations. Consider two general, noncausal statements of accidental succession:

(1) All U.S. Senate speeches on marine life are followed immediately by the death of a European Head of State.

(2) Whenever libraries receive new books, a record of receipt is immediately placed on file.

Suppose the sequence in the first example has occurred only once, while the second generalization has countless confirming, and no disconfirming, instances. It is indefinite whether the generalizations are unrestrictedly true, but this indefiniteness is irrelevant to a determination of whether the generalizations are lawlike. In the case of the first generalization, even if one were in a position to know that there would be several further instances and no disconfirming ones, such evidence would be regarded as insufficient for further predictions and as inadequate support for subjunctive conditional statements such as "Had there been a Senate speech on marine life yesterday, a European Head of State would have died." One might suspect that a connection exists, but the suspicion would not constitute a well-founded belief unless further data were forthcoming.

Neither the first nor the second generalization has sufficient inductive support to be treated as lawlike—by Hume's or any other reasonable set of inductive rules. Yet the second generalization is noticeably different from the first, for it certainly supports, even though it does not entail, the counterfactual "If this book were a newly received library book, a record of its receipt would immediately appear on file." Generalizations following this second pattern are unrestrictedly true, partially because of their foundation in general policies and because of reliable em-

30. Two analyses in the empiricist tradition reach a similar conclusion. Cf. Mackie in Footnote 44 below and R. S. Walters, "The Problem of Counterfactuals," *Australasian Journal of Philosophy* 39 (May, 1961), pp. 30–46.

ployees—in this case, library policies and librarians. Such generalizations state a factual relation of succession, and so are either true or false; but they also are based on a prescriptive policy that is more than a simple factual regularity. Policies, of course, do not bear truth values. If one did not understand the prescriptive component in the policy, one would not adequately grasp the significance of statement (2). It is because we are aware both of the policy and of the fact that failures in executing policies do occur that we consider the generalization nonlawlike, in spite of massive inductive evidence supporting it. In this case we are willing to venture "inferences beyond the actual," and we feel quite confident about them. But they are ventured with less confidence in their truth than are inferences from lawlike generalizations, because our knowledge that failures in execution do occur tends to undermine complete confidence.

Now contrast statements (1) and (2) with the accepted lawlike generalization

(3) Whenever large amounts of arsenic are swallowed by humans, death ensues.

It is clear that some stronger connectedness between antecedent and consequent events is assumed without reservation in this case. Counterfactual inference is therefore made without hesitation. Of course there are borderline generalizations such as

(4) Prolonged pipe smoking causes a weakening of lip and mouth tissue.

One may be inclined to think (4) supports counterfactuals, but only hesitantly because one considers the evidence less than conclusive.[31]

Hume discusses "the several degrees of evidence" that distinguish examples in the range of (3) and (4) (T, 124). He maintains that while we think of (3) as *proved* by an inductive argument that is *"free from* doubt and uncertainty," we think of (4) more reservedly in terms of *probability,* because the evidence is "attended with *uncertainty."* He argues that there are "many dif-

---

31. Still another type of generalization, involving temporal restrictedness, is called a "quasi-law statement" by P. F. Strawson. Cf. his *Introduction to Logical Theory* (London: Methuen & Co., Ltd., 1952), pp. 198f. Our discussion of the second example is indebted to Strawson's treatment.

ferent kinds of certainty," including demonstrative and non-demonstrative kinds—a view he defends both in his technical writings and in his correspondence.[32] Hume argues that there exists a "gradation from probabilities to proofs" that is in "many cases insensible" (i.e. undetectable), even though it is easy to see the "difference betwixt kinds of evidence" if widely varying types of generalization are compared (T, 131; cf, EHU, Sec. 87). This thesis that there are not two primary grades of universality, but many, betrays considerable sophistication. It is held by Strawson, for example, virtually without alteration. Indeed, although Strawson hardly intended his discussion as an interpretation of Hume, it could easily serve that function:

It is important to notice the shading continuity of that line which runs from high-grade natural law-statements to those "all *s* are *p*" statements which one has no good ground for making short of independent evidence, in the case of each individual member of the subject-class, that it is *p*. At various points in between these extremes lie the majority of empirical general statements. Seeing this should make us look for the difference between them in things which can alter gradually: in the character of our grounds for making them, and in the *extent* of our commitment in making them; and not in an abrupt cleavage in type of truth-conditions at some point near one end of the line.[33]

According to our interpretation, Hume regards lawlikeness, causal generalizations, inductive support, and subjunctive conditional statements as closely linked. Yet he does not think inductive support ever sufficient to guarantee the truth of lawlike generalizations or counterfactuals; at best he maintains that a proper foundation for inductive inference to counterfactual claims can be established. His explanation concerns how we come (rationally) to believe that some claims are justified and to regard some types of sequence, but not others, as lawlike.

The distinction between laws and lawlikeness, as we have drawn it, is here critical, yet it has been widely neglected or misunderstood in the interpretation of Hume. In one of the more illuminating studies of Hume's account of "laws of nature," J. C. A. Gaskin argues that "for Hume, a law of nature is, very

32. See Letter 91 in *The Letters of David Hume*, Vol. 1, ed. J. Y. T. Greig (Oxford: Clarendon Press, 1932), p. 187.
33. Strawson, *op. cit.*, p. 202.

roughly, the way in which we describe what always happens in our experience together with an expectation that our experience will be the same in the future as it has been in the past."[34] Gaskin proceeds to offer a sustained criticism of Hume, claiming that he is only entitled to speak of the highly improbable, not the absolutely impossible or what could not happen. Gaskin's critique refers roughly to what we have been calling *lawlike generalizations,* but it ignores the central distinction between these and true *laws of nature.* The support for his interpretation comes largely from the essay "On Miracles" in the first *Enquiry,* where Hume admittedly says that "a firm and unalterable experience has established these laws" (EHU, Sec. 90). In context, this passage clearly means that experience has established a *belief* in laws. As Gaskin later admits, Hume's more cautious statements reveal that he is "perfectly well aware" of the law-lawlike distinction.[35] In the essay on miracles, he propounds the degrees-of-evidence theory discussed previously (EHU, Sec. 87), and he explicitly ties the latter theory to his account of "proofs" of laws—i.e., lawlike status (EHU, Secs. 88f, 98). His view is that the miraculous must violate a law, whereas the "marvellous" merely violates our expectations of lawlikeness (EHU, Sec. 90).

Hume knows that the generalizations people manage to formulate are different from the laws themselves. We believe that Hume's imprecise statements about "laws" are best understood epistemically, in terms of the inductive evidence gained in experience that leads to the *acceptance* of lawlike generalizations. If Gaskin's formulation were correct, many telling points against Hume's whole account of miracles would readily follow. If our interpretation is accepted, however, such criticisms fail, and Hume's accounts of both causation and miracles make better sense. We cannot here analyze in detail Hume's views on miracles, but it is important to notice once again how the distinction between universals of law and lawlike generalizations can play a significant role in the interpretation and assessment of his philosophy.

34. J. C. A. Gaskin, *Hume's Philosophy of Religion* (New York: Barnes and Noble, 1978), pp. 121f.
35. *Ibid.,* p. 124.

IV

The Condition of Predictive Confidence. Extensive inductive support is not alone sufficient to account for the distinction between lawlike and accidental generalizations, for a comparable quantity of factual information may support the two types of generalizations, and a contrary instance would refute both in the same way. However, Hume identifies a second factor that is essential to the distinction. This feature is the *confidence* people place in factual evidence. In the end, confidence in a generalization may rest entirely on the inductive evidence supporting it. Even so, such confidence may be a necessary condition of the acceptance of generalizations as lawlike, and certainly confidence cannot be reduced to inductive evidence.

A. J. Ayer has perspicuously updated Hume's distinctive approach to the law-accident distinction. Ayer suggests that the distinction between generalizations of law and generalizations of fact "lies not so much on the side of the facts which make [law statements] true or false as in the *attitude* of those who put them forward."[36] The attitude is one of greater confidence in generalizations of law, because we see no reason to doubt the invariable conjunction they express. On this account, the way we regard universal causal generalizations is as important as the facts they express, and Kneale's ideas about necessity and possibility are gratuitous, because "saying that something is impossible is [saying] just that it is *inconsistent* with some natural law."[37] A similar view, though one rooted in an "epistemic commitment" rather than a psychological attitude, has been developed by Nicholas Rescher. He holds that lawlike status is "superadded" by human thought to the empirical evidence: *"Lawfulness is a matter of imputation:* when an empirical generalization is designated as a law, this epistemological status is *imputed* to it. . . . It is we the users who accord to a generalization its lawful status thus endowing it with nomological neces-

---

36. A. J. Ayer, "What Is a Law of Nature?," in his *Concept of a Person* (London: St. Martin's Press, 1963), p. 230 (italics added); and a later restatement in *Probability and Evidence* (New York: Columbia University Press, 1972), pp. 15–17, 129–32. (Ayer's suggestions have foundations in Braithwaite, Ramsey, and Weinberg.)

37. Ayer, *Probability and Evidence*, p. 17 (italics added).

sity and hypothetical force. . . . We must *decide* upon the epistemic status."[38]

Ayer's and Rescher's suggestions are but modern renditions of Hume's second theory of causation, as incorporated in his second definition of "cause," Df_2. Hume explains that, in addition to the factual concomitance mentioned in his first definition, Df_1, it is necessary that one who believes in a lawful sequence be mentally disposed to connect antecedent and consequent conditions for all similar situations. The extra strength of the connection in causal relations is not exhausted by factual concomitance alone; there must also be a mental preparation, including *belief*, which he characterizes as an attitude of "reliance and security" (EHU, Secs. 46, 98).[39] This mental preparation is for Hume the source of the idea of necessity, and he agrees even with his opponents that necessary connection in turn accounts for our distinction between causal sequences and noncausal sequences.

Without this background of both information and attitude, Hume maintains, one may observe objects to be prior and contiguous to others and yet not consider them causally related (T, 77, 87f). He is also careful to point out that the appropriate attitude alone is insufficient to distinguish a lawlike from an accidental generalization, since a sequence once deemed lawlike may remain strongly connected in the imagination long after tests have shown that the antecedent accompanies but does not produce the effect (T, 149). Hume, Ayer, and Rescher are all at pains to emphasize that although an epistemic or psychological commitment is required for lawlike status, there must also be well-founded evidential grounds. To be *justified*, the commitment must have the support of inductive evidence (and, in scientific contexts, at least, the theoretical support of other generalizations).

Hume's explanation of belief in causal laws is itself causal

---

38. Nicholas Rescher, "Lawfulness as Mind-Dependent," in N. Rescher, *et al.*, eds., *Essays in Honor of Carl G. Hempel* (Dordrecht, Holland: D. Reidel, 1969), pp. 185f (italics in original). Rescher weakly agrees with Hume on pp. 189f.

39. It is worth noting that just as there are degrees of inductive support, so there are degrees of confidence. Hume speaks of "degrees of belief and assurance" (T, 143; EHU, Secs. 46, 70, 87). A strong degree of confidence seems present when contingent laws have virtually become analytic truths and when laws function as rules of inference.

(T, 98ff), of course, and this fact has often been considered problematic. From his account, it follows that belief in the lawlike status of statements of regular sequence is a psychological effect regularly preceded by causal conditions that minimally include observations of some empirical regularity and a habit of expecting the consequent of that sequence upon the imagined or real appearance of its antecedent. Sometimes the causal conditions also include data acquired by inductive test procedures (T, 141–44, 154, 175; EHU, Sec. 41). Belief grows progressively stronger, Hume claims, as habits become more "perfectly" developed, as the volume of corroborating instances increases, and as argument in support of the belief is strengthened (T, 98, 133–37; lengthy argument involving a complex set of inferences, however, is said to weaken belief). The more entrenched a habit or attitude of expectation becomes, the more firmly established is belief in a necessary connection.

Though Hume leaves the details lamentably obscure in his well-known discussion of belief, he apparently intends to say that belief in lawlike generalizations is caused by the same impression (of reflection) of which the idea of necessary connection is a copy; the impression causes the idea (T, 5) and also causes it to be "formed" in an "elevated and enlivened" way, i.e., the impression causes belief in the idea (T, 98, 101). Hume demonstrably regards both ideas and beliefs as the causal consequents of impressions (T, 5, 98); and it is virtually certain that he regards a particular belief in a particular lawlike generalization as a feeling of "assent either caused by the idea of necessary connection" (T, 106, 169), or caused along with that idea by the original impression from which the idea is derived (T, 86, 94, 97, 103, 119).

Hume is fully aware that his theory is not as intuitively satisfying as an objectivist theory such as Kneale's and that necessity is commonly believed to be a feature of empirical facts. But he is not interested in elucidating what he calls "the frequent use of words" such as "necessity." That such terms have a referential function in ordinary discourse he never doubts. He is sceptical only that a justification can be given for the belief that natural necessity is an objective feature of the facts. He can find no empirical foundation other than regularity of sequence (the inductive component), plus an additional impression of reflection (the attitude component). He takes these conjointly to be the "true meaning" of modal terms in causal contexts:

> As to the frequent use of the words, Force, Power, Energy, etc., which everywhere occur in common conversation, as well as in philosophy; that is no proof, that we are acquainted, in any instance, with the connecting principle between cause and effect, or can account ultimately for the production of one thing by another. These words, as commonly used, have very loose meanings annexed to them; and their ideas are very uncertain and confused. (EHU, Sec. 60n)
>
> As 'tis more probable, that these expressions do [in causal citations] lose their true meaning by being *wrongly apply'd,* than that they never have any meaning; 'twill be proper to bestow another consideration on this subject, to see if possibly we can discover the nature and origin of those ideas, we annex to them. (T, 162)

The "true meaning" of causal statements involves a revision of the ordinary meaning, but Hume is not primarily interested in analyzing ordinary usage. His aim is to remove a metaphysical misconception (cf. EHU, Sec. 32). The general direction of his thinking can be reconstructed as follows: In causal contexts, the word "necessity" does not function to describe or to convey information about events in themselves. Rather, it marks a distinction between lawlike generalizations and accidental generalizations needed for certain uses of predictive and subjunctive expressions. It is not the facts referred to by both sorts of generalization that differ, those denoted by lawlike generalizations being modal while the others are not; instead it is the two types of generalization that differ, in accordance with the strength of our commitment to their unrestricted universality. Rather than it being the case that general causal statements are initially used for prediction exclusively because they are recognized as distinctively lawlike on the basis of empirical observation, it is instead the case that general statements are recognized as lawlike because they reward our confidence by faithfully serving predictive functions.[40] There are, then, practical reasons for employing the notion of necessity, but there are no grounds for the belief that some objective natural necessity is denoted. Moreover, if there is a generic difference between the two relations "necessary connection" and "nonnecessary con-

---

40. This sentence draws inspiration from Nelson Goodman's "Humean idea" in *Fact, Fiction, and Forecast* (Indianapolis: Bobbs-Merrill Co., 1965), p. 21.

junction," there must be some empirical characteristic manifest whenever there is a necessary connectedness that is universally absent in the case of mere conjunction. That is, there must
be an empirical difference that justifies a distinction between
asserting the existence of necessity and denying it. Yet no
philosopher has ever successfully identified such a difference. It
has never even been adequately described; and we scarcely possess
a concept of the characteristic (EHU, Sec. 60; T, 162–66). Necessitarian accounts also suggest that there is a relation of implication
between natural events. While we understand logical implication,
we have no clear conception of what it would be like to observe
empirical implication, and certainly if it is required that we
observe such physical connections in order to warrant causal
inference, we are far from being justified in making such
inferences.

The letter of Hume's writings is, of course, never quite as
clear as this interpretation suggests. But our construal of his
arguments is patently plausible, for Hume was clearly sensitive
to the nondescriptive, inferential uses served by modal discourse
in causal contexts (EHU, Secs. 32, 59, 60). Whatever the exact
content of his message, his most important legacy is the claim
that "x is necessarily connected with y" is not a factual statement about nature because it does not describe a nonsubjective
state of affairs (except to the extent that it expresses the state
of the evidence). However, to say that the world can be described
without modal terminology is not to say that such terminology
serves no important function.[41] Modal terminology survives in
our language because it may serve an explanatory function; or
it may serve to refer to inferences that are justified; or it may
serve to mark a distinction. Hume never denied these facts
about causal discourse, though it is true that he was not chiefly
concerned with them and that his impression/idea theory of
meaning somewhat limited his vision.

41. The following statement is an example of a use of modal terminology
that Hume would not wish to challenge: "provided that the scientist has
correctly identified the situation . . . and therefore knows what principles
and laws he can appeal to, it is the very business of the theory to tell him
what *must* happen, i.e., what he must expect to happen, in such circumstances." From Stephen Toulmin, *The Philosophy of Science: An Introduction* (New York: Harper Torchbooks, 1960), pp. 92f.

The Humean and Hume himself thus at least implicitly distinguish between lawlike generalizations and merely accidental generalizations. It simply will not do to maintain, as Barry Stroud does, that Hume never makes the distinction and could not have countenanced belief in accidental but universal regularities.[42] Hume's distinction is drawn in terms of differing attitudes to general statements in the light of available evidence. To this argument a philosopher such as Kneale may rejoin that even if these considerations explain why we make the distinction, they do not take account of the philosophically justifiable, bona fide metaphysical difference between causal regularities and accidental regularities. After all, the objection runs, even undiscovered universals of law support counterfactual conditionals, while unnoticed universals of accident do not sustain their associated counterfactuals. Yet Hume's account only explains why we draw distinctions between diverse general statements we are actually in a position to entertain; his account fails to distinguish relations of which we have as yet no acquaintance. The follower of Kneale will argue that there are real necessities in nature and that we are committed to the truth of synthetic claims about unactualized possibilities beyond empirical facts. Hume again stands accused of not taking seriously counterfactual statements associated with laws, and of failing to offer an account of their content and relation to laws, as contrasted with an account of our epistemic situation in formulating lawlike generalizations. The follower of Kneale will insist that these issues are metaphysical, not epistemological, and that the Humean epistemological and psychological theories we have canvassed are therefore irrelevant.

We shall consider this challenge throughout the remainder of the chapter, but before doing so we need to recast the Humean position in light of the argument thus far. That position should be distinguished from Rescher's "Kantian" claim that we are "driven to a law-idealism." Rescher argues that *"the very concept of a natural law"* is mind-dependent.[43] In our Humean view,

---

42. Barry Stroud, *Hume* (London: Routledge & Kegan Paul, 1977), pp. 63, 93–95.

43. Rescher, *op. cit.*, pp. 190f. Rescher's most precise statement of his general thesis is the following: "the *claim* of lawfulness, unlike the *claim* of factuality, involves something . . . that would be infeasible in the face of a postulated absence of minds."

the very concept of *lawlikeness* and the acceptance of causal generalizations are mind-dependent, but universals of law and the regularities to which they correspond are not. The Humean considers lawlikeness, and so the *acceptance* of statements as universals of law, to be contingent upon an epistemic context. Counterfactuals too, as we shall now see, are tied to an epistemic context. But universals of law, causal laws, are mind-independent, as are the regularities they describe. Lawlikeness thus depends on the propositional attitude taken toward universal generalizations, for logically there is no difference between the form of lawlike and accidental generalizations. Of course propositional content is entirely independent of a propositional attitude: a belief is correct if and only if the entertained proposition is true. But truth conditions will not settle the matter of lawlike status; only attitude will, once it has been determined that a belief in the truth of a universal generalization is justifiably held.

In the remainder of this chapter we directly address the latter issues. But we may conclude this section confident in the recognition that, on the textual evidence, Hume did not simply ignore the issue of lawlike and accidental generalizations.

V

The key to the Humean approach to counterfactuals is the observation, accepted by almost all parties to the dispute, that the inductive evidence substantiating belief in any singular causal counterfactual statement is identical to the evidence for whatever lawlike generalizations are thought to support such a conditional. This observation enables the Humean to assimilate counterfactual statements to the regularity theory without embracing commitments to natural necessities, or to empirically untenable unactualized possibilities. The apparent commitment of counterfactual statements to unactualized possibilities can be construed, not in terms of truth conditions in the objects of causation, but in terms of the conjunction of inductive evidence and a high degree of confidence in that evidence, which conjunction leads users of such information to advance a counterfactual.

We shall argue that there is more to a lawlike generalization than what is expressed by the semantic meaning of the law statement, and that counterfactuals do not follow merely from the semantic meaning of these generalizations. To understand lawlike generalizations, as we have seen, one must be acquainted with both the evidential basis and the conditions under which speakers use such terms as "cause" and "law." It is this basis and these conditions that allow us to classify semantically identical general statements as lawlike and accidental universals.

The problem of possible instances can be resolved once an explanation has been provided both of the purposes to which lawlike generalizations are put and of the epistemic and contextual conditions under which people come to accept those generalizations and come to believe in the counterfactuals supported by them. Hume himself sees no reason for a stronger interpretation of lawlikeness; and any interpretation that removes the role of belief from the analysis of lawlikeness he considers deficient (T, 95ff). On the other hand, Hume denounces neither belief in nor language denoting causal necessity, and he would accept the language of possible cases, so long as one understands this language in terms of the practical need for customary expectation and "reasonings upon a supposition." Lawlike generalizations cover possible as well as actual cases solely in this restricted sense of supposition.

This account may still seem to leave Hume in the unenviable position of claiming that law-governed counterfactuals can be analyzed fully in terms of indicative statements. But this interpretation misses the point. For Hume, counterfactuals are analyzable in terms of the (indicatively expressible) evidence supporting lawlike generalizations plus the aforementioned component of pragmatic meaning. Hume is committed to saying that law-governed indicative conditionals and law-governed counterfactual conditionals are supported in exactly the same way and that the only difference between them—that antecedents of the first can be true whereas those of the latter are never true—is a negligible difference. Future indicative statements and counterfactuals, if this construal is correct, are formulated in different moods and have different meanings; but they commit one to neither more nor less in terms of natural possibilities than one is committed to by uttering factual generalizations, especially in their predictive employment. In both cases predictive language and modal terminology are used when one has firm confidence that nothing happens in violation of the law.

We may turn this brief strategy for analyzing counterfactuals into a detailed analysis by taking over the account that Mackie has elaborated in several places, including contexts in which he explicitly embraces views attributed to Kneale. Undoubtedly Kneale, like most who have agonized over counterfactuals, presupposes that they have truth values. This supposition has been one of their chief sources of difficulty. But neither a necessity theorist nor a Humean need accept this supposition, and Mackie in fact describes a strikingly different view.

Mackie claims that "To advance a counterfactual is not to assert any proposition, . . . it is rather to run through the condensation of an argument."[44] For him a counterfactual describes an imaginary situation and connects it to another such situation. Such connections can only be nonimaginary if they are inferred without supposition from considerations believed to be true or correct. Thus to state a counterfactual is to express an argument from imaginary supposition to imaginary conclusion through nonimaginary connections. The connections are more often than not grounded on suppressed or even unknown additional premises, and therefore counterfactuals are condensed, incomplete, telescoped arguments. One reason we understand and sometimes even embrace counterfactual claims, in ignorance of the evidence of lawlikeness needed to sustain them, is this characteristic of condensation. Thus, although we know no laws of human action, we understand and embrace counterfactuals about what someone would have done if his beliefs had been different from what they were.

We can and do read through the arguments that counterfactuals express without knowing all their premises, or all required intermediate steps. To *entertain* a counterfactual is thus to make a supposition while withholding assent to the existence of further true premises that together with the supposition imply the conclusion; but to *embrace* a counterfactual is to make a supposition while assenting to the truth of premises that together with the supposition imply the conclusion—i.e., that would constitute a valid argument for the counterfactual's consequent. In either case the required additional premises may actually be unknown and disagreements about their relevance,

---

44. J. L. Mackie, "Counterfactuals and Causal Laws," in *Analytic Philosophy*, Series I, ed. R. Butler, as reprinted in Beauchamp, ed., *op. cit.*, p. 97.

availability, and truth may explain the indeterminacy and ambiguity that notoriously surrounds counterfactual utterances. Mackie notes that "If we interpret counterfactuals . . . as arguments, we cannot say that they are true or false or that they are implied by other statements,"[45] even though counterfactuals may be sustained by premises, particularly general laws, that together with the supposition of their antecedents entail their consequents.

Mackie's exposition contains an important passage so congenial to Hume's account that Hume would no doubt have been pleased to have written it himself:

> If we ask, "Why is it that causal laws sustain counterfactuals whereas generalizations of fact do not?" we are formulating the puzzle in a misleading way. We are suggesting that we must look for some special virtue in causal laws, over and above universality, that enables them to sustain counterfactuals, mysterious truths that go beyond the actual world. . . . The real puzzle is, "Why do some generalizations of fact, . . . 'accidental' generalizations, fail to sustain counterfactuals which a corresponding causal law would sustain?" The problem is not to find any extra virtue in causal laws, but to find what special deficiency there is in "accidental" universals.[46]

Mackie's argument is framed in terms of the considerations of evidence and confidence on which Hume bases his distinction

---

45. *Ibid.*, p. 97. The denial that counterfactuals have truth values, which the following account substantiates, is of course not to be taken as a report on ordinary language, or indeed informal philosophical usage. Undoubtedly, counterfactual claims are normally thought of as true or false in ordinary talk. Throughout the course of this work we occasionally follow convention in characterizing counterfactuals as true and false. But, if the full analysis we offer is accepted, then such expressions need to be treated for the most part as circumlocutions for the analysans we present. Just as the expression "valid" is often attributed to statements, when in fact it is more properly restricted to arguments, the expression "true" may similarly be applied to arguments, even telescoped ones, with no harm done. It is clear in both cases what is meant. Ordinary usage would present a problem for our account if it included contexts in which the counterfactual statements acknowledged by commonsense reflection as true could not be accommodated by our analysis as supported or sustained arguments. Though we occasionally speak of *true* counterfactuals, it is our doctrine as well as Mackie's that such expressions do not have truth value. Such lapses should be construed as stylistic variations to accommodate a context of argument or the views of another, not as inconsistencies.

46. *Ibid.*, pp. 98–99.

between lawlike and accidental generalizations. A generalization sustains a counterfactual if our reasons—our evidence for embracing the generalization—are not undermined by the supposition of the counterfactual's antecedent. Thus if the evidence for a generalization is finitely enumerable, as in the case of typical accidental generalizations, then the supposed counterfactual's antecedent will describe an unexamined bit of evidence whose existence would undermine our confidence in the generalization. The difference between lawlike generalizations that sustain counterfactuals and accidental generalizations that do not, lies not in the meaning of these two different sorts of statements. As Mackie writes: "The difference lies in the kinds of evidence we have. We are justified in using a universal as a causal law if we have good inductive evidence for it, so that our reasons for believing it are not impaired when it is combined with a supposition" that either predictively goes "beyond cases for which the law has been checked" or counterfactually alters "the extension of the [law's] subject term." Mackie concludes that "the problem of sustaining of counterfactuals by causal laws is nothing more than the problem of induction."[47] It is only the traditional misunderstanding of Hume's views about induction that might blind one to the similarities between the theory Mackie advances and Hume's own discussion of the role played by evidence and confidence in the distinction between lawlike and accidental generalizations. In short, Hume anticipates Mackie's explanation of how one can believe that "causal laws differ from 'accidental' universals in their ability to sustain counterfactuals without assuming that a causal law, in its content, is anything more than a simple universal."[48]

We may now collect all that has been said in previous sections about Hume's account of the distinction between lawlike and accidental generalizations and bring it to bear on the analysis and support of counterfactuals. Within this framework law-governed counterfactuals are well supported by lawlike inductive generalizations only to the extent that the generalizations themselves are well supported. Three examples should make this point clear:

(1) All South African politicians are white.

47. *Ibid.*, p. 100.
48. *Ibid.*, p. 100.

may be omnitemporally true, but it certainly does not warrant the counterfactual

(1c) If Muhammad Ali were a South African politician he would be white.

because the supposition expressed by the antecedent of (1c) undermines acceptance of (1) as lawlike. However, the generalization

(2) All generals with mediocre soldiers fear a stronger enemy.

sustains, but to a lesser degree than a lawlike generalization (since there is inferior evidence and less than full confidence), the counterfactual

(2c) If Patton had been given mediocre soldiers, he would have feared a stronger enemy.

In contrast, the generalization

(3) A kerosene-soaked wick ignites when touched by an open flame.

strongly supports (since there is excellent evidence and the fullest degree of confidence)

(3c) If this kerosene-soaked wick were touched by an open flame, it would ignite.

Why is (3c), but not (2c), regarded as a law-governed counterfactual? Natural necessitarians think it is empirically possible (a real possibility in nature) in the case of (2c) that Patton might not have feared the enemy even if he had been given mediocre soldiers, because there is no natural causal necessity prohibiting such a state of affairs. But they also think the contradictory of (3c) is not empirically possible, because laws report empirical necessities of which the contradictory of (3c) would be a violation. Humeans, by contrast, regard the distinction in terms of empirical possibility and necessity as otiose and ill-founded. They think we do not regard examples resembling (2) as lawlike, because we lack firm evidence and conviction that cases like (2c) will always occur, while we do not lack such evidence and conviction about cases resembling (3c).

Kneale believes the resort to modal terminology is lethal

for Hume's theory of causation, since it reintroduces necessary connection as an essential feature. But if the language of possible cases is exhaustively analyzable in terms of suppositions and suppressed, nonmodal premises, then from the fact that lawlike generalizations sustain counterfactuals, no conclusion whatever follows in support of a natural necessity thesis. At most, it follows that lawlike generalizations are used to make "inferences beyond the actual." These are hypothetical suppositions moving from known data to the inductively insufficient conclusion that something must be the case. Inductive sufficiency cannot be obtained for such a conclusion, for the lawlike generalization is being used to project beyond the actual world into so-called possible worlds that are counter to fact. These hypotheticals do not report what is the case; they are mind-dependent projections. By contrast to factual reports, hypothetical counter-to-fact assertions have no standing independent of the minds that report them. Since the Humean view is that lawlikeness itself is a contribution of mind, this conclusion is hardly surprising. Lawlikeness and counterfactual support alike can be treated as a function of the degree of confidence generated by and vested in the supporting evidence.

VI

How does this theory of counterfactual support, suggested by Hume and detailed by Mackie, fare against the important criticism (mentioned near the end of Section IV) that these are metaphysical issues, not epistemological or psychological ones? The criticism, in the words of George Molnar, is that "what is possible or impossible does not depend on what anyone knows, or on the manner in which such knowledge is acquired, or on the evidential grounds on which the hypotheses are accepted." In a ringing defense of Kneale against the reduction of nomological necessity to epistemic features of universal general statements, Molnar notes that "there are . . . nomic regularities at present unknown to anybody. It would be absurd to deny that they, too, limit what is possible. Or suppose that, contrary to fact, there exist no intelligent beings and that consequently nothing is known. In that case, too, certain things and states of affairs would be possible and others impossible; some events could happen and others could not." Molnar considers his view incompatible with the Humean notion "that the concept of law has epistemic criteria built into it."[49] His criticism has special force for Humeans—as distinguished from certain idealists and Kantians—since the Humean admits that there are universals of law and causal regularities that are mind-independent.

The major issue raised by Molnar is whether *any* epistemic approach to laws and counterfactuals could be adequate to account for a metaphysical distinction. This question, he would insist, is plainly ignored by a circular appeal to an epistemic interpretation of counterfactuals and laws. Both the problem and the accusation might be put as follows: Hume's theory is merely an account of *lawlikeness* (lawlike generalizations), not of *laws* (universals of law). The latter are independent of our statements about them. Molnar argues that possibility and necessity, for example, are not epistemic concepts and that what is possible or impossible depends neither upon what some one or some group of scientists knows, nor upon the manner in which they acquire their knowledge, nor upon the evidential basis used to accept hypotheses. Unknown law-governed regularities determine what is possible no less than do known ones.

Moreover, universals of law arguably bear some connection or other to unknown counterfactual statements, while unknown accidental generalizations do not. Even before Faraday discovered the fact, electric currents were generating magnetic fields; and the counterfactual "Had Socrates produced an electric current—which he did not—he would have generated a magnetic field" is in principle *supportable* whether or not anyone

---

49. George Molnar, "Kneale's Argument Revisited," *Philosophical Review* 78 (1969). Reprinted in Beauchamp, ed., *op. cit.*, pp. 110–11. Molnar is arguing not only against Mackie but also against Ernest Nagel (*op. cit.*) and others who have taken the following line sympathetic to Hume: counterfactuals should be analyzed as statements about what can be deduced from a system of statements *S* (which includes law statements and statements of assumed boundary conditions) when some antecedent condition statement *A* is introduced as a supposition. A consequent *C* follows necessarily from *A* and *S*, but this necessity is strictly logical. Introduction of natural necessity to account for counterfactuals seems gratuitous on this account; indeed no necessity is attributed at all, other than the necessity of inferences warranted by the laws.

has evidence for the relevant law and its associated counter-factual. The Humean must not be caught denying these claims, for he will thereby be condemned to an uncritical idealism with regard to universals of law and indeed to all causal relations. Furthermore, Hume's first definition of "cause" would then stand in danger of being assimilated to the second definition, in a way he might be eager to avoid (see Chapter 1). In the end opponents of Hume would appear triumphant. By attributing natural necessity to law-governed causal regularities, indepen-dent of our evidence for their status, Kneale, Molnar, *et al.*, seem to avoid every difficulty. So, is there or is there not an answer to the claim that Humeans have simply confused the epistemic with the metaphysical, the lawlike with laws?

The Humean response to this straightforward way of putting the problem is equally straightforward: if law-governed coun-terfactuals are supported by unknown universals of law (on some different account of counterfactuals from the one presented above), this feature of the universe's secrets does not support the claims that there are empirically unaccountable, unrealized possibilities and that there is some esoteric cosmic necessity that places a limit on possibility. Universals of law for the Humean are simply universal statements of regularities that are exhaus-tively analyzable in terms of conjoined events. To say, counter-factually, that if an instance of the antecedent in an unknown universal of law were to occur, then an instance of the conse-quent would also occur, admits nothing metaphysically beyond a causal regularity that conforms to the requirements for laws delineated in Chapter 3. It does not follow that Humeans can-not account for the universal-of-law/universal-of-accident dis-tinction, for Humeans no less than necessitarians such as Kneale and Molnar acknowledge that there are boundaries or limits on empirical "possibility." These boundaries of empirical possibil-ity are set by the regularities that always hold no matter what the conditions. Any universal proposition is merely accidental, and so not an expression of a universal regularity, if there exist conditions in the actual world under which the antecedent and the consequent could fail to be conjoined. These conditions might, of course, be unknown. The Humean maintains only that adequate testing or manipulation of empirically possible conditions (as empirical possibility is understood above) *would* indicate that some generalizations are lawlike and others accidental.

If constant conjunctions prevail on a universal scale, then events of the cause (or effect) type do not occur without the occurrence of events of the effect (or cause) type. There is no reason to say that events of the cause (or effect) type cannot occur without events of the effect (or cause) type—except as interpreted through the limited notion of possibility just offered. Indeed, so far as we know, all events of the effect type and all events of the cause type could have occurred apart from a constant conjunction relation by which they are attached, for things might be otherwise on a cosmic scale than we know them to be.

This perspective on Molnar's argument helps show how the Humean draws the universal-of-law/universal-of-accident distinction. It is drawn on the basis of epistemic considerations, yet without reducing the notion of universal of law to an artifact of sentient cognition. A Humean holds that Molnar's position fails because it refuses to take seriously the analysis of counterfactuals offered above, together with the regularity view of the distinction between lawlike generalizations and universals of law. How can it be, on the Humean analysis of counterfactuals, that undiscovered universals of law support associated counterfactuals and that unknown universals of accident fail to support their associated counterfactuals? If counterfactual conditionals are themselves always mind-dependent and are not true or false propositions, they do not follow from the existence of undiscovered universals of law, even though such universals do hold independently of our knowledge of them. If counterfactual statements are condensed or telescoped arguments, then they are exclusively the creations of intelligent beings. If there are no such beings there are no arguments, and a fortiori no condensed ones either, and so no counterfactuals. And if there are such creatures but they have not entertained particular counterfactuals, then qua arguments these "counterfactuals" do not yet exist to be supported or not by their associated general statements. Accordingly, the distinction drawn between undiscovered universals of law and unknown universals of accident is simply irrelevant to questions about counterfactuals, for it fails to respond to the Humean claim that there is no such thing as a counterfactual independent of the cognition of sentient creatures.

Unknown universals of law, however, do have a property closely related to their *alleged* support of counterfactuals that is not possessed by accidental universals. This is the property of being so related to evidence that if there are or could be sentient creatures adequately acquainted with the evidence, they would embrace the relevant counterfactual. For any statement that correctly reports an undiscovered universal of law L, the only way to interpret its connection to counterfactuals is through the earlier account of evidence and lawlikeness; if evidence existed for L, it would sustain L's associated counterfactuals. But if L were instead an accidental universal, and if evidence existed for L, this evidence would be insufficient to allow reports about L to sustain its associated counterfactuals. These two subjunctive conditionals, proposed to distinguish unknown universals of law from unnoticed universals of accident, are themselves condensed or telescoped arguments. They are as good as we can reasonably hope to find, for we cannot have *arguments* about the unnoticed or unknown that do not themselves either depend on evidence or turn the unnoticed and unknown into the noticed and known. The regularity theorist is thus freed from the incubus of being unable to distinguish universals of law from universals of accident.

This employment of Mackie's treatment of counterfactuals, as telescoped arguments without truth values rather than as statements with truth values, is ironical. Mackie considers his contribution to the subject of causation to consist in an empirical replacement of the general theses Kneale defended against the Humean. Yet Mackie's own summary of his treatment of counterfactuals is stunningly Humean:

The inductive evidence that supports or corroborates the laws justifies the use of the counterfactuals which they seem to sustain, and the continuities, when observed or inferred, give at least further psychological encouragement and perhaps further justification for their use. Thus the counterfactual conditionals which emerge from the analysis of causal statements, though not themselves true, are surrogates for clusters of statements which can be true.[50]

We thus have a ready answer to the popular criticism that in the end there is no difference on Hume's account between a universal of law and a statement of a universally instanced

50. Mackie, *The Cement of the Universe*, pp. 229f.

cosmic accident (such as, let us hypothesize, "In certain regions densely populated by birds, eclipses are always followed by decreases in the production of their eggs") that survives all attempts at falsification and all changes in the order of nature. The answer is simple: there is indeed, so far as we know, no difference whatever. Such statements are nothing less than universals of law. An allegedly "accidental" universal that meets the tests of survival we have proposed is a universal of law. That there is nothing beyond these tests to distinguish accidental and lawful universals is the proper interpretation of "heroic Humeanism." So understood we are pleased to embrace it.

VII

While we take the epistemic and nonepistemic replies tendered in previous sections to be sufficient to refute natural necessitarians who rely on analyses of counterfactuals, a chicken-and-egg problem remains: Should the analysis of lawlike generalizations rest on an accepted understanding of counterfactuals, or should the analysis of counterfactuals rest on some accepted understanding of lawlike generalizations?

The analysis of counterfactuals has been a major postwar industry in Anglo-American philosophy, quite apart from any direct bearing it may have on causation. The project of explicating the "truth conditions" of counterfactual utterances has occupied philosophers at least since the seminal papers of Roderick Chisholm and Nelson Goodman, respectively entitled "The Contrary-to-Fact Conditional" and "The Problem of Counterfactual Conditionals."[51] The discussion, however, has persistently been plagued by the aforementioned chicken-and-egg problem. Most accounts of counterfactuals have included in their truth conditions some lawlike generalization and in their falsity conditions the absence of a true universal statement with nomological force. The strategy of such analyses suggests that their proponents find the notion of lawlike generalization less problematic than the notion of counterfactual support, and lawlike generalizations in some respect easier to distinguish

---

51. Roderick Chisholm, "The Contrary-to-Fact Conditional," *Mind* 55 (1946), pp. 289–307; Nelson Goodman, "The Problem of Counterfactual Conditionals," *The Journal of Philosophy* 44 (1947), pp. 113–28.

from true but accidental generalizations than "true" counterfactuals are distinguishable from false ones. And yet as often as some philosophers have offered accounts of counterfactuals that depend on an implicit understanding of laws, others (especially from Kneale onwards) have offered accounts of laws that depend on an implicit understanding of counterfactuals. These two approaches cannot be combined into a single theory of laws and counterfactuals, because each treats the analysandum of the other as less problematic and therefore as a more suitable analysans.

A rather significant problem of circularity thus emerges for philosophers such as Kneale and Molnar: laws are analyzed in terms of counterfactuals, which themselves rely on an implicit appeal to laws. Until a clear and independent account of one or the other notion is forthcoming, neither notion can help explicate the related notion of nonaccidentalness. This problem is especially acute for Hume's opponents, who have appealed to one of these notions to explain the other in order to object to the Humean theory of causation. Their method of strictly distinguishing lawlike from accidental generalizations trades on alleged differences between the counterfactuals associated with these two different sorts of statements. Yet again the argument is circular: the differences between the counterfactuals cited are grounded in assumptions about the lawlike-generalization/accidental-generalization distinction. Thus the supposed death knell of the regularity theory ultimately goes unexplained by Hume's opponents.

In the circumstances, the attraction of "heroic Humeanism" is understandable: its parsimony, its refusal to credit unexplained distinctions no matter how widespread, and its dissolution of conventional philosophical problems are considerable assets. In particular the Humean avoids a circular explanation of lawlike generalizations and counterfactuals by analyzing both in terms of epistemically warranted attitudes. In all of these respects Hume's theory seems superior to any available substitute.

VIII

A non-Humean alternative to strategies that reciprocally explain lawlike generalizations and counterfactuals has recently attained considerable celebrity in philosophical circles. In conclusion we must consider this alternative.

New accounts of counterfactuals, as statements allegedly susceptible of truth or falsity, have been offered that ground truth conditions in considerations free from appeal to universals of law. These accounts are the so-called possible worlds semantic theories for counterfactuals, given their most detailed statement by Robert Stalnaker and David Lewis. The significance of these theories for causality and for Hume's explanation is clear: an analysis of counterfactuals that does not appeal to universals of law or lawlike generalizations provides an alternative to Hume's account of causation, because it enables one to tie causal sequences directly to true counterfactuals without any reference to laws whatever. Such an approach is a striking departure both from the postwar tradition of linking laws with counterfactuals, and from the Humean one of linking causation with laws. Causal necessity, too, is expounded in terms clearly incompatible with Hume's theory, for the nomological force of lawlike generalizations is itself accounted for by the connection between such generalizations and nonlaw-governed counterfactuals. Whether or not Humeans can accomodate possible worlds by treating them as abstract objects or conceptual fictions,[52] exponents of the new possible worlds theory of counterfactuals believe they can provide a better theory of *causation* than did Hume. In the present section we examine Lewis's version of this counterfactual theory and consider whether it does represent a tenable improvement on Hume's theory.

Lewis's theory is complex, and involves formidable technicalities and intermediaries between the analysans "*c* causes *e*" and its ultimate analysandum. Causation is defined in terms of causal dependence, and this notion in turn is explicated by appeal to the truth of a counterfactual about *c* and *e*. The counterfactual's truth conditions themselves include the truth of a conjunction of statements about the occurrence or nonoccurrence of *c* and statements about the occurrence and nonoccurrence of *e* at the possible world most similar to the actual world. Causal dependence is then distinguished from what

---

52. As Mackie argues in *Truth, Probability, and Paradox* (Oxford: Oxford University Press, 1973).

Lewis calls "nomic dependence," a conditional relation that reflects the operation of laws. Lewis explicates causal dependence and nomic dependence separately through their relations to counterfactual dependence and to his account of the truth conditions of counterfactual expressions. On Lewis's view, the defects in a Humean account of causation can be identified and explained once we have distinguished these separate issues. In fact it is because the matters are so complex that these distinctions have gone unnoticed, and the result is that "the regularity analysis gives conditions that are almost but not quite sufficient for explicable causal dependence."[53]

The wider aim of Lewis's account of causation is to solve problems that he believes Hume's approach cannot solve: problems mainly concerning the nature of causal directionality, "distinguishing genuine causes from effects, epiphenomena, and preempted potential causes."[54] These problems are addressed from the Humean point of view in Chapter 6. Here we shall examine first Lewis's claims about the relation of his views on causal dependency to his views about truth conditions for counterfactuals, focusing especially on his claim that the vagueness of counterfactuals generally infects causation, and makes it a relation whose reports must inevitably be vague. Then we turn to his argument for the independence of counterfactuals from nomological dependence; and, applying our criticisms of claims about the vagueness of counterfactuals, show that his views are at least as problematic as those whose conclusions he seeks to supplant. In the end both counterfactual and causal dependencies must be based on lawlike generalizations, as the Humean consistently claims.

According to Lewis,[55] if two events c and e occur, then e is causally dependent on c only in cases where the proposition that e does not occur depends counterfactually on the proposition that c does not occur, that is, where a counterfactual of

---

53. David Lewis, "Causation," *Journal of Philosophy* 70 (1973), pp. 556–57, reprinted in E. Sosa, ed., *Causation and Conditionals* (Oxford: Oxford University Press, 1975), pp. 180–91; quotation p. 189. Cf. also his *Counterfactuals* (Cambridge: Harvard University Press, 1972), p. 189. Page references in the text are to the reprinting in Sosa's collection or to Lewis's book, unless otherwise noted.
54. Lewis, "Causation," p. 181.
55. *Ibid.*, p. 186.

the following form is true: Since both c and e have actually occurred, $\sim O(c) \square \rightarrow \sim O(e)$ [where $O(c)$ is to be read as "c occurs"]. If e is causally dependent on c, then c causes e. $\sim O(c) \square \rightarrow \sim O(e)$ is true if a possible world where both $O(c)$ and $O(e)$ are true is more similiar to the actual world than is any possible world where $O(c)$ is false and $O(e)$ is true. Unlike regularity accounts, this analysis of causation nowhere makes reference to laws. Comparative determinations of similarity or closeness of possible worlds to the actual one involve judgments of comparative similarity between worlds, and since similarity is a vague concept, Lewis concludes that "the vagueness of similarity does infect causation; and no correct analysis can deny it."[56]

It is by no means as clear as Lewis maintains, however, that the vagueness of similarity infects either causation or his counterfactual account of it. This is not to deny that "similar" is a vague term. But the (supposed) truth or falsity of counterfactual statements does not turn on the truth or falsity of statements infected by the vagueness of "similarity." Their truth turns on how the three-place relation "x is more similar to y than to z" is instantiated. The predicate expressing this relation is not vague in the way that "similar" is, for, unlike "similar" alone, it is a comparative predicate. In general, sentences that employ the three-term relation in question *can* be indeterminate in truth-value because of the number of dimensions along which comparisons between the terms are made. But from this it does not follow that they *are* vague. This contention deserves further exposition.

If we could specify the seemingly diverse dimensions in which worlds differ in general ways, we would still have no clear procedure for weighting them in order to make "overall" judgments of comparative similarity. Worlds y and z might differ from one another only in two different nonvague dimensions—say, in the shape and size of their constituents. Without a method of weighting differences along such diverse dimensions we could make no reasoned judgments of overall degrees of similarity between x, a third world differing from both in, say, material composition of constituents, and y, or between x and z. If the dimensions (like shape, size, and composition of constituents)

56. *Ibid.*, p. 184.

along which worlds can differ are not comparable at all, then judgments of relative overall similarity are not vague; they are senseless. If on the other hand they are comparable, then our failure to find a well-justified measure is no reason to describe relations of overall similarity as vague. The multidimensionality of comparative overall similarity would be a reason for calling statements of such comparative similarity vague only if one of the dimensions of the similarity were itself vague in a way that precluded comparisons along it *alone*. Moreover, a strong case can be made that there are no vague *properties* at all, only vague *predicates*.[57] Consequently, if the comparisons to be made concern the degree to which worlds differ in the instantiation of certain properties, then there is simply no scope for vagueness in the relations of comparative similarity between worlds. Any indeterminacy of *comparative* overall similarity is, then, not a semantic indeterminacy (just because it is a comparative relation); it is an indeterminacy that hinges on the absence of a means for aggregating and comparing the nonvague dimensions along which worlds may differ. Accordingly, Lewis need not defend himself against objections to his account that appeal to the vagueness of counterfactuals and the exactitude of causation, for the *causal* counterfactuals at issue are not vague at all.

As we shall argue, a closer examination of the dimensions along which Lewis permits causally different worlds to vary reveals that these dimensions are not merely comparable, they are identical. The dimensions relevant to determining comparative similarity appear to be only two: the laws operative in each world, and the chain of events constituting what may be called the "histories" of the worlds to be compared. According to Lewis, a world that differs from our own because of differences in laws may be closer than one that differs in respect of history; and thus the supposed truth or falsity of counterfactuals and their associated causal statements does not unavoidably turn on the presence of associated laws, as a regularity theorist would hold.

Both in order to show that causal counterfactuals are not vague in the way Lewis suggests, and to assess his argument against the Humean, we need to consider Lewis's account of

57. Kenton Machina argues cogently for this view in "Vague Predicates," *American Philosophical Quarterly* 9 (1972), pp. 225–34.

laws: according to Lewis, "A generalization is a law at a world *i* . . . if and only if it appears as a theorem in each of the best deductive systems true at *i*."[58] The best deductive systems are roughly those that balance axiomatic simplicity and informational content in the description of *regularities* that obtain at *i*. Lewis provides six excellent reasons for adopting this view of laws (lawlike generalizations for the Humean): it explains why a proposition's being both general in form and true is not sufficient for its being a law; it explains the contingency of laws (since they are relativized to worlds for each of which the best axiomatic systems may differ); it therefore explains how we can exhaustively enumerate all the instances of a generalization without knowing it to be true; it explains why being a law is different from being believed to be a law; it explains why we take actual theoretical axiomatizations to be our best guesses about what the universals of law at this world are; and it explains the vagueness and difficulty of the concept of laws in terms of the parallel difficulty in the notions of simplicity and strength.

Lewis's restriction of laws to generalizations that fit into the best axiomatic systems for the description of their worlds makes the relations between the laws at a world and the history of that world transparent. If laws restrict actualities at a world, but not possibilities, and if two worlds are *identical* in histories (the chain of events down to the most fundamental levels that occur "in" them), then they must also be identical in laws. Yet if laws restricted possibilities as well as actualities, this conclusion would not hold; for then two different sets of laws might both be consistent with the same history of actual events, while differing in their consistency with various logically possible alternatives to this history. Since on Lewis's view laws describe only actualities at a given world, if the set or sets of laws applicable in two worlds differ, then their histories must differ also.[59] However, two worlds may be alike in laws, though differing in histories—as, for instance, when their initial conditions differ. Thus, the following principles for comparing worlds that differ by laws or histories may be attributed to Lewis:

---

58. Lewis, *Counterfactuals*, p. 73.
59. The plural qualification is added to cover histories not systematized by a *unique* set of laws, but described with equal economy and strength in more than one set of laws.

(A) For any two possible worlds: if they share the same history, then they share the same set(s) of laws.

(B) For any two possible worlds identical in initial conditions: if they do not share the same history, then they do not share the same set(s) of laws.

Of course, A and B both presuppose, per Lewis's stipulation, that the worlds in question are deterministic. As suggested above, leading opponents of the regularity theory would be unwilling to accept these principles. They would hold, for example, that two worlds might be identical in history, although their laws differ in the maximum velocity with which they permit objects in the worlds to travel. For present purposes, the upshot of Lewis's principles is that every difference between possible worlds that is relevant to the "truth" of counterfactuals in this world comes down to differences along only one dimension: the dimension of histories. Worlds that differ in law must differ somewhere in their histories if only at the most microphysical levels; and this difference in history exhausts their nomological differences. Accordingly, the comparison between possible worlds and their degrees of similarity to the actual one turns only on the kind of events and the order in which events occur in the worlds at issue.

These considerations may shed a new light on Lewis's claim that:

The respects of similarity and difference that enter into the overall similarity of worlds are many and varied. In particular, similarities in matters of particular fact trade off against similarities of law. The prevailing laws of nature are important to the character of a world; so similarities of law are weighty. Weighty, but not sacred. We should not take it for granted that a world that conforms perfectly to our actual laws is *ipso facto* closer to actuality than any world where those laws are violated in any way at all. It depends on the nature and extent of the violation, on the place of the violated laws in the total system of laws of nature, and on the countervailing similarities and differences in other respects. Likewise, similarities or differences of particular fact may be more or less weighty, depending on their nature and extent. Comprehensive and exact similarities of particular fact throughout large spatio-temporal regions seem to have special weight. It may be worth a small miracle to prolong or expand a region of perfect match.[60]

---

60. Lewis, "Causation," p. 184.

The possible worlds to which we appeal in testing a causal counterfactual do not differ from our own or from each other in "many and varied" respects. Their denizens, at least up to the time of the occurrence of the effect, are identical, or at any rate are counterparts of one another; and the events that constitute their histories are also the same until the time of the effect. Contrary to Lewis's claim, worlds like these conform perfectly to the laws of our world. They are *ipso facto* closer to actuality than any world where those laws are violated. These worlds do not differ in history from the actual world *at all,* and therefore must be closer than worlds that differ from ours by even the most trivial departure from our laws. Even a trivial departure must make a difference in history if the initial conditions are the same.

Furthermore, Lewis's account of laws leaves no room for the miracles to which he appeals (in the above quotation) in order to "prolong or expand a region of perfect match." The interpolation of a "miracle" among a prolonged sequence of events constituting a history thereby changes the laws that govern that history, since we must add to our axiomatic accounts of this (deterministic) world's regularities a statement covering the causal conditions of the singular event in question. Also, depending on the account of miracles accepted, we will probably have to delete laws the "miracle" violates—or at least qualify them by an exception clause (as Hume in effect argues in his essay "On Miracles"). Thus, what Lewis calls "the nature and extent" of departures from the facts and violations of laws are commensurable: both consist simply in differences among the histories of the worlds under comparison.

Whatever indeterminateness infects our identifications of these differences is a consequence of the want of a theory for individuating events, and for counting them up. Since there is no reason in principle why such a theory cannot be provided, there seems no reason to describe the counterfactuals necessary for assessing causal claims as unavoidably vague. Moreover, since we already have some clear standards of individuation, the prospects for agreement about the status of causal counterfactuals may be better than Lewis supposes; we may even be able to reach reasonable conclusions at variance with his own. Before considering particular cases, however, we need to explore Lewis's treatment of "counterfactual independence" and its relation to "nomic dependence." As noted, Lewis introduces these crucial concepts in order to expound his view of the relations among causality, counterfactuals, and general laws. He then employs them to diagnose alleged defects in the Humean theory about these items and their relations.

First, Lewis defines "nomic dependence." A set of propositions $C_1, C_2, \ldots C_n$ *depends nomically* on a set of (mutually incompatible) propositions, $A_1, A_2, \ldots A_n$ only when there is a nonempty set of laws L, and a set of propositions describing particular facts F, such that L and F jointly and nonredundantly imply all the material conditions $A_1 \supset C_1, A_2 \supset C_2, \ldots A_n \supset C_n$. Under these circumstances, according to Lewis, the family of propositions $C_1, C_2, \ldots C_n$ is *counterfactually dependent* on the family of propositions, $A_1, A_2, \ldots, A_n$, if "(all members of) *L* and *F* are counterfactually independent of the *A*'s. . . . In that case, we may regard the nomic dependence in virtue of *L* and *F* as explaining the counterfactual dependence."[61]

However, on the accounts of laws and counterfactual independence that Lewis offers, no set of laws like L can be shown to be counterfactually independent of a family of propositions like the A's. A law set L "is *counterfactually independent* of the family of propositions $A_1, A_2, \ldots$, if L would hold no matter which of the A's were true . . . ." If, as seems to be assumed, A-statements describe the occurrence of particular events, then, given a world in which an event described by A_1 occurs, the closest possible world to it in which A_1 is not true will differ from it in history at least by the absence of the A_1 event. This absence will be due either to the possible world in question having different initial conditions (and thus an utterly different history up to the A_1 event) or to different laws obtaining at this world, though its history (before and possibly after) matches that of the actual world almost perfectly. In these circumstances, Lewis would regard a world with an *almost* perfect match in history as the closest. Because the match is almost but not completely exact, the laws of this world must be different from L: worlds with parallel "pasts" and ever so slightly divergent "futures" are governed by at least some different laws. Accordingly,

61. *Ibid.*, pp. 187–88; quotation p. 188.

if the set L bears the logical relations to the family of propositions, $A_1, A_2, \ldots$ required for the nomological dependence of
$C_1, C_2, \ldots$ on the former, the set set L cannot be counterfactually independent of the A's. Therefore, the C's cannot be counterfactually dependent on the A's.

To see this point more clearly, consider Lewis's own example:
the current barometer reading depends counterfactually on the
current air pressure, where the former is nomically dependent
on the latter in virtue of the conjunction of (1) the gas laws
governing air pressure and the operation of barometers, and (2)
the particular fact that the barometer in question is currently
operational. According to Lewis, both the latter fact and the gas
laws are counterfactually independent of the actual air pressure;
that is, *they would obtain no matter what the air pressure is.*
For this counterfactual to be true, as Lewis supposes, it must
be the case that at the world most similar to the actual world, in
which the current air pressure is different from the actual value,
the same laws governing air pressure and barometer mechanisms
obtain (and the barometer remains operational). But this closest
of all relevant possible worlds is either different in its history
up to the event in question (in virtue of the operation of the
same gas laws on different initial conditions), or else (in virtue
of the singular departure in air pressure at this moment from
the actual value) it is different in total history, and therefore in
laws governing air pressure and the readings of barometers.[62]
Because the second alternative describes what, on Lewis's view is
a closer world, the counterfactual that the same laws would hold
regardless of the actual air pressure cannot be asserted, contrary
to Lewis's supposition.

This result has significant implications for Lewis's position. If
no set of laws is counterfactually independent of a set of singular statements A, together with which they make for the
nomological and thus counterfactual dependence of another set
of singular statements C on A, then this second set C cannot be

62. It is important for the purposes of this argument to remember that
the same set of laws governs the behavior of both the atmosphere and
barometers in our world. Of course, in a world that differed from ours very
greatly, different laws might govern both the relation among thermo-
dynamic properties of the atmosphere that account for our weather and
the relation among these properties, and mechanical ones that account for
the operation of barometers.

shown to be counterfactually dependent on A. Therefore C cannot be said to describe the *effects* of the events that the propositions in set A describe. Yet, on Lewis's view, it is precisely such effects that these counterfactually dependent statements are supposed to describe. Our argument here turns on Lewis's requirement that laws be counterfactually independent of singular statements. Waiving this requirement would of course avoid the difficulty, but it would also commit Lewis to what he calls a regularity theory weaker than his own counterfactual account. He says the regularity theory seems to work only because it "gives conditions that are almost but not quite sufficient for explicable causal dependence."[63] Missing from this theory, says Lewis, is "the supposition that L and F are counterfactually independent" of the assertion that the cause occurred.

One of the chief virtues that Lewis claims for his counterfactual account of causation is its ability to circumvent problems that allegedly bedevil a regularity approach to causation. Lewis lists the problem of effects as chief among these problems: "Suppose that *c* causes a subsequent event *e,* and that *e* does not also cause *c*. . . . Suppose further that, given the laws and some of the actual circumstances, *c* could not have failed to cause *e*. It seems to follow that if the effect *e* had not occurred, then its cause *c* would not have occurred."[64] The truth of this counterfactual is incompatible, on Lewis's treatment, with the argument's assumption that *e* did not cause *c*. According to Lewis, the solution of this problem is

flatly to deny the counterfactuals that cause the trouble. If *e* had been absent, it is not that *c* would have been absent. . . . Rather, *c* would have occurred just as it did but would have failed to cause *e*. It is less of a departure from actuality to get rid of *e* by holding *c* fixed and giving up some or other of the laws and circumstances in virtue of which *c* could not have failed to cause *e,* rather than to hold those laws and circumstances fixed and get rid of *e* by going back and abolishing its cause *c*. . . .

To get rid of an actual event *e* with the least over-all departure from actuality, it will normally be best not to diverge at all from the actual course of events until just before the time of *e*.[65]

63. Lewis, "Causation," p. 189.
64. *Ibid.*
65. *Ibid.*, p. 190.

But the problem of the counterfactual dependence of laws on histories, given Lewis's conception of the former, vitiates this approach to the so-called problem of effects, and so deprives Lewis's conception of its chief alleged advantage over the regularity view. The truth of the counterfactual that had e not occurred c nevertheless would have, which is required by this solution, simply cannot be derived without undercutting the counterfactual Lewis wishes to assert in this case—that had c not occurred, e would not have happened either. Since, *ex hypothesi*, c caused e, e must be counterfactually dependent on c in virtue of its nomological dependence on c. That is, there is a set of laws L which, together with c, materially implies e. (For simplicity assume that no further initial conditions are required to imply e.) Furthermore, it is required that L be counterfactually independent of c, i.e., L would hold whether c occurs or not. On the other hand, since e is not the cause of c by the same hypothesis, Lewis asserts that it is not the case that had e not occurred c would not have happened either.

Consider three worlds, with the same histories up to the occurrence of c. In the first c and e occur; this is the actual world. In the second, c occurs, but e does not; this is the world that Lewis deems closest to the actual world, because it is just like the actual world, except that e does not occur. The third world is just like the actual world, except that neither c nor e occurs in its history. Since these worlds are all deterministic, it follows, given Lewis's treatment of laws, that their laws will differ, because the histories differ while initial conditions are the same in all three worlds. But if the laws of world three differ from those of world one in part because of the nonoccurrence of c (and e) then L is not after all counterfactually independent of c. Accordingly, it cannot be shown that with respect to the actual world, e is counterfactually dependent on c, since it cannot be shown that it is nomologically dependent on c with respect to a set of laws L that are themselves counterfactually independent of c. But if causal dependence, and therefore causation itself, depends on counterfactual dependence, it follows that we cannot on Lewis's account show that c caused e, which is what we began by assuming.

Notice that if Lewis were to surrender the requirement that laws be counterfactually independent of histories, this result would not obtain. The result rests on the joint assumption that the histories of the three deterministic worlds in question are identical up to and after c and e, and principle B, that different histories consequent on identical initial conditions imply different laws. Neither of these assumptions can plausibly be surrendered. To surrender the requirement that the laws at a world be counterfactually independent of the causal sequences they govern at that world, is, as Lewis insists, tantamount to embracing the regularity theory. For all the latter lacks on his view is the requirement that we here suggest should be relaxed: that laws are counterfactually independent of causal sequences. However, so far as Lewis's solution to the problem of effects is concerned, giving up this assumption deprives it of its force. For, if the world in question is a deterministic one, and is governed by the set of laws L that sanctions the counterfactual, and therefore the causal dependence of e on c, then it can be shown to sanction the counterfactual dependence of c on e as well (just in case there are no additional conditions, F, distinct from c). For if L and the statement that c occurred jointly imply the statement of e's occurrence, then by *modus tollens* the denial of e's occurrence plus L will imply the denial of c's occurrence. In that case, c will be nomologically, and therefore counterfactually, dependent on e, and ultimately causally dependent on e as well.

The real thrust of Lewis's counterfactual account of causation, however, is his discussion of the problem of causal asymmetry, and his belief that regularity theories of causation founder decisively on this problem, while a counterfactual account can surmount it. Thus, his paper "Causation" begins with a doubt "whether any regularity analysis can succeed in distinguishing genuine causes from effects, epiphenomena, and preempted potential causes . . . without departing from the fundamental idea that causation is instantiation of regularities. I have no proof that regularity analyses are beyond repair. . . . Suffice it to say that the prospects look dark."[66] Lewis concludes this paper by rejecting the solution to some of these problems that has traditionally been associated with the regularity theory: the stipulation that a cause must always precede its effect. Even if we

66. *Ibid.*, p. 181.

adopt Lewis's arguments against this solution, the fact that his own account does not seem free of difficulties[67] suggests that we need to turn to the problem that provided Lewis's original motivation: the problem of causal asymmetry.

We devote Chapter 6 to this problem. We there conclude that the defect Lewis finds in the regularity theory's account of causal directionality is no essential part of the theory. Indeed, arguments that the heoric Humean musters against some forms of the law-accident distinction are even more attractive in the context of problems of causal directionality. This outcome is to be expected, since much of the initial plausibility of the attribution of necessity to causal sequences rests on our firm conviction of their directionality. The Humean account of this directionality is very much a part of its complete treatment of law, accident, necessity, and counterfactuality.

67. Lewis's solution to the problems of epiphenomena and of preempted potential causes involves the same considerations as his treatment of the problem of effects.

5

Contiguity and Succession

HUME'S ARGUMENTS about causation early in the *Treatise* are intended to show that contiguity and succession are individually necessary conditions of causation.[1] These arguments and their aims have generally been ignored or misinterpreted. In particular Hume's claims about the spatial and temporal contiguity of causes and effects have been taken for epistemic strictures about causal knowledge and its employment. In the first four sections of this chapter we argue against these interpretations and ex-

---

1. The pertinent passages in Hume's writings are found exclusively in the *Treatise* and its *Abstract*. (EHU only incorporates succession into the definition of "cause." However, as we shall see, "contiguity" and "succession" contain an important similarity of meaning in Hume's arguments. Also, Wade Robison has offered reasons for believing that Hume's *second* definition of "cause" Df_2 does not include the relations of contiguity and succession. "Hume's Causal Scepticism" in G. P. Morice, ed., *David Hume: Bicentenary Papers* [Edinburgh: University of Edinburgh Press, 1977], p. 165, note 12.) There is evidence in the *Treatise* that he takes these criteria of causation seriously, despite the brevity of his arguments and his notorious remark that if his argument for succession is not satisfactory "the affair is of no great importance" (T, 76). The criteria of contiguity and succession appear early in the analysis of causation, reappear in his discussion of natural and philosophical relations, and emerge again in his two definitions of "cause" (T, 75–77, 93f, 170–72). These passages acknowledge that there are three ways in which the temporal relation between causes and effects might conceivably be construed: (i) as separated by some interval of time; (ii) as perfectly contiguous, so that the effect succeeds the cause in the very next period of time; (iii) as perfectly contemporaneous, existing during the same period of time. Hume defends (ii) and denies both (i) and (iii). In this chapter we contend that, when properly qualified, this position is correct.

hibit the compatibility of contiguity requirements with causal assumptions commonly considered incompatible with them. We then analyze Hume's claims about the temporal succession of effects and causes, revealing unnoticed connections to the contiguity requirements and defending his views against counterarguments. Our discussion of these problems is continuous with our treatment of the problem of causal asymmetry, to which Chapter 6 is wholly devoted.

I

Let us first consider Hume's general pronouncements about contiguity. He maintains that contiguity in *time* is an essential feature of all causal relations, while contiguity in *space* characterizes only such relations as can properly be denominated spatial.[2] His rather compressed argument for this general thesis consists largely in an appeal to the maxim that "nothing can operate in a time or place, which is ever so little removed from those of its existence" (T, 75). While he recognizes that proximate causes are commonly distinguished from remote causes, he seems to reject the idea that remote items can be *causes*. On a literal interpretation of his text, each member of a set of conditions forming a causal chain is a cause only of that succeeding member with which it is connected contiguously; all noncontiguously related members are not causally related. Hume, then, seems to hold that:

> For all x and for all y, x is a cause of y only if:
>
> (i) x is temporally contiguous with y,
>
> and (where relevant)
>
> (ii) x is spatially contiguous with y.

This claim is certainly controversial, for it does not conform either to ordinary or to scientific causal judgments. We commonly attribute causality to events that are spatially distant or that occurred hours and even years prior to their effects. We

2. Hume holds that there are nonspatial, nonquantitative, causally related objects. Passions, moral reflections, sounds, etc. are examples. These objects are "nowhere" and so have "no particular place" (T, 235f).

readily grant, for example, the truth of such general and singular causal statements as the following:

(1) Cirrhosis of the liver is often caused by a protein deficiency in childhood.
(2) Hypnotic suggestion caused him to pull the trigger that resulted in death.
(3) Planetary activity causes the tides.

According to a strict reading of Hume's theory, based on condition (i) above, each of these three claims is false, because the alleged cause and effect are not contiguous. Indeed the second example states a doubly false causal judgment. The hypnotist did not cause the trigger finger to move, and neither the hypnotist nor the triggering-agent is the cause of death. If Hume is interpreted literally, the hypnotist causes a state of mind and the trigger finger's motion causes the trigger to move—no more, no less. If a person lingers after the bullet passes through his body, then even the bullet is not a cause of death, though its effect might be a cause. Hume's contentions seem false because our everyday concept of causation has a flexible character, allowing the remote relatedness he seems to repudiate. For this reason, his contiguity criterion initially strikes us as *ad hoc* and legislative.

The first pertinent question is whether the counterintuitive character of Hume's claim is significant. As we have observed in previous chapters, Hume is not concerned to analyze the ordinary concept of causation, nor does he attempt to provide a descriptive definition of "cause." Accordingly, criticisms that presuppose the adequacy of reports about the ordinary concept of causation stand in danger of begging the question. Before these matters can be decided, however, both Hume's motivation to hold this view and his arguments for it must be considered. This procedure may help us understand why his position seems intuitively implausible and why he is led to embrace what some regard as counterintuitive conclusions.

Two reasons lead Hume to stipulate that contiguity is a necessary condition of causation. First, he has in mind the model of explanation advocated by the natural science of his period, according to which contiguity seems to be a requirement of the causal relation.[3] This model leads him to think that because a *causal chain* can have no gaps, a *cause* must therefore be contiguous with its effect (T, 75). The inference is of course eccentric when judged by the standard of common causal judgments. On many occasions both scientists and the common man would certainly refuse to submit to Hume's seemingly extreme stipulation, as examples (1) and (3) illustrate. Cirrhosis of the liver is not caused merely by a sudden attack, nor the tides by immediately contiguous conditions. These conditions are known scientifically to be causally insufficient (though perhaps they are sufficient for certain explanatory purposes). Moreover, it is usually difficult to isolate *any* relevant contiguous conditions for effects that either have an enduring character or have indeterminate boundaries—whether or not they are events subject to explanation by natural science. The difficulty in specifying contiguous conditions, and sometimes the irrelevance of doing so, is evident in the case of such effects as the gradual collapse of a financial empire, being late because one forgot to set an alarm, the glowing of a steel rod recently removed from a heat source, and population decreases caused by plagues. Such examples naturally lead us to be sceptical of Hume's conclusions.

Second, Hume is influenced by his enthusiasm for the maxim that nothing "ever so little removed" can be causally efficacious. From this notion he seems to reason that an event or object at all removed from an effect is never really its cause, though we often believe removed events to be causes—much as he thinks we do not really see external objects yet believe we do. Here Hume once again departs from ordinary causal language, and this departure creates the paradox that remote "causes" cannot be *causes*. Our sense of paradox is deepened by our awareness that even in science, contiguous conditions are not requisite for causal laws. Consider, for example, laws in psychology. A physiological psychologist may explain a duck's behavior at any given moment in terms of temporally contiguous brain conditions, but

---

3. For an orientation to the relevant scientific background of Hume's contiguity criterion, cf. M. S. Kuypers, *Studies in the Eighteenth Century Background of Hume's Empiricism* (New York: Russell & Russell, 1966), Chapters I–IV; *The Leibniz-Clarke Correspondence*, ed. H. G. Alexander (Manchester: Manchester University Press, 1956); and A. Koyré, *From the Closed World to the Infinite Universe* (New York: Harper & Row, 1958).

a behavioral psychologist must often cite more remote conditions in framing laws. The phenomenon of "imprinting" provides an illustration.[4] Whenever, in the twenty-four hours following hatching, normal baby ducks are exposed to a moving decoy duck—one bearing only a vague resemblence to an adult duck— the ducklings proceed to follow the decoy. If such objects are first presented later than twenty-four hours after hatching, no such result occurs; imprinting can happen only within a strictly limited temporal period. Of interest here is that the imprinting stimulus comes to have prepotent effects during the subsequent life of the affected duck. During early adulthood, for example, it will choose a cardboard decoy as a sexual partner rather than an adult duck of the opposite sex. The causal conditions that explain the duck's later behavior are remote, not contiguous; and they exert an influence even in the face of more proximate antecedents. Whereas physiological laws incorporate contiguous antecedents and consequents, behavioral laws often incorporate no contiguous conditions. Yet both may genuinely be causal explanations that invoke causal laws, by Hume's own regularity account of causation. For reasons not unlike those presented through this example, Thomas Reid and Richard Taylor (but not their usual ally C. J. Ducasse) have contended that Hume's contiguity criterion is absurd and irrelevant to the analysis of causation.[5]

But are Hume's claims irrelevant and absurd in the light of such criticisms? We think not, for two reasons. First, quite apart from the important consideration that Hume's analysis is revisionary of the concept of causation, his requirement of contiguity need not entail the actual falsity of statements 1-3 above. Hume can consistently be understood as claiming that these statements are *true only if there exist interval-less causal chains* linking remote antecedents to their later consequents. On this reading, which is textually more plausible than any previously

4. E. H. Hess, "Imprinting," *Science* 130 (1959), pp. 133-41.
5. Cf. Taylor's representative statement in the first three chapters of *Action and Purpose* (Englewood Cliffs, N.J.: Prentice-Hall, 1966). For Ducasse's view, cf. *Causation and the Types of Necessity* (Seattle: University of Washington Press, 1924; New York: Dover Publications, 1969), pp. 43-50; *Nature, Mind, and Death* (La Salle, Ill.: Open Court, 1951), pp. 133-38; " 'Cause' and 'Condition,' " *Journal of Philosophy* 63 (1966), p. 239.

mentioned interpretation, Hume intends only to deny that there can be action at a distance through which there exists no causal chain; he does not deny remote causation *per se*. As we show in the next section, the natural science of his period and his self-styled appropriation of the Newtonian method together led Hume to this conclusion.

Hume merely holds that wherever there is causation there is contiguity, either immediately between cause and effect or mediately through links in a causal chain; causation never involves action at a distance. He gives many examples of causal relations that conform to this model. The following passage hardly admits of an alternative interpretation:

Two objects are connected together in the imagination, not only when the one is immediately resembling, contiguous to, or the cause of the other, but also when there is interposed betwixt them a third object, which bears to both of them any of these relations. This may be carried on to a great length; tho' at the same time we may observe, that each remove considerably weakens the relation. Cousins in the fourth degree are connected by *causation,* if I may be allowed to use that term; but not so closely as brothers, much less as child and parent. In general we may observe, that all the relations of blood depend upon cause and effect, and are esteemed near or remote, according to the number of connecting causes interpos'd betwixt the persons. (T, 11f; cf. T, 427ff)

Hume hesitates to use the term "causation" here because contiguity is not strictly required in order that causal statements about blood relatedness be true. But he allows such statements to be causal when it is recognized that there are "connecting causes." His point concerns not merely the imagination in its role as the faculty of causal judgment; it is a point about causation, as the last sentence makes clear. Hume states his position even more explicitly later in the *Treatise* when he turns specifically to the question of causal contiguity:

Tho' distant objects may sometimes seem productive of each other, they are commonly found upon examination to be link'd by a *chain of causes,* which are contiguous among themselves, and to the distant objects; and when in any particular instance we cannot discover this connexion, we still presume it to exist. We may therefore consider the relation of CONTIGUITY as essential to that of causation. (T, 75; italics added)

When Hume comes to his final discussion of causation in the *Treatise* ("Rules by which to judge of causes and effects"), he never argues that a noncontiguous "causal" condition is not a cause. Rather, he argues that it is "not the *sole* cause of that effect, but requires to be assisted by some other principle. . . . [When noncontiguous] these *causes* are not compleat ones" (T, 174, italics added). The same theme is reiterated in the first *Enquiry,* where Hume says the relation of cause and effect "is either near or remote, direct or collateral" (EHU, Sec. 22).

Second, statements such as 1–3 above are usually cited for purposes of causal *explanation*. But causal explanations that describe remote causes are perfectly compatible with an account of temporally and spatially contiguous links in a causal chain required for causation *per se*. Explanatory exigencies direct investigation to particular links or sets of links in a causal chain, and these may well be remote links. Protein deficiencies in childhood do indeed *explain* the occurrence of cirrhosis of the liver, but it is a dubious inference from this truth to the claim that what is *now causing* a person's cirrhosis is an earlier diet. The contemporary cause is the diffuse fibrosis destroying the normal lobular architecture of the liver tissue. It is when we want to know why *this* phenomenon is occurring that we begin to trace the sources (through a series of causal chains, if they can be reconstructed) back to a protein deficiency, and perhaps even beyond to the level of predictive medicine that studies the effect of the mother's dietary habits on the fetus. No one seriously thinks that there are periods without causal chain connections between fetal protein deficiencies and a much later condition of cirrhosis. Hume would certainly agree that causal laws may correctly report regular conjunctions between remote sets of events and may be useful for explanation; but he would not concede that there need be no interlocking causal chain each link of which can, in principle, similarly be explained. Indeed he would deny the legitimacy of an explanation that did not at least allow for such links. If this interpretation of Hume's view of causal chains is correct, then he is not subject to the criticisms offered above and is probably not even subject to the claim that his contiguity requirements are counterintuitive.

While Hume's commentators seem not to have noticed that the interpretation defended here is *textually* plausible, it has not gone unnoticed that the position is a *philosophically* tenable one. Ernest Nagel, for example, could scarcely be in closer agreement:

The event frequently picked out as the cause is normally an event that completes the set of sufficient conditions for the occurrence of the effect, and that is regarded for various reasons as being "important." . . . [But] the relation holds between events that are spatially contiguous, in the sense that the [cause and effect] occur in approximately the same spatial region. Accordingly, when events spatially remote from each other are alleged to be causally related, it is tacitly assumed that these events are but termini in a cause-and-effect chain of events, where the linking events are spatially contiguous. . . . [Also] the relation has a temporal character, in the sense that the event said to be the cause precedes the effect and is also "continuous" with the latter. In consequence, when events separated by a temporal interval are said to be causally related, they are also assumed to be connected by a series of temporally adjacent and causally related events. And finally, the relation is asymmetrical. . . .[6]

Nagel's appeal to causal chains helps tie Hume's temporal contiguity claim about events to the view that causal explanations of effects need not explicitly appeal to temporally contiguous events. The legitimacy of such explanations requires the existence of intervening events (known or not) between the explanans-conditions and the explananda-phenomena. We shall return to this problem later in the present chapter, again in Chapter 7, and for a final time in Chapter 8.

II

Let us turn now exclusively to Hume's views on *spatial* contiguity. Hume's insistence on contiguous spatial relations poses a threat to his empirical theories of language and knowledge, for this insistence leads him to deny that gravity or any other natural phenomenon can be understood in terms of causal action at a distance unless a connecting medium is postulated:

6. Ernest Nagel, *The Structure of Science* (New York: Harcourt, Brace & World, 1961), p. 74. See also his statement of a motivation similar to Hume's, p. 171. Hume's account of contiguity, succession, and causal chains is adopted virtually unaltered by A. J. Ayer, in *Probability and Evidence* (New York: Columbia University Press, 1972), esp. p. 135.

When we talk of gravity, we mean certain effects, without comprehending that active power. It was never the meaning of Sir ISAAC NEWTON to rob second causes of all force or energy; though some of his followers have endeavoured to establish that theory upon his authority. On the contrary, that great philosopher had recourse to an etherial active fluid to explain his universal attraction. . . . (EHU, Sec. 57n)

This passage betrays the regulative power of the belief in causal chains. No scientifically oriented philosopher in Hume's time wished either to return to earlier conceptions of occult forces from which science had been liberated by mechanical philosophies or to postulate an intuitively repugnant remote causation. Hume follows, apparently without reservations, what he takes to be Descartes's and Newton's requirement of contiguous causation. On this basis he declares the notion of noncontiguous causation scientifically unacceptable. Because he accepts Newton's view that the idea of action at a distance involves "so great an absurdity" that no "competent philosopher could ever believe it,"[7] he is disposed to agree that "an ethereal active fluid" or some other "second causes" must be assumed. Indeed the action-at-a-distance controversy was so prominent at the time that it should probably be regarded as the paradigm for Hume's postulation of "second causes." This postulation renders Hume epistemologically inconsistent, however, for he is insisting, without empirical warrant, that there *must* be connecting causes (continuous media), even if they cannot be observed. Theoretical constructs thus replace perceptual evidence in explaining observed planetary motions; but this explanation is no more empirically justified than the Cartesians' resort to the "sole efficacy of the Deity," which Hume delights in denouncing (EHU, Sec. 57n; T, 157-59).[8]

Were his empiricism given overriding significance, Hume should maintain that laws of gravitation express universal empirical regularities between distant objects. All assumptions

7. *Isaac Newton's Papers and Letters on Natural Philosophy*, ed. I. B. Cohen (Cambridge, Mass.: Harvard University Press, 1958), pp. 302f.
8. Indeed, Hume seems guilty of the *a priori* causal legislation for which he censures rationalists as well as of the "enquiry beyond the senses" he everywhere denounces. He does occasionally mention our "profound ignorance" in such matters (EHU, Sec. 57; T, 638f). But this again strikes him as good grounds for deriding Cartesianism.

concerning continuous media should be rejected. Belief in gravitation as a causal phenomenon commits him, as an empiricist, either to believe in noncontiguous causation or to suspend any commitment to contiguity other than as a regulative principle. On either alternative he must deny that spatial contiguity is an *essential* criterion of causal relatedness between extended objects. The same could be said of magnetic phenomena where cause and effect might be thought more "observable" than gravitational phenomena, even though the observed connection is not contiguous. Just as Berkeley was led by his empiricist principles to dismiss the concept of absolute space because it was unperceivable, so Hume should have dismissed the notion of an ethereal medium.[9]

While this rebuke is deserved and reflects an inconsistency in Hume's thought, it is not a telling criticism against his philosophy of causation. The objection rests on an assumption that Hume must be unyielding in the protection of his empiricist demand that for every idea there exists a corresponding impression. This assumption can easily be overemphasized in the philosophical assessment of Hume's work. Discerning critics have never regarded his primitive empiricist epistemology as an ideal to be protected at all costs, and his most important contribution to philosophy, the theory of causation, ought not to be tarred with the brush of his defective theories of knowledge and language. If Hume's empiricist strictures against theoretical entities are qualified or ignored, then he is left free to accept the existence of the ether or some other entity as a *theoretically justified* belief.

This line of defense is certainly not implausible, especially in light of later developments in mechanics. Historians of science have often maintained that the ultimate rejection of the ether theory led to the overthrow of the Newtonian notion of gravitation, in favor of Einstein's conception. The entire sequence of events thus supports Hume's rejection of action at a distance, as well as his commitment to the existence of causal chains underlying apparently noncontiguous causes. It is his insistence on the

9. Berkeley, *Principles of Human Knowledge*, Secs. 110–17. In *Siris*, Berkeley also rejects postulation of an ethereal medium for causal transmission as unproved and gratuitous. Cf. *Works* (London: Thomas Nelson and Sons, 1948), ed. A. A. Luce and T. E. Jessop, Vol. V, pp. 108–18.

latter point about the relations between causes and their effects that determines his unwillingness to accept explanations of gravitational phenomena dependent on the possibility of action at a distance. Here again, admissible causal explanations are governed by the character of the causal relation, and not vice versa.

III

As we have reconstructed his arguments, Hume's position can be paraphrased in the following way. Although we do cite spatially and temporally distant happenings as causes, and even as *the* cause, philosophical reflection reveals that we do not admit distant events to be solely sufficient for their effects. At least one contiguous standing condition can always be uncovered and shown to be causally relevant, though such conditions may not themselves be sufficient causes, if by "sufficient" is meant solely sufficient.

Two potentially important objections might be lodged against this position. First, the claim that a contiguous causal condition or event could always be uncovered may not be defensible in the light of quantum mechanical considerations, if quantum mechanics is understood as permitting noninstantaneous action at a distance where no energy exists in the space across which the action occurs. Indeed, Ernest Nagel, whom we earlier cited in defense of Hume's criterion of spatial and temporal contiguity, hints at a possible scientific need to dispense with the criterion:

It is even debatable whether the [spatial and temporal contiguity] conditions just mentioned are in fact fulfilled in alleged illustrations of this notion of cause . . . when the illustrations are analyzed in terms of modern physical theories. Nevertheless, however inadequate this notion of cause may be for the purposes of theoretical physics, it continues to play a role in many other branches of inquiry.[10]

It is always open to the Humean who believes in continuous media to insist that, at every level of inquiry, apparent action at a distance must ultimately be explicable in terms of "second causes" in an as yet unobserved medium. But, if Nagel's admission is taken seriously, then this Humean strategy is subject to a

10. Nagel, *op. cit.*, pp. 74f.

rebuttal having more or less the same force as the Humean gambit: a believer in noncontiguous causation can always reply that contiguous causation is merely apparent at present levels of inquiry and that research into the yet uncharted depths of quarks and antiquarks will reveal that these subtle elements and their aggregates conform to macroscopic models of action at a distance. Thus, there seems to be an empirically unresolvable, metaphysical stand-off.[11]

This quantum-mechanical problem was, of course, undreamed of in Hume's age. Like the quantum-mechanical considerations that seem to undermine Hume's regularity requirement, vast interpretative difficulties stand in the path of broaching these matters, and their presence leaves the Humean many options. One may, for instance, invite an opponent to explain why at a certain microphysical level a feature like contiguity, otherwise present in cases of causal relations, should cease to be. The admission that it is simply absent, and that this absence is fundamental and inexplicable, should raise the Humean question of how microphysical causal but noncontiguous relations invariably aggregate into spatiotemporally contiguous ones at the level of macroscopic objects.

The answers to these questions may ultimately satisfy the Humean that spatiotemporal contiguity is in fact not a fundamental feature of the causal relation "in the objects" alone, but rather depends on the perceptual faculties of creatures who observe causal relations only at macrophysical levels of aggregation. This outcome would be consistent with the way Hume analyzes causal necessity, for he makes an appeal not just to the objects of causation, but also to the observer's capacity for generating impressions of reflection. So analyzed, the requirement of spatiotemporal contiguity would continue to play a regulative role in causal inquiry, and would remain an essential feature of causal relations beyond the level of microphysics.

A second objection is that interpretative reliance on causal chains raises the well-known dilemma that a sufficient cause may be nothing less than the entire set of causal links pro-

11. We have borrowed much of this objection from Mary Hesse, *Forces and Fields* (London: Thomas Nelson and Sons, 1961), pp. 279–86, and "Action at a Distance and Field Theory," *The Encyclopedia of Philosophy*, Vol. I, p. 13.

ductive of its effect. This conclusion seems to many philosophers ridiculous, as each sufficient cause (or causal chain) potentially includes the entire sequence of events in the history of the universe. Yet we never regard such lengthy and complex chains as causes, however revisionary our analysis. If the requirement of contiguity leans heavily on the appeal to causal chains and if these chains lead backwards without end, requirements of contiguity preclude citation of *the* causes for any effects.

This objection, like others, fails to distinguish Hume's aims in analyzing causation *simpliciter* from the quite different objectives of those who analyze causal *explanation*. As we have previously noted, Hume is analyzing the causal relation, not the language of "cause" and not the structure of causal judgment. There exist many prudential, scientific, moral, legal, and historical reasons for citing as causes some particular links in causal chains, while excluding other links. Our purposes in doing so are usually those of explanation and accountability (the determination and ascription of responsibility). Such reasons, and their governing principles of selection, have been appropriately analyzed in the accounts of causation offered by Collingwood, Hart and Honoré, Gasking, Gorovitz, Hanson, and many others. But from the fact that we isolate in justifiable ways certain links or causal conditions, while excluding others, it would be an egregious *non sequitur* to infer that there are no other links. The need to account for these links is no doubt one of the main reasons Hume introduces the contiguity criterion.

The distinction between causes and conditions first emerged in the literature of causation in order to distinguish not only causally relevant conditions from causally irrelevant ones, but also to distinguish conditions that are *merely* causally relevant from *the* cause, where "the cause" judgments are determined by principles of explanation and accountability (including "the cause" judgments in history, "the cause" judgments in law, etc.). Even Collingwood, an ardent devotee of this method of analyzing causation, points out that our explanatory purposes determine which links in the chain of causal events can properly be cited, *except* where we have in mind the scientific or Humean "sense" of causation (as distinct from its practical senses). In this case Collingwood agrees that the connections are "tight" and nonrelative. He even argues that *actio in distans* is nonsense in this (Humean) sense of "cause" and that it is perfectly consistent to say that most of our causal *judgments* are governed by explanatory purposes while at the same time insisting that there exists a chain of contiguous causes.[12] This unexpected defense of Hume seems to us essentially correct.

Unfortunately not all of Hume's opponents are so agreeable as Collingwood. Norwood Hanson has developed a position that, if correct, would invalidate the account of causal chains underlying our defense of the contiguity criterion. We turn next to Hanson's arguments, for it is with them that the illicit assimilation of issues surrounding causation and contiguity to those involving causal explanation reaches its contemporary apogee. While we shall reserve a more extended discussion of causal explanation and its relation to causation *simpliciter* to Chapters 7 and 8, it is important to make clear at this juncture how the Humean views the general relation between these two matters.

IV

Hanson directly links Hume's epistemology to both the criterion of contiguity and the causal chain account.[13] He argues that Hume and his followers make major mistakes in conceiving of causes and effects as chains of sequential events and in requiring that cause and effect be logically distinct, individually describable items. Hanson argues that a close look at actual causal language reveals it to be "theory-loaded." His point is that the concepts used to identify an item as a cause or as an effect of a certain type tacitly incorporate semantic connections, which presume a background of theory, between any cause and effect items of that type. Hanson holds that, without background knowledge of the linkage, no request for an effect item would be intelligible.

Hanson points out that in statements such as "The scar on his arm was caused by a wound he received when thrown from

---

12. R. G. Collingwood, *An Essay on Metaphysics* (Oxford: Clarendon Press, 1940), pp. 304–7, 313f. A substantially similar point is made in Hume's spirit by C. J. Ducasse, in " 'Cause' and 'Condition,' " *op. cit.,* pp. 239f.

13. Norwood Hanson, *Patterns of Discovery* (Cambridge: Cambridge University Press, 1958), Chapter 3, "Causality." (Cf. also Hanson's earlier article, "Causal Chains," *Mind* 64, pp. 255ff.)

his carriage," an effect can be understood only in terms of its cause. "Wound" is an explanatory word, and "scar" denotes the explained item. To see something as a scar is already to diagnose it through at least an embryonic knowledge of pathology. The identification itself, says Hanson, commits one to a causal judgment. In other contexts these words might function differently; and in the present context other theory-loaded concepts might provide an explanation of the scar. Hanson proposes that there are as many *causes* of the scar as there are *explanations* of it. Which word is a cause-word and which an effect-word is determined by a specific context of explanation. "Causes certainly are connected with effects," says Hanson, "but this is because our theories connect them, not because the world is held together by cosmic glue."[14]

He ascribes to the chain analogy a pervasive influence affecting the central issues in the analysis of causality. Specifically, the analogy's alleged implications include the following: (1) it suggests that causal relations can be detected by "normal vision" independent of theory; (2) it gives singular sequential occurrences (to which causal chains exclusively apply) an unwarranted place among the topics of scientific inquiry; (3) it leads us to misunderstand the role of theories and theoretical notions in the detection of causes; (4) it fails to accommodate differences in "theoretical level" between a cause and its effect; and (5) it obscures a continuum of theoretical "richness" that moves from higher to lower levels in a causal hierarchy. We think that the notion of causal chains is innocent of these alleged crimes; but clearly the charges deserve careful examination.

Hanson first alleges that Humean causal chain explanations are unsatisfactory because they make causes out to be "visual data *simpliciter*": "The chain model encourages us to think that only normal vision is required to be able to see" a causal connection, while in fact causes and effects "are not simple, tangible links in the chain of sense experience. . . ."[15] Hanson nowhere substantiates this charge, and the question remains open whether there is such a connection between causal chaining and normal vision. Hanson's "normal vision" theme may reflect

14. *Ibid.*, pp. 54, 59.
15. *Ibid.*, p. 54.

oversimplified treatments of causation in terms of pairs of events, taken one pair at a time. But these interpretations are not committed to the chain analogy, nor is the chain analogy committed either to isolated pairs or to explication in terms of "normal vision." For example, in order to explain why an elastic gas-filled container expands on heating, one recounts a chain of events, one that includes items quite outside the reach of "normal vision" (molecules, in this case). Even if causal chain accounts were taken to imply that all causal connections are to be appreciated by an analogy with the connections displayed in paradigm cases of observable causal relations, such as the collision and recoil of billiard balls, Hanson's original charge would not follow.

Hanson wants to show that the alleged reliance of the chain analogy on the view that causes and effects are visible data is a defect. He thinks it obscures the fact that "what we refer to as 'causes' are theory-loaded from beginning to end. They are not simple, tangible links in the chain of sense experience, but rather details in an intricate pattern of concepts."[16] Literally taken, Hanson is saying that *events,* the relata of causal relations, are "theory-loaded" and that events are "details in an intricate pattern of concepts." He must mean that the *terms* in which a causal explanation is offered or the terms in which a causal relation is expressed are theory-loaded and are details in an intricate pattern of concepts. But if this interpretation of his account is correct, his larger argument fails. One can hold his conceptual theory without surrendering the view that causal relata fall into chain-like sequences that causal explanations describe. We shall return to this problem in Chapters 7 and 8.

Another of Hanson's charges is that chain-like accounts are suited only to singular occurrences, to what he calls fortuitous accidents. "The chain analogy," Hanson says, "is appropriate only where genuine causal connexions cannot be expressed." This is another *non sequitur.* Even if Hanson were correct in claiming that the analogy works only when there exists "a series of striking accidents," this contention would not entail that the causal chain model cannot express genuine causal relations and explanations. Accidents themselves are the results

16. *Ibid.,* p. 54.

of perfectly genuine causal connections and have equally genuine causal explanations, both for ordinary observers and for scientists. (Consider Hanson's own remarks about the work of Kepler, Boyle, Faraday, Röntgen, and Curie.)[17]

Hanson also charges that the causal chain analogy, partly because of its alleged reliance on visible data, obstructs us from appreciating the role of theories in the detection of causes: "Galileo can say what causes [the clock] to do what it does, because the blind Galileo has . . . a knowledge of horological theory. Though the apprentice has what Galileo lacks, normal vision, he cannot detect the cause of the clock's motion."[18] This charge is no more telling than the others. Whether theory would provide Galileo with an advantage in detecting every sort of cause is doubtful; but let us admit that his horological notions enable him to detect a cause not detectable by his apprentice. It hardly follows that Galileo's findings cannot be expressed in a chain-like account. Nor does it follow that if we express his findings in a chain-like account we shall be obstructed from appreciating the role of Galileo's theoretical insight in detecting the cause.

Hanson also complains that the chain analogy fails to accommodate the difference in "theoretical level" between a cause and its effect. Hanson says that causal connections can only be expressed in languages that are "many-leveled" in their explanatory power. But what is a "level" in this context? Suppose e_1 is on a different theoretical level from e_2, which e_1 causes. In turn e_2 may be a cause of e_3. Does this fact elevate e_2's theoretical status? If only two levels are allowed, does it follow that e_2 is on the same level as e_1, or that it is both on that level in one context and not in another? If the latter, then presumably Hanson would not reserve a higher, more exclusive status for e_1 except in contexts where it is the cause-event. Perhaps in his view there is a general hierarchy of levels to which events are assigned, with cause-events always assigned to a level higher than the effects to which they directly relate—the difference being that causes explain effects, but not the other way around. Alternatively, there may be such a hierarchy for all the types

17. *Ibid.*, pp. 59 and 190, n. 3.
18. *Ibid.*, p. 59.

of events within the scope of a given theory. As they stand, both of these suppositions seem consistent with the chain analogy.

Causal relata, Hanson supposes, are always hierarchically ordered: events on the causal level can only be described in a language theoretically richer than events at the effect level. Consider complex servomechanisms and feedback loops. These organic, electronic, or mechanical systems are composed of causes and effects that can satisfy Hanson's hierarchy requirement only on pain of contradiction. In such systems e_1 causes e_2, which causes e_3, where e_1 and e_3 are not the same event, but are identified and described in a language of identical theoretical richness. On Hanson's view e_3 is at once on the same theoretical level as e_1 and below it, a description that is plainly nonsensical. Consider a specific mechanical example, an account of the automatic control of a steam engine:

One of the oldest devices for automatic control is the governor . . . invented by Watt (1788). When the engine runs too fast [event e_1], balls [attached to the drive shaft] move outward [event e_2], and by doing so they tend to close the throttle [event e_3], thus slowing down the speed of the machine [event e_4]. And when the engine runs too slowly, the balls tend to open the throttle.[19]

The types of events in this example—e_1 . . . e_4, connected in a feedback loop—can be represented as linked in a causal chain. Such applications of the chain analogy suffice to counter Hanson's allegation that the chain model fails to accommodate the fact that there is always a decline in theoretical richness as we move along a causal series. There simply is no such fact. In our example there are genuine causal connections leading from e_1 to e_4. But temporal priority aside, there is no hierarchy in which e_1 is richer or higher than e_4. Theoretically e_1 is the same type of event as e_4; they both amount to changes in the rate of revolutions per minute of the drive shaft. Moreover, returning to an earlier point, the causal chain explanation of the self-regulation of the engine is not an explanation of a merely singular or fortuitous occurrence.

Hanson's charges against causal chains largely rest on their alleged connection with Hume's ideas/impressions empiricism.

19. Mario Bunge, *Causality* (Cambridge, Mass.: Harvard University Press, 1959), p. 154.

If our discussion in Section II is accepted, then Hanson's accusations could hardly be correct. In that section causal chains were cited, together with what Hume calls "second" and "secret" causes, in order to show how Hume's claims about contiguity can be separated from and preserved against objections that wed these claims to his strictly empiricist accounts of language and knowledge. By showing in this section that arguments such as Hanson's should give us no pause, we further support the spatial contiguity condition as Hume originally offered it.

We turn now from the spatial to the temporal contiguity criterion, which will lead directly to a consideration of Hume's succession criterion.

V

Hume commonly refers to causes and effects both as objects and as events,[20] but even when he uses the language of objects it is easy to interpret his referents as events. (Cf. Chapter 7 for a fuller discussion of events as the relata of causation.) Presumably such events take time and are divisible into earlier and later stages. As normally conceived, time is a continuous and not a discontinuous magnitude in which events occur. Because events take time, they have duration, do not occur merely instantaneously, and are infinitely divisible without termini unless there are discontinuous atomic causal units.[21] The question we must now consider is whether earlier segments of cause-events are either less productive of effects than later segments, or perhaps not parts of the cause at all. Are we to say that an event

20. Cf., e.g., EHU, Sec. 59: "When any natural object or event is presented, it is impossible . . . to discover . . . what event will result from it." In the *Treatise* Hume even speaks of "bodies, motions, or qualities" as causes (88). That he is indifferent to which terms are used is obvious from his mixing of categories in the same passage. For example: "[The mind must] imagine some event, which it ascribes to the object as its effect" (EHU, Sec. 25).

21. Hume does defend a doctrine of "indivisible parts" of space and time, though these arguments are weak and hard to understand. The temporal discontinuity thesis would now be almost universally rejected by philosophers; but, as Ducasse points out, their claims are *a priori* hypotheses, and one could assume (*a priori*) a discrete time series, as Hume apparently does (cf. T, 29–31; EHU, Sec. 125). See Ducasse's comment in *Causation and the Types of Necessity*, p. 45n. We shall eventually show that nothing of importance turns on these arguments.

is a real cause only if it exists in (and perhaps perishes in) the instant directly adjoined to the instant inaugurating the effects? If so, is the real cause itself divisible into earlier and later stages? If not, do we ever experience real causes?

Hume provides no direct answers to these questions. He does at one point say that "extended things" are contiguous *by degrees* and that this idea is one which "custom and reflection alone make us form" (T, 235). This remark is obscure. If Hume means to endorse a looser sense of contiguity, meaning more or less near by, he thereby weakens his position so severely that the only important matter is whether cause and effect are sufficiently proximate that the imagination is able to make a connection. This conclusion would be tantamount to jettisoning contiguity as a necessary condition of causation, for it would permit temporal gaps between a cause and its effect.

Let us suppose, however, that Hume means strictly what he elsewhere says and so accepts the strong rather than the weak sense of contiguity, viz. that there can be no interval between a cause and its effect. One reason sometimes proffered in support of this claim is that if cause and effect were not contiguous, some factor could intervene and prevent the effect, even though "the cause" had occurred. Cause and effect must, then, individually represent the latest and the earliest respective segments of two processes, segments that yet occur *at the same instant;* or, following the interpretation we have been developing, the two causally related events must at least be connected by a chain of events standing in this temporal relation. Presumably this conclusion is required because point-instants are not stretches of time but rather are the durationless, indivisible limits of time-stretches. Since the series of point-instants is dense, there exists an infinite number of instants between any two instants. Accordingly, in order to avoid the problem of temporal gaps, it must be maintained that, at a minimum, contiguous causes perish and their effects begin in the *same* instant. That is, the terminal instant and the commencement instant must be identical.[22]

---

22. This analysis of causation and time is explored, but not necessarily endorsed, by Bertrand Russell, "On the Notion of Cause," in *Mysticism and Logic* (New York: Doubleday, 1917), pp. 178–82; C. J. Ducasse, *Nature, Mind, and Death* (LaSalle, Illinois: Open Court, 1951), pp. 133ff; and W. Kneale, *Probability and Induction* (Oxford: Clarendon Press, 1949), pp. 62–64.

But if the Humean were to take this route, he would have to confront its damaging implications for the criteria of contiguity and succession. Some philosophers have argued on virtually identical grounds that causes and effects occur simultaneously— not successively, as Hume requires. These philosophers first point out that in the familiar example, a billiard ball does not move until the moment it is hit by another. They claim that nothing that happens prior to the moment of impact is in fact *the cause* of the effect, even if it is causally relevant; and they conclude that all causal relations must so be analyzed. This thesis is generally supported by the following line of thought, which we shall call the *Simultaneity Paradox*:

(1) An effect takes place only at the instant the final condition C_f of a jointly sufficient set of conditions occurs.

(2) If there is the slightest interval T between occurrence C_f and the effect, then there must be some other condition C_n still to take place after C_f (in which case C_f is not the final condition at all). Otherwise: (a) the effect would occur immediately upon the occurrence of C_f (in which case there is no intervening period T); (b) something might occur in the environment to prevent the effect during T (in which case C_f is not a causal condition).

(3) Therefore, cause and effect must be perfectly simultaneous.[23]

This argument makes it increasingly difficult to differentiate cause from effect. Suppose, for example, that what causes a downward hurtling beer stein to break is simply its final impact with the floor. If this latter event is the only one cited, and both the owner's inebriated and somnolent condition and the distance of the fall are ignored, we not only fail to adduce a relevant cause for purposes of explanation, we seem to achieve nothing beyond designating the effect itself (breakage on the floor). This conclusion is even clearer in cases such as cutting

---

23. The argument, as we have stated it, seems to be held by: Richard Taylor, "Causation," *Monist* 47 (1963), pp. 311–12; William H. Riker, "Causes and Events," *The Journal of Philosophy* 55 (March 1958), pp. 281–91; and Russell, *op. cit.* Unfortunately, Russell's analysis is complicated by the fact that he is operating with a definition of "cause and effect" that he rejects. The argument is carefully analyzed by Ducasse, *Causation and the Types of Necessity, op. cit.*, pp. 44ff.

cheese by moving a knife, where the terminal point of one event seems identical with the starting point of another.

Hume would certainly be dissatisfied with this example and with the above conclusion (3). To endorse such an argument would apparently be to contradict his claim that successiveness is a necessary condition of causal relatedness. Accordingly we must first understand Hume's argument for succession before we will be in a position to assess the paradox as an objection to the temporal contiguity requirement.

VI

What position is Hume defending with the argument that it is "absolutely necessary" that an effect succeed its cause (T, 75f)? He holds that *experience* "in most instances" confirms that temporal succession is a necessary condition of causation, and he provides a complex metaphysical argument in support of this claim. This argument does not directly establish the temporal precedence of causes. Rather, it is a nullifying argument pretending to show an absurdity in the supposition that effects are contemporaneous with causes:

> 'Tis an establish'd maxim both in natural and moral philosophy, that an object, which exists for any time in its full perfection without producing another, is not its sole cause; but is assisted by some other principle, which pushes it from its state of inactivity, and makes it exert that energy, of which it was secretly possest. Now if any cause may be perfectly co-temporary with its effect, 'tis certain, according to this maxim, that they must all of them be so; since any one of them, which retards its operation for a single moment, exerts not itself at that very individual time, in which it might have operated; and therefore is no proper cause. The consequence of this wou'd be no less than the destruction of that succession of causes, which we observe in the world. . . . For if one cause were co-temporary with its effect, and this effect with *its* effect, and so on, 'tis plain there wou'd be no such thing as succession, and all objects must be co-existent. (T, 76)

This argument is atypical of Hume, for it is both obscure and ill-arranged. It must be reconstructed and analyzed before any question of its merits can be broached.

The structure of the argument is that of a *reductio ad absurdum* purporting to prove that if it were possible for even

a single event to be both truly a cause and perfectly contemporaneous with its effect, then any cause that did not act con-
temporaneously with its effect would not be a proper or sole
cause, for any proper cause acts as soon as possible. The conclusion is that all causes, under such an assumption, would be
contemporaneous, which is absurd because all temporal succession would thereby be eliminated. The argument is divisible
into two stages, the second of which is dependent upon the
important conclusion reached in the first.

Stage One:

Consider first the idea of *imperfect contemporaneity* of cause and
effect. Here cause and effect overlap, the cause being partially prior in
time. According to this notion certain causes, at the peak of their
strength, exist for some duration unaccompanied by their alleged
effects. Some degree of succession is admitted, because effects occur later
than some phases of their causes. But, according to an established
maxim, such precedent objects are not *sole* causes. Indeed, they are
not causes *at all* unless assisted from their inactivity by some additional
causal condition or else aided by the removal of some retarding condition so that they act *at that particular time* on the effect and not
previously. Only then, when the effect is being produced, would they
become, properly speaking, causes. (All preceding conditions, if any,
are noncausal.) Hence, if causes are contemporaneous with their effects,
they are, *qua* causes, perfectly contemporaneous.

Stage Two:

Consider then the idea of *perfect contemporaneity*. Any object that is
properly a cause (following Stage One) exerts its causal influence only
at the instant when it is actually producing the effect; i.e., it brings its
effect into existence nonsuccessively. Accordingly, all events linked in a
whole causal chain are perfectly instantaneous, for all possibility of
succession has been cancelled by their perfect contemporaneity. This
conclusion is obviously absurd, since we observe the succession of causes
and effects.

While this two-stage outline clarifies Hume's argument, the
strategy behind the argument is still unclear. The argument is
a *reductio* best stated in the form of a dilemma where an Axiom
is presupposed:

Axiom ("Established Maxim"): Sole or proper causes act as
    soon as is possible.

Suppose C: "One or more causes are contemporaneous."

Then, either

    (A) Causes are perfectly contemporaneous with their effects.

or

    (B) Causes are not perfectly contemporaneous (and exist for some period during which they are unaccompanied by their effects).

If A,   then all causes and effects are contemporaneous and there is no succession, which is plainly absurd.

If B,   then the cause's duration unaccompanied by its effect is noncausal (and, if the cause is at full strength, would require assistance to become causal). This means it is a proper cause only when the effect is actually being produced, in which case it is perfectly contemporaneous and reduces to A.

Therefore, one must either accept the absurd conclusion of Hypothesis A or accept precisely the same absurdity by following B.

And therefore, not-C: It is not the case that some causes are contemporaneous. Hence, all causes are successively related to effects.

Hume supposedly proves the necessity of succession by assuming C (contemporaneity) and deducing the false statement A. Accordingly, he thinks it best to recognize the intrinsic absurdity of the very notion of contemporaneous causation and to exclude it as an element in the *idea* of causation.

The "established maxim" axiom is the locus of any remaining opacity in Hume's argument. This maxim leads him to conclude that sole or proper causes act to produce effects *as promptly as is possible in succession.* But what is the sense of "succession" in this argument? The term appears to be restricted quite rigidly in meaning; and the meaning involved renders the argument similar to the previously examined *contiguity* argument against temporally remote, noncontiguous causation. In both cases, if an apparent cause is retarded but acts later or remotely, then Hume claims its prior action is not, properly speaking, a cause of the effect-event. The reason is that there is some interval in the chain during which the cause is "retarded" from producing the effect (efficacy being contingent upon the addition or removal of other conditions). The term "succession" thus refers strictly to the *noncontemporaneity of events where there is interval-less contiguity between the events.* We shall hereafter refer to this relation of contiguity and succession between the events as "conjunction," for it is precisely the relation that Hume has in mind when he adds the element of invariability and uses the favored term "constant conjunction."

It is not surprising that in Hume's philosophy the notion of temporal succession entails that of temporal contiguity. The separate maxims cited in support of the criteria governing these notions are strikingly similar. The first maxim, supporting contiguity, says "nothing can operate in a time . . . which is ever so little remov'd from those of its existence" (T, 75). The second maxim, supporting succession, says that any cause "which retards its operation for a single moment, exerts not itself at that very individual time" (T, 76). Hume appends to the first the note that "whatever objects" are causes are not temporally removed, and he adds to the second that anything so retarded is not a "proper cause." The locutions "retarded for a single moment" and "ever so little removed" both indicate that there must not be an interval between a cause C and its effect E during which intervening conditions either could prevent E or could themselves serve as causes of E—hence denying the remote object any real causal efficacy. The presumption in each case is that a set of conditions is causally sufficient, and thus the cause of E, only if there is no temporal interval between that set and E.

This clarification of the meaning of the terms "contiguity" and "succession" nonetheless leaves our account deficient. The two terms are not *identical* in meaning, and their differences remain obscure. We must now return to the *Simultaneity Paradox* as an objection to Hume in order both to assess its power and to understand these differences in meaning.

VII

Bertrand Russell and Richard Taylor have exploited the *Simultaneity Paradox* to argue that causes cannot be temporally contiguous with their effects. Russell's argument, the more rigorous of the two, is stated in the following way:

No two instants are contiguous, since the time-series is compact; hence either the cause or the effect or both must . . . endure for a finite time. . . . But then we are faced with a dilemma: if the cause is a process involving change within itself, we shall require (if causality is universal) causal relations between its earlier and later parts; moreover, it would seem that only the later parts can be relevant to the effect. . . . Thus we shall be led to diminish the duration of the cause without limit, and however much we may diminish it, there will still remain an earlier part which might be altered without altering the effect, so that the true cause . . . will not have been reached. . . . [On the other hand, it cannot be accepted] that the cause, after existing placidly for some time, should suddenly explode into the effect, when it might just as well have done so at any earlier time, or have gone on unchanged without producing its effect. This dilemma, therefore, is fatal to the view that cause and effect can be contiguous in time.[24]

The moral Russell and others apparently draw is not that all causes and effects are contemporaneous. Rather, they maintain that Hume's criterion of contiguity and his two assumed axioms are so rigid that, when conjoined with normal assumptions about the continuity of time, they entail that all causes and effects are either contemporaneous or separated by a finite time-interval— the very possibilities that Hume denounces as absurd.

The *Simultaneity Paradox*, however, contains conceptual presuppositions rendering it innocuous as an argument against Hume. The term "instant" as it appears in the argument presumably means a durationless point or indivisible slice of time in which no event, however infinitesimally small, could occur. Instants in this sense cannot be said to be contiguous, as Russell correctly observes, because there is an infinity of instants between any two instants. This much of the argument is definitional, and may be accepted without reservation. But it follows neither that *events* do not take time (they do, by definition—just as instants do not), nor that events cannot be contiguous *at* an instant (they obviously can be), nor that any two events cannot be both contiguous and successive if the first begins at instant t_1 and ends at instant t_2, while the second begins at t_2.

24. Russell, *op. cit.*, pp. 184f. Cf. Taylor's argument by examples, *op. cit.*, esp. pp. 311f. Russell's argument continues to be influential. J. R. Lucas, for example, seeks to avoid Hume's account of contiguity in time on grounds of the "impossible paradoxes" demonstrated by Russell. "Causation," *Analytical Philosophy*, Second Series, ed. R. J. Butler (Oxford: Basil Blackwell, 1957), p. 38.

If this account of temporal conjunction is accepted, then the *Simultaneity Paradox* vanishes. The paradox can be resolved in the following way: Causes are events (as Russell rightly supposes), and events take time (by contrast with instants, which do not); the succession of causes and their effects in the time order occurs when the instant of the cause-event's termination is temporally *identical* with the instant of the effect-event's commencement. Cause and effect do occur at the same time in the sense of "at the same instant," and in this respect they are simultaneous; but they do not each occur in the same temporal interval, and in this respect they are nonsimultaneous.

While this line of argument seems sufficient to defeat the *Simultaneity Paradox,* as sketched in Section V above, it is not sufficient to defeat Russell's extended position. Russell goes on to argue that, because the duration of the "cause" can be diminished without limit (an early and alterable part remaining *ad infinitum*), neither the true cause nor the true contiguity relation is in principle reachable. But this argument has its own problems, including certain conceptual presuppositions that are fatal. Russell's view assumes that there are events (as when he speaks of "a process involving change within itself"); yet one consequence of his argument is a denial that events exist. Consider the following paraphrase of the argument, where "event" is substituted for "cause": "If the event involves changes within itself, we shall require (if time is universal and continuous) earlier and later parts of the events—parts that are themselves events. Since the later parts are needed to complete the events, yet are themselves infinitely divisible into earlier and later parts, there always will remain an earlier part required for the later part, and therefore events cannot in principle attain completion." On Russell's own grounds, then, the duration of an event is always diminishable so that an earlier part could be altered in such a fashion that the event could not be completed. It follows that we can never have true events, just as Russell thinks it follows that there are no contiguous cause-effect pairs—and, as part of the larger argument in his essay, that there are no causes.

As we note in Chapters 3 and 6, there may be quantum-mechanical grounds for denying that causes exist: sheer indeterminism will obliterate the distinction between causal sequences and accidental ones. But we cannot imagine what argument would show that there are no events with beginnings and endings. We again follow Hume: the *experience* of events in succession provides our primary grounds for rejecting this extended part of Russell's argument—though we would agree that if there are no events, then we have neither refuted Russell nor successfully defended Hume. The assumption that events exist seems to us minimal in the present connection; but it nevertheless is an obviously important assumption. If events are not infinitely incompletable, then neither are causes (being events), and Russell's argument fails.

Our position enables us to see not only the deficiencies of the *Simultaneity Paradox* but also why "temporal contiguity" and "temporal succession" are not identical in meaning in Hume's philosophy, even though they are broadly similar. In using the term "contiguous" and explicating its temporal meaning as "not in time ever so little removed," Hume means that two contiguously related events occur at the same instant in their respective last and first phases. The relation of temporal contiguity, then, is one kind of relation of identity—viz. overlaps of time, or partial simultaneity. This meaning is not shared by the term "succession." Hume denies that there can be "retardation for a single moment" and yet insists that the cause-event and the effect-event are not contemporaneous. This specification seems to entail that despite being contiguous in their respective last and first phases (a logically necessary condition of their being immediately successive, in Hume's sense, though not logically sufficient), the events take time, and one has a *"priority* in time" over the other. This difference in meaning resolves the problems mentioned at the end of Section VI.

While our interpretation does introduce a distinction between contiguity and succession not specifically mentioned in Hume's text, we do not know how to understand either his arguments or why he would think contiguity different from succession unless this distinction marks the difference. Moreover, the interpretation is consistent with Hume's language and his examples. In explicating contiguity he speaks of the cause and effect as having "touched" one another where "there was no interval betwixt them." In the same passage he says the "motion, which was the cause, is prior to the motion, which was the effect" (A, 12). Since motions are events that take time, Hume's choice of words conforms to our account of his meaning. But most importantly this construal of his theory renders his arguments impervious to the *Simultaneity Paradox*.

VIII

A surprising conclusion follows from our findings. Far from Hume's argument being thoroughly antagonistic to the *Simultaneity Paradox*, the two arguments share certain conclusions. Hume argues for two main theses: (a) a cause cannot be perfectly simultaneous ("co-temporary") with its effect; and (b) any temporal interval whatever between cause and effect is a delay that violates the established maxim(s). Thesis (a) requires event-nonsimultaneity and preserves temporal succession, while (b) states a thesis found in the *Simultaneity Paradox*.

Hume's contentions, however, are not paradoxical in the way those of the *Simultaneity Paradox* are, despite their shared thesis. Indeed Hume's criteria of contiguity and succession conform to many common views about causation. This feature of Hume's account is clearly expressed through an example and explanation offered by R. G. Collingwood:

If I set fire to one end of a time-fuse, and five minutes later the charge at its other end explodes, there is said to be a causal connexion between the first and second events, and a time-interval of five minutes between them. But this interval is occupied by the burning of the fuse at a determinate rate of feet per minute; and this process is a *conditio sine qua non* of the causal efficacy ascribed to the first event. That is to say, the connexion between the lighting of the fuse and the detonation of the charge is causal in the loose sense, not the tight [Humean] one. If in the proposition "*x* causes the explosion" we wish to use the word "cause" in the tight sense, *x* must be so defined as to include in itself every such *conditio sine qua non*. It must include the burning of the whole fuse; not its burning until "just before" that process reaches the detonator, for then there would still be an interval to be bridged, but its burning until the detonator is reached. Only then is the cause in sense III [Hume's sense] complete; and when it is complete it produces its effect, not afterwards (however soon afterwards) but then. Cause in sense III is simultaneous with its effect.

Similarly, it is coincident with its effect in space. The cause of the explosion is where the explosion is.[25]

25. Collingwood, *op cit.*, pp. 314f.

Collingwood oversteps his premises by arguing for simultaneity and coincidence in space. As we have seen, it makes a major difference how one analyzes *"when* the cause is complete." Otherwise the passage stands.

If our contentions throughout this chapter are correct, then Hume's insistence on the necessity of contiguity and succession in the causal relation seems unrefuted, and his arguments in favor of these claims undamaged. This conclusion further supports positions discussed in earlier chapters. Hume relies heavily on the description of causes and effects in purely spatiotemporal terms to substitute for the dramatic terms "necessity," "power," "force," "impact," "collision," etc. If the latter terms can be reduced to purely spatiotemporal ones, Hume's opposition to necessity theories and his reliance on the relation of constant conjunction are strengthened. We do not conclude, however, that every major problem connected with causal contiguity and succession has now been resolved. Hume's claims require the adoption of what he described as "established maxims of natural philosophy," maxims he never troubles to substantiate. Without them he cannot infer that no causes are simultaneous with their effects merely from the falsity of the claim that all causes are simultaneous with their effects. Furthermore, we may question Hume's argument that if all causes and effects were simultaneous there would be no succession at all. His argument has not excluded the possibility of the noncausal, temporal succession of events that indeterminism, for example, would allow.

Such problems raise the larger issue of how time order and causal order are related. These issues are especially important for Hume because so many philosophers have taken him to believe that causal priority or directionality is determined exclusively by temporal priority. If this received interpretation is correct, then Hume's principles preclude some types of simultaneous causation, and Hume is apparently committed to the independence of time and the temporal order from causation and the causal order. We think there are good reasons for rejecting this understanding of Hume. But since in the next chapter we treat exclusively the problem of the direction of causation, this interpretative issue can temporarily be postponed.

6

The Nature
of Causal Directionality

ONE FEATURE of causation upon which almost all philosophers have agreed is the asymmetrical character of the relation: if the singular causal claim "*a* causes *b*" is true, then it must be false that *b* causes *a*. Philosophers have not agreed, however, on what constitutes this directionality or asymmetry, or how it can be detected. Hume seems to have claimed that causal directionality consists wholly in the temporal priority of the cause to its effect. The last chapter examined the arguments he offered for this claim, and this chapter takes up a number of contemporary alternatives to his account.

These alternatives have been developed by Douglas Gasking, G. H. von Wright, J. A. Aronson, J. L. Mackie, and David Sanford. Their accounts of causal priority reflect a range of conceptions of causality widely different from Hume's. In assessing them we must consider whether they surmount problems that Hume's treatment of causal priority allegedly cannot overcome, and whether they solve other problems better than Hume's theory does. Accordingly, before turning to these recent accounts, we will present general criteria of adequacy for alternatives to Hume's temporal priority condition. We argue in the early and middle sections of this chapter that the several philosophical accounts we consider either fail to satisfy these criteria or give incorrect answers about particular cases of causal directionality. In the later sections we reexamine Hume's original account and advance a novel suggestion about its implications and defensibility.

I

What criteria of adequacy must any account of causal priority meet in order to qualify as a serious alternative to Hume's account? First, it deserves notice that asymmetry is generally supposed to be only one feature of the causal relation, though an essential one. Any account of causal priority should therefore describe one logically necessary condition for the truth of sentences of the form "*a* caused *b*." When conjoined to the other truth conditions, the result should be a set of conditions jointly sufficient for the truth of sentences of the form "*a* caused *b*." This first condition of the adequacy of any account of causal asymmetry suggests a second condition. The description of causal priority must be independent of the descriptions of other conditions in combination with which it provides jointly sufficient conditions. Otherwise, causal priority would be indistinguishable from the remaining features of the causal relation.

Suppose, however, that the necessary condition of causation that an account of asymmetry describes cannot be expressed without appeal to the notion of causation itself. That is, suppose asymmetry is so analyzed that it cannot obtain or cannot be established to obtain unless the causal relation also obtains or can be shown to obtain. In that case, the condition that causes be causally prior to their effects would involve a form of circularity depriving it of systematic import. If causal priority is a necessary (but not sufficient) component of causation, an account of its nature must be a proper *part* of an account of causation as a whole. But if this latter notion is in turn an ineliminable part of any account of causal priority, the analysis of such priority will be vitiated by circularity. These considerations suggest that any acceptable treatment of the nature of causal directionality must enumerate conditions of causation that are necessary but *not sufficient* for that relation's obtaining between two events. It must provide a necessary condition because it is to describe one among several components of the causal relation; it cannot provide a sufficient condition on pain of being uninformatively circular. In order to reflect the motivation of these complementary criteria of the adequacy of competing accounts, we shall refer to them respectively as the criteria of *necessary conditionality* and of *noncircularity*.

The criterion of noncircularity is potentially controversial.

Some philosophers argue that causation is not susceptible of a noncircular analysis. They suggest that causation is a relation among items not reducible to components that do not themselves presuppose an understanding of causation. In so doing, they openly admit that all accounts of the causal relation must ultimately be circular.[1] Because circularity in the characterization of a metaphysically controversial notion is often taken to be vicious enough to suggest the incoherence of the notion or to recommend its elimination, such philosophers must explain why the circle they acknowledge is virtuous. In the absence of such a demonstration, a reductive analysis that distinguishes the components of the causal relation and that satisfies criteria of necessary conditionality and noncircularity would certainly seem preferable. As we shall see, Hume clearly meets these two strictures, while others do not.

A third criterion must also be satisfied by any account of causal priority that competes with Hume's. Any real alternative to his claim that causal directionality is a reflection of temporal priority cannot simply repeat his criterion. Such an alternative should not be proscribed from making *any* mention of the temporal position of causes and effects; but if an account is to be contrasted with Hume's, it cannot appeal to relative position in time of the cause and effect as the *main* feature in which causal asymmetry consists. In short, an adequacy criterion for alternatives to Hume's treatment of causal asymmetry is that these accounts not entail that the temporal order of two causally connected events be a *logically sufficient* condition of their causal order.

These three criteria—necessary conditionality, noncircularity, and nontemporality—provide the framework for assessing theories of causal directionality that we shall employ in this chapter.

II

"The notion of causation is essentially connected with our manipulative techniques for producing results." So claim Douglas Gasking and G. H. von Wright, who in separate works offer

1. Michael Scriven argues for such a view in "Causation and Explanation," *Nous* 9 (1975), pp. 3–16, as does G. E. M. Anscombe, "Causality and Determination" in E. Sosa, ed., *Causation and Conditionals* (Oxford: Oxford University Press, 1975), pp. 63–81.

both a general analysis of causality and an account of causal directionality in terms of the notion of "bringing about one event by doing some action."[2] Consider, for example, the statement "Heat causes metal to glow."

> We have a general manipulative technique for making anything hot: we put it on a fire. . . . We find, too, that certain . . . things, such as bars of iron, when manipulated in this way do not only get hot, they also, after a while, start to glow. And we have no general manipulative technique for making things glow: the only way to make iron glow is to apply to it the general technique for making things hot. . . . We do not speak of making iron hot by making it glow, for we have no general manipulative technique for making things glow. And we say that the high temperature causes the glowing, not *vice versa*.[3]

Thus, given two events we suppose to be causally connected, the direction of the causal relation between them is determined by asymmetries in the manipulative techniques for bringing about events of the types in question. The one for which such techniques are present is the causally prior event; the one for which no technique seems available is the causally posterior event. But what is a "manipulative technique"? It is not helpful to answer that it is a method someone may use to bring about a state of affairs, event, or situation. This answer trades on the controversial expression "bring about," an expression whose clearest meaning is "cause to occur." The employment of such locutions runs the manipulability theory afoul of the noncircularity criterion, for the concept of manipulability and its surrogates are laden with causal notions. The reason is clear: a particular series of actions constitutes a manipulative technique only if there is more than an accidental connection between the actions and another distinct state of affairs.

Gasking's application of this notion is vitiated by still further

2. Douglas Gasking, "Causation and Recipes," *Mind* 54 (1955), pp. 479–87, as reprinted in Tom L. Beauchamp, ed., *Philosophical Problems of Causation* (Encino, Ca.: Dickenson, 1974), pp. 126–32; G. H. von Wright, *Explanation and Understanding* (Ithaca: Cornell University Press, 1971). Von Wright quotes Gasking's arguments at length, describing them as "the position most similar to mine which I have found in the literature."
3. Gasking, *op. cit.*, pp. 128f.

circularity. On his account, we have a manipulative technique for making things hot, but none for making them glow. How can Gasking respond to the claim that we do in fact have a manipulative technique for making things glow: the very same technique we use to make them hot? Plainly, he cannot reply by appealing to considerations of temporal asymmetry, for to do so would implicitly be to adopt Hume's criterion for causal priority. Indeed, the manipulative techniques for *making* iron hot (that is, *causing* it to become hot) is also, on considerations of transitivity, the cause of the iron's subsequently glowing. Therefore, if availability of manipulative techniques is to be a criterion for distinguishing causes from effects, it will have to be combined with a method for distinguishing subsequent from immediate effects in a single causal chain. But this latter method requires that we characterize nothing less than causal priority itself, and in a way that does not allow for the reintroduction of manipulative techniques. Our original problem of distinguishing cause from effect thus remains unsolved.

Gasking might reply that the technique for heating iron does not itself make it glow, because in other circumstances and with other materials the technique will result in heating without glowing. "We speak of making iron glow by making it hot, i.e., by applying to it the usual manipulative technique for making things hot, . . . which in this special case, also makes it glow."[4] Gasking's argument here suggests that a manipulative technique must be causally sufficient. One difficulty with this way of characterizing manipulative techniques is that manipulative techniques are never actually causally sufficient, and those that are necessary for their results are also necessary for the effects of these results. One general manipulative technique for making things hot is to place them in or near a fire, but doing so is clearly not sufficient for heating something. Between the item and the fire there might be any number of insulating materials or cooling apparatuses. In most circumstances such interfering factors will not obtain, but this admission is just a way of recognizing that the manipulative technique in question is at best causally sufficient in certain causally relevant circumstances themselves not analyzable in terms of manipula-

4. *Ibid.,* p. 129.

bility. Under those circumstances the technique is also causally sufficient for the glowing. On the other hand, putting a piece of iron near a fire is necessary neither for its becoming hot nor for its glowing. The upshot is that there seems no way either to characterize manipulative techniques or to associate them with the "right" relatum in the causal relation without violating our general stricture against circularity.

There remains still another respect in which Gasking's theory is vitiated by circularity. One traditional objection to manipulability analyses of causation and causal directionality has been the charge of anthropomorphism; these analyses have been said to tie causation too closely to human action. This allegation has at least two variants: first, it is claimed that the analysis precludes a causal relation between events for which no manipulative techniques are or could be available; and second, it is claimed that the analysis precludes causal relations independent of human actions of any kind. Gasking is sensitive to the first of these charges, and has offered a reply:

> a statement about the cause of something is very closely connected with a recipe for producing or preventing it. It is not exactly the same however. . . . Sometimes one wishes to make a theoretical point. And one can sometimes properly say of some particular happening, A, that it caused some other particular event B, even when no one could have produced A, by manipulation, as a means of producing B. . . . But when one can properly say this sort of thing it is always the case that people can produce events of the first sort as a means to producing events of the second sort. . . . We could come rather closer to the meaning of "A causes B" if we said: "Events of the B-sort can be produced by means of producing events of the A-sort."[5]

This position avoids a charge of anthropomorphism at the cost again of appealing covertly to a prior understanding of causation. Consider another of Gasking's examples. We can say that a rise in the mean sea-level was caused by the melting of the polar ice-cap, even though we cannot ourselves melt the ice-cap, because we can raise the water-level in a bucket by melting ice into it. (Gasking's paper was written before the greenhouse effect was envisaged.) Both the example and the analysis trade on our ability to sort events into similar classes

5. *Ibid.*

in order to extend the attribution of causal relationships from manipulable, producible events to events in those same causal classes that we cannot produce. On what basis can we generate the required classes? What general features of events permit us to sort them into classes of causally similar events? For example, what is it about the motion of one billiard ball toward another, the motion of one gas molecule toward another, and the motion of one meteor toward another, that enables us to group these three types of events into a class, and say that each causes the motion of the second object? Is it because we can cause one billiard ball to move by manipulating another? The answer, we suggest, is that these events are of the same sort because of causal relations and the general laws governing them. The criteria we require to sort events into the appropriate classes, thereby enabling us to make theoretical claims about causal relations that transcend our manipulative powers, are the *causal* similarities between events. Because by Gasking's own admission there are no manipulative techniques for producing many of the events in these classes, it follows that despite his precautions Gasking is ultimately committed to an account which is either anthropomorphic, in the first sense noted above, or uninformatively circular.

Gasking's account of causation is not, however, guilty of anthropomorphism in the second sense described above, for it links the truth of causal claims not to the existence of the human actions that constitute the exercise of manipulative techniques, but only to their possibility. Von Wright, whose views are otherwise similar to Gasking's, seems freely to plead guilty to anthropomorphism in this second sense. He writes: "I would maintain that we cannot understand causation, nor the distinction between nomic connections and accidental uniformities of nature, without resorting to ideas about doing things and intentionally interfering with the course of nature."[6] If von Wright is correct in this claim, and if the charges leveled here against the manipulability theory are borne out, then the only reasonable conclusion seems to be that we cannot understand the concept of causation at all. For we cannot explain "doing things" or "interfering with nature" unless we already have a grasp

6. Von Wright, *op. cit.*, pp. 65f.

of causation. Accordingly, we now turn to accounts of causal directionality that are independent of such notions.

III

According to a tradition in the analysis of causation at least as old as the one for which von Wright and Gasking argue, causation consists in the transference of a quantity from one object to another. One of its recent exponents, J. A. Aronson,[7] offers this doctrine as an alternative to the manipulability theory, which he too charges with anthropomorphism. The purpose of his account is to "justify the use of 'cause' in the theoretical sciences by supplying . . . nonanthropomorphic conditions for determining the direction of the cause-effect relation."[8] According to Aronson, causes may be distinguished from their effects by appeal to the fact that

Prior to the time of the occurrence of [the effect], the body that makes contact with the effect-object possesses a quantity (e.g. velocity, momentum, kinetic energy, heat, etc.) which is transferred to the effect object (when contact is made) and manifested as [the effect].[9]

Thus the direction of causation between two events is to be explicated by appeal to differences between distinct objects. Prior to the causal sequence one object has the quantity; subsequent to the causal sequence the other object manifests the quantity. The sequence is causal in part because the quantity manifested by one and then the other object has been transferred between them; and the direction of the transfer constitutes the direction of causation. The fact that this treatment seems to require that causal sequences involve changes in at least two distinct objects presents an immediate problem. It is unclear how the account applies to causal sequences involving only a single object, substance, or system. Thus prior states of a closed system or an undisturbed object such as a pendulum causally determine its subsequent states, even though this process does

---

7. J. A. Aronson, "On the Grammar of Cause," *Synthese* 22 (1971), pp. 414–30. Cf. also his "The Legacy of Hume's Analysis of Causation," *Studies in History and Philosophy of Science* 2 (1971), pp. 135–56.
8. Aronson, "On the Grammar of Cause," p. 414.
9. *Ibid.*, p. 422.

not involve the transfer of quantities between distinct objects.

But even in cases when distinct objects are in question, Aronson's analysis of causal directionality faces serious difficulties. One immediate issue is its apparent dependence on the time order of events in a causal sequence, a dependence so heavy as to suggest a possible violation of the nontemporality criterion imposed on any alternative to Hume's account. The transference doctrine determines the direction of causation by identifying the object that possesses a privileged quantity *earlier in time*. If the privileged quantity can itself be identified *only* as that quantity manifested first in time by the cause object and second in time by the effect object, the transference doctrine will transparently fail the nontemporality criterion; it will turn out to be more a version of Hume's theory than an alternative to it. This problem should be kept in view during the following examination of how the transference account deals with cases of allegedly simultaneous causation. These cases constitute the acid test of any alternative to Hume's view, for the latter apparently denies the possibility of simultaneous causation.

To put Aronson's account to this test, let us suppose that the quantities he describes can be transferred instantaneously and continuously. In cases of simultaneous causation, a quantity can presumably be transferred continually during the entire temporal interval occupied by the cause and the effect. To make the supposition more concrete, consider a simple gear system composed of two cog-gears, a and b, such that during an interval the turning of a causes the turning of b, although neither is connected to a motor. On Aronson's view, the motion of gear a is the cause of the motion of gear b, since a quantity, in this case kinetic energy, is being transferred from a to b. In this situation, however, it is logically impossible to determine that a is transferring kinetic energy to b (and not vice-versa) without presuming that a's motion is the *cause* of b's motion. And if, logically speaking, this presumption is identical to the claim on the basis of which the direction of transference is determined, then transference is superfluous to an account of the determination of causal priority.

Consider the two sentences:

(1) At t, gear a, which is perfectly enmeshed with gear b, is in motion.

(2) At t, gear a is transferring kinetic energy to gear b, with which it is perfectly enmeshed.

(1) describes the event we would consider the cause of b's motion. But (2) describes this same event: kinetic energy is a measure of the product of mass and velocity; if it is being transferred, it must be non-zero, and consequently the angular velocity of a must be non-zero as well, i.e., a must be in motion. That (1) describes the same event as (2) can be similarly shown. Indeed, given the definition of kinetic energy, (1) entails (2). If they describe events uniquely, they describe the same event. And if, *ex hypothesi*, (1) describes the cause of b's motion, so does (2). On the other hand, (2) is supposed to describe the condition (transference) in virtue of which one of two simultaneous causally connected events is the cause of the other. It turns out to do so only in the trivial sense that it redescribes the cause: the occurrence of the "transfer" is—so far as we can detect—nothing but the occurrence of the cause. But if these two events are identical, it is no easier to detect a transfer and its direction than it is to determine which of two simultaneous (or non-simultaneous) causally connected events is the cause and which the effect. Indeed, the theory's "application" requires that we already know which of a pair of events is the cause.

One reply is to suggest that if (1) describes the cause, then there *must* be some quantity besides kinetic energy transferred from a to b. Unfortunately, other physical quantities such as inertia and force similarly fail to clear the noncircularity hurdle. Moreover, the transfer of mechanical quantities from causes to effects is invariably associated with the transfer of other mechanical quantities from the effect to the cause. Consider again gears a and b. The concrete motion in which a participates causes the particular motion of b, and their joint motion involves a transfer of kinetic energy from a to b. But it also involves a transfer of another mechanical quantity from b to a. Because neither a nor b is attached to a motor, the motion of a during the interval t involves a continual reduction in its velocity throughout t, consequent on a's transfer of kinetic energy to b. Thus the motion of b, the effect, transfers a quantity of negative kinetic energy to a. How are we to distinguish which of these two quantities determines the cause and which its effect? What is it about positive kinetic energy that negative kinetic energy lacks, and that enables the direction of its transfer to determine the direction of causation? Nothing. So far as mechanical quantities are concerned, Aronson's criterion for causal asymmetry requires a prior partitioning of quantities into those whose transfer confers directionality and those whose transfer does not. But this partitioning, like Gasking's manipulability theory, presupposes a prior determination of the existence and direction of causal relations.

The transference doctrine apparently rests on a mistaken view about the relations between causal assertions and the attribution of transferable quantities. As the example of the mechanical concepts to which Aronson appeals makes clear, the attribution of transferable quantities is made possible by a scientific theory, one that systematizes and quantifies the interrelations between propositions describing physical relations antecedently determined to be causal. Having once decided what causal relations exist, we begin to hypothesize about the properties exemplified in causal relata that will explain the regularities they are supposed to manifest. The citation of transferable quantities enables us to bring apparently diverse causal relationships into the same class. It provides unified quantitative explanations of these relations, and it permits the identification of yet undiscovered causal connections. Thus, Newtonian mechanics enables us to systematize previously agreed upon causal relations. It does so by appealing to the transference of quantities that bring diverse causal relationships into the same class of interactions. But the direction of causation among members of this diverse class was known long before Newton's systematization.

To the extent that these determinations predate physical theory, Gasking correctly claims that judgments of causal priority in unobservable causes are dependent on judgments with respect to observable ones—judgments that do not conceptually turn on the transferability of specified quantities. But just as Gasking's claims about judgments of manipulability presuppose causal notions, so do Aronson's claims about judgments of transfer and directionality. We conclude, then, that Aronson's transferability arguments make no significant advance beyond the manipulability theory.

IV

Among writers on causation, J. L. Mackie has devoted the most sustained attention to the problem of causal directionality. He first broached the question in his influential "Causes and Conditions,"[10] where he considered whether causal priority can be analyzed through the notions of causal necessity and sufficiency. The largely negative findings of this paper are important in their own right, and we must review them before turning to his positive account of the nature of causal asymmetry.

In this early paper Mackie considers whether an event cited as the cause of another is causally necessary for the effect, causally sufficient for it, or neither. He concludes that events cited in singular causal judgments are insufficient but necessary components of a complex of conditions that obtained at the time the cause occurred, where the conditions comprising the complex are not themselves jointly *necessary* for the occurrence of the effect but are nevertheless *sufficient* for it. To denote cause-events on this account of causal conditionality, Mackie coins the acronym "inus condition"—an insufficient but necessary part of an unnecessary but sufficient condition. An example of Mackie's own description will make clear why cause events are the inus conditons of their effects. To assert that a particular short circuit caused a specific fire is not to suggest that the short circuit was by itself either necessary or sufficient for the fire; it could have been caused by arson, or prevented by a sprinkler system. But there was a complex of conditions present on the occasion in question such that together with the short circuit these conditions were sufficient for the fire; and yet without the short circuit they would not have been sufficient. Nor is it the case that these conditions and the short circuit together were necessary, for an altogether different complex of conditions would also have been sufficient for the fire. In other words, the claim that the short circuit caused the fire means that the cause was an inus condition of the fire.

The view that causes are the inus conditions of their effects is tantamount to the claim that they are necessary and sufficient

10. J. L. Mackie, "Causes and Conditions," *American Philosophical Quarterly* 2 (1965), pp. 245–64, as reprinted in Sosa, ed., *op. cit.*, pp. 15–38.

in the circumstances for their effects. Seen in the actual circumstances in which it occurs, the cause is all that is required to produce the effect, and is the only thing that could produce the effect. Mackie's analysis of causal priority presupposes this inus condition analysis. While this approach has considerable plausibility as an analysis of singular causal statements, inus conditionality cannot alone account for causal asymmetry, as Mackie himself later argues in "The Direction of Causation":

> To say *A* was . . . an *inus* condition of *B* is not to say that *B* was an *inus* condition of *A*. *This* asymmetry, however, cannot constitute the causal priority. . . . For if *A* is an *inus* condition of *B*, then, provided that there is some necessary and sufficient condition for *A* itself, *B* will *also* be an *inus* condition of *A*. Since [for instance] the short circuit was, given the circumstances, nonredundant [i.e., necessary] and also sufficient for the fire, the fire, together with these circumstances, formed a sufficient condition for the short circuit, and of this sufficient condition the fire was a nonredundant part. . . . Thus although the relation "is an *inus* condition of" is not symmetrical, an effect usually is in fact an *inus* condition of its cause. . . .[11]

Every event's effects, together with the circumstances in which the event takes place, are jointly sufficient for the occurrence of that event, and its effects are necessary for it as well. (Events having no causally sufficient conditions constitute an exception.) The symmetry of conditionality, and the fact that causes are necessary and sufficient (in the circumstances of their occurrence) for their effects, guarantee that effects are necessary and sufficient in the circumstances for their causes. These same considerations also imply that the only events without causally sufficient conditions are those having no effects at all. The question of causal directionality does not even arise for events of this kind. Mackie's conclusion is therefore too weak: an effect is not just usually an inus condition of its cause, it is invariably one.

In the later article, Mackie provides the following characterization of causal priority:

(I)   If *A* and *B* are causally connected in a direct line, then *B* is causally prior to *A* if there is a time at which *B* is fixed while

11. J. L. Mackie, "The Direction of Causation," *Philosophical Review* 75 (1966), p. 446.

A is not fixed otherwise than by its causal connection with *B*.[12]

The notion of fixity is characterized as follows:

(II) An event *E* is fixed at time *t* if, and only if, *either E* has occurred at or before *t*, *or* a sufficient cause of *E* has occurred at or before *t*.[13]

Mackie's analysis appears to differ from Hume's chiefly by finding causal directionality in fixity in time, not position in time. Presumably this difference allows for the simultaneous occurrence of events fixed at different times, as well as for the formal possibility of causes fixed before their effects even though occurring after them. Thus, fixity in time permits causal directionality in the absence of temporal priority, and even in spite of it. The notion of fixity is not otherwise specified by Mackie except in terms of condition (II) above, but the notion is evidently coined to reflect the intuitive conception that certain events are settled and unalterable at times when others are not. While this seems true of events in the past, and seems false for some events that will occur in the future, it may well be the case that there are future events that are no more open to alteration now than events in the past. For example, their occurrence might follow from already fixed past events in accordance with deterministic laws. Fixed events of this type could be causally prior to simultaneous or earlier events in a way that Hume does not allow. More will be said about problems with Mackie's notion of fixity in Section V below. As the analysis stands, however, (I) and (II) both run afoul of the adequacy criteria adduced at the beginning of this chapter, for the expression "sufficient cause" figures in (II), which itself gives the meaning of the key term in (I). The employment in (I) of the expression "causal connection," however, engenders no difficulty. It describes a symmetrical relation presumably analyzable in terms of *other* features that, together with causal priority, are sufficient for the relation of causation. We thus may understand "*x* and *y* are causally connected in a direct line" to mean "*x* is the cause of *y* or *y* the cause of *x*."

12. *Ibid.,* p. 457.
13. *Ibid.,* p. 459.

Can we, however, provide a substitute for "sufficient cause" in (II) that will preserve Mackie's intentions without violating our adequacy conditions? Presumably a sufficient cause is an event causally sufficient in the circumstances of its occurrence for the occurrence of another event. This notion of "causal sufficiency in the circumstances" itself describes a nonsymmetrical relation, and may be analyzed in terms of those general features of causation that are independent of the presumed asymmetry. Substituting "causally sufficient condition" for "sufficient cause" in (II) would thus render Mackie's analysis consistent with the requirement that an account of causal directionality not presuppose a prior account of causation in general. The question now to be asked is whether, so interpreted, (I) and (II) provide a sufficient condition for causal priority.

Let us apply this corrected analysis to a case of allegedly simultaneous causation—for example, Gasking's claim that an iron bar's being at a certain temperature is the cause of the bar's simultaneously glowing with a characteristic color. Call the former event x and the latter y. *Ex hypothesi, x and y are* causally connected in a direct line, and y occurs through its causal connection with x; that is, y's occurrence satisfies the requirement for being fixed by x, which is clearly sufficient (given the circumstances and relevant laws) for y's occurrence. Thus, (I) and (II) correctly certify the causal priority of x (the temperature) to y (the glowing). But notice that (I) and (II) also certify y as causally prior to x. Insofar as x is an inus condition of y, it follows that (in these circumstances, as governed by relevant laws) y's occurrence is a sufficient condition for the occurrence of x as well. The bar's being at a certain temperature at t is just as much fixed by its glowing as the glowing is fixed by the heat of the bar. The heating could not have occurred, given the laws of nature and the circumstances involved, otherwise than through its causal connection with glowing. To deny this is to deny that the heating was necessary in the circumstances for the glowing; and if causes are necessary in the circumstances for their effects, the latter conclusion cannot consistently be denied. In a case of apparent simultaneous causation, the relation that obtains between x and y can only be such that in the circumstances each event is fixed through the occurrence of the other.

The culprit in this untoward outcome for Mackie's proposal is our substitution of "condition causally sufficient in the circumstances" for his term "sufficient cause," coupled with the symmetry of necessary and sufficient conditionality. In Section VI we examine the consequences of dispensing with this latter assumption, but here we may consider the merits of our substitution in the former matter. Can it be that although glowing and heating are both sufficient for each other in the circumstances that obtained, the heating was also sufficient for the glowing in some stronger sense—for example, sufficient for it independently of some or all of the circumstances in which the two events occurred? We think not. The fact that the alleged cause in this case manifested the property of heating simply is not sufficient *simpliciter* for the occurrence of an event that manifests glowing. Accordingly, treating the expression "sufficient cause" as meaning "condition sufficient simpliciter for the effect" entails that the heating was not causally prior to the glowing, for it was not a sufficient cause of it.

Suppose now that by "sufficient cause" we should understand "that complex of conditions which, in the light of operative causal laws, was sufficient for the effect." On that reading the heating was certainly part of such a sufficient condition of the simultaneous but distinct event of the glowing. But, in a thoroughly deterministic world, the glowing is equally part of a sufficient condition for the heating. From the occurrence of the glowing, together with the occurrence of the actual circumstances and the same laws, the occurrence of the heating invariably follows. Accordingly, if we are to understand the notion of sufficient cause in this way, Mackie's account will be incompatible with at least some versions of determinism. However, the question of whether determinism reigns or not is distinct from the question of what causal directionality consists in, and our answer to the latter question should not preempt answers to the former. The claim that some events have no causes is a denial of determinism, but it is consistent with the further claim that some events do have causes. If these latter events have causes, then presumably their causes will be causally prior to them. An interpretation of "sufficient cause" that compels us to deny the consistency between these claims produces more difficulties than it solves. We must add to this consideration the fact that we cannot give a finitely long enumeration of the conditions, positive and negative, that are in fact sufficient *simpliciter* for an effect. Therefore, we cannot in a finite length of time establish the order of fixity among actual fixed events, and Mackie's account becomes in consequence inapplicable to actual cases. The irrelevance of his definition, so construed, is another reason for treating "sufficient cause" as "condition sufficient in the circumstances" instead of "causally sufficient *simpliciter*."

If we adopt the reading of sufficient cause argued for above, it is easy to show not only that Mackie's proposal cannot account for directionality in alleged cases of simultaneous causation, it cannot even explain the direction of causation between non-simultaneous events—except through appeal to temporal priority, and thereby in violation of another of our adequacy conditions. Suppose Jones consumes a fifth of gin at t_0, which results in the onset of drunkenness at t_1, which in turn causes an auto accident at t_2. How can we avoid the patently absurd claim that his accident at t_2 caused his drunkenness at or during t_1? We cannot do so by pointing out that the drunkenness at t_1 was fixed at t_0 by the drinking, while the auto accident at t_2 was not fixed at t_0. If the drinking fixed the drunkenness, it did so only because it was sufficient in the circumstances for the latter. On any other account of sufficiency it did not fix the drunkenness at all. If the drunkenness was sufficient for the accident in this same sense, then, in virtue of the transitivity of sufficiency, it follows that the accident was fixed at the same time as the drunkenness (t_0). Because the drunkenness at t_1 was not fixed otherwise than through its causal connection to the drinking at t_0 and because the drunkenness at t_1 and the accident at t_2 are causally connected in a direct line, it follows that the accident caused the drunkenness.

Of course, there were circumstances absent during the interval from t_0 to t_1, but present in the interval between t_1 and t_2. These circumstances were necessary for the occurrence of the accident at t_2, given the drunkenness at t_1, but were not part of the circumstances obtaining during the earlier interval and were not necessary for the drinking to result in the drunkenness. We can appeal to these interim states, conditions, and events to denominate the drunkenness the cause, and the accident the effect.

But in making such an appeal we are founding our judgment of causal priority not on the fixity in time of events, but rather on their temporal position with respect to other events. This solution is tantamount to embracing Hume's criterion, and so offers no alternative.

The upshot of these considerations is that Mackie's account fares poorly both with respect to hard cases involving simultaneous causation and with respect to easy and obvious ones. Mackie subsequently became disenchanted with his initial effort and developed a modified successor—though he cited quite different reasons for his dissatisfaction from those we have described. We shall now argue that his second alternative fares no better than its predecessor.

V

Mackie describes the account of causal directionality expounded in *The Cement of the Universe*[14] as substantially different from the one just considered, although he still claims to allow for the logical possibility of both simultaneous and backward causation. In this allowance he *seems* to be clearly at variance with Hume, who excludes both phenomena. Mackie's later account, unlike its predecessor, is offered within the context of a broad general theory of causation. Our assessment of it will therefore be complicated by the introduction of other issues which are integral to Mackie's second treatment of causal priority.

Before turning to the details of this analysis, two of its general features deserve comment. First, Mackie cheerfully allows that his treatment is incompatible with causal determinism:

if determinism does not hold, the concept of causal priority which I have tried to analyze will apply to the objects, but if determinism holds it will not. If you have too much causation, it destroys one of its own most characteristic features. . . . If total determinism holds . . . our present concept of causal priority will not be true of the real world.[15]

This admission has several startling ramifications. As noted above, the question of what constitutes causal asymmetry is

14. J. L. Mackie, *The Cement of the Universe* (Oxford: Clarendon Press, 1974), Chapter 7.
15. *Ibid.*, p. 191.

quite independent of the question of whether every event has a cause. The first question concerns the nature of the relation between paired events, provided they are causally connected. The second is a question about whether all, some, or no events have causes. Insofar as asymmetry is a necessary part of causality "in the objects," determinism would not merely, in Mackie's words, "destroy one of [causation's] most characteristic features." It would "destroy" causality altogether, in Mackie's account, as a relation between events. This conclusion is ironical if only in light of the fact that many opponents of the Humean conception of causality argue that the causal relation either logically can or actually does obtain in indeterministic circumstances, and that the Humean explanation is false just because it is deterministic.[16] Some commentators have found Mackie's admission so bizarre that it has alone been a sufficient reason for them to reject the account. (An alternative thus motivated is considered in the next section.)

There is a second remarkable feature of Mackie's analysis. Although he wishes to provide an account that will allow for the possibility of retrocausation, he insists that temporally backward causal directionality must "stop short of offering us means of bringing about the past."[17] Many philosophers have argued against Hume on grounds that backward causation is at least a conceptual possibility,[18] but Mackie's contention is unique in important respects. An opponent of the claim that the future can cause the past will be comfortable with a notion of causal directionality that licenses backward causation solely on the

---

16. Cf. for instance, G. E. M. Anscombe, *op. cit.*, and F. Dretske and A. Snyder, "Causal Irregularity," *Philosophy of Science* 39 (1972), pp. 69–71.

17. Mackie, *The Cement of the Universe*, p. 168.

18. For one philosopher who seems to argue in this way, see Lawrence Sklar, *Space, Time, and Spacetime* (Berkeley: University of California Press, 1974), pp. 375–78. Richard Taylor's arguments, analyzed previously in Chapter 5, make an overt appeal to simultaneous causation and the possibility of retrocausation. For a sustained argument in favor of the actuality of retrocausation, cf. John Earman, "An Attempt to Add a Little Direction to 'The Problem of the Direction of Time,'" *Philosophy of Science* 41 (1974), pp. 15–47. For a detailed refutation of Earman's arguments, cf. Adolf Grünbaum, "Is Preacceleration of Particles in Dirac's Electrodynamics a Case of Backwards Causation? The Myth of Retrocausation in Classical Electrodynamics," *Philosophy of Science* 43 (1976), pp. 165–201.

condition that it *not* provide a way of bringing about past events. Indeed, he might argue that such a restriction on retro-causation is tantamount to surrendering altogether the belief that there is causal directionality of any kind, either forward or backward in time. Suppose the same causal relation can obtain between x and y when x is earlier than y and when x is later than y. If a necessary component of that relation is causal asymmetry, then, whatever causal asymmetry consists in, it will be the same whether it operates forward or backward in time. Consequently, if causal asymmetry moving backward in time must stop short of *bringing about* past events, it must also stop short of bringing about (causing) future ones as well. And yet it is the ability of events to bring about other events that we explain by a causal asymmetry between them. If there is no such "production," "necessitation," or "determination" of one event by another to be explained, then there is no scope for causal asymmetry among causally connected events. On these grounds, there is no such thing as causal asymmetry.

Mackie thus seems implicitly committed to the gratuitousness (as well as the nonexistence) of causal priority—unless, of course, he can successfully argue that retrocausal directionality differs from other sorts of causal directionality. Such an argument would, of course, have to show that retrocausation is different in kind from temporally forward causation. But to do so would either be to beg the question or to change the subject, and Mackie gives no hint that he is changing the subject to a new kind of causation. (One alternative to this line of reasoning is simply to admit that Mackie's restriction on retrocausation is too strict, and that if his account of causal priority allows for the possibility of retrocausation, we *do* have a means of bringing about the past!)

As noted above, Mackie's analysis of causal priority is nested in a wider account of causation. He maintains that "the basic requirement for the judgment that x caused y" is "that x and y are individual events, and x is seen as necessary (and sufficient) in the circumstances for y." Given such a relation between events, x is causally prior to y if one of the following three conditions obtains:

(I) x was fixed at a time when y was unfixed;

(II) x was fixed only at the time of its occurrence, but y was fixed as soon as x occurred;

or (III) there is a causal chain linking x, y and some other event z, such that x is between y and z, and z was not fixed until the occurrence of x.

Fixity is not explicitly defined, but it seems reasonable to assume that an event is fixed if it satisfies the characterization of fixity given in Mackie's first account: an event is fixed at time t, if it or its sufficient cause has occurred at or before time t.[19] This account rests on an analysis of causation in terms of conditions necessary-in-the-circumstances, an analysis Mackie expounds and defends in detail. The chief problem faced by a necessity-in-the-circumstances theory of causation is that of causal overdetermination. What are we to say when an event occurs for which there was no single necessary condition, because each of several events might have been necessary (and sufficient) in the circumstances for the effect, had not the others been present? Consider Mackie's example of a man who sets out across the desert with a canteen that, unbeknownst to him, contains poisoned water. The canteen has also been punctured, and its entire contents leak out before the opportunity for a first drink. The cause of death in this case was the puncturing, for the death resulted from thirst rather than from poisoning. Yet the puncturing was apparently not necessary in the circumstances for the death. Mackie convincingly solves this puzzle by noting that "what we accept as causing each result, though not necessary in the circumstances for that result described in some broad way, was necessary in the circumstances for the result *as it came about*."[20] Because the death was a death from thirst, the poisoning of the water was neither necessary nor sufficient in the circumstances for the death *as it came about* (though it might have been for an event that could have occurred at exactly the same time and place as the actual death).

Unfortunately, these same considerations make the effect, *as it came about*, equally necessary in the circumstances for its cause. Consider the counterfactuals Mackie uses to substantiate his claims about causal necessity: "if in these circumstances x had not occurred, then y would not have occurred either" means that in all possible worlds in which the same circumstances obtain and in which the same laws of nature are included, if x does

19. Mackie, *The Cement of the Universe*, p. 190.
20. *Ibid.*, p. 46.

not occur, neither does y.[21] Now substitute the traveler's death
(as it actually came about) for x, and substitute for y the puncturing of the canteen. These substitutions result in the true
counterfactual claim that in every relevantly similar possible
world in which the same circumstances obtained, had the death
(as it actually occurred—a death by thirst) not occurred, then the
puncturing would not have occurred. This counterfactual is
true provided the laws relating the puncturing and the death
are deterministic, in the sense that the puncturing and the circumstances jointly lead and can only lead to the death by
thirst. This proviso is one Mackie must accept, since he wants
to say that the puncturing caused, and was therefore causally
prior to, the death. To make this assertion he must assume the
puncturing to be fixed before the death and sufficient in the circumstances for its occurrence. If this counterfactual is sustainable, it follows that the death, as it came about, was necessary
in the circumstances for its cause, the puncturing. Mackie's
commitment to a necessity-in-the-circumstances analysis of causation thus commits him to the necessity-in-the-circumstances of
effects for their causes.

This commitment is acceptable, as far as we are concerned,
but it is incompatible with Mackie's account of causal priority,
as the following case illustrates: At time t_1, event a causes event
b to occur at t_2 and c to occur at t_3. An account of causal
priority must show that the direction of causation
between the three events moves only from a to b
and a to c, but not in any other way. Mackie's account meets the first part of this condition, since a
was fixed at a time prior to the times at which b and
c were fixed. But it also permits us to make the *ex
hypothesi* false claim that b is causally prior to c for
the very same reasons a is causally prior. Both a and b occurred,
and a was necessary in the circumstances for b, *as it occurred*. It
follows that b was necessary, given these same circumstances,
for the occurrence of a. Now, b is assumed to have been fixed
at t_2, prior to the time t_3, at which c was fixed. Therefore, if
necessity in the circumstances is a transitive relation, and if b
is causally necessary for a, then b bears exactly the same relation

t_1 a
t_2 b
t_3 c

21. *Ibid.* See Chapter 2, esp. p. 53.

to c that a does. But if a is causally prior to c, then b is causally prior to c as well.

This unfortunate outcome follows directly from Mackie's analysis, because he is explicitly committed to the transitivity of necessity in the circumstances. He introduces transitivity in order to show that the necessity-in-the-circumstances view can explain causal judgments in a variety of explanatory contexts: common sense, the law, and continuing processes characterized by functional laws. In the former two contexts he claims that we trace causal chains back from effects through intermediate causes to a deliberate human act, in order to attribute responsibility for the effect to a particular human agent.[22] Additionally, while discussing "functional laws" Mackie notes that a continuing process (e.g., the rotation of a top) is causally explained by its connection with prior phases, each of which is necessary in the circumstances for its successor.[23] In all three of these contexts our causal claims rest on inferences of the following form:

x causes y

y causes z

Therefore x causes z.

And, given the contention that x causes y means x is necessary in the circumstances for y, the following sort of inference must be countenanced:

x is necessary in the circumstances for y

y is necessary in the circumstances for z

Therefore x is necessary in the circumstances for z.

Mackie is thus committed to the transitivity of necessity in the circumstances. To surrender it would appear minimally to require a new explanation of the consistency of his theory with common sense and legal causal claims, as well as with those about continuing processes. Nevertheless, Mackie must surrender transitivity, for, on his counterfactual account of necessity, the arguments he adduces for it are invalid.

22. *Ibid.*, p. 119.
23. *Ibid.*, p. 157.

It was noted above that Mackie understands "necessity-in-the-circumstances" in terms of counterfactuals of the form "If x had not occurred, then y would not have occurred either." One natural way of expressing this proposition in modal terms is as follows:

$$\sim x \square \to \sim y$$
$$\sim y \square \to \sim z$$
Therefore $\sim x \square \to \sim z$.

However, as both David Lewis[24] and Robert Stalnaker[25] have shown, inferences of this form are fallacious.[26] In consequence, unless Mackie can present a general treatment of counterfactuals that preserves transitivity, he may be forced to surrender either the counterfactuals in terms of which necessity-in-the-circumstances is defined or the explication of common sense, legal, and process causal language by means of necessity-in-the-circumstances. Or, more drastically, he may have to surrender the necessity-in-the-circumstances view altogether.

Independent of whether this inference form is generally fallacious, the same counterexample to Mackie's treatment of causal directionality could still be produced. The argument on behalf of the counterexample would simply proceed without imputing to Mackie any commitment to the transitivity of necessity-in-the-circumstances. As Lewis shows,[27] arguments of a form close to that of the transitivity thesis are valid. In particular, the following form of argument is valid:

---

24. David Lewis, *Counterfactuals* (Cambridge, Mass.: Harvard University Press, 1973).
25. Robert Stalnaker, "A Theory of Conditionals," in N. Rescher, ed., *Studies in Logical Theory* (Oxford: Basil Blackwell, 1968).
26. Lewis offers the following counterexample to transitivity:

> If Otto had gone to the party, then Anna would have gone.
> If Anna had gone, then Waldo would have gone.
> If Otto had gone, then Waldo would have gone.
> The fact is that Otto is Waldo's successful rival for Anna's affections. Waldo still tags around after Anna, but never runs the risk of meeting Otto. Otto was locked up at the time of the party, so that his going to it was a far-fetched supposition; but Anna almost did go. Then the premises are true and the conclusion is false.

The fallacy of transitivity is treated on pp. 32ff in his *Counterfactuals*.
27. Lewis, *op. cit.*, p. 33.

$$\sim x \square \rightarrow \sim y$$
$$\sim y \square \rightarrow \sim x$$
$$\underline{\sim y \square \rightarrow \sim z}$$

$$\sim x \square \rightarrow \sim z.$$

This scheme simply reproduces the transitivity argument with the addition of a premise strengthening the relation between x and y. But the events b, a, and c of the above box-diagram illustration satisfy, *ex hypothesi*, the three premise-schemata of this inference, and thereby support the false conclusion that b is causally prior to c.

Still worse for Mackie, the stock of counterexamples is not exhausted here. Consider the following problem. Because the account in question is supposed to be independent of temporal priority, it should be able to account for directionality in cases of allegedly simultaneous causation. But imagine a causal chain of three simultaneous events, a, b, c, such that a is fixed before its occurrence but fixes b only at their joint occurrence, and b fixes c at that time as well. If c and its cause b are fixed simultaneously, and the cause, b, is necessary in the circumstances for the effect, c, then the effect, c (*as it came about, remember*), must bear the same relation to the cause b. Because in this case b was not fixed prior to the occurrence of c, the effect of a simultaneously occurring cause is, on Mackie's analysis, causally prior to that cause. This conclusion demonstrates that Mackie's analysis cannot account for the directionality of simultaneous causation at any but the simplest level of complication.

Mackie's revised analysis of directionality thus seems to accommodate difficult cases no better than his first attempt. It is burdened with highly counterintuitive features of its own, and its central position in his larger analysis of causality as a whole renders that analysis problematic at best. It also deserves note that Mackie's account may yet fail our adequacy criterion in its potentially question-begging employment of the concept of "fixity." What is it about one event's being fixed before the time at which another is fixed that makes the first the cause and the second the effect? It cannot simply be the temporal priority of the first. Nor can differences in fixity merely reflect differences in our abilities to prevent or interfere with some events (the unfixed ones) and not others. If fixity reduces to this basis, it suffers the fate of Gasking's and von Wright's accounts. And if causal priority is supposed to rest on the notion that, once fixed, an event transfers its fixity to its effect, which thus becomes fixed, then fixity is open to the objections that bedevil Aronson's treatment of cause.

Perhaps we can legitimately treat "fixity" as an undefined primitive term. After all, an account of causal priority must begin somewhere, and "fixity" may seem as good a place as any to begin. The best response to this line of defense (which amounts to an abdication of the quest for causal directionality) is to point out that we might just as well treat "causal priority" as a primitive, and be done with the whole issue. Since in any case Mackie evidently does not treat fixity as an unanalyzable primitive, it seems incumbent on him to offer some explanation of the nature of fixity and to explain why it makes for causal asymmetry.

Many of the criticisms and counterexamples offered in this section have turned on the relations between the concepts of necessary condition and sufficient condition. It has occasionally been noted that if these conditions were not symmetrical, our arguments against Mackie would be forestalled and our counterexamples undercut. Perhaps an account of causal priority that avoided these assumptions about the nature of conditionship would stand a better chance of success.[28] We turn to such an account in the next section.

28. Mackie seems to agree with this suggestion. In "Mind, Brain, and Causation," *Mid-west Studies in Philosophy* 4 (1979), pp. 19–29, he seems to despair of providing an account of causal directionality in terms of symmetrical notions of conditionship, for reasons similar to those canvassed in these last two sections. He notes that David Sanford's account, to be discussed in the section that follows, has convinced him of the possibility of an analysis of causal priority that makes use stipulatively of nonsymmetrical notions of conditionship. But he neither embraces Sanford's account nor provides one of his own in this paper. Rather, he opts for an explanation of our convictions about the direction of causation, in particular cases, that hinges on the counterfactuals that we are willing to embrace. Mackie recognizes that he "cannot offer [his counterfactual account] also as a factual analysis, as an answer to the ontological question about causal asymmetry." For he writes: "I deny that counterfactual conditionals with unfulfilled antecedents . . . can be simply and straightforwardly true" (p. 26). This denial is of course a reflection of his account of such counterfactuals, which we endorses in Chapter 4.

In the 1980 "Preface to the Paperback Edition" of *The Cement of the Uni-*

VI

David Sanford finds Mackie's accounts of causal priority inviting, but rejects them because of their incompatibility with determinism: "Mackie himself draws a consequence from his account which I cannot swallow. . . . I do not believe that total determinism is incompatible with the existence of causal priority."[29] Sanford rightly traces this spurious incompatibility thesis to Mackie's notion of fixity. Yet, Sanford suggests, "perhaps we can keep the advantages of Mackie's account and reduce its disadvantages by finding a replacement" for the notion of fixity.[30] His substitute for fixity is in effect an account of causal conditionality that does not entail the symmetricality of the causal relation.

According to Sanford, x is causally prior to y if and only if

C. (C1) x and y are causally connected in a direct line, and
    (C2) x is a causal condition of y, but y is not a causal condition of x,
or D. x is causally between y and some event that causes x, or y is causally between x and some event that y causes.

Sanford recognizes at least some of the strictures on acceptable accounts of causal directionality that have been employed in this chapter. To begin, he renders (C1), the condition of direct causal connection, as the stipulation that x causes y or y causes x. But he notes that this disjunction "cannot itself be regarded as an adequate partial analysis of causation to be completed by an account of causal priority. Such an adequate partial analysis must give us a way of determining that the disjunction is true without first determining which disjunct is true. The determination of which disjunct is true is left to the account of causal

verse, Mackie refers to this article and notes that "the objective asymmetry is, I admit, obscure and elusive" (p. ix). He "concedes" that "the positive account" offered in his book "is not altogether satisfactory" and that "the analysis actually offered on page 190 will not do" (pp. xiii-xiv).

29. David Sanford, "The Direction of Causation and the Direction of Conditionship," *Journal of Philosophy* 73 (1976), p. 196.

30. *Ibid.*, pp. 196–97.

priority, which thus completes the partial analysis."[31] In effect, this contention commits Sanford to the requirement that an account of causal asymmetry not presuppose an account of causality as a whole, and that the account of asymmetry describe one necessary condition of the causal relation. Similarly, he says of disjunct D that "regress or circularity can be avoided here if the causal priority of the other event to X or of Y to the other event obtains in virtue of satisfying clause C. And, even if such a causal priority obtains in virtue of satisfying clause D, vicious regress is avoided so long as the regress ends . . . with a causal priority that satisfies clause C."[32]

Sanford's departure consists principally in his new account of necessary and sufficient conditions. On the conventional philosophical treatment of necessary and sufficient conditionality, these relations are *symmetrical* with one another: x is a necessary condition of y if and only if y is a sufficient condition of x. By redescribing conditionship so as not to sanction this symmetry, Sanford hopes to show that causes satisfy certain conditionship requirements that effects do not, and that causal asymmetry rests in this difference.

As Sanford explains conditionship, to say that x is a causal condition of y and that y is not a causal condition of x is to say that there are "admissible circumstances"[33] in which everything causally necessary for x is causally necessary for y, but at least one thing causally necessary for y is not causally necessary for x. Sanford analyzes causal necessity by invoking a notion of logical necessity and appealing to laws. This strategy can be given a quasi-symbolic form: if x and y state the occurrence of events, z describes a state, condition, or other event (whose nonoccurrence can be expressed as "$\sim z$"), d_i is a law, and c_i is a statement of background conditions, then the event x describes is a causally necessary condition of y if and only if there are admissible circumstances in which:

31. *Ibid.*, p. 195.
32. *Ibid.*, p. 196.
33. Sanford leaves the notion of "admissible circumstances" unexplained, though he offers illustrations of these circumstances. These conditions reflect what we believe the laws of nature to be. Thus, for example, he claims that it is beyond the range of the "admissible," for the presence of higher forms of life to be a condition of the presence of oxygen, whereas the reverse is within the range of admissible conditions.

(z) [(logically impossible that $(x \cdot \sim z \cdot d_i \cdot c_i)$) → (logically impossible that $(y \cdot \sim z \cdot d_j \cdot c_j)$)]

and

($\exists z$) [((logically impossible that $(y \cdot \sim z \cdot d_j \cdot c_j)$) and (logically possible that $(x \cdot \sim z \cdot d_i \cdot c_i)$)]

The laws—d_i, d_j—are in Sanford's words "modal differentiators" that turn statements of causal impossibility into statements of logical impossibility. He writes, "It is natural to assume that causal laws are the appropriate modal differentiators, and here I shall neither question this assumption nor attempt to say what makes a causal law a causal law."[34]

Sanford tests his analysis by considering the common belief that a pendulum's having a certain length is causally prior to its having a given period, even though it possesses both simultaneously:

A pendulum's having a certain length is a causally necessary and sufficient condition, in the circumstances, of its having a certain period. Everything necessary in the circumstances for its having that length is necessary in the same circumstances for its having that period. But something necessary in the circumstances for its having that period, for example, the amount of gravitational force acting upon it, is not necessary in any admissible circumstances for its having that length. So its having a certain period is not a causal condition of its having a certain length. The length is thus causally prior to the period. . . .[35]

Sanford explains why the length is prior to the period by citing the fact that gravity satisfies the existential quantification in the second part of the definition. In particular, while there are natural laws making it impossible for the pendulum to have a certain period in the absence of a certain force of gravity (given the other circumstances), there are no such laws making it impossible for the pendulum to have a certain amount of length in the absence of a certain force of gravity (given the other circumstances).

Sanford's illustration is mildly marred by the falsity of this latter contention. Given the other circumstances, gravitational force does have an effect on the length of the pendulum. In the

34. Sanford, *op. cit.*, p. 200.
35. *Ibid.*, p. 206.

case of strings of the same material composition, their lengths will vary directly with their elasticities and the force of gravity. For a given elasticity, diameter, and mass, the length of a string is a function of the gravitational force acting upon it. In virtue of this law, gravitational force is necessary for the length of the pendulum in the actual, and therefore admissible, circumstances.[36] However, this deficiency is but the failure of an example, albeit a central one to the issue of causal directionality. More seriously, the analysis of causal priority Sanford offers suffers from the same defect as Mackie's account—the very defect that led Sanford to reject Mackie's treatment in the first place. As noted above, Sanford believes that his theory of causal priority manifests all the advantages of Mackie's account, without the disadvantage of being incompatible with total determinism. If certain sorts of determinism hold, however, then Sanford's own characterization of causal priority can be shown to be as incompatible with determinism as the account for which it is a replacement.

Consider a wholly deterministic world in which every event is a member of a single causal chain, such that it is fixed (predictively and retrodictively) by both its causes and its effects: for instance, an endless lineup of dominoes, each falling and causing its successor to fall. The laws governing this world dictate that, given the circumstances in which each event occurs, it can have but one outcome and one cause. Thus, each event is causally prior to the event directly after it in its chain, and causally posterior to the event before it. (It goes without saying that the events in question are causally connected in a direct line.) Given the occurrence of an event e_1, the fall of a domino, the laws governing its occurrence, d, and the background circumstances c, the occurrence of its cause, e_0 (the fall of the previous domino), can be retrodicted, and the occurrence of its effect, e_2 (the fall of the next domino), can be predicted. This situation will support the following statements of logical impossibility:

$$\text{logically impossible } (e_1 \ \& \sim e_2 \ \& \ d \ \& \ c)$$
$$\text{logically impossible } (e_2 \ \& \sim e_1 \ \& \ d \ \& \ c)$$

36. This difficulty shows how judgments of admissibility turn on acquaintance with causal laws. Because Sanford overlooked one of these laws, he made an erroneous judgment of admissibility.

The first of these, on Sanford's view, expresses the fact that the cause, e_1, is necessary for its effect, e_2. The second asserts that the effect is necessary for the cause. If Sanford's account of causal priority is correct, there must be something necessary for the effect that is not necessary for the cause. What can this be? The only things necessary for the effect, given circumstances c, are e_1, the cause, and the effect itself. We here assume the reflexivity of necessity that Sanford uses in his characterization. In virtue of this reflexivity, e_1 is necessary for itself, and given the determinism described above, e_2 is necessary for e_1 as well. Accordingly, nothing is necessary for e_2 that is not also necessary for e_1. Therefore, e_1, the cause, cannot be shown to be causally prior to e_2, its effect. But e_2 bears exactly the same relation to its consequent, e_3, that e_1 bears to e_2, and therefore e_2 is not causally prior to e_3 either. And so on. The upshot is that in a world as "tightly" deterministic as this one, Sanford's analysis entails the breakdown of causal priority altogether. Thus, if causal priority is a necessary component of causation in general, his analysis leads to a denial of the causal order.

On Sanford's behalf it might be argued that this conclusion follows only because we restricted the admissible circumstances in which e_2 could have occurred to the actual circumstances in which it did occur. Sanford admits that he has no theory about the legitimate scope and content of admissible circumstances relevant to a judgment of causal directionality. Nevertheless, he might argue that in general these circumstances cannot be restricted in a way that would obviate, as c does, something necessary for e_2 (the falling of the later domino) but not necessary for e_1 (the falling of the previous one). For example, Sanford could argue that admissible circumstances must permit the later domino's being glued to the ground, a situation which would have prevented e_2 while not interfering with e_1. This construal of the admissible circumstances requires that we stipulate, as a causally necessary condition, that the later domino not be glued to the ground. And since this condition is clearly necessary for e_2 but not for e_1, it follows that e_1 can be shown to be causally prior to e_2.

The trouble with this argument is that it purchases escape from the objection at the cost of a circularity that vitiates the whole analysis. For how do we decide whether an actual or an imagined factor falls among the admissible circumstances relevant to determining causal necessity and sufficiency? The counterargument presumes that we cannot exclude from the admissible circumstances factors that would be *sufficient* for the nonoccurrence of the effect (in this case, factors such as the presence of glue). But sufficiency rests on judgments of admissibility, which in turn appeal to considerations of sufficiency. Given Sanford's characterization of sufficient conditionality in terms of admissible circumstances, the admissibility of conditions sufficient for the nonoccurrence of the effect cannot be determined in a noncircular way. Moreover, in a wholly deterministic and simple world of the sort imagined, the only admissible circumstances— i.e., those countenanced by the laws at work in the context of a single causal chain—will reduce to c, the actual circumstances. Here there is no scope for factors relevant to the impossiblity of one event but not relevant to the impossibility of any other event temporally anterior or posterior to it.

It is not open to Sanford to reply that the world we have described is simply without causal priority. To say this is tantamount to admitting that his treatment is incompatible with (at least some versions of) determinism—a serious charge for someone who rejects other accounts of causal priority because of a like incompatibility. Moreover, even if our present world is not as deterministic as the one described above, at least some events in our world are necessary for their causes in Sanford's sense. To the extent that these events are necessary for their causes, Sanford's account will not allow that they are causally posterior to their causes.

Sanford's account faces another problem of circularity or regress that is of equal seriousness. His appeal to causal laws as the modal differentiators of statements of logical impossibility describes a role for causal laws that cannot be fulfilled. The class of laws required for even a single statement of impossibility to be true may well turn out to contain an infinite number of members. Consider the example of the pendulum described above. According to Sanford, its having a certain length is causally prior to its having a certain period because, given the law of the pendulum, the amount of gravitational force acting on the pendulum is necessary in the circumstances for its period, but not necessary in any admissible circumstances for its length.

Assuming the correctness of this description, let us focus on the relation that must obtain between gravitational force and the period of the pendulum. To begin, it is agreed that the gravitational force is necessary for the period. From this fact alone we cannot infer whether the period is necessary or sufficient for the amount of gravitational force. Conditionality, it may be recalled, is nonsymmetrical in Sanford's account. If the period is not a condition of the amount of gravitational force present, then there must be something necessary for the period of the pendulum that is not necessary for the amount of gravitational force. What can this be? One obvious candidate is the length of the pendulum, a factor apparently necessary for its period without being necessary for its gravitational force. But this factor cannot be cited without circularity. The initial question is whether length is a causal condition of period, and we can hardly assume an answer to the question in order to substantiate its conditionality. Some other factor must be identified, one that is necessary for the period but not for the strength of the gravitational force. But this will require a new modal differentiator in the form of another law relating the new item to the period, as necessary for it, while not being necessary for the gravitational force.

Once we identify such an item and the relevant law, the same cycle begins again. Each stage involves a new law and requires the satisfaction of a further claim of necessary conditionality. And there is no stopping point for this regress. Of course the regress could not commence if the pendulum's having a given period is after all necessary or sufficient for the amount of gravitational force present. But the presence of gravitational force is causally prior to the period of a particular pendulum, and so a causal condition of it. An account of causal priority that denied this particular directionality would in effect deny causal priority altogether as a feature of causation. The denial of causal priority to factors that figure in the fundamental laws of motion is a step toward the dissolution of the problem of causal directionality, and not a proper solution to it, as we shall argue in the last section of this chapter.

Short of surrendering the existence of causal directionality, then, Sanford's treatment requires that a single assertion of causal priority turn not on the truth of one law (or two) of nature, but on an indefinitely large number of them. Although problems of induction may render somewhat tentative any of our particular judgments of causal priority, surely they do not reflect so large a burden of unavoidable causal ignorance as Sanford's analysis entails. If Sanford is correct, the evidence supporting any claim of causal priority is always formally incomplete, not merely because the evidence for some particular causal law is incomplete, but because we cannot even enumerate the laws whose truth our judgment of causal priority requires. This consequence suggests that Sanford's account may be beyond revision.

The difficulties thus far described reflect only on the second of the two criteria Sanford offers for causal priority: that the cause be a *condition* of the effect (in his sense of condition), not vice versa. But what are we to say about the first criterion, that the events be causally connected in a direct line, just in case A is the cause of B or B is the cause of A? Can we, as Sanford rightly requires, determine the truth of this disjunction without first determining which of the disjuncts is true? The question is crucial, because on the view in question, "the determination of which disjunct is true is left up to the account of causal priority, which thus completes the analysis."[37] If the truth of the whole disjunction rests on a prior determination of causal directionality, then there will be nothing left for the analysis of this priority to complete, and the whole account will turn out again to be uninformatively circular. The question is especially important in the context of hard cases where causation and its direction are not revealed in the temporal separation of cause and effect. Thus, is it possible to determine causal connection in a direct line, where the simultaneity of events A and B is consistent with their being joint effects of a third event, C, and equally consistent with their being parts of a causal chain C-A-B? The second of these two alternatives will satisfy the disjunction, for here A is the cause of B, while the first will not, because in cases of causal forks neither of the joint effects is the cause of the other. If these two cases cannot be distinguished independently of an appeal to causal priority, then Sanford's first condition of causal priority will fail his and our criterion of noncircularity.

37. Sanford, *op. cit.*, p. 196.

Now consider a case where A and B are causally connected in a direct line. In addition to the relation of causal priority obtaining between them, A and B also satisfy the relations of spatiotemporal contiguity and constant conjunction (of events of their type). These latter two properties also obtain when two events are joint effects of some single cause. If a cause and its effect exhibit no further property or relation besides causal priority, then there will be nothing by means of which an account of causal priority could distinguish cases of causal connection in a direct line from those of joint effects. And if this is indeed the case, then "in the objects" the disjunctive relation of being causally connected in a direct line can only be distinguished from the relation of being joint effects by detecting the direction of causal priority. More generally, "A and B are causally connected in a direct line" will be true when and only when "A is causally prior to B, or B is causally prior to A" is true. Since there is nothing except one of the relations of priority to distinguish the case of a causal fork—joint effect—from causal connection in a direct line, we cannot at least in these cases determine whether the first of Sanford's two conditions of causal priority is satisfied without knowing beforehand the direction of causal priority. In Sanford's defense it must be said that he nowhere gives a definition of "causal connection in a direct line" and that he would consider the problem of providing such a characterization to be one of explicating the symmetrical relation of causal order, a different and more general relation than that of causal directionality. In effect, our argument hinges on the claim that a complete account of this symmetrical relation must presuppose an appeal to the asymmetrical notion of causal priority. Without such an appeal, no determination of order among simultaneous causally connected events seems possible.

We have detected three defects in Sanford's treatment of causal directionality. Despite these defects, and perhaps because of what they suggest about causal directionality, we consider Sanford's attack on this problem the most impressive and incisive of the alternatives to Hume's supposed views Unlike other accounts, it recognizes certain adequacy criteria for informative accounts of causal priority and their relation to analyses of causation as a whole. It leaves few crucial notions unexplained, and honestly admits its incompleteness in respect of those notions that are assumed in the exposition. Its attempt to supply a non-symmetrical account of conditionship not only appeals to strong intuitions long ignored in logic and the study of causation, but opens up a large and novel territory for the employment of these notions. Even the problems in this theory help us to understand the notion of causal priority more than they tend to discredit Sanford's account of it. Our criticisms consist in the claims that, on his account, causal directionality is incompatible with determinism, that causal directionality is only circularly detectable in alleged cases of simultaneous causation, and that for central cases a choice must be made between no directionality and one that generates an infinite regress in the causal laws required to ground it. These criticisms amount more to a general scepticism about the existence of causal directionality in the objects than to a refutation of Sanford. If so, it would appear that we embrace a scepticism about causal directionality that is not embraced by either Sanford or Hume, for Hume is not conventionally taken to have been a sceptic about causal asymmetry. However, as we show in the last two sections, there is much in Hume's arguments that suggests such a scepticism. In the end the difference between Hume and Sanford may, in Hume's words, be "of no great importance." For Sanford admits "the possibility that some causes do not precede their effects."[38] And if Hume should turn out not to be committed to the asymmetry of causation, this is a conclusion that he too can accept. Let us now see in what special sense he might find it acceptable, despite his claim that effects succeed their causes.

VII

The failure of so many accounts of causal priority either to give correct answers about the direction of causation (in both "hard" and "easy" cases) or to satisfy general conditions of adequacy must not lead us to think that no adequate account of the matter is possible. Like any negative existential claim, the conviction that no alternative to Hume's account is available can ultimately be defended only by critical analysis of the argu-

38. *Ibid.*, p. 193.

ments of Hume's competitors—as we have attempted throughout this chapter. But we must also consider what can be said on behalf of Hume's original suggestion that causal priority is nothing but temporal priority. One important argument, now to be considered, questions the widespread assumption that there are actual or possible cases of simultaneous causation on grounds that apparent cases of simultaneous causation involve events which either are not causally related or are not simultaneous.

If there are no cases of causes and effects that are simultaneous, there are many more "causal forks" in nature than hitherto supposed. Nonetheless, it may be that all cases of allegedly simultaneous causation actually involve *joint* effects of some third event. For example, an iron bar's being hot and its glowing may both be the effects of some temporally prior event of heating; and the turning of two enmeshed gears may not be related as cause and effect, because they are the joint effects of some third event. This fact, if it is a fact, would be surprising, but it would not be a *conceptually* intolerable surprise. It would be an empirical surprise, and no more intolerable than the discovery that the behavior of rigid rods and clocks depends on their velocity. Given the inadequate alternatives, it would certainly be worthwhile to retain the Humean analysis if the cost of doing so were merely an empirically surprising but logically coherent result.

A preferable defense of temporal priority, however, would provide a response to the alleged counterexamples that is neither empirically surprising nor conceptually impossible. The second alternative mentioned above—that of denying simultaneity instead of causation—is just such a preferable defense. Instead of denying that either of two apparently simultaneous events causes the other, we can insist that they are not in fact simultaneous and that the event that began first is the cause. On this view we must conclude that the iron bar's being hot did precede its glowing and that the motion of one gear did precede the motion of the second, even when available instruments cannot detect a temporal lag. This claim adds a condition to the analysis of causation that in some cases might never conclusively be established. While this outcome is unfortunate, the advocates of simultaneous causation are in no position to insist on the preferability of their view as against a firm insistence that cause and effect pairs are never simultaneous. The assertion that two events are simultaneous requires that there be no temporal gap between them, not even one shorter than detectable by available instruments. This negative existential is no more susceptible of conclusive verification than the opposite claim that there are no cases of simultaneous causation.

Even if we cannot conclusively establish the nonexistence of simultaneous causes and effects, we have broad and impressive theoretical reasons to doubt that simultaneous causal relations occur. Atomic theory and the theory of relativity both provide for a lag between the motion of one gear and that of a second, and between the heating and the glowing of an iron bar. No two gears are perfectly rigid, and no two gears are perfectly enmeshed; accordingly, a lag between the motion of the first and that of the second is to be expected. Similarly, the heating of an iron bar involves absorption of energy by its constituent atoms, and its glowing consists in the radiation emitted from their outer-shell electrons. Within such chains of events and their aggregation into detectable glowing there is vast scope for temporal asymmetry between cause and effect.

Current scientific theory does not commit us to the occurrence of any simultaneous events related to one another as cause and effect. It does, however, allow for the occurrence of perfectly contemporaneous states of objects or substances, in which one state is the cause and the other the effect. Any two temporally overlapping events will contain a number of perfectly contemporaneous segments, and if the overlapping events are cause and effect, these simultaneous segments, or states, will naturally be described as cause and effect as well. We may allow for the possibility and indeed the actuality of this sort of simultaneous causation in a way that is perfectly compatible with a Humean temporal priority criterion: if x causes y, than either x is temporally prior to y, or x and y are contemporaneous parts of two events such that one event is temporally prior to the other. Since x and y are themselves divisible, the temporal priority of causes will not require that every part or time-slice of x be causally necessary for the occurrence of each time-slice of y, nor that every time-slice of y be determined by some time-slice of x. Thus, for example, if the motion of one gear during the interval t_1

to t_2 causes the motion of a second gear during the interval $t_1 + \epsilon$ to $t_2 + \epsilon$, then there will be contemporaneous states of the two gears during the interval $t_1 + \epsilon$ to t_2 (where ϵ depends on the speed with which mechanical forces can be transmitted). The states can be described as cause and effect, but that part of the cause-state obtaining between t_2 minus ϵ and t_2 will not bear any causal relation to the effect-state. Similarly, that part of the effect-state occurring between $t_1 + \epsilon$ and $t_1 + 2\epsilon$ will not be causally dependent on the state of the first gear during the interval of contemporaneousness.

Is this enough simultaneity to satisfy those who oppose the temporal priority criterion? Does the fact that scientific theory precludes a more perfect simultaneity than this carry any weight with those who reject Hume's theory? Perhaps not. His opponents may argue that it is not the actuality but the possibility of simultaneous causation that an account of causal asymmetry must allow for. It may be that the transmission of causal signals at speeds greater than that of light is physically impossible. But that fact does not make simultaneous causation logically impossible or conceptually incoherent, so the argument goes, and any account of causation must allow for these conceptual possibilities.

There is of course a competing tradition according to which it is a logical necessity that causes precede their effects. All such conceptually based arguments are controversial and suspicious; and most of them rely on an action-based or manipulability account of causation that Hume could not accept.[39] Hume never explicitly held the view that the temporal priority of causes is a necessary truth. As we saw in Chapter 5, his argument proceeds from what he describes as "an established maxim in natural philosophy." The force of Hume's conclusions about simultaneous causation therefore turns on the force of the established maxim, plus his claim that we *experience* only succession in the relation. If we treat the maxim as one that reflects physical necessity, and not logical necessity, then Hume's

39. For example, see Antony Flew, "Can an Effect Precede Its Cause?" *Proceedings of the Aristotelian Society*, Supplementary Volume 28 (1954); Max Black, "Why Cannot an Effect Precede its Cause?" *Analysis* 16 (1956); and Richard Gale, *The Language of Time* (London: Routledge & Kegan Paul, 1968).

argument at most underwrites certain claims of modern science that simultaneous causation is physically impossible.

It is worth remembering that Hume may not have been offering an account of causal asymmetry in providing his argument for the temporal priority of causes, or even embracing the view that causation is an asymmetrical relation. Merely to assume or argue that causes are in fact prior to their effects is not to account for causal priority. Philosophers can and have developed avowedly nontemporal accounts of causal priority, while insisting that, as a matter of fact, all causes are temporally prior to their effects. Surely those physicists who recognize the temporal priority of causes do not thereby commit themselves to any among the wide range of competing accounts of causal directionality. Their belief in this priority stems from a relativistic definition of simultaneity conjoined with the claim that the fastest causal signals are light rays, which travel at finite speeds. Hume's argument for the temporal priority of causes is conceptually no stronger than theirs; for it too relies essentially on premises that are contingent. By parity of reasoning, Hume's argument does not commit him to any particular analysis of causal priority.

VIII

Even if one accepts Hume's established maxim and the validity of his argument, the question remains, "Why does temporal priority make for causal priority?" That is, does priority in time reflect or bestow on causes any priority other than the temporal one? What is it about the temporal position of an event that makes it the cause of another instead of its effect? It might be said that, in arguing that causes are temporally prior to their effects, Hume has not yet established in what *causal* priority consists. Perhaps Hume did not propound a doctrine about causal priority, or perhaps he was mistaken if he thought he did. If we nevertheless attempt to answer with Humean or empiricist strictures the question about causal and temporal priority, we may find ourselves committed to denying the existence of causal priority. These considerations suggest the possibility that had Hume considered the matter of causal directionality at further length, he might have rejected altogether the claim that there is such a thing.

Let us reflect on how this sceptical argument could be developed. In the spirit of Hume's doctrine that for every idea there is an impression, we may well ask from what impression the idea of causal asymmetry is derived. We have in effect already ruled out many potential answers to this question by showing that accounts based on "impressions" of manipulation, transference, and fixity fail to satisfy certain general adequacy criteria. These criteria are in part modern equivalents of Hume's test for the adequacy of any conceptual analysis—that it must break down the complex concept's "reductive" pedigree into observational statements. We have required that any account of causal asymmetry not presuppose a prior understanding of causation as a whole. We have done so in an attempt to produce a reductive analysis of causation that relates it to observation by exchanging its components—such as directionality—for detectable relations between events. If we assume empiricist strictures that deny the meaningfulness or the applicability of a concept for which there is no empirically determinable "mark," we must ask what the empirical mark of causal priority or asymmetry is. Notoriously, Hume argues that from an exhaustive examination of events considered in isolation, no general empirical mark either of causes or of their effects can be determined: "If we reason a priori, anything may appear able to produce anything" (EHU, Sec. 131). In other words, there is no detectable feature common and peculiar to all causes or all effects, in virtue of which they can be identified as such. This conclusion ultimately leads Hume to the regularity theory.

Philosophy has of course long since surrendered Hume's impressions-and-ideas doctrine, as well as its verificationist successors. Nevertheless, much of the continuing justification for the regularity analysis rests at least implicitly on the following empiricist inference: because there is no mark of causation detectable "in the objects," considerations of economy dictate that a theory of causation countenance no metaphysical glue between cause and effect. Similarly, the failure to find an empirical mark of asymmetry should suggest that a commitment to its existence is no less superfluous than a commitment to the existence of secret "causal powers." To say that, as a matter of contingent fact, causes precede their effects in time, is not to detect such an empirical mark, for this conclusion is consistent with any of a number of accounts of causal priority. On the other hand, to say that causal priority is reducible to temporal priority is tantamount to denying that there is asymmetry "in the objects." That is, a conflation of the two kinds of priority implies that there is no difference in the properties of events sufficient to make some of them causes and others effects. If the temporal asymmetry of causation itself has no explanation, and if there is no other asymmetry "in the objects," then an empiricist might well wish to hold that there is no special causal directionality and that causation is not an asymmetrical relation in the objects at all.

We may illustrate this line of thought by the following example. Consider a universe governed by totally deterministic symmetrical laws such as those of Newtonian mechanics. In this universe events at any time determine all future events, in the sense that once these events occur, the operation of the laws fixes all future events as well. Events at any given time also fix all events prior to them. That is, future events determine past ones just as fully as the reverse, under the Humean assumption that there is no power in causes that determines their effects. To insist that causation, as a relation "in the objects," is an asymmetrical relation, amounts only to a decision about how to *label* members of event-pairs, each of which causally determines or fixes the other to exactly the same extent, and in exactly the same way.

Of course, a sentient creature in such a world might suppose causation in the objects to be asymmetrical—that is, might suppose that the future is open in a way that the past is not, or that the past determines the future in a way the future does not fix the past, or that his own actions can constitute uncaused interventions on the basis of which he can determine the direction of causation. Yet it is possible that human creatures are mistaken in these suppositions. If our world conforms to the one described— and there is no definitive reason to think that it does not—then it is at least logically possible that causation "in the objects" is not an asymmetrical relation. Hume, as a confirmed Newtonian and empiricist, was certainly committed both to Newtonian symmetrical laws of a totally deterministic kind and to the non-existence of relations for which there is no observable sign. Accordingly, consistency alone seems to demand not only that causation *may not* be asymmetrical, but that in fact it *is not* asymmetrical. This conclusion is a matter of ascription, and not of textual interpretation; but its consistency with Hume's explicit beliefs cannot be denied, and so it must at least be judged Humean in spirit.

The question remains, however, whether the actual world is in fact governed by symmetrical laws, and whether they are deterministic in the way the laws of the aforementioned possible world are. If not, it may after all be the case that causal priority is more than a mere label for temporal priority. The possibility is even livelier for those who have no truck with empiricist strictures and the liberal employment of Ockham's razor. Still, classical and quantum laws of mechanics—which we believe do govern events in our actual world—are symmetrical in the way the laws of our possible world are. Of course, it remains highly controversial whether quantum mechanics represents a set of indeterministic laws (cf. Chapter 3). What is clear about these laws is that their operation does not allow the sort of forward or backward determinism in the classical mechanical states of the universe provided for by the laws of classical mechanics. Whether it follows that such laws are in fact "less" deterministic than classical laws, or are altogether indeterministic, depends on complex issues in the physical interpretation of its formalism. At least some philosophers have argued that quantum mechanics is quite as deterministic as classical mechanics, but differs from it in the state-descriptions with respect to which it is totally deterministic.[40] If this view is correct, then nothing stands in the way of a parallel between the actual world and the aforementioned deterministic world devoid of any causal priority "in the objects." Insofar as both of these worlds reflect the operation of symmetrical and deterministic laws, there is no scope in either for any physical or theoretical asymmetry among the events that constitute their histories.

IX

On the other hand, if, as some would have it, our actual world is indeterministic and therefore incompatible with Hume's conception of deterministic laws, then a Humean commitment to

40. Cf., for instance, Ernest Nagel, *The Structure of Science* (New York: Harcourt, Brace & World, 1961), Chapter 10.

empiricism leads to a quite different conclusion. Under assumptions of indeterminism, any conception of causation purporting to describe relations "in the objects" will for the Humean reflect an empirically groundless superstition that expresses systematically mistaken beliefs about powers and efficacy, necessitation and agency. On this view, if Hume's conception of causality is not applicable to relations "in the objects," then neither is anyone else's applicable. The reason is simple: we know already, on empiricist grounds, that the alternatives cannot be acceptable accounts of causation. This is a matter of great importance, for to say that no conception of causation is applicable to relations between events, is to say that *there is no causation* at all. And if causation does not obtain between events, then one of its components, causal directionality, does not obtain between them either. Accordingly, there may be no such thing as causal priority in any case, whether the universe is deterministic or not.

The plausibility of ascribing this view to Hume may be enhanced by a consideration of the relation between time order and causal order. As noted in Chapter 5, Hume's argument for the temporal priority of causes proceeds by showing a triad of beliefs inconsistent: (1) the belief that there is at least one case of simultaneous causation; (2) the belief in an "established maxim of natural philosophy"; and (3) the belief that the existence of temporal succession is contingent on the existence of causal directionality. The conclusion of his argument for the temporal priority of causes is that its denial entails "the utter annihilation of time" (T, 76). Accordingly, it may be that for Hume the more fundamental relation is that of causality, and the less fundamental that of time order. It is of course well known that in the *Treatise* (T, 35f) Hume provides a reductive analysis of time and temporal relations to the causal succession of events and the changes in objects. In this account causal relations provide the analysans for time, which is the analysandum. Thus the simple attribution to Hume of the view that causal priority is nothing but temporal priority under another name is questionable.

Let us nonetheless assume that causal directionality is analyzable in terms of temporal directionality. If this is the case, then the question of what the latter asymmetry consists in also remains to be answered. And if the character of temporal asymmetry is accounted for by appeal to some other asymmetrical relation, then the nature of that further asymmetry would arise. This regress might suggest that temporal and/or causal asymmetry reduces to some form of directionality that is ultimately unanalyzable. Those who would reject such an appeal to brute unexplainable facts of asymmetry must identify a relation among events that is symmetrical, or at least not asymmetrical, and in terms of which causal and/or temporal asymmetry may be explained. Let us formally describe this possible relation as *nonasymmetrical.*

If causation is itself a nonasymmetrical relation, then it may account for the directionality of time. This thought reflects the strategies of Kant in the eighteenth century, Boltzman in the nineteenth, and Reichenbach in the twentieth. The latter two attempted to explain the direction of time by appeal to causal processes underlying the processes described in statistical thermodynamics. This theory is expressed in symmetrical laws, and governs reversible processes—that is, it only permits types of sequences that may occur in either temporal order. On Boltzman's view, for example, the operation of the symmetrical laws will, given different local conditions, produce sequences of events in exactly opposite orders. This account led him to suggest that the direction of time is a "local phenomenon," an artifact of local conditions, and reflects no intrinsic asymmetry among the events it orders:

Then in the universe, which is in thermal equilibrium throughout and therefore dead, there will occur here and there relatively small regions of the same size as our galaxy . . . which . . . fluctuate noticeably from thermal equilibrium. . . . For the universe the two directions of time are indistinguishable, just as in space there is no up and down. However, just as at a particular place at the earth's surface we call "down" the direction towards the center of the earth, so will a living being in a particular time interval of such a single world distinguish the direction of time towards the less probable state from the opposite direction (the former towards the past, the latter towards the future).[41]

41. Ludwig Boltzman, *Lectures on Gas Theory,* as quoted in Bas C. van Fraassen, *An Introduction to the Philosophy of Time and Space* (New York: McGraw-Hill, 1971), p. 94.

This view accounts for temporal asymmetry by appeal to a nonasymmetrical relation; and it thereby provides those who believe that temporal relations are founded on causal relations further motivation to deny that causation is asymmetrical. For it is only on this latter assumption that a non-question-begging analysis of time order can proceed.

Our conclusion is ironic, in a way that Hume might have appreciated. We began by suggesting that no one has yet refuted Hume's claims about causal priority, despite a long tradition that assumes him to be mistaken. We then examined a range of alternatives, whose failures naturally strengthen the case for Hume's own claims. Eventually we questioned whether Hume can consistently hold that causation is an asymmetrical relation at all. If this ascription to Hume of a certain form of sceptical doubt seems plausible, it may shed new light on his own general comment about this issue. In the *Treatise* (76), while concluding his discussion of causal priority, Hume writes: "If this argument appear satisfactory, 'tis well. If not, I beg the reader allow me the . . . liberty . . . of supposing it such. For he shall find, that the affair is of no great importance."

7
Events, Facts, and the Extensionality of Causal Contexts

CAUSATION IS a relation, and every account of causation presupposes an implicit characterization of the objects of this relation, for these relata must have properties consistent with their relational character. Unlike contemporary students of causation, Hume does not attend explicitly to questions about the nature of causal relata. Nevertheless certain suppositions about causal relata are implicit in his theory of causation, and these suppositions deserve consideration together with more probing contemporary analyses of the problem.

Hume loosely refers to the relata of a singular causal relation both as "objects" and as "events," where events, like objects, are presumably locatable, datable, concrete particulars. Philosophers subsequently have come to prefer the language of events and conditions, but until recently no analyses of such notions had been provided that would clarify and distinguish them. Of late one question about causation to which considerable attention has been paid is whether causes and effects are *events*, or whether causes and effects are better construed as *facts*. Donald Davidson, Jaegwon Kim, J. L. Mackie, and Zeno Vendler have all considered this issue to be one of the more pressing ontological problems about causation. As Mackie puts it, the issue emerges from "anxieties about the exact ontology of causation."[1]

1. J. L. Mackie, *The Cement of the Universe* (Oxford: Clarendon Press, 1974), p. 31.

Most of these discussions begin with an examination of the view we treated in Chapter 3, and advanced most notably by Davidson, that causes and effects are events in the sense of concrete occurrences exemplifying features over and above the ones we hit upon for describing them. On this view causation is a two-place relation between particular events, whose (definite) descriptions are freely substitutable in causal sentences without changing their truth value, so long as reference is preserved. Hence causal statements are extensional.

We begin our discussion of these matters with a general analysis of Hume's account, devoting the remainder of the chapter to the above currents in contemporary philosophy—especially to controversies about whether causes are facts or events and controversies about whether causal contexts are extensional or intensional. These issues may not at first seem directly relevant to the defense of Hume and Humeanism. As we shall show, however, it is critical for Humeans to be able to defend the extensionality of causal contexts, while rejecting a fact ontology.

I

In the *Treatise* Hume generally describes the relation of causation as holding between "objects," while in the *Enquiry* the relation is often said to hold between "events." These expressions may suggest that the relata of causation are spatiotemporally localized particulars; but for several reasons Hume's terminology alone can hardly settle the question. In many passages throughout his work Hume clearly treats facts, states, perceptions, and substances as constituents in causal relations. Moreover, several passages in the *Enquiry* and the *Treatise* strongly suggest that Hume does not consider either objects or events *as wholes* to be the actual or minimal units of causation. Hume implies in these passages that some particular quality or feature of a causal occasion instead constitutes the relevant cause or effect. Thus he writes, "where several different objects produce the same effect, it must be by means of some *quality*, which we discover to be common amongst them. . . . We must always ascribe the causation to the *circumstance*, wherein we discover the *resemblance*" (T, 174, emphasis added).

Such passages need not be supposed to reflect any incompatibility with Hume's description of the relata of causation as objects, for Hume employed this concept in so general a way that its extension includes an extremely heterogeneous set of kinds and categories. Items of at least the following six different sorts are alike referred to as "objects" in Hume's writings:

(1) Ideas, impressions, sensations, perceptions (for instance, see T, 169, 201ff, 239–42).
(2) Material objects (T, 202, 206, 193ff).
(3) Actions or motions (T, 12, 88).
(4) Qualities (T, 87f; EHU, Sec. 38).
(5) Mathematical items (T, 42, 49).
(6) The self (T, 277, 286).

Almost anything might qualify as an object in Hume's usage. Indeed it might be construed as one of Hume's intentions to show that the class of possible causes and effects is ontologically heterogeneous. This conclusion seems implicit in one of his most paradoxical dictums: "Any thing may produce any thing. Creation, annihilation, motion, reason, volition: all these may arise from one another, or from any other object" (T, 173). Hume seems to be saying that not only may events cause events, and qualities cause qualities, but that there is some sense in which events may cause qualities, qualities may cause events, bodies may cause motions, substances may cause changes, states may cause actions, etc.

By now it should be clear not only that Hume did not address the question of the ontology of causation directly, but that no consistent theory about what kinds of items are causally related is likely to emerge solely from textual analysis. Accordingly, it would be more reasonable to extract an account of the ontology of Hume's theory from reflection on the central components of his analysis of causation. These components undeniably provide at least the necessary conditions for the ontological character of causal relata. It may turn out that further consideration of them will reveal sufficient as well as necessary conditions for being a cause or an effect, for through such consideration we may isolate an arguably basic ontological category—one by means of which apparently heterogeneous ways of describing causes and effects can be systematized. If our investigation answers the question of what the relata of Hume's account of causation *must* be, then a comparison of this result with wider ontological views will provide an important test of the adequacy of Hume's theory of causation as a whole.

II

The conditions of causation that Hume advances may initially seem no more promising for inferring a coherent ontology of causation than do his casual remarks about causes and effects, for each of his three conditions appears to contemplate a different sort of item. Consider first the requirement of spatiotemporal contiguity. Spatial contiguity is fundamentally a relation between objects and substances—particular items that can be moved about in a spatial framework, that can endure over time, and that are variously identifiable by appeal to their properties and relations. Temporal contiguity, however, is not obviously a relation that obtains among spatially extended objects. Its primary locus of application is rather the class of events, states, and conditions that have beginnings and endings relatively close in time (compared with the substances to which they happen). As with items satisfying a spatial contiguity requirement, these entities are reidentifiable particulars; but they do not necessarily have the obvious spatial borders objects have. On the other hand, objects may turn out not to have the intuitively clear temporal boundaries that events seem to possess. The requirement of spatiotemporal contiguity thus apparently selects an ontologically heterogeneous class of causes and effects.

The situation is further complicated by the implications of Hume's other two conditions of causation. Temporal priority obviously obtains between certain kinds of items, yet it is not a relation that need be satisfied by objects in *causal* relations. Objects cited in the description of an effect may exist before the objects cited in a description of the cause without Hume's requirement being violated. What is more, while the first and second requirements are at least consistent in requiring that causation be a relation between reidentifiable particular items, the central requirement of constant conjunction makes no sense as a relation between particular objects or events. Whatever is regularly conjoined must be capable of *repeated* appearance or recurrence, and particular items are conceptually incapable of such repetition. Only abstract entities such as properties and relations can satisfy this condition of causality. Thus, the implications of Hume's third requirement make the class of causal relata still more heterogeneous—indeed so heterogeneous as apparently to render Hume's dictum that anything may cause anything a hollow *reductio ad absurdum*.

Jaegwon Kim has tried to bring ontological order out of these seemingly conflicting constraints, and to provide an ontologically coherent treatment in the spirit of Hume's account of causation. After canvassing the difficulties and apparent inconsistencies recounted above, Kim brings the time-like, the space-like, and the abstract items that Hume's account seems to require together under the category of a structured *event*. He takes this category to include the exemplification by a concrete object of a property or relation at a time or during a time-period. An event thus characterized may be capable of satisfying the constraints of Hume's analysis of causation because each component of Hume's analysis can be represented. Kim's is a promising approach to the ontology of causation and its ramifications, and we should therefore pursue it in some detail.

Kim represents events by expressions of the form $[(x_1, \ldots, x_n, t), P^n]$. "An expression of this form refers to the event that consists in the ordered n-tuple of concrete objects $(x_1, \ldots, x_n)$ exemplifying the n-adic empirical attribute P^n at time t."[2] The following existence and identity conditions for events are adopted:

(1) $[(x_n, t), P]$ exists if and only if the n-tuple of concrete objects (x_n) exemplifies the n-adic empirical attribute P at time t.

(2) $[(x, t), P]$ is identical to $[(y, t'), Q]$ if and only if $x = y$, $t = t'$, and $P = Q$.

Kim generalizes this latter condition to account for the identity of permutations of n-tuples of objects and n-adic properties. Events meeting the existence and identity conditions can satisfy the requirements of contiguity and temporal priority because their objects and times are contiguous and the time of the cause event is prior to that of the effect event. How such events satisfy the requirements of regularity is a more complicated matter. Kim notes: "There appears to be a general agreement that the

2. Jaegwon Kim, "Causation, Nomic Subsumption and the Concept of an Event," *Journal of Philosophy* 70 (1973), p. 222.

requirement of constant conjunction for causal relations for individual events is best explained in terms of lawlike correlations between generic events. Constant conjunction obviously makes better sense for repeatedly instantiable universals than for spatio-temporally bounded particulars." Each event, according to Kim, is the instantiation of a universal, a type, which he calls its generic event. Because each event has a unique constitutive property that is a generic event (the instantiation of the property constitutes the particular event in question), "it follows that each event falls under exactly one generic event, and that once a particular cause-effect pair is fixed, the generic event that must satisfy the constant conjunction requirement is uniquely fixed."[3]

Kim holds that "generally the cause event will be a dyadic or higher-place event involving, as one of its constitutive objects, the constitutive object of the effect event; and the first term of a constant conjunction will in general be a relational generic event rather than a monadic one."[4] Thus, the requirement of constant conjunction may be expressed in Kim's notation as follows: $[(a,b,T)P]$ is a cause of $[(b,T'),Q]$ only if (i) $[(a,b,T)P]$ and $[(b,T'),Q]$ exist, and (ii) $(x)(y)(t)([(x,y,t),P]$ exists $\rightarrow$ $[(y,t + \triangle t),Q]$ exists), where $\triangle t = T' - T$, and "$\rightarrow$" carries the nomological force of a universal of law.

Despite Kim's avowed intentions, there is reason to believe this account does not reflect an ontology entirely compatible with Hume's analysis of causation. It can be shown, for example, that Kim's claims about the relation of particular events to generic events and the relation of these latter to constitutive properties of particular events is incompatible with the constant-conjunction view. Consider the following example: Oedipus married Jocasta, who, unbeknownst to him, was his mother. Some time after this event Oedipus suffered acute mental anguish. It seems reasonable to suppose that the first event caused the second. Oedipus's marriage to Jocasta can be expressed in Kim's notation as

a [(Oedipus, Oedipus's mother, t_1) married].

It is also true that Oedipus married Laius's widow. This event can be described as

3. *Ibid.*, p. 226.
4. *Ibid.*, p. 234.

b [(Oedipus, Laius's widow, t_1) married].

On Kim's criterion, $a = b$, since their constitutive objects, properties, and times are identical. *Ex hypothesi, a* caused Oedipus to experience mental anguish at some later time; therefore, so did b. The effect can be expressed in Kim's notation as

e [(Oedipus, t_2) having mental anguish].

If, following the regularity theory, the constant conjunction of generic events, i.e., constitutive properties, is a necessary condition for singular causal relations, then neither a nor b could properly be said to have caused e. The unique generic events of marriage and mental anguish are instantiated respectively by a and e. As the occasional happy marriage attests, there is no lawlike correlation between these generic events or constitutive properties. There is, let us assume, a constant conjunction between marrying and mental anguish when the persons related by the constitutive property of marriage are also mother and son, and for that reason we consider a the cause of e. If Kim's ontology is to sanction this claim, something in his account must be modified.

For the Humean, however, Kim's account is beset by a still more serious difficulty. Specifically, we may wonder whether his criterion of event identity is compatible with the claim that constant conjunction of unique generic events, i.e., of constitutive properties, is a necessary condition of causal relations between particular events.

Consider the following events, which parallel a and b:

c [(Oedipus, Oedipus's mother, t_1), incestuously marrying];

d [(Oedipus, Laius's widow, t_1), incestuously marrying];

$c = d$, on Kim's criterion, for the same reasons that $a = b$; and c (or d) causes e, in part because of the constant conjunction of their constitutive properties. On the same criterion, however, it is false that $c = a$, because the constitutive properties, marrying and incestuously marrying, are plainly not identical. Since on Kim's account[5] every event falls under exactly one generic event determined by its constitutive property, a and b must instantiate a generic event different from the one c and d instantiate. This conclusion entails that they cannot satisfy the same statements of constant conjunction, and that therefore they cannot have

5. *Ibid.,* p. 226.

the same effect, contrary to the assumption with which we began. The denial of identity among *a, b, c,* and *d* is plainly implausible. One simply cannot pick out features of the event described by "*a*" or "*b*" that are not possessed by the event described by "*c*" or "*d*." Their times are all the same, as are the spatial locations and features of their constitutive objects. There is nothing observable by which they could be distinguished. Faced with a choice between denying the mutual identities of *a, b, c,* and *d* and surrendering the regularity theory whose ontology Kim is attempting to expound, many will prefer the latter alternative of rejecting Humeanism. *Mutatis mutandis,* the Humean can hardly adopt Kim's exposition in the face of its counterintuitive implications for the identity of *a, b, c,* and *d.* The Humean must either modify it or reject its claims.

The denial of identity between *a* and *c* on the basis of Kim's criterion has other equally untoward consequences for the constant conjunction requirement. It seems undeniable both that *a* caused *e* and that *c* caused *e.* The consequence for Kim must be that marriage uniformly causes mental anguish, and that incestuous marriage does as well. But unless incestuousness plays no role in the cause of mental anguish, these two causal regularities are incompatible. According to one, marriage without incest is sufficient to produce an effect which, according to the other, requires the added presence of incestuousness. If *c* causes *e,* then *incestuous* marriage is necessary, and marriage alone will not suffice. On the constant conjunction view developed in our earlier chapters, *a* and *c* could not equally be the cause of *e.* If we insist that they both are causes, then either they are identical or causation does not involve the constant conjunction of generic events. If they are identical, Kim's criterion of identity as well as his claims about the character of generic events and their relations to particular ones need revision.

Any revision of Kim's account should achieve at least the following things. It should preserve the ontological homogeneity that Kim has provided for the regularity theory: i.e., it should show how one type of object can satisfy all three of the Humean conditions on causation. The revision must also be consistent with firm convictions about the identity of events whose descriptions may vary from occasion to occasion. And of course it must in consequence of these requirements explicitly allow for the most central of Hume's claims about causation: that it consists in the instantiation of constant conjunctions expressed by universals of law. The following revision suggests itself as satisfying the foregoing requirements while entailing only minor modifications in Kim's account.

Instead of holding as Kim does that particular events manifest one and only one constitutive property, let us permit multiple constitutive properties, and revise Kim's identity criterion along the following lines: events are identical if and only if their constitutive objects are identical, their times are identical, and their respective objects all share the same constitutive properties, of which there can be more than one. How does this reconstruction apply to the case of *a, b, c,* and *d?* Given the identity of Laius's widow and Oedipus's mother, we can deduce that if *a, b, c,* or *d* contains the constitutive property of marrying, then it will contain the constitutive property of incestuously marrying. In consequence, we can show that $a = b = c = d$ on the strength of a modified criterion.

The difficulty with this procedure is that we cannot *show* that two events are identical where the objects and properties do not bear the neat logical relations the constituents of *a, b, c,* and *d* bear to one another. To address this problem, we can capitalize on the Humean's demand that if two events are identical then a statement of their identity should be compatible with the theory that causal connections rest on constant conjunctions of generic events. That is, the assertion that two putatively identical events both caused some other event should not commit one to inconsistent causal laws. Whether events are identical, however, cannot be determined merely by their descriptions, since these may make use of differing predicates, or cite differing constitutive properties. In order to determine event identity we must resort to a causal criterion of event identity: events are identical if and only if their causes and effects are identical. The criterion is Donald Davidson's,[6] and its effect is to make Hume's causal laws the determinants of identity among events. For events will be identical only if they instantiate the same uni-

6. Donald Davidson, "The Individuation of Events," in Nicholas Rescher, *et al.,* eds., *Essays in Honor of Carl Hempel* (Dordrecht, Holland: D. Reidel, 1969), pp. 216–34.

versals of law. In order to determine these same identities, Kim's criterion must be rendered compatible with the regularity theory in the way we have suggested.

In fact, the connection between Kim's criterion and Davidson's is more intimate than might at first appear. The combination of either of these two criteria with the constant-conjunction-of-generic-events view of causality entails the other criterion. If two events possess the same constitutive objects, times, and properties, then we can infer that the constitutive properties of each event will appear in the same set of laws no matter what causal laws associating constitutive properties apply. Consequently, the particular events in question will have precisely the same particular causes and effects. Conversely, since the causes and effects of events are determined by their constitutive properties, two events having the same particular causes and effects will also have the same constitutive objects, properties, and times.

The upshot of this discussion is an account of the objects of causation as structured particulars or concrete events that consist in the exemplification of sets of properties at or during times, and which are causally connected in virtue of the constant conjunction of unique generic events that they exemplify. These generic events are to be characterized in terms of properties constitutive both of the particular events and of the particular objects that manifest these constitutive properties. Now we must consider whether this event analysis, which provides a coherent ontology for Hume's theory of causation, can stand against arguments that oppose all event ontologies.

III

Our modification of Kim's treatment is consistent with Hume's account of causation, but it still must confront certain difficulties and alternatives. One important alternative is the theory that causes and effects are *facts*, not *events*, and that facts are the exclusive relata of causation.[7] This view incorporates a commitment to the intensionality of causal statements, and it therefore has serious metaphysical consequences for the Humean

7. See Zeno Vendler, "Causal Relations," *Journal of Philosophy* 64 (1967), pp. 703ff, for an influential exposition of this view. For limited support, see John L. Pollock, *Subjunctive Reasoning* (Dordrecht, Holland: D. Reidel Publishing Co., 1976), pp. 145–57.

theory of causation. On the view we have tentatively embraced, events *a* and *c*—Oedipus's marrying Jocasta, and his incestuously marrying her—are identical events. Yet Jocasta's giving birth to Oedipus is causally necessary for event *c*, but apparently not for event *a*. Accordingly, either *a* is not identical to *c*, or the substitution of coreferring descriptions of the unique event that both "*a*" and "*c*" describe, changes the truth value of causal statements containing "*a*" or "*c*" as descriptions of the cause or effect.[8] This apparent intensionality presents a difficulty for any account of the objects of causation, and showing how it can be circumvented should add further dimensions to our Humean account. Ultimately, consideration of this issue will lead to our defense of an event theory of causal relata as against a fact theory.

On their face, questions about whether causal statements are extensional or intensional seem far removed from the regularity theory, or for that matter from the ontological issue of whether causal relata are events or facts. After all, Hume knew nothing of the distinction between extensional and intensional discourse. That issue pertains to the logical form of statements of a certain kind, whereas the events/facts question is ontological. If we can show that the explanation of whether a type of statement is extensional or intensional depends on critical ontological commitments, or vice versa, then the two issues will turn out to be intimately related. Their bearing on ontological matters of the sort that Hume does face would thus become transparent.

Roughly speaking, a sentence is extensional if coreferring singular terms are substitutable for its substantives without affecting the truth value of the sentences, or if the substitution of coextensive predicates is truth preserving. Otherwise, a sentence is nonextensional or intensional. A more general and precise characterization might proceed as follows. Consider a sentential context, $C(x)$, that takes sentences as arguments. $C(x)$ is extensional if there is no sentence s, such that replacement of singular terms or coextensive predicates in s preserves s's truth value, while changing the truth value of $C(s)$. A sentential context that takes singular terms as arguments is extensional if

8. This apparent difficulty for the analysis at hand was originally broached in Monroe Beardsley, "Actions and Events: The Problem of Individuation," *American Philosophical Quarterly* 12 (1975), p. 272.

there is no singular term t such that replacement of coreferential terms of coextensive predicates in t preserves the reference of t while changing the truth value of $C(t)$.[9] This sort of extensionality is also known as referential transparency.

Among sentential contexts that seem clearly intensional are those reporting psychological attitudes such as knowing that . . . , fearing that . . . , and descriptions of other characteristically human activities such as explaining. The truth of propositions involving these descriptions is, in an old fashioned way of talking, "mind-dependent." Their intensionality rests upon this mind-dependence. That is, the explanation of why substitution of coreferring terms and coextensive predicates does not preserve truth value in these sentential contexts usually invokes human logical lapses, or ignorance that some item satisfies different descriptions, or some other feature of the mental states of persons.

It is worth illustrating this point by reflecting on the intensionality of causal explanation.[10] Consider the following example of the sentential context ". . . explains . . .":

(1) Oedipus's marrying his mother explains his subsequent madness.

9. This characterization of extensionality is found in a number of places. For example, Adam Morton offers it in "Extensionality and Non-Truth-Functional Contexts," *Journal of Philosophy* 66 (1969), p. 159:

(a) extensionality: if t is obtained from s by substituting predicate B for predicate A, then
$$(x)\ (A(x) \equiv B(x)) \supset (C(s) \equiv C(t))$$
(b) referential transparency: if t is obtained from s by substituting a name of b for a name of a, then
$$(a = b) \supset (C(s) \equiv C(t)).$$

10. Rational reconstructions of the concept of explanation, like the deductive nomological model, are in part attempts to provide an unrelativized "explication" of this notion—one that expresses a purely formal relation between sentences and that is not bedeviled by problems of intensionality. Uniform substitution of coreferential terms or coextensive predicates should leave the truth values of the sentences in such an explanation unaffected, and thereby, the explanation intact. The claims made here are not about explanation thus reconstructed, but about our ordinary notion of explanation—as examined, for instance, in Peter Achinstein, "Explanation," *Studies in the Philosophy of Science, American Philosophical Quarterly*, Monograph Series, No. 3 (Oxford: Basil Blackwell, 1969). For further discussion of these issues cf. Chapter 8.

Someone might complain that (1) is misleading since events do not explain other events; rather, sentences do, even though we ordinarily speak of events and facts as explaining other events and facts. In order to accommodate this complaint, we may say that events explain other events *only under a description*. This observation makes it clear why explanatory contexts are intensional. Descriptive substitutions in the arguments of explanatory contexts may change the truth value of the whole sentence without affecting the truth values or references of the sentences or terms that figure in the whole sentence's arguments. Thus, most well-informed persons treat (1) as true, because they are generally familiar with the events to which (1) refers under the descriptions it employs. On the other hand, the following sentence referring to the same events under other descriptions would usually be considered false by well-informed persons:

(2) Oedipus's marrying Laius's widow explains his subsequent madness.

(2), of course, varies from (1) only in respect of the way that Jocasta is described. Since this variation in truth value results from a change in description that preserves reference, explanatory statements seem to be intensional. Their intensionality consists in what we have called their mind-dependence: whether one event explains another depends on us, and on how we describe the events in question. More precisely, let us call a sentential context mind-dependent if its truth entails the truth of other statements that assert (or deny) the existence of mental conditions such as belief, desire, intention, fear, etc. Thus, for example, the truth of (1) turns on the general belief that marrying one's mother leads to deleterious consequences, while the falsity of (2) hinges on not knowing that Oedipus's mother is identical to Laius's widow and to Jocasta. In the sense we have described it above, mind-dependence is thus a sufficient condition for the intensionality of a sentential context. *A fortiori*, the extensionality of a statement should entail its mind-independence, i.e., should guarantee that its truth does not entail the truth of other statements that assert or deny the existence of mental states.

It is at this point that issues of concern to Hume and his followers become manifest. On their views, causal relations between events are presumably *not* mind-dependent. Hume insists that the course of nature is objective, and independent of the beliefs and descriptions of mortal minds. If we were all swept away, our desires, fears, hopes, explanations, and artifacts would all disappear with us. Nature, in contrast, is no artifact. The relations between natural events would continue unimpaired; and paramount among those relations is that of cause and effect. That is why the Humean takes the truth of statements about causes and their effects to be independent of human beliefs, desires, and linguistic descriptions. There is a powerful statement of this view in the *Treatise* (167f): "[causes] operate entirely independent of the mind, and wou'd . . . continue their operation, even tho' there was no mind existent to contemplate them, or reason concerning them. Thought may well depend on causes for its operation, but not causes on thought. This is to reverse the order of nature, and make that secondary, which is really primary. . . . The operations of nature are independent of our thought and reasoning. . . ." As we saw in Chapters 1 and 4, the Humean will go to considerable lengths in order to avoid any tincture of "idealism" or mind-dependence in his characterization of causation or the laws that underlie it, despite Hume's beliefs about the subjectivity of necessary connection.[11]

If causal relations are not mind-dependent, then—subject to the proviso that mind-dependence is necessary for intensionality, or at least for intensionality in the case of causal statements —it follows that *the Humean is committed to the extensionality of causal statements.* The mind-dependence proviso is critical to this contention, and it requires that we corroborate at least one of the two following claims: (1) mind-dependence is not only a generally sufficient condition for intensionality, it is also a universally necessary one; or (2) the only reason to suspect that causal statements are intensional is their similarity in form and employment to statements such as explanatory ones whose intensionality does consist wholly in their mind-dependence. If

11. Hume of course argues that whatever power, efficacy, or necessity we attribute to the objects of causation is not independent of the mind, and that causation involves beliefs about necessary connection. But these claims should not be construed as assertions of the mind-dependency of causation "in the objects." See our discussion of these matters, including this passage, in Chapter 1, and related issues in Chapter 4.

neither of these claims is established, it is open to someone to argue that the intensionality of causal relations does not rest on their mind-dependence. There might, after all, be other sorts of intensional contexts which are not mind-dependent, and it could be claimed that causal contexts are members of this further class of intensional contexts. Such arguments would completely undercut any simple inference from mind-independence to extensionality. We need to ask, then, whether (1) and/or (2) can be demonstrated, or at least convincingly defended. Demonstrating (1) would of course entail a substantial analysis of intensionality well beyond the scope of the present work. We shall therefore attempt to sustain only (2). Not only will this task suffice for present purposes, but it will bear on the claims of Chapter 8 about the nature of causal explanation.

One prominent tradition in the literature on causation attempts to analyze the causal relation into explanatory relations, or even to assimilate causation to explanation—as we saw in Chapters 3 and 5. Norwood Hanson has expressed such a view, asserting that "there are as many causes of x as there are explanations of x. . . . In fact what we refer to as 'causes' are theory-loaded from beginning to end." More explicitly, Michael Scriven has written, "a cause is *an* explanatory factor (of a particular kind). Causation is the relation between explanatory factors (of this kind) and what they explain." According to Monroe Beardsley, "to specify the cause of an event is to give a causal explanation of it, and *if* explanatory contexts are nonextensional, as many would hold, then I don't see how causal contexts could fail to be nonextensional as well. They stand or fall together." Finally, in "Causal Relations," when faced with apparently nonextensional causal statements, Davidson suggests that "the 'caused' of [such statements] is not the 'caused' of straightforward singular causal statements, but is best expressed by the words, 'causally explains.' The affinities between causation and explanation are manifest."[12]

Moreover, both causal contexts and causally explanatory ones seem capable of taking either fact-describing or event-describing expressions as arguments (a topic to which we shall turn below),

12. Norwood R. Hanson, *Patterns of Discovery* (Cambridge: Cambridge University Press, 1958), p. 54; M. Scriven, "Causation as Explanation," *Nous* 9 (1975), p. 11; M. Beardsley, *op. cit.*, p. 272; and D. Davidson, "Causal Relations," *Journal of Philosophy* 64 (1967), p. 703.

and many features of causal language are distinguished by their connections with explanation. For example, it is often claimed that the distinction between causes and conditions turns on whether one of an effect's necessary conditions provides its causal explanation rather than merely one of its conditions.[13] Thus, even if those who assimilate causation to explanation are wrong about the intensionality of the former notion (as we shall argue), they are certainly warranted in finding a close relation between the two concepts. Explanations typically appeal to causes, and it is mainly to satisfy explanatory demands that events and facts are both cited as causes. It is just this similarity of function and form between causal and explanatory contexts that encourages philosophers incautiously to treat causal statements as intensional. These similarities suggest the conclusion that the *only* reason causal statements are taken to be intensional is their similarity in form and employment to statements, such as explanatory ones, whose intensionality does consist wholly in their mind-dependence. If so, it follows directly from this conclusion and from the mind-independence of causal statements that such statements are extensional.

IV

The conviction that causal sentences are extensional is based on the even stronger conviction that the truth of intensional statements entails the truth of other statements about the existence of cognitive states, while the truth of at least some[14]

---

13. See, for example, J. L. Mackie, "Causes and Conditions," *American Philosophical Quarterly* 2 (1965), as reprinted in E. Sosa, ed., *Causation and Conditionals* (Oxford: Oxford University Press, 1975), pp. 21–23; Samuel Gorovitz, "Causal Judgments and Causal Explanations," *Journal of Philosophy* 62 (1965), pp. 695–711, as reprinted in Tom L. Beauchamp, ed., *Philosophical Problems of Causation* (Encino, Calif.: Dickenson Publishing Company, 1974), pp. 235–47; and A. Collins, "Explanation and Causality," *Mind* 75 (1966), pp. 482–500. Some of the issues broached in these papers are treated in Chapter 8 below.

14. We introduce the qualification "at least some" because certain causal statements describe causal relations between mental events. Even in these cases the relation a causal statement asserts to obtain between mental events is not the kind of relation that is mind-dependent in the sense described above. Thus the statement that "belief *b* caused action *a*" expresses a relation between *b* and *a* that also obtains between nonmental events, like a short circuit and a fire.

causal statements does not entail the truth of any such statements about mental conditions. It rests, in short, on nothing less than our belief that causal relations are "independent of the mind, and wou'd . . . continue their operation, even tho' there was no mind existent to contemplate them, or reason concerning them" (T, 167). Yet this conclusion undercuts the account of particular events as causes and effects we defended in Section II. Recall that, on the view there embraced, events consist in particular objects manifesting sets of constitutive properties at or during times. We were obliged to expand the number of properties exemplified in a single event in order to allow for variable reference to the same particulars. We thereby sought to preserve the compatibility of an account of events as the fundamental relata of causation with a constant conjunction analysis of this relation.

Yet the compromise between doing justice to events and their descriptions, on the one hand, and to a Humean account of causation, on the other, seems now to entail that causal statements are intensional. For the same event under different descriptions that pick out different properties apparently both *is and is not* the cause or effect of some other event. In the example cited in Section II, Jocasta's giving birth to Oedipus was causally necessary for their *incestuous* marriage; yet the birth does not seem causally necessary for their *marriage,* even though the marriage and the incestuous marriage were one and the same. The same event cannot at once be the cause or effect of another event and not be the cause or effect of that other event. Only an event whose descriptions determine its identity can have so varying a causal efficacy. But such events, "events *under descriptions,*" now seem incapable of serving as the mind-independent causal relata to which Hume is so firmly committed.

Thus, the Humean faces a number of unattractive alternatives. The constant conjunction analysis of causation cannot be surrendered; and the Humean is equally unwilling to deny that causation exists independently of the mind (except as Hume is committed to the psychological theory of causal necessity that we sketched in Chapter 1). At the same time, the Humean should be able to account for our actual citations of causes and effects and for our well-grounded judgments about their identities. The only way to render these claims consistent would appear to be by surrendering the last mentioned task. If Hume had recognized this problem, we suspect he would have chosen to revise at least some of our ordinary causal citations and beliefs about event identity in the interest of certain broader and more systematic considerations. In other words, he would have maintained that causation is extensional and that the countervailing intuitions that apparent counterexamples express are mistaken. If it can be shown that cases such as the marriage/incestuous marriage example are in fact extensional, despite contrary appearances, then the constant conjunction view can be preserved, together with the commitment to particular concrete occurrences as the fundamental relata of causation.

This general stategy is the one we shall pursue. In the next section we offer a criterion of extensionality that causal statements clearly pass, and in the following section we show that apparent cases of intensional causal statements can consistently be handled. These conclusions will reveal the final ontological commitments of Hume's account of causation.

V

Causal sentences can be analyzed into sentential contexts and their arguments, where these arguments may either be singular terms or sentences themselves. Typically, when the sentential context is ". . . because . . . ," the arguments are sentences. An example involving *terms* as arguments is

(3) The Titanic's striking an iceberg *caused* the sinking of the Titanic.

An example involving *sentences* as arguments is

(4) The Titanic sank *because* it struck an iceberg on 14 April 1912.

To say that sentences such as these are extensional is to say that if a substitution of coreferring terms of coextensive predicates in their arguments leaves the argument's references unchanged in the case of a term-type argument, and leaves the argument's truth value unchanged in the case of a sentence-type argument, then the whole sentence will also be left unchanged in truth value.

The singular terms of (3) and (4) pass this test without difficulty. We could substitute identicals from any of the following descriptions in (3) or (4) while preserving their truth values:

The Titanic = the largest passenger liner afloat before 1930 = the newest ship in the White Line in 1912 = the sistership of the Olympic = the ship which struck an iceberg and consequently sank on the night of 14 April 1912.

The sinking of the Titanic = the event about which Walter Lord wrote his first best-seller = the event which cost Lloyd's of London more money than any other in 1912 = the event which resulted in the only mass grave in the Halifax cemeteries.

Some of these substitutions would be unusual, and might never find their way into versions of (3) or (4) formulated in order to *explain* the sinking or state the effect of the Titanic's striking the iceberg. But this consideration has no bearing on the *truth* of (3) and (4) when they embody such substitutions. We may therefore conclude that at least some causal contexts are extensional, in that they are referentially transparent.

But what of the substitution of coextensive predicates in a sentence such as "*x* struck an iceberg on 14 April 1912"? Because this sentence is coextensive with "*x* carried Lady Astor among its passengers for the last time," substituting coextensive predicates in (4) could yield the patently false sentence

(5) The Titanic sank because it carried Lady Astor among its passengers for the last time.

Must we infer from this substitution that, as some have suggested, the causal relation is intensional?[15] One way to circumvent this sort of counterexample is simply to argue that the apparent failure of extensionality in (5) results from a misconstrual of the underlying logical form of such sentences. On this view, the appropriate logical form of (4) is that of sentences in which causation is a relation between *events,* and is correctly represented by the more cumbersome sentence

---

15. Dagfinn Føllesdal seems committed to this conclusion on the strength of a similar argument in his "Quantifying into Causal Contexts," M. Wartofsky and R. Cohen, eds., *Boston Studies in the Philosophy of Science* (New York: Humanities Press, 1965), p. 264.

(6) There is an event y, the sinking of the Titanic, and an event x, the striking of an iceberg by the Titanic on the night of 14 April 1912, and x caused y.

This thesis leaves no scope for counterexamples such as the inference from (4) to (5). It treats all sentence-taking causal contexts as implicitly term-taking ones. The tactic parallels Frege's suggestion about the logical form of " . . . after. . . . " Although this operator takes sentences as arguments, and although its truth value *may change* when its sentences are substituted for, *salva veritate*, Frege argues that its actual logical form involves events and a claim that one follows the other in time.[16] This approach is both attractive and plausible, but it ties the thesis of extensionality for causal contexts so directly to the claim that causes and effects are particular events as to beg the question here at issue. Moreover, it provides sentence-taking causal contexts with nothing like the direct and more formal test of extensionality that applies to term-taking causal contexts. Its plausibility as an argument for the extensionality of sentence-taking causal contexts rests entirely on the strength of the claim that logical form differs from apparent form (for reasons that transcend issues in the philosophy of language alone). A more convincing argument for the extensionality of such causal contexts would show that these sentences pass a test for extensionality that paradigm cases of intensional sentence-taking contexts do not pass—where the argument does not resort to allegations about underlying logical form. Let us sketch such an approach.

The admission that causal statements fail the test of extensionality when certain coextensive predicates are substituted in sentence-arguments is not very damaging. It is tantamount only to admitting that causal statements are not truth-functional, which is already well known.[17] More importantly, we may

16. Gottlob Frege, *Philosophical Writings*, trans. M. Black and P. Geach (Oxford: Basil Blackwell, 1952), p. 77.
17. There is of course a well-known and controversial argument to the effect that if a context is extensional then it is truth-functional. This argument originated in the work of Frege, but its contemporary statement is W. V. O. Quine's "Three Grades of Modal Involvement," reprinted in *The Ways of Paradox* (New York: Random House, 1966). Quine employs the argument in advancing objections to modal logic, but it has been ap-

revise our criterion of extensionality so that such causal statements will accommodate the substitution of coextensive predicates in their contained sentences where other sorts of statements
—such as those expressing beliefs, modalities, or explanatory relations—will not. The original criterion stipulated that
an extensional statement must permit the substitution of coextensive predicates in contained sentences without changing
the whole statement's truth value. But we may legitimately revise this criterion so that a sentence-taking context is extensional
if the *references of the gerundive nominalization of the contained sentences remain the same*. Every sentence has at least
one nominalization. For example, the gerundive nominalization
of "the Titanic sank" is "the sinking of the Titanic." Such
nominalizations assume the logical form of singular terms. For
this reason causal contexts taking them instead of sentences
as arguments pass the conventional test of extensionality without difficulty. If we require that the nominalizations associated
with coextensive predicates retain the same reference, then we
can take advantage of the fact that term-taking causal contexts
pass our test. We can thus formulate a new test of extensionality that sentence-taking causal contexts pass, but that intensional
contexts do not pass.

By using our revised criterion, it turns out that the substitution that took us from a true causal statement such as (4) to
a false causal statement such as (5) provided no fair test of
extensionality. The nominalizations of the sentence arguments
of (4) and (5) in which coextensive predicates have been substituted are: "The Titanic's sinking" and "The Titanic's carrying
Lady Astor among its passengers for the last time." These

---

plied in the analysis of causal statements by Anscombe, Føllesdal, and
Davidson. In this connection, the argument has been used to show that since
causal contexts are acknowledged to be non-truth-functional, it follows
that they are extensional neither for substitution of predicates nor for substitution of terms. The argument has been criticized as invalid by Arthur
Smullyan, "Modality and Description," *Journal of Symbolic Logic* 13 (1948),
pp. 31–7, by R. Cummins and D. Gottlieb, "On an Argument for Truth-
Functionality," *American Philosophical Quarterly* 9 (1972), pp. 256–59, and
by J. L. Mackie, *The Cement of the Universe*, Chapter 10. These authors
have, in Mackie's words, "drawn the claws of an argument to which excessive
deference has been shown" (p. 254).

nominalizations are clearly not coreferential. We may therefore conclude that the predicate substitution in question produces a false causal statement not because causal contexts are not extensional, but because the substitution fails to meet the proper criterion of extensionality.

By contrast, while the substitution of coextensive predicates can preserve both the reference of gerundive nominalizations and the truth value of causal statements, it fails to do so for explanatory contexts of psychological attitude statements. For example, the true statement

(7) The fact that Oedipus went mad is explained by the fact that he married his mother.

is made arguably false when we substitute "married Laius's widow" for "married his mother"—even though this substitution preserves the reference of the gerundive nominalization.

Similarly the true statement

(8) Steve believes that Larry is his brother.

may be turned into a false one by substituting the coextensive predicate "male sibling" for brother, even though such a substitution would preserve the reference of the nominalization. And again, the presumably true statement

(9) Necessarily $(9 > 5)$.

is made false when "the number of the planets" is substituted for "9," even though "9's being greater than 5" and "the number of planets being greater than 5" have the same reference (recognizing, of course, that it may be difficult to say precisely what their reference is). Thus, we conclude that causal contexts satisfy our revised criterion of extensionality while intensional ones do not.

It may be objected that our revision amounts to a wholesale transformation bearing no interesting connection to the traditional criterion and so lacking significant implications for the question whether causal contexts are extensional. If so, our criterion would simply beg the question at issue. In reply, it should be noted that our new criterion does isolate some real differences between causal contexts. These differences reflect the permissibility of substitutions preserving reference. Whether

the differences strictly pertain to the extensionality versus intensionality discussion may be a terminological issue. Perhaps
we should coin a new term to describe the property in question.
Nominal Extensionality seems appropriate, because it reflects
both the appeal to nominalizations and the doubts there may be
about whether its referent really is a kind of extensionality.

There is, however, at least one consideration that would favor
describing nominal extensionality as a form of extensionality:
Ruth Barcan Marcus has argued that "we cannot talk of *the*
thesis of extensionality, but only of stronger and weaker extensionality principles."[18] Marcus shows that the strength of a principle of extensionality varies with the sense of the equivalence
demanded between intersubstitutable arguments of a context
under examination. Adapting this thought to our purposes,
we could maintain that denying our criterion the title of a
principle of extensionality involves a denial that equivalence
of reference under transformation to gerundive nominalization
is any sort of equivalence at all. Such a denial will be difficult
to accept if, as Noam Chomsky has suggested,

> Gerundive nominalizations can be formed fairly freely from proposi-
> tions of subject-predicate form, and the relation of meaning between
> the nominal and the proposition is quite regular. . . . Gerundive
> nominalization involves a grammatical transformation from an under-
> lying sentencelike structure. . . . The semantic interpretation of a
> gerundive nominalization is straightforward in terms of the gram-
> matical relations of the underlying proposition in the deep structure.[19]

We conclude, then, that "nominal extensionality" is a genuine
and relevant form of extensionality.

VI

The Humean's commitment to the mind-independence of causation motivates the claim that causal statements are extensional,
and our criterion of nominal extensionality offers an argument
for this conclusion as well. But both motive and argument must

18. Ruth Barcan Marcus, "Extensionality," *Mind* n.s. 69 (1969), pp. 55–62,
as reprinted in L. Linsky, ed., *Reference and Modality* (Oxford: Oxford
University Press, 1971), p. 46.
19. N. Chomsky, "Remarks on Nominalization," *Studies on Semantics in
Generative Grammar* (Hague: Mouton, 1972), p. 16.

confront important counterexamples to the extensionality of causation. If these counterexamples cannot be accommodated or defeated, a serious objection to Hume's conception of causation will remain unanswered. In considering these counterexamples, we will attempt to preserve the ontological simplicity of the Humean account, which countenances only particular events subsumed under general laws connecting unique generic events. The cost of this attempt, as we shall see, is a multiplication of the absolute *number* of events that occur beyond our ordinary intuitions.

The most serious obstacle to a Humean extensional account of causation is the so-called problem of adverbial or predicate modification.[20] Events such as sinkings can occur rapidly or slowly, fatally or harmlessly, detectably or undetectably, expectedly or unexpectedly. In short, there seem to be different ways in which the same event can occur. For instance, the Titanic's sinking was rapid, fatal, unexpected, etc. Thus an intensionalist might argue that the invalidity of the following inference demonstrates the nonextensionality of causation:

(4) The Titantic's striking an iceberg caused the sinking of the Titanic.

The Titanic's sinking was a rapid sinking; and therefore:

(11) The Titanic's striking an iceberg caused the Titanic's rapid sinking.

This conclusion could well be false. After all, the rapidity of the sinking might more properly be blamed on the captain's giving incorrect orders, or the failure of the crew to execute those orders, or the passengers' panic which impeded emergency operations. So, the argument continues, the only way the Humean can preserve extensionality is to deny that the Ti-

---

20. Alvin Goldman, *A Theory of Human Action* (Englewood Cliffs, N. J.: Prentice-Hall, 1970), p. 3, presents this problem. More recently, Beardsley takes it up in "Actions and Events." Jaegwon Kim and Donald Davidson discuss the problem in their papers—notably, Kim's "Events as Property Exemplifications," in *Proceedings of the Winnipeg Conference on Theory of Action* (Dordrecht, Holland: D. Reidel, 1976), and Davidson's "The Logical Form of Action Sentences," in N. Rescher, ed., *The Logic of Action and Decision* (Pittsburgh: University of Pittsburgh Press, 1967), pp. 81–103, and "Causal Relations."

tanic's sinking is identical to its sinking rapidly. If this stategy is admitted, there will be no way to limit the number of nonidentical events to two, for there can be as many events as there are adverbs applicable to the event of the sinking. Since the number of such applicable adverbs is indefinite, it follows that the extensionality of causation commits us to an indefinite number of events, where common sense countenances only one. Opponents of the extensionality thesis think this result is so evidently absurd that it renders the thesis indefensible.

This anti-Humean argument is questionable in several respects. It can be shown that (a) where adverbial modification renders certain causal claims false, it truly has multiplied events; (b) where adverbial modification does not change the truth value of a causal claim, there is no multiplication of events; and (c) where a multiplication of events does occur, it is innocuous.

On what basis is it claimed that the Titanic's sinking is identical to its sinking rapidly? We suspect the basis is the assumption that it could not, logically speaking, sink rapidly without also sinking. From this fact, however, it does not immediately follow that sinking rapidly is the same event as sinking. Intuition that the two events are the same presupposes some kind of direct relation between sinking and rapid sinking, but this unanalyzed relation is not alone sufficient to establish *identity*. Moreover, there may be conflicting intuitions about such cases, especially when we individuate events on the basis of their causal relations. Consider a sphere that is simultaneously spinning and changing color. In this case, we have no difficulty saying that two events occur—a color change and a spinning—even though they both happen to the same object and at precisely the same time and place. The multiplication of events is here intuitively admissible, because we believe that the *causes* of the spinning and the color change are different. In other words, at least some of our event-individuating intuitions are based on beliefs that causes are not identical. If we consider the Titanic episode in the light of such intuitions, we are led to the following conclusion: because the cause of the rapid sinking (say, a failure of command) is believed to be different from the cause of the sinking (the striking of an iceberg), there is at least some intuitive basis for holding that the rapid sinking and the sinking are distinct events.

The dispute thus comes down to a clash of intuitions, and the conflicting intuitions have equal force. The more plausible the claim that two event descriptions entail different truth values for the causal context in which they figure, the more the differences between the events described seem to mount up. But the more these differences mount up, the stronger becomes the intuition that they describe different events. After all, the *sinking* of the Titanic was arguably nothing that anyone's orders or execution of orders or panic could have done anything about, but the *rapidity* with which it sank was something that these three conditions did affect. To the extent that these considerations weigh against the truth of (11), they also weigh against the putative identity of the sinking and the rapid sinking. The intensionalist cannot without argument refuse to embrace one of our methods for individuating events, while insisting on exclusive use of the other. The extensionalist, by contrast, can accept both of these criteria for event individuation. If the criteria conflict, and one criterion is better fulfilled, extensionality may still reign. Depending on which is better fulfilled, we will prefer to multiply events or to deny the truth of some causal assertions.

Consider, for instance, how the opponent of extensionality would defend the claim that (11) is false. He would do so by pointing out that although the striking was necessary for the rapid sinking, it was not sufficient for it. This is an insufficient ground for denying the truth of (11), but if it is even *a* reason to suppose (11) false, it is an equally strong reason to believe in the falsity of (4), "The Titanic's striking an iceberg caused its sinking." But if (4) is false, it is not surprising that an alleged falsehood such as (11) should follow from it without undercutting its extensionality. The mistake in the argument is the supposition that causes are ever *cited* in a way that supposes them to be anything more than necessary for their effects. The extensionalist may reason that if events are cited in true causal statements under descriptions which suppose them to be only causally necessary for their effects, then citing the striking as a cause of the rapid sinking is perfectly in order. Thus, an argument for the truth of (11) might be mounted.

Such an argument would again invoke Davidson's dictum (cited in Chapter 3) that deletions from (or additions to) the description of an event are not deletions from (or additions to) the event described.[21] The terms selected to describe the cause in (11)—the Titanic's striking an iceberg—pick out a particular event, but cite only some of its features in designating it. To cite others of its features would make no difference to the question of which event was described, but it might lessen any pre-analytical reluctance to accept the truth of (11). In the present example, "The Titanic's striking an iceberg" cites an event that also had properties involving a ship with insufficient lifeboats, relatively inexperienced crewmen, a complacent captain, etc. Similarly, "The Titanic's sinking" refers to an event with properties that the expression does not cite—properties such as being rapid, fatal, and unexpected. These considerations support the truth of (11), and thereby deprive the intensionalist of his argument. They also show how the extensionalist accommodates the identity of an event whose description is adverbially unmodified with one whose description is so modified. He simply exploits our occasional inclination to individuate events by reference to their *inclusiveness*.

Sometimes this rough criterion seems to give implausible results, in contrast with one that individuates events by reference to *causes*. Can the extensionalist accommodate these cases? Consider the following sentence:

(12) The Titanic sank rapidly because the captain gave incorrect orders.

If we accept the view that the Titanic's sinking = the Titanic's rapid sinking, we must infer the obviously false statement that:

(13) The Titanic sank because the captain gave incorrect orders.

But perhaps the nominalizations of "the Titanic sank" and "the Titanic sank rapidly" do not refer to the same events. If so, then they fail our test of nominal extensionality. When we ask for the cause of the Titanic's sinking *rapidly,* emphasizing rapidly, we are asking for the cause of an event's (the sinking) having a *particular* property (being rapid). An event's taking place is not the same as an event's taking place rapidly, or fatally, or unexpectedly. It is equally clear that an event's taking place

---

21. Davidson, "Causal Relations." Davidson himself says nothing about additions.

rapidly, fatally or unexpectedly may have effects or causes quite different from those of the unvarnished event itself. Insofar as a rapid or fatal or unexpected event can participate in causal relations, it is reasonable to suppose that the event's being rapid or fatal or unexpected is itself an event, or at least an entity quite distinct from the event modified. This line of argument of course results in a multiplication of events, where ordinary intuitions might promote a contrary inclination to posit event identity. But as we have seen, these intuitions do not hold the field uncontested, and the Humean has independent grounds that encourage the multiplication of the objects of causation.

Our long digression into questions of extensionality has brought us back to the characterization of Humean causal relata that we initially elaborated in the exposition of Kim's analysis of events (in Section II). There we examined the view that causal relata had to be spatiotemporally bounded particulars of a certain sort: the manifestation of *unique* constitutive properties by particular objects at specific times. But this account set our intuitions about event identity at variance with our commitment to constant conjunction as the basis for causation, a problem which led to a multiplication of constitutive properties manifested by particular objects in a single event. Plausible as this move appears, it was found to generate an intensional character for causal statements. The Humean can no more embrace this consequence of a causal ontology than he can accept an ontology incompatible with the requirement of constant conjunction. Faced with this inconsistent triad of beliefs, the Humean must surrender something. We conclude that what must be surrendered is the ontology of causal relata reflected in our ordinary intuitions about event identity. Such intuitions are no more likely to give a Humean pause than like intuitions about causation. If his ontology renders the regularity theory consistent with the extensionality of causal statements at the cost of a counterintuitive multiplication of the sheer number of events that make up the history of the universe, then this is a consequence he should willingly embrace.

In the present case, the Humean will insist that the Titanic's sinking and its sinking rapidly are two distinct spatiotemporally restricted particulars. The former is an event. The latter may not be so classified by ordinary thought, but it is surely as much a concrete particular item with its own causes and effects as the former. Whether we call it an event or not is merely a matter of nomenclature. What is crucial for the Humean is that the resulting multiplication of events makes possible a coherent and defensible ontology, a commitment to the extensionality of causal sentences, and an analysis of events that complements the regularity theory.

VII

In conclusion, we may test the adequacy of the Humean commitment to particular events as the objects of causation by comparing it with the sustained alternative view offered by J. L. Mackie, who embraces facts as well as particular events as causes and effects.

In Chapter 10 of *The Cement of the Universe*, Mackie takes up two questions: (1) Are causes and effects facts or events? (2) Are statements that describe causal relations extensional or intensional? His answer to the first question is that we must recognize both facts and events as the relata of causal relations, although facts "seem to have every advantage over" events.[22] His answer to the second question is that causal assertions are only occasionally extensional, and that when they are it is because of our ignorance about the causal relata we are describing. Mackie does not explicitly say why these two questions—concerning the ontological nature of causes and concerning the statements that describe them—go together; but our arguments in Section III of the present chapter provide the main lines of an explanation. As we there noted, some philosophers have embraced an intensional account of causal contexts just because it accords with their view that causation is to be understood in terms of explanation (or, more radically, that it consists in explanation). Mackie is influenced by these views, but nonetheless writes, "I would reject any . . . theory that what is there is constituted or determined by how things appear to us (or to me)."[23] Since he explicitly warns that "the causation that I want to know more about is a very general feature . . . of

---

22. J. L. Mackie, *The Cement of the Universe*, p. 262.
23. *Ibid.*, p. 2.

the way the world works," it seems natural to expect that Mackie will reject any treatment of the causal relation as mind-dependent, and will defend the extensionality of causal sentences. This expectation turns out to be mistaken.

Before we assess Mackie's views, let us ask what the question of extensionality has to do with the issue of whether causal relata are events or facts. Roughly, an events ontology seems to be substantiated by an extensional treatment of causal statements, while a facts ontology goes hand in hand with an intensional account. Events are particulars, and they are designated by singular terms. The relations between pairs of such items should not be affected by the terms we hit on to refer to them, and from this observation it is a short step to the conclusion that the descriptions of these relations are extensional. A facts ontology, by contrast, suggests a quite different conclusion. While it remains unclear what facts are (a controversy Mackie fails to advance), they do seem to bear affinities to *propositions* rather than to concrete particulars. Moreover, the only extensional relations between propositions appear to be truth-functional. Causation is certainly not a truth-functional relation. Accordingly, an ontology of causation in terms of facts leads naturally to an intensionalist theory of causal statements.

Mackie first considers the view, defended most notably by Davidson[24] (and embraced by us in modified form above), that causes and effects are events (concrete occurrences) with features beyond and sometimes even entirely different from the ones we hit upon for describing them. According to this treatment, we can specify the whole cause of an event without wholly specifying it, for "the event *qua* concrete occurrence includes everything that was relevant to the production of the effect and much more besides."[25] On this view, causation is a two-place relation between particular items whose (definite) descriptions are freely substitutable in causal sentences without changing truth value, so long as reference is preserved. That is, causal statements turn out to be extensional. Although Mackie admits that "We can . . . and sometimes do, take causes (and effects) as concrete occurrences and causing as a two-place relation between such

24. Donald Davidson, "Causal Relations," *passim*.
25. Mackie, *The Cement of the Universe*, p. 256.

events," he goes on to maintain that "it is far from clear that this is the best treatment, and it is certainly not the only possible one."[26]

If Mackie's arguments against extensionalist views such as Davidson's are sound, they are equally strong objections to the view we have embraced as an account of the Humean causal ontology. We think, however, that Davidson's views can be defended against Mackie in a way that will demonstrate the general adequacy of the theory we have sketched in this chapter. Let us, then, take up Mackie's objections against events and extensionality.

Mackie objects to Davidson's position principally on grounds that "it seems a disadvantage of concrete occurrence causes that they will nearly always include *irrelevant components*," while "we are, sometimes at least, interested in a more selective, more discriminating relation than can hold between concrete occurrences."[27] Facts allegedly enable us to land on the causally relevant features of events in a way that reference to the entire event does not; entire events are individuated merely "by their spatio-temporal regions," not by their causally relevant features.[28] Facts are said to be ontologically compelling, because "it will be such facts only that can be explained, rather than a concrete occurrence in all its infinite detail."[29] Mackie raises the question, "Why, then, do we bother to recognize producing causes [events] as well as explanatory causes [facts]?"[30] He answers, quite simply: our ignorance. His meaning is that when we are ignorant of the particular causally relevant features of whole events, we refer to the event as best we can. When our knowledge permits the requisite precision, we cite facts.

Mackie argues additionally that by using the Method of Difference we can "progressively localize" a cause. For example, after it was discovered that drinking wine causes intoxication, we eventually were able to distinguish between relevant and irrelevant causal factors. By making observations and performing experiments, the precise cause of intoxication was "progressively

26. *Ibid.*, p. 257.
27. *Ibid.*, p. 258 (italics added).
28. *Ibid.*, p. 257.
29. *Ibid.*, p. 260.
30. *Ibid.*, p. 262.

localized." This process constitutes an "important kind of advance in knowledge," since it identifies the aforementioned irrelevant components of concrete occurrences and so removes a barrier to the increase of knowledge.[31]

Whatever its ontological significance, Mackie's notion of an irrelevant feature of an event needs sharpening. Mackie cannot mean by an irrelevant component of an event a feature that plays no role in bringing about the event's effects. If this is what an irrelevant component of an event is, then events have no irrelevant components. Features of an event may well be irrelevant to some of the event's causes and effects under various descriptions, but for them to be irrelevant to all of an event's causes and effects under all possible descriptions would entail an implausible causal indeterminism, as well as introducing a large number of "nomological danglers." Thus, for example, that the Titanic's striking the iceberg had the feature of involving a ship with insufficient lifeboats is irrelevant to the description of its effect as the sinking of the Titanic, but it is clearly relevant to another description of the effect as the sinking of the Titanic with fearful loss of life. Thus, there appear to be no causally irrelevant components of events, although there may be many causally irrelevant ways of describing an event. Mackie presumably would not disagree.

Mackie's contention is probably better interpreted as the claim that a component is irrelevant if it plays no role in bringing about some particular effect. A feature of an event may thus be relevant for its effect under some descriptions, and irrelevant under others. But relevance will then turn out to be not an *ontological* distinction about features of events, but an *epistemological* distinction about which features are important for *explanations* of why a particular event had the cause or effect it did have. This interpretation may reasonably be attributed to Mackie, for he describes the isolation of such a feature as "an important kind of advance in *knowledge*." Understood, then, as a point in causal epistemology, the claim that concrete occurrences include irrelevant features is correct, but the objection has no force as a complaint against the view that causes (independent of our descriptions or knowledge of them)

31. *Ibid.,* p. 258.

are concrete occurrences. To show that a feature of some event is irrelevant to the occurrence of *one* of the event's effects is hardly to demonstrate that it is not a feature of the causing event in question. *Whether* one event caused another is a separate issue from *why* one event caused another. The description of an event through its causally irrelevant features will pick out the same cause, even though it will not provide an explanation of why it had this particular effect. To infer that irrelevant features are not parts of the cause—i.e., features of the cause in question—or that it is the features themselves that are *the* cause, amounts to an illicit inference from epistemological truths to ontological falsehoods.

Mackie's appeal to relevant and irrelevant features, on the one hand, and to explanatory considerations on the other, determines his preference for facts over the concrete event analysis of causes. What are we to say regarding his alternative, the notion of "fact"? Mackie provides no explicit definition of a fact, but it is easy to cite passages in his book where a fact is described not as a proposition but as a "feature of an event."[32] Exploiting the claim that facts and not events are employed in explanations, Mackie introduces the notion of a *minimally complete causal account*; it is "one which mentions all the features that were actually causally relevant to some event."[33] He describes the typical form of a minimally complete causal account as follows: "*a*'s being *B* and there being an *x* such that *x* is *C* and *x* has relation *R* to *a* and . . . caused there to be a *z* such that *z* is *D* and *z* has relation *S* to *a*." Such an account will single out from a concrete occurrence "in all its infinite detail" a single set of explanatory facts:[34]

What is here said to cause something may be called an *explanatory* cause. An explanatory cause is a fact, but of an unusually pure sort. Everything causally relevant about it is expressed by general terms and existential quantifications; the individual that this fact is about, the only item with respect to whose description the expression that states this fact is referentially transparent, is causally irrelevant, everything that is causally relevant about this individual having been covered by explicit monadic, dyadic, or polyadic predicates. . . .

32. *Ibid.*, pp. 265–67 and the passages quoted below.
33. *Ibid.*, p. 260.
34. *Ibid.*, pp. 260–61.

A minimally complete causal account is explanatory in at least two ways. The conjunction of features in the cause will be related to that in the result by some regularity. . . . Also, since the first conjunction includes all the features that are causally relevant to the latter, this regularity will be . . . a pure law of working. . . .

Pushed to this extreme, facts as causes seem to have every advantage over events. Why then, do we bother to recognize producing causes as well as explanatory causes? The reason lies, as so often, in the extent of our ignorance. A minimally complete causal account is an ideal which we can hardly ever reach.[35]

Mackie gives a number of more particular reasons why we might take concrete events rather than facts as causes:

We may know that a certain event caused another without knowing what features of the former event were relevant, and therefore without being able to specify any facts as causes. And since less knowledge is needed to pick out an event as a cause, the knowledge that is needed is more easily acquired. One event's causing another is observable whereas the identification of a fact as a cause requires some theory, some assumptions, or some comparison of cases with one another.[36]

Mackie's rationale for choosing facts over events relates exclusively to the limitations of knowledge—ignorance in knowing which specific features of an event were causally relevant to the production of a second event. As knowledge increases, the possibility for citing features or facts increases. Thus, on Mackie's view, producing causes and explanatory causes differ in degree, not in kind; and the difference that makes the critical difference is epistemological, not ontological.

The quoted passages from Mackie's book raise many questions. We think the answers to these questions all lead back to the view of causes as events, as concrete occurrences, and away from Mackie's conclusions that causal relata are facts. Apparently, facts are explanatory causes because they are the features of events cited in the regularities and theories we employ to explain why one particular event caused another. When we do not possess such laws and theories, we may refer to one event as the cause of another, but we shall not be able to say why it was

---

35. *Ibid.*, pp. 261–62.
36. *Ibid.*, p. 265. In his 1980 "Preface to the Paperback Edition" of *The Cement of the Universe*, Mackie offers further clarifications of his views, but the position remains unaltered (see pp. ix, xv).

the cause—i.e., in virtue of which of its features it had this result. These claims about causal explanation are correct and important, but they have no bearing on the *ontological* issue of the objects of causation. That Mackie's theory of explanatory causes cannot be a correct ontological account of causal relata becomes clear when we consider what a *feature* of an event is. A feature of an event is a property or aspect of it. It is not a particular item or occurrence; it is a universal. Universals do not cause things (or explain them); only their instantiations do. Similarly, effects are not features, but the instantiations or exemplifications of features. The items that exemplify features are particulars: either substances or events. When a substance exemplifies a feature, the "result" is an event, and when an event exemplifies a feature (for instance, the Titanic's sinking exemplifying the feature of being rapid, or fatal, or unexpected), this too is a particular. It is the *having* of a feature by *particular* items that constitutes the feature's causal role. A feature is an explanatory cause only because of its exemplification by a substance or an event—that is, only because it is "part" of a producing cause or concrete occurrence.

How, then, shall we express the relationship between features, intensional facts, and explanatory causes, on the one hand, and events, concrete occurrences, and producing causes, on the other? To answer this question we need to recall Davidson's treatment of events and their descriptions, the treatment Mackie rejects as an exhaustive account. What Mackie calls explanatory causes are merely those features of events that are mentioned in descriptions of the events for purposes of causal explanation. Our quest for these features is likely to be interminable, as a result of the impossibility of specifying an event under a description that shows it to be sufficient for its effects or causes. Mackie therefore describes a minimally complete causal account as "an ideal which we can hardly ever reach."[37] Additions to the list of causally relevant features by which we describe the events constitute additions to our knowledge about causal relations, and so "explanatory causes" are of epistemological importance. But this importance is again no reason to offer them as ontological alternatives to concrete occurrences. Moreover,

37. *Ibid.*, p. 262.

if a fact is the exemplification of a feature by an event, then that exemplification is as much a particular concrete datable occurrence as the event itself. As such, it too is a subject of referentially transparent description. Surely the feature or features themselves could not be causes or effects unless exemplified by some event.

What is the upshot of this comparison of events and facts for the issue of extensionality with which we began? We may agree with Mackie that "statements about producing causes will be extensional, since in them predicates are used only to identify concrete occurrences. . . . But this is not true of explanatory cause statements."[38] We can agree with Mackie only subject to the qualification that explanatory causation is not a relation *in the objects*—independent of, and by contrast with, producing causation. Explanatory causation reflects the purposes and interests we bring to causal inquiry. Subject to the same qualification, we may also accept Mackie's more general conclusion: "We need then, to recognize both kinds of cause, events and facts, and at the same time to distinguish them, in order to understand what we think and say about causal relations."[39] This distinction turns out, however, to be the distinction between causation *simpliciter* and causal explanation, a distinction between an ontological relation, and an epistemological one. Mackie's conclusion that an ontology of facts has "every advantage over" an ontology of events thus seems to confuse ontological and epistemological accounts of causation.[40] Once they are distinguished, the Humean ontology of causal relata remains intact.

---

38. *Ibid.*, p. 268.
39. *Ibid.*, p. 265.
40. Is it fair to conclude that there is nothing of metaphysical significance in Chapter 10 of Mackie's book (on grounds that Davidson's ontology is not directly challenged and that facts turn out to be features of events)? This metaphysically neutral outcome would be surprising, since the proclaimed topic of the chapter is the ontology of causal relata. We think nonetheless that it is the right conclusion. The reason the chapter fails to have metaphysical import is that it is really only tangentially about ontology. Primarily it is an elaboration of the epistemology of causation begun in his Chapters 2 and 3, where Mackie introduces "causal fields" and "progressive localization" as epistemological accounts of how we *know* causes (cf. pp. 35, 63, 73). A careful examination of the roles "a minimally complete causal account" and "explanatory causes" play in his Chapter 10 would show them merely to be extensions of his earlier epistemological views.

8

Causal Judgment
and Causal Explanation

PHILOSOPHERS HAVE long believed that problems of causation are closely connected to problems of causal explanation and causal judgment. This belief has no doubt derived much of its authority from the traditional assumption that effects are explainable or understandable in terms of their causes. Aristotle's influential theory of the "four causes," for example, is as much an analysis of basic principles of explanation as of types of causal relatedness. Since his time accounts of causal explanation and judgment have figured prominently in treatments of such fundamental philosophical problems as induction, free will, time, moral and legal responsibility, the nature of human action, and historical understanding.

Throughout our exposition and defense of Hume we have maintained that causation and explanation present substantially different problems. Chapters 5 and 7 defend this view in detail. Nevertheless, we do not deny that there are important connections between causation and explanation, if only because many requests for explanation are properly answered by the citation of causes. Indeed, almost every theory of causation has implications for the construction and evaluation of causal explanations. Hume's account is no exception. He offers and assesses explanations in a wide variety of contexts, always in the light of his own theory of causation. In this chapter we consider the question of how Hume's theory of causation bears on issues of causal explanation and causal judgment. We also describe Hume's actual approach to these issues and the commentary on that approach offered by Mill and other defenders of the regularity theory.

Because Hume's account of causation is revisionary, we should not be surprised if its application to the analysis and assessment of causal judgment and explanation turns out to be revisionary as well. Yet a revisionary account of judgment and explanation would be more difficult to defend than such an account of causation. Unlike causation, explanation is not fundamentally a relation between spatiotemporal particulars, nor could it be supposed to obtain independently of its discovery or description by sentient creatures. If explanation is a relation at all, it involves more than two relata. To say that one event explains another seems to be an elliptical way of describing a three or more term relation between the two causally connected events and sentient creatures who cite one event to explain the other. By contrast to causation, causal judgments and explanations are human practices shaped by purposes and beliefs.

A revisionary reconstruction of judgment and explanation that made rationally warranted causal explanations and judgments unattainable would therefore be unacceptable. Indeed, we would do well to question any account that ruled out the bulk of common judgments and explanations. The structure of judgment and explanation as a human enterprise sets limits on the degree of revision that is permissible. No successful analysis of these notions can transcend the established limits. On the other hand, some attempts at causal judgment and explanation are clearly inadequate, and an acceptable theory cannot endorse them.

In this concluding chapter we first canvass leading analyses of singular causal judgments. Many of these analyses have been treated in earlier chapters, at least insofar as they constitute objections to Hume's theory of causation. Here we briefly expound the constructive side of these accounts of causal judgment, and then consider whether they identify errors of either omission or commission in the regularity theory. Our intent is to show that despite the contributions made by possible alternative analyses of causal judgments, their aims differ fundamentally from Hume's, and consequently these analyses constitute no threat to his conception of causation. We argue that this conclusion applies as well to Hume's successor John Stuart Mill.

In later sections we shift from causal judgments to issues of explanation. The central topic that we address there is the relation between Hume's theory of causation and the contemporary covering-law account of explanation. We explore the possibility that Hume's theory entails an implicit commitment to this scheme of explanation. Finally, we consider whether defects in the covering-law model reveal faults that undermine Humean views.

I

Many philosophers have handled the concept of causation through an analysis of ordinary causal judgments. The most radical of these attempts assimilate all questions about causation to questions about causal judgment and explanation. Some even make the nature of causal judgment primary, and generate an account of causation from conclusions about causal judgment. Philosophers who defend singularist, manipulability, and contextualist theories of causation have generally challenged Hume's regularity analysis from this perspective. R. G. Collingwood, though a probing critic of Hume, is among the more moderate. He argues that there are three different senses of cause, and that Hume's account is inadequate because it neglects to take two of these senses into account. Gertrude Anscombe's reaction is at once more critical and more typical: "Contrary to the opinion of Hume, there are many different sorts of causality."[1] Based on such criticisms even some careful expositors of Hume's texts have accused him of philosophical error or at least of shortsightedness. For example, Antony Flew argues that Hume's theory errs significantly by overlooking the practical interests that inform causal judgments,[2] and Terence Penelhum complains that Hume does not account for our use of "cause" as a *sine qua non* or necessary condition—as in-

---

1. G. E. M. Anscombe, "Causality and Determination," in E. Sosa, ed., *Causation and Conditionals* (Oxford: Oxford University Press, 1975), p. 78.
2. Antony Flew, *Hume's Philosophy of Belief* (London: Routledge & Kegan Paul, 1961), p. 127.

stanced, for example, in historical judgments.³ Penelhum bluntly accuses Hume of failing to see that "it is not part of the notion of a cause as a necessary condition that it should also be a sufficient one."⁴

Let us begin our examination of causal judgment with an example of the (usually singular) causal assertions that prompt such philosophers to criticize Hume. Consider a circumstance that Collingwood considers typical of those calling for causal judgment and explanation:

A car skids while cornering at a certain point, strikes the kerb, and turns turtle. From the car-driver's point of view the cause of the accident was cornering too fast, and the lesson is that one must drive more carefully. From the county surveyor's point of view the cause was a defect in the surface or camber of the road, and the lesson is that greater care must be taken to make roads skid-proof. From the motor-manufacturer's point of view the cause was defective design in the car, and the lesson is that one must place the centre of gravity lower.⁵

Using such examples, Collingwood derives a "principle of the relativity of causes." He argues that persons who are differently situated will give different answers to the question "What is *the cause* of *y*?" Relativity of judgment occurs because the cause, for any given person, is that condition from the set of all relevant causal conditions that the person is capable of controlling or preventing, or at least the cause is that which is most naturally understood in terms of controllability. "The cause" judgments, on Collingwood's analysis, are thus relative to a specific context of investigation, determined by considerations of manipulability. Collingwood concludes that a person who is unable to control the conditions of an event's occurrence cannot use the term "cause" in one of its important meanings. There simply are no causes in this sense unless conditions are seen from the perspective of agent control.

Not everyone opposed to Hume believes in the contextual relativity of causes, or even that there are different senses of

3. Terence Penelhum, *Hume* (New York: St. Martin's Press, 1975), pp. 56f and p. 201, note 12.
4. *Ibid.*, p. 56.
5. R. G. Collingwood, *An Essay on Metaphysics* (Oxford: Clarendon Press, 1940), p. 304.

cause. Some are noncontextualists committed to a uniform analysis of singular causal statements. Ducasse's singularism is an example of a theory according to which the cause is the same for all, independent of context. Nevertheless, the subtle and significant differences between certain singularist theories, manipulability theories, and contextualist theories can be no part of our concern here. Our exclusive interest is their unified opposition to Hume and the grounds of that opposition. In considering the following positive proposals about the character of causal judgments, we shall therefore bracket the question of their many theoretical differences.

C. J. Ducasse

If it is the cause that we seek, we look for a *difference* in those circumstances between the moment when the phenomenon occurred, and the preceding moment. And the field among the entities of which the conditions lie is thereby also denied. It is that of circumstances which *remain constant* over the two moments.[6]

R. G. Collingwood

The term "cause," as actually used in modern English and other languages, is ambiguous. It has *three senses;* possibly more; but at any rate three.

Sense I. Here that which is "caused" is the *free and deliberate act* of a conscious and responsible agent, and "causing" him to do it means affording him a motive for doing it.

Sense II. Here that which is "caused" is an *event* in nature, and its "cause" is an event or state of things by producing or preventing which we can produce or prevent that whose cause it is said to be.

Sense III. Here that which is "caused" is an event or state of things, and its "cause" is another event or state of things standing to it in a one-one relation of causal priority: i.e. a relation of such a kind that (a) if the cause happens or exists the effect also must happen or exist, even if no further conditions are fulfilled, (b) the effect cannot happen or exist unless the cause happens or exists, (c) in some sense which remains to be defined, the cause is prior to the effect; for without such priority there would be no telling which is which.[7]

---

6. C. J. Ducasse, *Causation and the Types of Necessity* (Seattle: University of Washington Press, 1924; New York: Dover, 1969), p. 19.
7. Collingwood, *op. cit.,* pp. 285f (emphasis added).

H. L. A. Hart and A. M. Honoré

There is not a single concept of causation but a group or family of concepts. These are united not by a set of common features but by points of resemblance, some of them tenuous. Of this group the correlatives "cause and effect" mark off one member which is of fundamental importance in practical life and for that reason, if no other, has claim to be considered the central notion. . . . The notion, that a cause is essentially something which interferes with or intervenes in the course of events which would normally take place, is central to the common-sense concept of cause, and is at least as essential as the notions of invariable or constant sequence so much stressed by Mill and Hume.[8]

J. L. Mackie

I suggest that a statement which asserts a singular causal sequence, of such a form as "A caused P," often makes, implicitly, the following claims:

(i) A is at least an INUS condition of P—that is, there is a necessary and sufficient condition of P which has one of these forms: (AX or Y), (A or Y), AX, A.

(ii) A was present on the occasion in question.

(iii) The factors represented by the "X," if any, in the formula for the necessary and sufficient condition were present on the occasion in question.

(iv) Every disjunct in "Y" which does not contain "A" as a conjunct was absent on the occasion in question.[9]

This set of quotations presents the constructive side of several important non-Humean proposals. In previous chapters we evaluated aspects of Ducasse's singularism, Mackie's inus-condition analysis, and the manipulability theories of von Wright and Gasking. We found each wanting as alternatives to some aspect of Hume's theory of causation. The most instructive from among these theories of causal judgment for present purposes, however, is the eclectic and influential account offered by

---

8. H. L. A. Hart and A. M. Honoré, *Causation in the Law* (Oxford: Clarendon Press, 1959), pp. 26–27.

9. J. L. Mackie, "Causes and Conditions," *American Philosophical Quarterly* 2 (1965), pp. 245–64, as reprinted in Sosa, ed., *op. cit.*, pp. 15–38. On page 19, Mackie adds, "I do not suggest that this is the whole of what is meant by '*A* caused *P*' on any occasion, or even that it is a part of what is meant on every occasion."

H. L. A. Hart and A. M. Honoré. They draw heavily on uses of the term "cause" in legal, historical, and practical contexts, and they exhibit a special interest in "the cause" judgments of ordinary thought as expressed in singular causal statements.[10] They contend that careful attention to terms such as "cause," "effect," "result," and "consequence" reveals dimensions of meaning neglected in many philosophical treatments of causation, including those of Hume and the defenders of the regularity theory. Hart and Honoré find, for example, that the causal notions of "provision of reasons," "provision of opportunity," and "human intervention" are ignored in regularity theories. They hold that nonregularity principles govern the judgments of lawyers, historians, and the "plain man." The principles operative in these judgments, they claim, have more to do with the context of causal inquiry than with causal laws, which they regard as functioning primarily to justify causal judgments.

Hart and Honoré argue that a *cause* in practical life is a condition deviating from the normal or reasonably expected course of events, whereas a *mere condition* is a factor that is normal and inconspicuous. Criteria of normality, they maintain, are relative to one's context of inquiry, and this relativity indicates that use of the word "cause" is closely tied to the need to explain a puzzling or unusual occurrence. Their analysis follows the general lines of Collingwood's: they are contextualists who find the concept of causation to involve a cluster of related concepts and who also find the manipulability model essential. In their estimation, however, Collingwood misses the close connection between explanation and causation, and with it the crucial insight that causes are departures from the normal course of events.

Many contemporary philosophers interested in causation have taken Hart and Honoré's analysis as a point of departure. Samuel Gorovitz, for example, bases his account of causation on the Hart-Honoré thesis that causes are relative to context and selected because they are deviations from the circumstantially normal. Gorovitz finds Hart and Honoré's notion of "normality" both obscure and incomplete, and suggests a more technical

10. Hart and Honoré, *op. cit.,* pp. 17–48.

"differentiating-factor analysis."[11] But this contribution represents merely an improvement in the expression of a view whose essential features are shared with many others.

Let us now turn to the criticisms of the regularity theory that follow from these views. A common objection is that there are many cases in which we distinguish causes from their effects even though knowledge of regularities would not alone allow us to do so. Moreover, it is often observed that certain relations which are clearly not causal nevertheless satisfy the regularity theorists' criteria of causation. A traditional example of the second sort is the regularity of night following day, which is said on the regularity view to entail that the latter be the cause of the former. Examples of the first sort are often found in legal and practical contexts in which known regularities do not discriminate between causes and mere conditions. Thus the murderer's administration of poison and the victim's hunger must be distinguished as cause and mere condition of death, though both are equally implicated in regularities subsuming the effect in question. The nearly universal complaint is that the regularity theory is useless in these cases and that if one removes the manipulability, differentiating, or abnormality dimension, the causal relationship vanishes with it. Regularity theorists' analyses of causation are thus dismissed as one-sided accounts whose misplaced emphasis stems from an exclusive focus on scientific contexts.

These criticisms suggest two basic conclusions pertinent to the interpretation of Hume and the defense of a regularity theory of causation: (1) the regularity theory is too restricted to provide an adequate account of causation; and (2) theories of judgment and explanation are essential to an understanding of *the causal relation.* Insofar as the latter theories describe a crucial distinction in judgment between causes and conditions, they seem to highlight the inadequacies of a regularity theory blind to such differences.

---

11. Samuel Gorovitz, "Causal Judgments and Causal Explanations," *Journal of Philosophy* 62 (1965), pp. 695–711, as reprinted in Tom L. Beauchamp, ed., *Philosophical Problems of Causation* (Encino, Calif.: Dickenson Publishing Company, 1974), p. 240.

II

Hume and his successor John Stuart Mill together stand opposed to the views presented in the previous section. Hume provides no direct rejoinder to these claims, for reasons we shall elaborate, but he is forthright enough in stating his opposition to views that discriminate between causes and conditions. In a well-known passage of the *Treatise*, he writes, "we must reject the distinction betwixt *cause* and *occasion*, when suppos'd to signify any thing essentially different from each other" (T, 171; emphasis in original). Mill's answer is equally direct. He argues that "the real Cause is the whole of these antecedents; and we have, philosophically speaking, no right to give the name of cause to one of them exclusively of the others."[12] Hart and Honoré, Mackie, and many writers on causation have complained that this model is excessively idealized, even for physical causation.[13] Mill, however, is uncompromising: "Nothing can better show the absence of any scientific ground for the distinction between the cause of a phenomenon and its conditions, than the capricious manner in which we select from among the conditions that which we choose to denominate the cause."[14]

The grounds for this summary rejection of distinctions which, as Hume says, "we sometimes make," are to be found in many of our arguments in favor of the regularity theory of causation. Together they constitute a strong case against the criticism that Hume's theory fails to draw obvious distinctions and sustain widely shared beliefs. In Chapter 1 we argued that Hume's is a revisionary theory of causation, not a logical or conceptual investigation of ordinary language or common sense. In Chapter 4 we expanded this thesis, noting that Hume's stated interest is in the "true meaning" of causal statements and not in the "frequent use of words." In Chapter 2 we found that Hume's revisionary analysis is a constructive attempt to analyze the true nature of causation, and not a sceptical attempt to question the existence of causes or the workings of causal reasoning. In

12. John Stuart Mill, *A System of Logic* (London: Longmans, 1961), Book III, Chapter 5, Section 3.
13. Hart and Honoré, *op. cit.*, pp. 21, 41–43; and J. L. Mackie, *The Cement of the Universe* (Oxford: Clarendon Press, 1974), p. 118.
14. Mill, *op. cit.*

Chapter 3 we argued that singular causal statements entail causal laws (whatever else such statements may also involve) and that Ducasse's singularism collapses into the regularity theory. In Chapters 5 and 6 we noted the counterintuitive character of many of Hume's statements about contiguity and directionality. We mentioned that his views seem to deviate from common convictions and to be inconsistent with apparently successful causal explanations. Finally, and most importantly, we argued in Chapter 7 that Hume's theory constitutes a metaphysical account of causation that renders sentences reporting this relation extensional, and thus that Hume's theory is not intended as an epistemological account of causal explanation and judgment.

These contentions all suggest a firm conclusion regarding the theories of causation and consequent criticisms of Hume outlined in Section I of this chapter. However prescient these accounts of causal judgment, they provide inadequate grounds for the criticism of Hume, because their philosophical purposes diverge too widely from his. The philosophers we have cited are motivated by philosophical interests in the epistemological principles governing judgments in a variety of contexts. Judgments of causal responsibility in law and morals, for example, are based on principles that make it possible to determine whether a particular human action is a cause. An action's *being* "the cause" is in turn influenced by the need to identify responsible agents. Likewise in ordinary and historical causal judgments, practical concerns fashion the truth conditions of "*x* caused *y*." Contrary to the opinions of Hart and Honoré, Anscombe, and innumerable others, no Humean will deny that there are various "senses" of cause, not all of which are controlled by empirical truth conditions. The principles involved may well be "man-made," as Hart and Honoré note in citing such statements as "The gardener's failure to water the flowers caused their dying."[15] Indeed, these senses may in the end depend on moral, or at least normative, considerations. As William H. Dray points out:

A causal explanation is often . . . designed to show what went wrong; it focuses attention not just on what was or could have been done, but on what *should* or *should not* have been done by certain historical

15. Hart and Honoré, *op. cit.*, pp. 35f.

agents. Thus, selecting the causal condition sometimes cannot be divorced from assigning blame.[16]

The language of "selection" is common in these theories. Though constrained by governing principles, one selects from a range of causal conditions, any one of which may truly be "the cause." There is a deficiency in the regularity theory only if it pretends to analyze these *senses* of "causation" and offers an account of the principles by which causes are "selected." But the regularity theory is not of this order. Hume has multiple interests, but this aim is not among them. He is concerned with the metaphysical, epistemological, and psychological problems of causation and causal inference spawned by his overarching intent in the *Treatise* to produce a science of human nature. But he is not interested in the nature of ordinary causal judgments. At most he advances a theory on the basis of which the misleading directives of custom and imagination can be counteracted and corrected:

> Tho' custom be the foundation of all our judgments, yet sometimes it has an effect on the imagination in opposition to the judgment. . . .
> We may correct this propensity by a reflection on the nature of these circumstances. . . .
> We shall *afterwards* [Sec. 15] take notice of some general rules, by which we ought to regulate our judgment concerning causes and effects. (T, 147–49; emphasis added)

Hume here manifests a subsidiary interest in what he calls both "principles" and "general rules" that guide causal judgment in selecting true causes from accidentally conjoined conditions (cf. T, 97n, 170–75). But he does not intend to analyze practical, historical, and legal judgments about causation; and there is no indication in his work that he regards the regularity theory as directly relevant to this task. Of course, Hume and Mill may be chasing rainbows, for it may be the case that all causal judgments and explanations are context bound—scientific and metaphysical ones no less than the practical. Hanson's critique of the regularity theory seems to reach this conclusion. Should such a broad alternative account of causation turn out to be correct, Hume and Mill can be faulted for total failure; but let

16. W. Dray, *Laws and Explanation in History* (Oxford: Clarendon Press, 1957), p. 99.

us at least be clear about their enterprise. They ought not to be faulted for neglecting to provide analyses they never intended to provide and had no philosophical reason to undertake.

III

Three apparent problems are raised by the arguments thus far advanced. First, our suggestion that Hume has no theory of causal judgment may be deemed unacceptable because large sections of the *Treatise* are devoted to causal inference and thus to circumstances under which causal judgments are formulated. Second, the belief, apparently shared by Mill and Hume, that a cause is the whole set of the antecedents of an effect may seem incompatible either with the regularity theory altogether or with the very possibility of causal judgments. Either outcome would of course threaten the regularity view. Third, any claim that Hume and Mill are concerned with causation and not with the analysis of causal judgments seems to leave no room for them to handle the problems of causal explanation we promised to treat in this chapter. We shall consider the first two issues in the present section, reserving the third for the remainder of the chapter.

Hume plainly did develop a theory of causal inference that is intimately connected to the regularity theory. It is predominantly descriptive and psychological in character, but contains important logical and epistemological elements as well (some of which were discussed in detail in Chapter 2). For example, Hume distinguishes the psychological process of causal inference from causal inference that *successfully* locates the cause. He further distinguishes both forms of inference from the true cause itself. His theory of inference is based on a psychological account of observation and association, and of course it explains the movement of thought from cause to effect in terms of custom. In certain passages Hume exhibits a belief that causal judgment involves a selective picking out of causes. He treats this process, however, in the way psychologists explain selective attention and discrimination; he evidently does not think it has anything to do with the logical principles regulating proper selection of causes. Thus it is no surprise that his enterprise differs starkly from that of the philosophers such as Collingwood mentioned in Section I.

According to Hume's philosophy causal judgments are based on experiences of constant conjunction. Yet Hume nowhere denies that there may be special reasons for selecting some set of constantly conjoined conditions over another set of constantly conjoined conditions—given the variety of purposes (practical, legal, historical, etc.) that influence human decisions. His real philosophical interest, however, is in context-independent judgments of the true cause, as illustrated by his account of inductive rules. He simply is not concerned with conditions dictated by practical contexts. The correctness or incorrectness of a causal judgment, then, is determined by true causal relations— the only cement of the universe—and not in any other way.

Mill's views are similar. Concerning the ordinary distinction between what is denominated the cause and what is considered merely a condition, he writes: "However numerous the conditions may be, there is hardly any of them which may not, *according to the purpose of our immediate discourse*, obtain that nominal preeminence" of being denominated the cause.[17] Following a series of examples of the distinction between *the* cause and its background conditions (with the variability and contextual determination discussed by Hart and Honoré), Mill concludes: "Thus we see that each and every condition of the phenomenon may be taken in its turn, and, with equal propriety in common parlance, . . . may be spoken of as if it were the entire cause."[18] Mill holds that what may be unexceptional in common parlance, and what may be permissible according to immediate discourse, is subject to systematic explanation, without thereby affecting our understanding of causation in the objects. According to Mill, "the real Cause is *the whole of these antecedents;* and we have, philosophically, no right to give the name of cause to one of them exclusively of the others."[19]

The notion that the cause is the whole of the antecedents of the effect can be variously interpreted, and different objections will be offered against Hume and Mill depending on the interpretation accepted. Sometimes the notion that the cause is the whole of the antecedents is treated as a claim about all of the causally relevant conditions *contiguous* with the effect. Let us call this sense 1. So interpreted, the whole-of-the-antecedents

17. Mill, *op. cit.*
18. *Ibid.*
19. *Ibid.*

view may be considered incompatible with the very possibility of true causal judgments. Alternatively the whole-of-the-antecedents view can be treated as a claim not about the spatiotemporally contiguous causal conditions of an effect, but as a claim about the entire network of causal chains that stretches backward in time from the effect, the whole of its antecedents over time. Let us call this sense 2. So interpreted, the whole-of-the-antecedents claim seems incompatible with the *regularity* theory, for there could be in principle no regularities of this order.

Even if sense 2 were the correct interpretation, the allegation of incompatibility with the regularity theory could not be sustained. The errors on which this argument trades were exposed in Chapter 5 when contiguity and causal chains were treated. We can all agree that there is no law connecting effects and the whole prior history of the universe leading up to them. If the whole-of-the-antecedents view required such a law, the regularity theory would indeed be undercut. But of course it does not require such a law. Let us allow that each of the events figuring in the vast network of causal chains leading up to a given effect is minimally necessary in the circumstances for the effect, as it came about. It does not follow that one or more laws connect each causally necessary prior event with the effect that constitutes the terminus of the network of causal chains in question. Hume and Mill are committed only to the view that laws subsume each pair of contiguous links in these chains— links that perhaps criss-cross and overlap in the case of any given effect. Behind an effect stand many chains constituting the whole of its antecedents (in sense 2), a whole that is causal not in virtue of one law, but in virtue of many. There are as many laws as there are causally distinct types of conjunctions in the network of causally necessary links. This full set of events leading directly to an effect is how the sequence of prior events looks when all anthropocentric and normative principles of selection, such as those cited by Honoré and Hart, are stripped away, and nature is left bare of human interest and interpretation.

Understood in sense 2, then, the whole-of-the-antecedents thesis in no way conflicts with the regularity theory's insistence that causal connections are law-governed. The only respect in which this interpretation is incompatible with Hume's theory of causation is in its suggestion that among the antecedents con-

stituting the cause are events that are not spatiotemporally contiguous with the effect, events that occurred long before and far
away from the effect. Because Hume is committed to the spatiotemporal contiguity of causes and effects, he cannot embrace
the whole-of-the-antecedents thesis when interpreted as a claim
that the entire network of chains is "the cause" of the effect.
A Humean must therefore reject this understanding of Mill's
claim that "the real cause . . . is the whole of these antecedents." "The cause" in Hume's regularity theory indicates the
set of all causally necessary circumstances obtaining at the time
and place the effect occurred, and this set alone (i.e., sense 1
above) must constitute the whole of the antecedents.

Yet when Mill's claim that the cause is the whole of the antecedents is interpreted in this way, it is often criticized on the
ground that it makes accurate causal reports impossible. This
charge is more serious than the contention that he failed to
analyze ordinary causal claims, a task neither he nor Hume set
themselves. J. L. Mackie, for instance, holds that analyses of the
cause as reflecting the sum of the antecedent conditions is logically incompatible with the truth of correct causal reports.
After advancing his own account of causes as inus conditions,
Mackie notes the following advantage they have over causes
treated as the sum of conditions sufficient for their effect:

> [It is a] well-known difficulty that it is impossible, without including
> in the cause the whole environment, the whole prior state of the uni-
> verse . . . to find a genuinely sufficient condition [for a particular
> house's catching fire] . . . because we should have to include, as one
> of the negative conjuncts, such an item as the earth's not being de-
> stroyed by a nuclear explosion just [prior to the effect]. . . . but it is
> easy and reasonable to say simply that such an explosion would . . .
> take us outside the field in which we are considering this effect. . . .[20]

Thus, on Mackie's view, Mill's claim is seriously defective,
because the sum of conditions would have to include a possibly
infinite number of negative conditions. If this infinite set is
part of the cause, causes could not be described in sentences of
finite length. To avoid this difficulty Mackie introduces "the
causal field," a notion that bears striking parallels to Colling-

20. Mackie, "Causes and Conditions," pp. 23–24.

wood's relativism as well as to Hart and Honoré's "causal contexts." Mackie notes that the question (1) "What caused this man's skin cancer?" may mean (1a) "Why did this man develop skin cancer now when he did not develop it before?" or it may mean, among other things, (1b) "Why did this man develop skin cancer, whereas other men who were also exposed to radiation did not?"[21] In (1a) the "causal field" is the cancer of the man, and one acceptable answer to the question is that the man was exposed to a certain amount of radiation. In (1b) the causal field is the class of men exposed to radiation, and in this case being exposed to radiation cannot be the cause. Mackie's account has the objectionable characteristic of treating causation through explanatory contexts. It merely explains why and how we select certain features from among the antecedents of the effect, and not others, in ordinary causal judgments. Perhaps it is for this reason that Mackie recognizes an interpretation of Mill whose conclusions he finds philosophically acceptable:

> Since even the choice of a field is relative to a purpose or a point of view [and may be] . . . closely related to our interests, there is much to be said for Mill's refusal to distinguish "philosophically speaking" between causes and conditions. As an analysis of ordinary language, this would be wrong; but from a theoretical point of view, as an account of causal processes themselves, it would be right.[22]

Despite this endorsement, it is important to note that the alleged difficulty leading Mackie to prefer his broad account to Mill's is not a difficulty for the regularity theory. Mill's account of the cause is actually *compatible* with ordinary distinctions between causes and conditions, and need not involve the "refusal" Mackie mentions. Mackie supposes that we cannot specify the whole cause if we cannot wholly specify it. He assumes that because a full description of the cause must be of infinite length on Mill's view, any lesser description is not a description of the cause; and consequently causes could never be cited. But merely because a particular description of the causal event is couched sometimes in terms of one aspect and sometimes in terms of another (depending on the context of inquiry, occurrence, or

21. *Ibid.*, p. 22.
22. Mackie, *The Cement of the Universe*, p. 120.

causal field), and thus is incomplete, it does not follow that the whole panoply of antecedents which characterize the cause event has not been referred to.

Davidson has expressed this point in an account we cited in Chapter 3: "Mill's critics are no doubt justified in contending that we may correctly give the cause without saying enough about it to demonstrate that it was sufficient; but they share Mill's confusion if they think every deletion from the description of an event represents something deleted from the event described."[23] Davidson's point actually can be used in defense of Mill, despite the apparent criticism. Certainly it misses the mark when it invokes "Mill's confusion." Mill explicitly allowed that in ordinary discourse we may cite the cause without saying enough about it to demonstrate sufficiency. It is also not clear that Mill asserted or even supposed that every deletion from the description of an event represents something deleted from the event described. There are several passages that at least strongly suggest a contrary position. Thus Mill writes: "If we do not, when aiming at accuracy, enumerate all the conditions, it is only because some of them will in most cases be understood without being expressed, or because for the purpose in view they may without detriment be overlooked."[24]

Davidson's point effectively answers Mill's critics, but not Mill himself. One of Davidson's own arguments will suffice to illustrate why:

"The cause of this match's lighting is that it was struck—yes, but that was only *part* of the cause; it had to be a dry match, there had to be adequate oxygen in the atmosphere, it had to be struck hard enough, etc." . . . [This] "yes, but" comment does not have the force we thought. It cannot be that the striking of this match was only part of the cause, for this match was in fact dry, in adequate oxygen, and the striking surface was hard enough. What is partial in the sentence "the cause of this match's lighting is that it was struck" is the *description* of the cause; as we add to the description of the cause, we may approach the point where we can deduce, from this description and laws, that an effect of the kind described would follow.[25]

23. D. Davidson, "Causal Relations," *The Journal of Philosophy* 64 (1967), as reprinted in Beauchamp, ed., *op. cit.*, p. 195.
24. Mill, *op. cit.*
25. Davidson, *op. cit.*, p. 195.

The positions defended by Mill and Hume on these matters are again not incompatible with the views of many contemporary philosophers who have attacked them. These critics have mistakenly thought that their special interests in the ordinary conception of causation offer grounds for criticizing Hume's and Mill's treatment of the causal relation itself. With Hume's actual intentions now firmly in mind, we may turn to the implications of the regularity theory for problems of causal explanation.

IV

We have argued that neither Mill nor Hume intends to analyze the principles regulating singular causal judgments. In light of this conclusion, how should the regularity theory treat problems of causal explanation, especially in light of the fact that Hume seems to have no greater interest in causal explanation than in causal judgment? His apparent indifference is compatible with a revisionary account or rational reconstruction of explanation. As we have repeatedly argued, Hume's account of causation is revisionary. The Humean may offer a parallel rational reconstruction of explanation, so long as the account does not render explanation an impossible or rare achievement. But what form could such a revisionary thesis assume?

A revisionary account of explanation that many Humeans have found attractive is the deductive-nomological or covering-law model of explanation, and we have left little doubt in earlier chapters of this book that Hume is in some measure committed to covering laws. In the remaining sections of this chapter we examine more precisely Hume's commitment to this model, and the difficulties, if any, which such a commitment generates for his regularity theory of causation. In this section we expound the broad outlines of the model and of Hume's investment in it. In the next two sections we consider objections to the model when construed as a sufficient condition for explanation, the degree to which these objections reflect on the regularity theory, and possible strategies for undercutting these objections. In the final two sections we assess the claim that the deductive-nomological account provides necessary conditions of adequate explanation, attending particularly to purposive or goal-directed behavior, which is often claimed to be non-Humean in its underlying causal mechanisms. We consider whether the explanations offered for human action by historians and social scientists, and indeed by Hume himself, are consistent with his theory of causation.

Hume offers no explicit characterization of causal explanation, but leading proponents of the covering-law analysis have traditionally appealed to certain key features of his theory of causation. Indeed, according to one version of this model, all explanations of contingent phenomena proceed by the subsumption of the item to be explained under a law that connects it to conditions *causally relevant* to its occurrence. The earliest explicit statement is found in Mill's *System of Logic:*

An individual fact is said to be explained by pointing out its cause, that is, by stating the law or laws of causation of which its production is an instance. Thus a conflagration is explained when it is proved to have arisen from a spark falling into the midst of a heap of combustibles; and in a similar manner, a law or uniformity in nature is said to be explained when another law or laws are pointed out, of which the law itself is but a case, and from which it could be deduced.[26]

Mill goes on, as have other followers of Hume, to argue that this account, suitably amended, holds for the explanation of all contingent occurrences in the natural and social sciences.

That Hume concurs in these claims seems evident from several diverse sources. For example, he holds that explanation of natural phenomena proceeds by subsumption under laws of successively greater generality:

It is confessed, that the utmost effort of human reason is to reduce the principles, productive of natural phenomena, to a greater simplicity, and to resolve the many particular effects into a few general causes, by means of reasonings from analogy, experience, and observation. But as to the causes of these general causes, we should in vain attempt their discovery; nor shall we ever be able to satisfy ourselves, by any particular explication of them. These ultimate springs and principles are totally shut up from human curiosity and enquiry. Elasticity, gravity, cohesion of parts, communication of motion by impulse; these are probably the ultimate causes and principles which we shall ever dis-

26. Mill, *op. cit.,* Book III, Chapter 12, Section 1.

cover in nature; and we may esteem ourselves sufficiently happy, if, by accurate enquiry and reasoning, we can trace up the particular phenomena to, or near to, these general principles. The most perfect philosophy of the natural kind only staves off our ignorance a little longer. (EHU, Sec. 26)

As we argued in Chapter 3, Hume suggests that explanation requires laws, and that the ultimate explanations of both particular occurrences and the generalizations that subsume them are the laws of physics. More importantly, he claims that we can expect no more from explanations than that they reveal the items explained as instances of the consequents of causal laws (of perhaps successively more general sorts). This restriction on what we can hope to discover from explanations is significant, for Humean theories of explanation are sometimes condemned on the ground that the mere subsumption of an event under a regularity is no explanation at all. As one contemporary opponent of covering-law explanations writes, "once the demand for explanation arises, an answer which does no more than represent what is to be explained as what we always find happening in such circumstances fails to explain it at all. . . . [S]ome sort of analysis besides mere certification as a recurring phenomenon, would seem to be essential."[27] The view that explanations must "go beyond certifying" something as "what always happens" is one that Hume and his followers ultimately reject, another reason for saying they defend a revisionary account of explanation. Most alternative theories connect explanation with subjective *understanding*. They stipulate, as at least a necessary condition of successful explanation, that it reduce puzzlement, make the explanandum comprehensible, and meet certain contextually determined criteria of appropriateness.[28]

On Hume's contrasting view, the most we can hope for by way of explanatory completeness, accuracy, and understanding is the demonstration that the occurrence to be explained reflects regularities of a perhaps fundamental but nevertheless

---

27. Dray, *op. cit.*, pp. 72f.
28. See for example Michael Scriven, "Explanation, Prediction and Laws," *Minnesota Studies in Philosophy of Science,* Vol. 3 (Minneapolis: University of Minnesota Press, 1962), pp. 170–229, and Peter Achinstein, "Explanation," *Studies in the Philosophy of Science, American Philosophical Quarterly,* Monograph Series, No. 3 (Oxford: Basil Blackwell, 1969).

wholly contingent type. This position strongly suggests that Hume would sympathize with those philosophers whose aim is to provide a revisionary analysis or rational reconstruction of explanation by appeal to covering laws. Notable among these philosophers has been Carl Hempel, who has defended the deductive-nomological pattern first elaborated by Mill. Hempel seeks to make the assessment of explanations as much a matter of formal considerations as possible. He deems inadequate the requirement that explanations provide understanding, construed as the subjective reduction of puzzlement. In its place, he proposes that explanations establish a formally determinable, deductive relation between sentences describing the event to be explained, the initial conditions (the cause), and a law or laws permitting the deduction of the former from the latter. In this way the notion of explanation is assimilated to that of proof, a procedure whose satisfaction is mechanically determinable for many problems.

Although Hempel and other empiricists have clearly endorsed some version of the regularity theory of causation,[29] none has ever offered the following simple argument as a rationale for their accounts of explanation: (a) to provide a causal explanation of an event is to cite its cause under an appropriate description; (b) causal connections obtain in virtue of laws that subsume events; and therefore (c) to provide a causal explanation (and not merely a true singular causal statement) involves the citation or presumption of a law or laws underwriting the connection between the event to be explained and the events described as its cause. These three simple parts of a Humean argument provide a more direct reason for accepting the deductive-nomological model of explanation than does the attempt to assimilate explanation to proof. They also seem superior to Hempel's so-called general adequacy requirement for explanations, according to which explanations take this form because only thus do they give good grounds for supposing that the explanandum event actually obtained.[30]

The deductive-nomological account of explanation has en-

29. C. G. Hempel, *Aspects of Scientific Explanation* (New York: Free Press, 1965), pp. 349ff.

30. Hume himself embraced this latter criterion of adequacy for explanations. Cf. his insistence that we can know of the occurrence of an event only through causal considerations (T, 108; EHU, Sec. 87).

countered many substantial objections, and it is understandable that a proponent would not want to carry an additional obligation to defend a particular theory of causality. Thus even *Humeans* interested in this account of explanation could not be expected to treat Hume's theory of causation in detail or to make it an essential part of their account of explanation. Furthermore, proponents of the covering-law account have held that its application, especially in the natural sciences, extends well beyond the bounds of explicitly causal contexts. Ernest Nagel, for example, treats explanations that appeal to the equation of state for an ideal gas, $PV = rT$, as covering-law explanations, but not causal ones, on the grounds that the equation's variables vary functionally and symmetrically in a way that causal sequences do not.[31]

The issues complicating the preceding seven chapters of this work perhaps testify to the wisdom of dissociating the covering-law account of explanation from the unnecessary demands of a full scale defense of Hume's theory of causation. On the other hand, if these chapters strengthen the grip of Hume's account of causation, they must improve the position of the covering-law account of explanation. More importantly, they lend credence to the rational reconstructionist aims of a covering-law theorist by providing independent reasons to suppose that we can expect no more of explanations than what the covering-law model offers. If Hume is right about the limits to explanatory pretensions, then we can only ask of an account of explanation that it conform to the standards for perspicuity and clarity already exemplified in the mathematical notion of proof.

In his account of scientific explanation, Hempel notes that "the terms 'empirical science' and 'scientific explanation' will . . . be understood to refer to the entire field of empirical inquiry, including the natural and the social sciences as well as historical research."[32] Hume is notoriously committed in the *Treatise* to an account of explanation that is uniform across all the nonmathematical disciplines in which explanations are advanced and assessed. His "science of human nature" was conceived both at the time he wrote it and subsequently as a novel

---

31. E. Nagel, *The Structure of Science* (New York: Harcourt, Brace & World, 1961), Chapter 3.
32. Hempel, *op. cit.*, p. 333.

and revisionary approach to scientific explanation. The following statement is indicative of his approach: "There is a general course of nature in human actions, as well as in the operations of the sun and the climate. . . . In judging of the actions of men we must proceed upon the same maxims, as when we reason concerning external objects" (T, 402–3). This position gives yet another reason for holding that Hume would concur in the broad outlines of the deductive-nomological treatment of explanation (at least as Hempel develops it).

We conclude, then, that though Hume did not offer such an account with the precision we might wish, he apparently holds that events are explained by subsumption under laws, that laws themselves are explained by subsumption, that both the natural and social disciplines can uniformly be treated, and that these claims have prescriptive or revisionary force for those regions of inquiry in which they are ignored in actual practice.

V

The natural affinity between the regularity theory and the deductive-nomological model has led each to be assessed by reference to the merit of the other. This association is problematic for the defender of Hume's theory of causation, for the deductive-nomological model has been subjected to extensive criticism on grounds remote from problems of causation. On this theory, explanations are usually given for events, but in fact particulars of other sorts are also involved, including states, conditions, facts, etc. The sentences that provide the explanation, the "explanans," must meet several substantial conditions: they must describe one or more general laws and must include an account of the initial or boundary conditions within which the explained or "explanandum" phenomenon occurred, arose, or obtained. These two components of the explanans must jointly imply the truth of the explanandum statement. When initially advanced by Hempel and Oppenheim,[33] the theory also required that the explanans have "empirical content" and that the explanans be true.

These last two conditions of an adequate explanation have

---

33. C. G. Hempel and Paul Oppenheim, "Studies in the Logic of Explanation," *Philosophy of Science* 15 (1948), pp. 135–75.

long bedeviled the covering-law theory. The aim of the em-
pirical-content stipulation is to exclude metaphysical, theological, and other scientifically "disreputable" accounts of phenomena which may pass muster on a commonsense account of explanation. The problem with this condition is a variant of one
that has haunted empiricism from Hume's day to our own: it
has proved impossible to expound an effective criterion of empirical content which is neither so broad as to legitimate much of
what Hume calls "school metaphysics," nor so narrow as to exclude much of what he calls "reasoning concerning matter of
fact and existence" (EHU, Sec. 132).

The second requirement, that the explanans be true, raises
a different problem of epistemic indeterminism for the revisionary covering-law model. Given that the explanans must contain
laws, and assuming that the evidence for any nomological statement is always incomplete, it follows that whether any set of
statements constitutes an explanation is never beyond inductive
doubt. The positive claim that a set of statements is an *explanation* will be as much open to revision as the lawlike statement it relies upon. This consequence is problematic for the deductive-nomological model, because many sentences seem to constitute an explanation whether or not they prove ultimately to
be true. For example, no one is inclined to deny explanatory
power to Newtonian accounts of the height of the tide at a
particular date and place just because the laws they cite have
turned out to be false.

On the other hand, to forgo entirely the requirement of
truth, or some similar epistemic stipulation, would result in
even graver counterintuitive consequences. Without such a requirement trivial explanations for events can be produced.
Given any explanandum statement, it requires only minimal
logical ingenuity to construct a set of sentences that includes a
false universal conditional and that implies the explanandum
sentence, thereby satisfying the covering-law model. To abandon
epistemic requirements of the explanans is thus to deprive explanations of their explanatory power.

One alternative in the face of this difficulty is to substitute for
the requirement of truth the requirement that the explanans
be "well supported by available evidence." This strategy may enable us to retain the covering-law model as an account of ex-

planation while remaining faithful to most of our ordinary views on the subject. The trouble with this alternative is that the notion of "evidential support" is no clearer than the concept of empirical content, as required by the condition discussed above; and, even weakened in this way, the covering-law model will diverge from ordinary beliefs about explanation. For according to ordinary notions, the distinguishing constituent of explanation is not a set of logical, semantical, and epistemological features, but rather a body of informal, context-dependent features such as reduction to the familiar and the allaying of puzzlement. Accounts that by common agreement satisfy these conditions and that satisfy ordinary demands for explanatory completeness may yet lack "evidential support." This divergence from ordinary conceptions reflects one respect in which the covering-law model offers a rational reconstruction of ordinary notions.

A still more controversial divergence from ordinary standards of explanation can be found in the model's requirement that explanation and prediction be symmetrical. Because an explanation involves the deduction of a statement describing the occurrence of a particular phenomenon from a lawlike generalization and a description of initial conditions, it follows that the lawlike generalization and the initial condition statement together justify belief that the explanandum phenomenon has occurred or will occur, and thus that the occurrence could have been either predicted or retrodicted. Accordingly, it will be a necessary condition of every adequate scientific explanation that it serve equally well as a prediction or a retrodiction. This requirement, which seems a fairly obvious inference from deductive-nomological strictures, flies in the face of common evaluations of explanations, for we customarily do not hold them to so rigorous a standard. Here again the covering-law analysis diverges from conventional views in offering a rational reconstruction.

These problems continue to plague the covering-law theory of explanation, but is there any reason to suppose that they also create problems for Hume's theory of causation? We do not see that there need be any significant spillover from problems of explanation to causation. For example, the complexity of defining "empirical content" and "evidential support" bears directly on Hume's epistemology and on the general philosophical program of his empiricist followers. But it does not present difficulties for the *regularity* theory. One might argue further that none of the counterintuitive implications of the covering-law model are relevant to Hume's theory of causation, because, despite appearances, the two subjects are utterly distinct. Such an argument rests on the premise that the deductive-nomological theory is not an analysis of *causal* explanation, so that problems for the former are not problems for the latter. In support of this claim, it is noteworthy that nothing in the covering-law theory's demands for initial conditions requires that explanans statements describe the spatiotemporally contiguous and temporally prior conditions of the explanandum phenomenon, i.e., its cause.[34] Indeed, covering-law theorists are prepared to accept as initial conditions certain events, states, and circumstances that are apparently not causes of the effect to be explained. Thus the dispositional states and macroscopic properties of an object can be explained by the object's simultaneous microstructure together with laws relating the macroproperties and the microstructure. It is also sometimes claimed that we may provide a covering-law explanation of a phenomenon by citing its effect and a teleological law relating them. (Even apparently nonteleological laws, such as Fermat's least-action principle in optics, occasionally permit such apparently noncausal explanation.)

Although these considerations suggest that covering-law explanations are not restricted to the class of causal explanations, they certainly cannot entirely obviate a Humean defense of deductive-nomological explanation and rational reconstruction in this domain. It was the intention of Mill and other followers of Hume, as we have seen, to extend Hume's account of causation to all explanatory contexts, so that all explanations would in the end be causal explanations. The Humean is committed to the view that even where the term "cause" does not figure in an explanation, and even where the initial conditions do not seem overtly to constitute the cause of the explanandum phe-

---

34. Hempel makes this claim in the course of attempting to distinguish causal explanation and deductive-nomological explanation in "Explanation in Science and History" in R. Colodny, ed., *Frontiers of Science and Philosophy* (Pittsburgh: University of Pittsburgh Press, 1962), pp. 9-33.

nomenon, *the power of the explanation must ultimately rest on processes that are causal in Hume's original sense.* Teleological explanations, for example, are not admitted by the Humean unless they rest on a Humean causal process. Least-action explanations such as those involving Fermat's principles are clearly causal in that reference to future events (in the explanation of past ones) neither entails retrocausation nor is ineliminable. And physical microanalytic explanations, though admittedly synchronic, are of the sort Hume would have sanctioned as causal, because they trade on the causal laws cited in their elaboration.

Thus, problems for the deductive-nomological model that stem from its status as a revisionary reconstruction of ordinary conceptions cannot simply be swept aside by defenders of Hume, for his theory of causation does have all the *implications* for explanation discussed in the previous section, and perhaps other implications as well. On the other hand, as we shall argue, greater explicit reliance on Hume's own insights into causal reasoning will assist defenders of the covering-law model in their attempt to circumvent the aforementioned objections. This strategy may require a revision in the outlines of the covering-law model, as many of its proponents have conceived that model. But this revision presents no problems for the philosopher bent on defending Hume's theory of causation.

VI

The covering-law model is challenged by technical objections and informal counterexamples. Both the objections and the counterexamples are contrived to show that a set of sentences can satisfy every demand of the model, and yet fail to explain the explanandum.

Consider first the technical problems. Hempel and other contemporary exponents of the covering-law model seek to provide an account of explanations that employs a formal language no stronger than that of first-order truth-functional logic. One reason for this commitment is their desire to treat explanation as objective, as a mathematical procedure modelled on proof. Another reason is their belief that a language no stronger than first-order logic suffices in all scientific contexts, in part because it seems sufficient for the mathematical formulae through which much scientific knowledge is expressed. Finally, first-order logic is a system that we thoroughly understand, and so promises to bring an especially high order of perspicuity to the analysis of explanation. In Hempel and Oppenheim's classic presentation of the deductive-nomological model,[35] an explanation is defined formally as follows: an ordered pair of sentences (T, C) constitutes an explanation for a singular sentence E if and only if

(a) C is a singular sentence, and T is a set of universally quantified sentences employing purely qualitative predicates;
(b) T and C are true;
(c) E is logically derivable from T and C jointly, but not from either alone; and
(d) T is compatible with at least one class of singular sentences which has C but not E as a consequence.

This apparently innocuous formalization of criteria already expounded informally has the unfortunate property of enabling us to construct an infinite variety of counterexamples that impugn the covering-law account. A simple example will suffice to illustrate this problem. Suppose T is the law that objects expand when heated, and E, the explanandum sentence, asserts that the moon is devoid of life. Suppose further that we add to T a statement such as "The moon is devoid of life or is heated but does not expand." This statement functions as C is required to by the formalization; E then follows from T and C, and all three sentences satisfy conditions (a) through (d). Yet the moon's being devoid of life has not been explained. Accordingly the multiple criteria in the covering-law model do not constitute a sufficient condition of explanation. They seem so trivially satisfiable as to shed no light on explanation whatever. It is not difficult to invent restrictions which when added to conditions (a) through (d) will circumvent this particular counterexample, but such restrictions require an independent rationale, and further counterexamples to the newly restricted account can easily be devised. Attempts to shore up the formal version of the analysis, and generally to thwart the criticism that the covering-law model provides only trivially satisfiable necessary con-

35. Hempel and Oppenheim, *op. cit.*

ditions of explanation, have thus far not succeeded. Indeed the project has by and large been abandoned.[36]

This criticism of the covering-law model is serious for several reasons. First, it shows that the covering-law model provides at best necessary conditions of explanation. Moreover, the objection suggests that the necessary conditions described are uninteresting and fail to restrict the class of admissible explanations. Any explanation sanctioned by ordinary convictions, and even some putative explanations rejected in ordinary contexts, can be phrased so as to pass the test of conditions (a) through (d), and whatever additional restrictions are added to them. In short, the covering-law theory so substantially revises ordinary explanatory commitments that it turns out to have no special relevance for explanation.

Let us now return to our central concern. Not only does this objection leave Hume's account of causation untouched, but that account can be called upon to explain what has gone wrong in the reconstruction offered. The objection does not impair Hume's theory because the regularity account is in no respect committed to the adequacy of first-order truth-functional logic. Indeed, nothing is more obvious than the non-truth-functionality of singular causal statements, both on Hume's account of them, and on commonsensical accounts as well. For instance, "the fact that the Titanic struck the iceberg caused it to be the case that the Titanic sank" is true (although it requires special analysis in terms of events on the regularity theory we have supported), while the same causal statement with the contained sentences reversed will be false even though their truth values remain unaltered. Accordingly, causal statements are not truth-functional. Because it is thus free from any commitment to the adequacy of first-order logic for expressing the causal relation, the regularity theory is not open to the same trivializing counterexamples as the covering-law model of explanation.

Moreover, the non-truth-functionality of causal statements

36. Crucial papers on this subject include Rolf Eberle, David Kaplan, and Richard Montague, "Hempel and Oppenheim on Explanation," *Philosophy of Science* 28 (1961), pp. 418–28; David Kaplan, "Explanation Revisited," *Philosophy of Science* 28 (1961), pp. 429–36; and Jaegwon Kim, "Discussion: On the Logical Conditions of Deductive Explanation," *Philosophy of Science* 30 (1963), pp. 286–91.

helps reveal what has gone wrong in the attempt to formalize the deductive-nomological model at the level of first-order logic. If, as suggested above, an adequate explanation must ultimately appeal to processes that are causal in Hume's original sense, then it will be no suprise if a concept of explanation cut adrift from this non-truth-functional relation falters because of counterexamples hinging on the conception's commitment to truth-functionality. In abandoning the causal rationale for covering-law explanations, covering-law theorists successfully avoided celebrated controversies in the philosophy of causation. But they thereby strayed too far from the actualities of explanation in ordinary contexts. As it turns out, explanation is not an objective, truth-functional relation among sentences, and it is not akin to proof in mathematics. It retains an essentially pragmatic connection to the purposes of sentient creatures, and must meet informal requirements determined by these purposes. The Humean can and should claim, on the basis of his theory of causation and in behalf of his commitment to a nontrivial covering-law model, that such informal requirements are best represented by a model that posits a causal connection between the explanandum and the explanans. The hopes for first-order formalization would consequently have to be surrendered, but the nontrivial character of deductive-nomological strictures on explanation could be preserved.

This suggestion can be illustrated by considering informal counterexamples intended to show the irrelevance of covering-law requirements. Suppose we wish to explain why the Empire State Building is 1200 feet high. We may give an account of the matter that meets covering-law requirements by deducing its height from the law of the rectilinear propagation of light, the necessary truths of trigonometry, the angle of incidence of the sun's rays, and the measured length of the shadow cast by the building. This account clearly fails to explain the height of the edifice in question. It would be fatuous to reply that, although the argument does not satisfy conventional strictures on explanation, it is nevertheless scientifically adequate. For there are reasonable limits on the degree to which a rational reconstruction of explanation can transcend common intuitions, limits that the deductive-nomological model has simply ignored.

This explanatory deficiency can be amended by introducing

Humean causal considerations. The Empire State Building counterexample does not constitute an explanation because the items cited in the statement of the initial conditions do not, in any sense relevant to human purposes and capacities,[37] causally determine the state of affairs to be explained. One of the initial conditions is a causal consequence of the explanandum phenomenon and the other is causally independent of it. The problem identified is thus solved by adding a requirement that explanans and explanandum stand to each other in some particular causal relation that cannot be expressed through first-order logic, or for that matter through any simple and straightforward terms. It would, for example, be excessively stringent to require that the initial conditions cite the cause of the explanandum phenomenon. As noted previously, some patently acceptable covering-law explanations do not mention among their initial conditions phenomena that constitute the cause of their explananda phenomena. Some explanations cite states simultaneous with the explanandum phenomenon: for example, explanations of the properties of diamonds in terms of their crystal-lattice structure, and explanations that employ the gas laws. Others cite events that occur after the event to be explained, such as explanations employing Fermat's least-action principle to account for the path of a light-ray in terms of the last point on the path.

In each of these cases there is at least an indirect Humean causal link. The analysis of causal connections between simultaneous states provided in Chapter 6 shows how an explanation employing the gas laws and simultaneous causal conditions can reflect a Humean causal connection. And the citation of events occuring after the explanandum event in accounts trading on Fermat's principle are legitimate causal explanations because the explanandum event and the later event cited in its initial conditions are causal consequents of prior events which fix them both. These considerations suggest that a suitable restriction might be formulated and added to the other requirements of the covering-law model. So revised, the model would circumvent

---

37. Relativization to human purposes and capacities reflects the fact that in a wholly deterministic universe later events may strictly determine earlier ones, but not in a way that would allow humans to bring about events in the past. Cf. Chapter 6 for further discussion.

both vexing formal puzzles and informal counterexamples to the conventional deductive-nomological account of explanation. The revision would also reveal the extent to which Hume's treatment of causation is independent of defects in the covering-law model, as traditionally conceived. It is of course unclear whether exponents of this model would accept an addition which binds it so closely to an account of causation, and which precludes its formalization. Furthermore, whether such a causal requirement will represent the final among a set of sufficient conditions of explanation—that is, whether it will enable the covering-law model to avoid all technical objections and counterexamples— is beyond our immediate task. What does seem clear is that such an explicit causal condition of explanations would strengthen the Humean conviction that all factual knowledge is founded on relations of cause and effect.

We shall not here attempt to formulate a specific additional requirement of causal relevance between explanans and explanandum. Not only would the task be arduous, but a Humean need not be committed to any particular version of the requirement. He must, however, be committed to the general view that a restriction of this kind represents the correct strategy in analyzing explanation. This general view places the Humean under a heavier obligation than that of articulating the details of an account of explanation. It demands that he defend the whole strategy of covering-law explanation against a set of objections entirely different from those expounded in this section. These objections are found in non-Humean theories that oppose the covering-law model on grounds that it fails to provide even a set of *necessary* conditions of explanation, let alone a set of sufficient conditions.

VII

Many philosophers accept the deductive-nomological model as an adequate account of explanation in the physical sciences, yet consider it inapplicable to the life sciences and the human sciences. They argue that explanation in those disciplines does not conform to the covering-law model because the phenomena to be explained do not reflect the operation of causation—at least not as Hume conceived it. This conclusion about explanation resembles the conclusions reached by Hart and Honoré, Collingwood, and others about the different senses of cause and the importance of a causal context. However, new problems beyond those discussed by these philosophers emerge in connection with explanation, and they are especially important for Hume's theory of causation.

The life sciences and the social sciences both treat their subjects as teleological or goal-directed systems. The behavioral patterns of living systems are described and explained by appeal to the ends or goals towards which they are directed. Because ends or goals cannot be causes (obtaining, if at all, only after the behavior they determine), it is often maintained that the behavior in question is not the product of Humean causal mechanisms, and cannot be accounted for in terms that satisfy the covering-law model. In this section we take up these arguments with reference to teleological phenomena generally, and in the last section with reference to a special subclass of such phenomena: human actions. In both cases, we argue, the range and applicability of Hume's account of causation and its associated commitments to a theory of explanation can be defended without alteration.

Hume certainly would not accept the view that purposive explanations fail to conform to his theory of causation. In both his theoretical account and his practical employment of purposive explanations, he treats the relation between explanans and explanandum as wholly causal. He notoriously argues that acts of free will aimed at human goals can be explained causally, while retaining their status as free acts for which we rightly hold persons responsible. He also argues the connected thesis that the inference from the presence of apparent design in nature to the existence of a designer is an inference from effect to cause, and he applies his analysis of the grounds of our causal knowledge to this inference. In the first *Enquiry*, for example, he writes:

You . . . have acknowledged, that the chief or sole argument for a divine existence . . . is derived from the order of nature; where there appear such marks of intelligence and design, that you think it extravagant to assign for its cause, either chance, or the blind and unguided force of matter. You allow, that this is an argument drawn from effects to causes. From the order of the work, you infer, that there must have been project and forethought in the workman. (EHU, Sec. 105)

Hume refers here to the possibility that the blind and unguided force of matter might be the cause of phenomena that seem to show the mark of intelligence, purpose, aptness, goal-directedness, adaptiveness, functionality, or design. Although the quoted passage alone is a tenuous basis for the interpretation, Hume is widely supposed to believe that a correct explanation of apparently teleological phenomena must appeal to this "unguided force of matter." While Hume never explicitly commits himself to the claim that teleological phenomena are explainable by causal laws of the type known in physics, reductive analyses of teleological explanations have always enjoyed the sympathy of Humeans, and we believe would have enjoyed Hume's sympathy as well.

But what are these teleological phenomena, and how might their explanation be achieved in Humean causal terms? Teleological characterizations fit the following general pattern.

A system S engages in behavior B for the sake of goal G, if and only if:

(i) B tends to bring about G; and
(ii) B occurs because it tends to bring about G.[38]

Such characterizations are employed in explaining the behavior of an organ such as the heart, the circulation of the blood being the end-state for the sake of which it beats (the function that it serves). Similarly, functional explanations are offered for human actions with conscious goals or purposes. The notion of "tending to bring about a state," as in (i), may be explicated causally (as reflecting the necessity in the circumstances through which B causes the occurrence of G); but the claim that "B occurs because it tends to bring about G," as in (ii), is not obviously causal. There are two reasons. Because G is attained only after (or at best simultaneously with) the occurrence of B, G cannot be the cause in Hume's sense. Additionally, behavior frequently fails to attain its goals, and since unattained goals are not actual

38. This version is adapted from Charles Taylor, *The Explanation of Behavior* (London: Routledge & Kegan Paul, 1964).

occurrences, they cannot be Humean causes. The formulation above permits both temporal posteriority and failure to attain goals by use of the expression "tends to." But the "because" expression in clause (ii) cannot be given a Humean causal reading. If characterizations of this sort are countenanced as having explanatory power in the life sciences and the social sciences, then these subjects must appeal to processes that are not causal in Hume's sense.

The Humean has two compatible alternatives. First, the independent cognitive standing of such explanations can be denied. The Humean may argue that there are nonteleological treatments of systems that engage in behavior "for the sake of ends," that these treatments are wholly causal, and that the evidence for them is preferable to that supporting teleological explanations. The Humean's second alternative is to provide an analysis of teleological accounts that shows them to be merely a species of causal explanations, despite appearances to the contrary. Such an analysis would characterize teleological accounts as innocuous conveniences without metaphysical or methodological implications that could cast doubt on their wholly causal character.

Humeans have profitably pursued both of these strategies. The plausibility of the first is illustrated by the history of biology since Darwin. Darwin's influential theory of natural selection provides purely causal, nonteleological descriptions of and explanations for phenomena previously supposed to be the products of design and purpose. His explanation of the fittedness of organs to their function, plants and animals to their niches, populations and species to their environment, in terms of small hereditary variations and their consequences for rates of reproduction, is a paradigm of the elimination of teleology endorsed by Humeans. The cause of design is, in effect, the "blind and unguided force of matter" cryptically mentioned by Hume. Since Darwin's time causal accounts of apparently goal-directed activities have been improved in detail and range. Few biological areas remain in which at least the outlines of a nonteleological replacement for obsolete teleological explanations have not been sketched. The causal laws of Darwinian evolution governing heredity, variation, and environmental interactions, can themselves be explained by appeal to causal laws at the level of genetics and physiology; and these in turn are explained by chemical and physical laws that reflect "the blind and unguided force of matter" at a still deeper level. The degree to which this strategy of supplanting teleological characterizations by causal ones can succeed is of course an empirical question, one that can only be settled on the strength of the experimental and observational evidence for the competing characterizations. But it seems clear that the evidence is mounting in favor of nonteleological hypotheses, and at an accelerating rate. As this process proceeds, the claim that there are important classes of phenomena not regulated by causal mechanisms grows increasingly less tenable.

The Humean's second strategy is not only compatible with the first, but acquires much of its plausibility from the success of the first. The second strategy views teleological characterizations as exhaustively translatable, at least for explanatory purposes, into causal characterizations. This reduction to Humean mechanisms also opens the door to covering-law explanations of ostensibly teleological phenomena. Central to this strategy is an analysis of condition (ii)—"B occurs because it tends to bring about G"—in the general pattern offered above. In one popular proposal that builds on Darwin's account, condition (ii) is treated as an elliptical expression. It stands for the claim that systems such as S exhibit B-type behavior because the disposition to do so is hereditary, because such behavior has historically tended to bring about the occurrence of G in these systems, and because that occurrence has been causally conducive to the survival of systems of type S.[39] However, a number of objections must be overcome in defending this proposal. It links its characterization of teleological statements to the truth of an empirical theory, a theory in the absence of which it cannot account for the meaning or employment of these statements. Indeed, the analysis ties teleology so closely to biological contexts that it seems inadequate to explain the large number of cases which apparently transcend such contexts. Thus, the proposal appears inapplicable to teleological behavior that is not determined by hereditary dispositions (e.g., goal-directed animal behavior and

---

39. For a good example of such accounts, cf. M. Ruse, *Philosophy of Biology* (London: Hutchinson & Co., 1973), Chapter 8.

the apparent purposiveness of such human artifacts as guided missiles or thermostats).

Larry Wright has noticed the possibility of generalizing Darwinian analyses of teleological descriptions beyond narrow biological contexts. On Wright's analysis the key to Darwinian explanations is the requirement that among the causally prior conditions of goal-directed behavior of a system are certain states of its ancestor systems. What makes phenomena goal-directed is the fact that these prior states are susceptible of description integrally referring to the subsequent goal states, i.e., those causally requiring the teleological behavior in question.[40]

This insight is important for the Humean. The fact that causal conditions of teleological phenomena may be described in terms referring to their effects entails neither that the effects bring about the phenomena nor that the phenomena are closed to causal explanation. Indeed, quite the reverse is true. If a particular behavior pattern is teleological, it must be open to causal explanation because its source is a set of causal processes. So formulated, this analysis accommodates cases of natural selection involving merely apparent purposive biological phenomena, goal-directed human or animal behavior, and human artifacts, as well as pre-Darwinian claims about the purposes of the deity. For instance, the teleological character of human behavior is explained by noting that the prior states of an agent exhibiting the behavior include a desire to attain G, the desire itself being specifiable in terms that also describe G. Equally, the goal-directed behavior of animals produced through conditioning will be the causal product of prior exposure to objects resembling G.

This analysis of teleological characterizations is tied to the first of the Humean strategies in that it helps explain the progressive elimination of teleological characterizations in biology. These characterizations have become superfluous in many areas as alternative descriptions of goal-directed behavior have been provided. Thus, the intricate dance of bees was once explained by reference to its function in the acquisition of food. Wright's analysis substantiates the legitimacy of this attribution by noting

40. Larry Wright, *Teleological Explanation* (Berkeley: University of California Press, 1976).

the hereditary character of the behavior and the fact that it resulted in the acquisition of food in past generations. With the advent of physicochemical descriptions of more immediate and causally prior conditions, this explanation was largely supplanted by one citing chemical interactions. At this stage it was no longer necessary to characterize the antecedent conditions of the phenomenon in terms that mentioned its causal consequences, and an adequate explanation lost even the appearance of being teleological. By the same token, of course, teleological characterizations may on occasion become entrenched rather than replaced by the discovery of underlying causal mechanisms. When the description of these mechanisms is richly complex, practical considerations of simple reference may dictate the continued characterization of these mechanisms in terms of their consequences. In such cases the teleological appearance of the account is enhanced, but this result does not signify that the explanation is noncausal.

Because it is consistent with Humean causation, the foregoing analysis can easily accommodate teleological phenomena to the minimal version of the covering-law model we have endorsed. If teleological processes are causal, their explanation ideally involves subsumption under universals of law. Most teleological explanations countenanced in ordinary contexts cannot formally pass this requirement, of course, because the full range of causal conditions is unknown. The Humean is nonetheless committed to the existence of such conditions and to the possibility of an account that will reveal them to be initial conditions in a covering-law explanation.

This solution to the problem of teleological explanation seems to leave two questions unanswered. First, what are we to say when there is no promising causal explanation for a process that is characterized teleologically? Second, what are we to say if the characterization of the prior conditions of a teleological process *must* refer to goals or ends, so that no wholly nonteleological, purely causal explanation is conceptually possible? Inadequate Humean answers to these questions will undercut the entire Humean project for establishing the ubiquity of causal processes and the universal appropriateness of covering-law explanations. Yet the answers can at present be no better than programmatic. To the first question we would respond that if no causal explanation can be found, either the search has not been thorough enough or the phenomenon is uncaused. The latter alternative reflects the contingent character of the Humean's claim to be able to provide a detailed causal explanation for every teleological process. If this goal *cannot* be achieved for some processes, the Humean must candidly admit the failure of his broad program and consequently concede that there are limits on the range of causation. The former alternative rests both on the increasingly well confirmed belief that the program will not fail, and on the conception of empirical science that Hume's theory of causation provides.

The second question is in a sense more pressing than the first, for it reflects a belief that one special subclass of teleological behavior is essentially and ineliminably noncausal, both in mechanism and in explanation. This subclass is almost certainly limited to human action, a form of behavior that deserves separate and detailed consideration.

VIII

Hume writes that "the philosopher, if he be consistent, must apply the same [causal] reasoning to the actions and volitions of intelligent agents" as he does in explaining the human body and all external objects (EHU, Secs. 67–68; T, 403f). Hume is thus committed to a causal account of human action, to the explanation of such action in terms of covering laws, and to the compatibility of determinism and commonsense attributions of free will to human agents. Human nature, he holds,

remains still the same, in its principles and operations. The same motives always produce the same actions: The same events follow from the same causes. Ambition, avarice, self-love, vanity, friendship, generosity, public spirit: these passions, mixed in various degrees, and distributed through society, have been, from the beginning of the world, and still are, the source of all the actions and enterprises, which have ever been observed among mankind. . . . Mankind are so much the same, in all times and places, that history informs us of nothing new or strange in this particular. Its chief use is only to discover the constant and universal principles of human nature . . . and furnishing us with materials from which we may form our observations and become acquainted with the regular springs of human action and behavior. (EHU, Sec. 65)

Hume here suggests that the factors commonly cited as determinants of human behavior operate with causal force. Motives explain actions, and there are regularities in the relation of motives to actions that transcend historical epochs and cultural differences. Human action does not generate the same problems as the wider genus of teleological phenomena of which, in its intentional varieties, it is a species. The problem posed by teleological phenomena is the difficulty of identifying a causal relation between behavior and the end that is said to explain it. In human behavior, by contrast, prior motives to attain the ends or goals can readily be appealed to as Humean causes. Such explanations are teleological because the motives are described in terms that mention the ends towards which the action is directed. As the earlier formula dictates: the action of raising one's arm in order to signal a turn is caused by the intention to signal a turn.

This analysis, however, is too simple. The most influential argument against it holds that the universal and general principles which, according to Hume, "history discovers" are as much a mystery today as they were in Hume's time. Yet a causal relation between motives and actions requires such principles; and a science of human action demands that we know them. It is easy to construct general statements that connect particular actions and motives, but the trouble with these candidates—as Hume notes (EHU, Secs. 67–68)—is that they are invariably false, because laden with exceptions. If phrased so as to exclude all exceptions, they seem repeatedly open to the charge of vacuity and tautology. For example, consider an explanation of a person's climbing a ladder: the action is explained by the persons' *belief* that his hat is on the roof to which the ladder leads and by his *desire* to retrieve his hat from that roof. It is easy to generalize this singular statement into a lawlike statement to the effect that whenever persons wish to retrieve their hats from roofs, and believe that climbing a ladder will enable them to do so, they climb a ladder. This general statement is plainly not a causal law.

Hume's unrefined principle that the same motives always produce the same actions may only manifestly be true when motives are *defined* in terms of actions, in which case the causes and effects of human action would therefore not be logically distinct entities. Yet, as one standard objection to Hume has it, the nondistinct character of these causes and effects means that the statements explaining human action are analytically true, and it follows that "no explanation in Humean causal terms of action is possible."[41] This argument is most conveniently expressed by means of the account of teleological processes given earlier. According to the Humean, action is goal-directed because its causes, human motives, are typically characterized in terms that mention the ends or goals of actions. Yet on the anti-Humean objection we have sketched, this assimilation is fatal, for motives can only be expressed by reference to the goals toward which their associated actions tend, and the actions they explain can likewise only be characterized in terms of these ends. All exceptionless general statements connecting motives and actions thus seem analytic. The logical inevitability of such characterizations is revealed by the intensionality of the descriptions of motives and actions. If a coextensive description of a goal is substituted in the description of an action or intention, the goal's identity may change. Thus, in our previous example, suppose the agent's act of retrieving his hat is also truly described as "the act which caused his fatal accident." Substituting this true description of his goal-state into a statement about his action or its intention makes the statement false. Surely his motive was not to bring about an event identical to the cause of his fatal accident. The same must be said about the action of attempting to retrieve the hat by climbing the ladder: it was not the attempt to attain that state which caused his fatal accident. The upshot is that if a particular motive explains a particular action and the connection between motive and action is a logical one, then this explanation cannot be causal; the motive consequently cannot be the cause of the action.

This argument constitutes a serious challenge to Hume's claims. It rests on considerations about the intensional nature of our characterizations and explanations of action. Though Hume was entirely ignorant of these issues, he was committed to the appropriateness of causal explanations of human actions,

41. A. I. Melden, *Free Action* (London: Routledge & Kegan Paul, 1964), p. 85.

and so presumably to the view that they are ultimately reducible to nonintensional characterizations and explanations. Yet the many contemporary efforts to analyze the apparent intensionality reductively have not succeeded. In addressing this problem, the most we can hope for here is to sketch lines along which the defender of Hume must argue if he is to circumvent the objection to his theory while continuing to do justice to our ordinary explanations of human action.

This last proviso deserves brief explanation. Following contemporary philosophers such as Quine,[42] a defender of the regularity theory and its applicability to human behavior might argue that the intensionality of terms which precludes a causal account simply reflects their unsuitability to the scientifically acceptable description of behavior. The latter descriptions must be extensional. Accordingly, intensional characterizations of human behavior and its determinants should be replaced by the nonintensional explanations of neurophysiology or behavioral psychology. Such a program would proceed on analogy with the elimination of teleology from explanations of natural phenomena. Without assessing the plausibility of this general strategy, it cannot be attributed to Hume himself (though it is certainly open to the contemporary Humean). Both the passage quoted at the outset of this section and Hume's vast outpouring of historical explanations in terms of motives and actions are evidence that he did not envision this strategy of elimination.

A Humean response to the objection we have paraphrased should focus instead on the problem of explanation. If a *logical* connection obtains between intentions and actions, how can the citation of an intention adequately *explain* the occurrence of a particular event described as an action? An explanation of ladder climbing in terms of the intention to reach a roof leaves unresolved the question of whether an agent's movement is an action. Any physical movement of a body can be given a topographic description that is neutral as between the movement's constituting an action of the agent or an instance of mere reflex behavior produced, say, by artificial stimulation of appropriate neurophysiological centers. In practice we seldom

42. W. V. O. Quine, *Word and Object* (Cambridge, Mass.: M. I. T. Press, 1961).

have any difficulty distinguishing mere movements of the body from actions. But a view that envisages a logical connection between action and motive cannot explain how such distinctions are made. We cannot explicate the distinction between movements and actions by claiming that an action has an appropriate intention. Like motives, intentions are logically connected to actions, with the result that the evidence for something's being the relevant motive is identical to the evidence on the basis of which a particular movement is classified as an action. The logical connection thesis thus shifts our context of inquiry from questions about why actions are performed to questions about whether particular events in which agents figure are actions.

In the absence of independent grounds to believe that an action has taken place, the mention of motives will not explain an instance of human behavior any more than noting that Hume was unmarried explains his being a bachelor. The only way to give such an independent description of the action would be to show that it exhibits some property which can be identified without reference to its motive and goal and which distinguishes it from mere movement. But if motives and actions are logically linked, no independent grounds of this sort can be provided. To provide such independent grounds for believing that a particular movement is an action would require a nonteleological description of the action, which is impossible on the thesis in question. Thus, on the one hand the logical connection thesis leaves open the question of whether there are actions distinct from mere movements, and on the other it precludes the existence of evidence that could answer this question by establishing the existence of actions. If, then, there are actions, it is impossible to say how, on the logical connection thesis, motives could possibly explain them. Since of course there are actions, and motives do explain them, it follows that this thesis must be false.

The false claim that particular motives logically determine their correlative actions must be distinguished from the deceptively similar logical truth that every action entails some intention. This necessary truth no more requires a logical connection between particular motives and actions than the necessary truth that every effect has a cause requires that particular causes logically necessitate their effects. The mistake is particularly easy to make if the terms we employ to state the reason and describe the action are the same, as they are in a teleological characterization. Indeed, to recognize this tendency helps explain why we accept, for instance, Hume's *Histories* as containing truths about particular historical events and their causes, even when we do not know the generalizations that on the covering-law model must connect them. Nonetheless, the Humean needs to explain why, unlike biology, social science and history have yet to discover applicable causal laws, and why in the absence of such laws we should credit singular causal statements about human action with explanatory force.

Hume's answer to these two questions rests on a disarmingly simple comparison between human action and biological phenomena. He describes the action of agents by analogy with the behavior of the body:

In the human body . . . when irregular events follow from any particular cause; the philosopher and physician are not surprised at the matter, nor are ever tempted to deny, in general, the necessity and uniformity of those principles by which the animal economy is conducted. They know that the human body is a mighty complicated machine: That many secret powers lurk in it, which are altogether beyond our comprehension: That to us it must often appear very uncertain in its operations: And that therefore the irregular events, which outwardly discover themselves, can be no proof that the laws of nature are not observed with the greatest regularity in its internal operations and government. . . .

[Similarly] internal principles and motives may operate in a uniform manner, notwithstanding these seeming irregularities; in the same manner as the winds, rain, clouds, and other variations of the weather are supposed to be governed by steady principles; though not easily discoverable by human sagacity and enquiry. (EHU, Secs. 67 and 68)

With this line of thought, Hume circumvents the difficulty of at once claiming truth for singular causal statements about human action and admitting ignorance of laws. We can treat general conclusions about the relations between motives and actions as rough-and-ready approximations to the strict generalizations that underlie them. In so doing, argues Hume, we reason no differently from our explanations of "the operations of body, nor can we conclude any thing from the one irregu-

larity, which will not follow equally from the other" (T, 404).
Our knowledge, in Hume's words, is "imperfect"; but ignorance
alone does not exempt us from the same methodological commitments in the explanation of human action that we accept
in the explanation of natural phenomena.

Given Hume's epistemological commitments and theory of
causation, the Humean can only await the development of laws
of human action that are now unavailable. If the many attempts to provide such laws continue to meet with failure, even
as the conditions of scientific inquiry approach the optimum,
the Humean will have no recourse but to allow that there
apparently are no laws relating reasons, motives, beliefs, and
desires to actions. However, there are many levels on which to
search for laws, and it would be vastly premature to give up
altogether the Humean position on the causal explanation of human actions merely because no motive-action connections seem possible. One Humean alternative that parallels Quine's aforementioned reductive strategy would be that the laws governing human
behavior do not describe causes and their effects in terms of *reasons*
and *actions* but rather, for instance, in terms of brain-state and
movement or operant and reinforcer. There are many such
strategies consistent with Hume's theory of causation. However,
the central conviction that can never be surrendered, while remaining faithful to Hume's broader philosophical program, is
that "in judging of the actions of men we must proceed upon
the same maxims, as when we reason concerning external objects" (T, 403).

Index